GEOFFREY PAKIS

MORE SAUCE MADAM?

THE ADVENTURES OF A
HOTEL MANAGER

Mereo Books

2nd Floor, 6-8 Dyer Street, Cirencester, Gloucestershire, GL7 2PF
An imprint of Memoirs Books. www.mereobooks.com
and www.memoirsbooks.co.uk

More sauce, madam?
ISBN: 978-1-86151-975-7

First published in Great Britain in 2021
by Mereo Books, an imprint of Memoirs Books.

Copyright ©2021

The address for Memoirs Books can be
found at www.mereobooks.com

Mereo Books Ltd. Reg. No. 12157152

Typeset in 10/17pt Sabon
by Wiltshire Associates.
Printed and bound in Great Britain

In memory of David Nixon and
Jonathan Hassell, two great mentors of mine.

I would like to thank my valued friends, some of whom I have known for a very long time, for their personal contributions to this memoir.

Contents

CHAPTER 1

The trials of a cadet

My first catering experience was a disaster. We were going on camp in the Lake District, 'we' being part of the CCF or Combined Cadet Force from Wellington College in Berkshire, one of the great public schools, of which I was privileged to be a pupil. I was both excited and anxious at the thought of the hard work involved.

We paraded around in military kit on Wednesday afternoons looking clean, green and proud, but for the most part it interfered with my life at school. As I was excused from playing the major sports due to asthma, I used to go cycling in the afternoons, time permitting, more often than not to the 'gravel pits', which consisted of nearby 'lakes' where I would smoke a cigar, such as a Hamlet, which made my head spin. It was obligatory to join the CCF. The military clothes all had that musty and oily smell that only goes with such clothes, either to help make them waterproof or to be different, and it used to set my asthma off, even without any exertion, so I never really liked wearing them.

The CCF did have its moments though, like the year we oversaw the tunnels. These were underground tunnels that each boy had to go through and they would have ascents, descents and corners. But we thought it a bit tame so, being sadistic schoolboys, we devised one that had, halfway along, a corrugated iron sheet at head level so that anyone crawling through would bump their head on the edge. We thought this was really clever of us! The normal reaction would be to go lower to get under it, however it would become quite narrow further along and end in a two-foot-deep pit, invariably filled with ten inches of water or so, through which they'd have to crawl, only to find a dead end. The way out, backwards, was above our corrugated iron sheet, around corners etc.

We had great fun smirking secretly at every 'lot' that went down. Invariably the tunnels were wet and slimy with mud, so they would get dirty. Great fun! Occasionally one of them would not appear at the other end, so we would have to go down and flush them out, but I would stop at the 'pit' and could just about crouch in the water and smoke a cigarette. It had its advantages! It was worth it, even though it meant getting dirty.

One afternoon we were called into the Captain's room to organize the food for the camp. Lawrence Simmons, a friend, and I were in charge of a tent, so it was up to us. My God, we were going to be responsible for ten cadets! We were seventeen or eighteen years old and the pupils thirteen or fourteen. How would we cope? What if we got it wrong?

I was very nervous, but at the same time I dismissed this because I could fall back on the fact that I was a schoolboy, not an adult, even though I was eighteen by then, and that's what adults are for – to sort out problems.

We went off with the food list and devised the weekly menu based on compo rations and Mars Bars, baked beans and the like. We had a set amount to 'spend', and as there was some allowance left over, on the day we were due to submit our personal kit and food menu to the officers I bought some fresh milk and sausages. I wanted to make it a surprise for the boys and produce a nice menu for the first meal. The officers took my order in and that was that. Thank God we had done something right – it had all gone OK.

A few days later I went home to Shropshire for a week and then went to a party held by Sophie and Jo, two Wellington girls, in Camberley somewhere. I recall from my diary that I did not enjoy it very much. I suffered from epilepsy as well as asthma, and as we lived in a little village in Shropshire, my main mode of transport was by bicycle, because I was not allowed to drive. So my social life was restricted and hence I was introverted, a state of being not helped by a strict father. My epilepsy drugs at this time were barbiturates, and they heavily sedated me.

Being a pupil at an all-male school certainly did not help as your interaction with that most godly of species, the female, was limited. There were about seven hundred and fifty pupils at Wellington, but when I was about to start 'A' levels, they admitted one girl, Polly Amos, as a sort of trial. She was the daughter of a teacher nicknamed Crater due to a large dimple on his forehead, so she was familiar with the school, although I had never noticed her before. I think her nickname became Polyfilla! She was worshipped by the whole school and treated as a goddess. Everyone got out of her way and those fortunate enough to be spoken to by her were in seventh heaven! She could have screwed anyone and must have had the time of her life, but equally it must have been hard on her being constantly leched at by seven hundred and fifty boys.

The next year about a dozen more girls were admitted for 'A' levels and had their own purpose-built dormitory, called Apsley, but one was 'adopted' by other dormitories; she chose whomever she became most friendly with, so several girls could have been adopted by one dormitory. Richard Allen, a friend from Lynedoch, had adopted Sophie, who was a nice blonde. Virginia Gilmour was a regular visitor to someone in Lynedoch. Jo was in my English class and a real beauty, with a tan and honey-blonde hair. At the beginning of term I was late for our first English lesson with 'Sniffer' Ridley, who sniffed from left to right like a dog sniffing out various bitches on heat. Every seat was filled except the one next to this gorgeous blonde who sat at the end.

'Oh my God I've got to sit next to her,' I thought. My brain panicked. It is human nature to sit as far apart from one another as possible, to give personal space and the like, but I could not grasp why no one had sat next to her.

'Is, er – there anyone sitting here?' I forced myself to say to her, in the hope that someone was already there.

'No there isn't,' she beamed back. Wow what a face! And I had dared to look at her and been spoken back to. What an event. I sat down gingerly, afraid that any wrong move might upset her. I could feel the heat from her body and sat tense and still. I imagined where the heat was coming from. No Geoff, concentrate... Do I speak to her? Will she laugh at me?

Then textbooks were handed out but as we were at one end, we had to share a book. Panic seized me; do I move closer to her? Who turns the pages? Who holds the book? How can I stop looking at her? What if I get a hard on? These questions, and others, raced through my head, having never sat so close to a babe like this in my life. I was also faintly proud that I was so privileged, alone amongst the whole class, and felt a bit elevated - in my head, I might add! She was the other girl having the party. I felt privileged at being invited, but also out of my depth because it is all very well going to a party at home, but this was in a strange place and I didn't know who was going to be there.

So we had the party, which I didn't enjoy. I've no idea where I stayed but it was a 3.30 am finish so I must have been pretty well pissed.

The next day I caught a train to Windermere. We were all supposed to check in at the railway station by a particular time, but I had missed a connection, so I would be late. I had telephoned ahead to inform the camp about this. I arrived at Windermere and got off, not knowing what to do next.

Ah, there was Dr Perry, the school doctor, just getting out of his soft-top sports car. 'Hi there!' I offered as a welcome.

'Don't you speak to me!' he thundered back. Fear gripped me. The doctor was my saviour at school and gave me all the medicines needed for my ailments and he was always nice. But this was different. I guess it was because I was late. It had seemed strange to me that there was no one else from school on the train, so alarm bells were beginning to ring up top; what had upset him?

'Why... what...?' I offered, as if to help the worsening situation.

'Do you realise that out of one hundred and twenty boys you are the only one that's late? Get in the car!' he shouted. Oh Christ.... things were racing around my head like never before, what to say, what to say...

'The train was late, so I missed my connection,' I heard myself say. This would stick I guessed as British Rail didn't exactly have a brilliant record with timings. Anyway it would have to do.

'Well how come no one else missed the connection?' he retorted. It hadn't occurred to him that no one else had missed the connection because they were not on the same train, but he was past reasoning by then.

'Well, I'm sorry but...'

'And then there's the food,' he interrupted.

'Food?' I replied blankly. What could he possibly mean by that? This sounded more serious and like something that could be blamed specifically on me. My lateness had been a sort of warm-up from him to get to the main event.

'You bought sausages and milk?' he continued.

'Yes.' Well he's clever isn't he, and observant. I began to realise that we were coming to the crunch and I was thinking 'come on man spit it out, I'm beginning to get a bit pissed off now'. 'How long do milk and sausages last for?' he said, a bit more coherently. He was beginning to calm down in relative terms and we were getting technical. How long do they last? I'd no idea but as they'd been bought about ten days ago, I thought that would do.

'Ten days or so, I guess?' I said hopefully.

'Ten days! They last about a week maximum in a fridge!' he replied with bewilderment as to how anyone could be so dim. Oh, so they're a few days out of date; that's not too bad I thought.

'And where's the fridge?' he carried on. We had only been driving for five minutes and I think the journey would have taken about half an hour. I've got to kill this one, I thought; I can't endure much more of this. But how? Calm down Geoff, think logically. We had taken the food to the collection point at school, and they had driven it up in three-ton trucks to a campsite. Fridge? Where would that be? It dawned on me then that there was no fridge, which was why we used compo rations, and dried and powdered products. I thought it best to climb down on this one and apologise.

'I'm sorry, I thought there'd be a fridge.' And, realising what a stupid statement that was in the situation, added, 'I'm sorry if I've let you down.'

'It's not me, it's your team. The milk and sausages have gone off and they stink to high heaven!'

Yes, they would have, what with being left at room temperature for ten days, I realised.

'Sorry,' I said quietly in defeat, hoping that was the end of it. It was, and the rest of the journey was spent in silence, much to my relief. I thought it best not to make any comment in case that would provoke further accusations.

We arrived at Stannah, found my tent and Lawrence, and apologised to him about the food mistake. Even though we had decided on this together, it had been me that had actually bought the fresh items, so I had taken the blame. I felt better knowing that as far as I was concerned, I could portion off half the blame on him, even if no one else was aware. Everyone seemed to be OK about it, but they did glare at me for a while, which was to be expected.

I finished checking off the food, minus sausages and milk, which had already been disposed of, and set about storing it and cooking the evening 'meal', which we did on stoves outside the tent on the grass. This would have been something like tinned Irish stew followed by tinned Apple Pudding. We were accommodated in a large tent in which we slept on the floor in our sleeping bags with our belongings next to us, with an officer on a raised section at the end in a camp bed. Maybe there were mattresses on the floor. All the food was stored at the end. To keep us relatively sane, some fresh foods were supplied for the evening meal when at the base camp such as sausages, potatoes, peas and carrots. Quite what we did to them was entirely up to us! This would be followed by a hot tinned pudding. All of these were heated in our 'mess tins', these being little metal rectangular containers that functioned as saucepans, plates and bowls. I believe the real military find the main meal and sweet to be more appetising if eaten mixed together as one meal, but we didn't put it to the test. I believe also we were civilized enough to be allowed to use cutlery.

Once we were all fed, we cleaned up, had a brief chat, set our alarm clocks for 7.15 am and went to bed.

After breakfast, which consisted of cereals and coffee, we cleared up and made sure that each pupil had got their lunch and kit sorted. Lunch consisted of sandwiches, a piece of fruit and sweets for energy, and a water flask. The first day was spent walking around Grasmere via Calf Crag and Steel Fell. We carried haversacks with our lunch, a flask of water, Mars Bars, sweets like Fisherman's Friends, maybe some extra clothing etc, and a couple of idiots had a second flask containing whisky or brandy. The scenery, once you had climbed up, was fantastic, with colours ranging from green to brown, along with various purples from heather, and even better if the sun was shining. It really was worth it.

We went as a group, led by the officers, who were mostly ex-military themselves and were teachers at Wellington. It was quite pleasant to know that they could get out of that 'schoolmaster' syndrome and act as if they were of the same species as us. The day passed without incident, which to me was a welcome relief after the goings-on of the previous day.

The second day saw us climbing and abseiling at Shepherds Crag, which was great fun, and a doddle compared to some of the things I had done in the CCF at school. We had an assault course and 'confidence area' in the school grounds. The assault course was bad enough, being designed to absolutely knacker you, but the confidence area was something else. The 'high wires' were two stainless steel cables high up in fir trees, consisting of an angled walk up a cable from ground level up to a tree, followed by a level walk of at least the height of a house to the next tree, followed by an angled descent. For a normal-sized person who stands on the lower wire, the higher wire reaches about chest height, which means that you can pull this higher wire in towards you, which offers some form of security and 'balance'. There is no safety net or rope attached to you in case you slip, which I guess is why it was called 'confidence area'. You know, team building, character building and all that. I, however, was short, so short and small that my feet were below the normal boot size, so I could not be issued the standard boot but had to buy my own. With the help of my parents we found some drill boots which were metal studded from toe to heel. It was bad enough marching on flat tarmac trying not to slip, but on the slope down to the Armoury I had to 'fall out' because they would slide on the tarmac. You can imagine trying to get up a high wire at an angle wearing these! The purchase offered was minimal, so it was quite an achievement getting to the top. However, when I moved off along the horizontal section, it was a different story. Being so short, the top wire was almost above my head, which meant that there was no way I could 'lean' against it and the further out I went, the further above my head the wire became until my arms were outstretched above me. Remember that my feet were slipping all over the place. I 'hung' there terrified, swaying to and fro.

'Get on with it!' the officer barked.

'You fucking try this!' I thought. Jesus I was scared. There was hardly any of my weight on the lower cable, so in effect I was crossing hand by hand. Boy did I hold on tight, but eventually, with sweat pouring off my face, I managed it. Never again, I thought.

Then there was the 'death slide', which involves getting high up a fir tree and grabbing two handles which are attached to a pulley and sliding down the cable at an angle to the ground. Great fun really, and we all enjoyed it. One day it was my turn and up I went, adrenalin flowing. I grabbed the handles and on cue, set off. Then suddenly after about four feet it jerked to a stop. Christ! I thought. This isn't right. What do I do now?

As we were playing soldiers, I assumed that some sort of action was needed and as they were doing nothing on the ground it was up to me; it was far too high to jump down – broken bones and/or death would have been the result of that – so what then?

There was a fir tree to my right so automatically, before I knew it, I found that I had launched myself off from the handles and attached myself to the tree like a koala bear! I clung there not quite knowing what to do next. For what seemed like an eternity I gazed at the bark admiring its colours and contours in the hope that it might give me a solution to my predicament, but no, don't be silly Geoff, it's only a bloody tree.

'Get off that tree!' barked the officer from far below. I'm not sure whether I was more terrified about what to do or of being shouted at, but it seemed irrelevant; I was in a world of my own up there. No one could get to me, no one could tell me what to do, and it was an unusual feeling. But back to reality... I've been shouted at and must do something NOW....

With what would easily have qualified for a stunt in a Rambo movie, I shot back from the tree and grabbed the two handles. What is amazing is that my hands were already horizontally below the handles whilst attached to the tree, so quite how I managed to defy gravity and rise to the handles is beyond me. But boy was it a relief to get back on the handles. A few seconds later I trundled off down the wire to the ground, picked myself up and walked casually back to the others, as if nothing had happened out of the ordinary.

'What the bloody hell do you think you were doing?' the officer snapped.

What? You're shouting at me? I should be shouting at you! You're in charge of this and it went wrong! I thought angrily. The adrenalin was flowing, I had done something heroic (as far as I was concerned anyway), and it was not my fault. Which of the above should I say?

'Well I had to do something,' I found myself saying.

'You don't bloody well jump on a tree up there you idiot! What got into you?' he bawled in bewilderment. There was no point in him getting angry because the event had been and gone. To my knowledge you cannot reverse time, so his rantings were futile. I changed the tack. 'What happened then?'

'It got stuck,' he replied, calming down.

'How?' I questioned, now feeling that I had got the upper hand.

'Nisbet's anorak cord got stuck in the pulley. Anyway you are OK, are you?' he added as an afterthought.

'Yes thanks,' I replied casually, and walked off as if to dismiss the situation. I felt quite proud of my actions and reckon the others must have been in awe of me.

After an orienteering course in the Lakes, we went on a three-day trip which involved climbing Helvellyn on the first day and walking to Seathwaite and Wasdale the next. That night, thank God, we stayed in a hotel, but I don't think we actually stayed in beds, probably slept on the floor in a barn. At least I was able to have a drink in the bar. The final day saw us traipsing to Langdale via Scafell and finally back to base camp in Stannah. That night was our 'liberty' night, and I can remember being refused service in a pub even though some of our tent (fourteen-year olds!) were drinking merrily away. It really pissed me off, but I met up with some others outside and we proceeded on a pub crawl. One of them was Rory Bremner, who was a real laugh at ripping off the teachers. They all had their nicknames, for instance Feck (Mr Wood), Wort, Crombie, Pog (POG White), Sniffer (Mr Ridley) and Shank. His comedy career began (I suppose) by taking the mick and acting like the teachers, which he was very good at, as evidenced by his successful career. He could also, to my constant irritation, come into my music practice, where I would be trying to play an Abba or Beatle song on the piano, and settle down and play it perfectly without reading the music. I could test him on anything and after finding the right key, he could play it from his head. It was an amazing ability.

The final day at camp consisted of an inter-tent competition. We were given about ten co-ordinates and were awarded points for every checkpoint we reached. These were at the tops of mountains. There was also a time element to it. The basic route was from Grasmere to base camp. Some were manned and some not; you could cheat but if caught out you would be disqualified. How you got there was entirely up to each team. This basically meant you could go as the crow flies, eg up a mountain to a checkpoint, down the other side and up the next one and so on. Or you could go the longer way by going up the first mountain, continuing more or less at that level and walking around the tops, which was further but less arduous. Our team, on a democratic basis, opted for the first one, ie as the crow flies.

I was depressed; Dr Perry did not want me to go on this because of my asthma and he knew how much of a struggle this would be for me, but I was determined to walk it. It was, to me, the ultimate challenge. When it dawned on me that our team wanted to win, as did every team, I am sure, I began to have second thoughts. It would be a feat of endurance just to finish the course, never mind compete against the other teams.

We plotted our course, got ourselves ready and waited our turn. Each team went off at intervals of ten minutes and then off we went. This is it! The beginning was fairly easy but as the mountain became steeper, it got harder. I kept up pretty well on the first one and we found the checkpoint (manned) and set off downhill. It was so sad to be going down, and we weren't walking but running as fast as possible. Remember that I was supposed to be in joint command, but I was at the back and definitely not in charge. Then we hit the next mountain. My asthma got worse and worse. I was lagging behind.

'Come on Geoff!' exclaimed one of them, beckoning with his arms.

Oh piss off, I thought. *I'm doing my best.* My asthma was bad and my Ventolin Inhaler had no effect whatsoever because I had already far exceeded the daily dosage, so I also had a chronic headache. Every so often they would stop for a breather to let me catch up but as soon as I reached them, off they would go again, much to my distress. 'I'm going to let them down', I thought, 'Got to keep going.' 'Fuck the bloody lot of you!' 'Who gives a shit?' 'Perhaps I'll give up and blame it on my asthma.' 'Can I stop for a minute?' 'Please slow down for me!' 'Grow up, be a man you wimp!' Those were some of the random thoughts passing through me as I gazed with frantic effort at each tuft of grass or piece of rock or stone below me as they appeared. This was sheer hell, and seemed to be never ending. I was beyond reasonable thought and had resorted to the one simple task in life. Left foot forward, right foot forward. Left foot forward, right foot forward. Mind you, don't twist your ankle. Do not let the team down. An occasional glance ahead.

Then we were level, and oh what a relief. I could actually stand up straight, or as straight as an asthma attack allows. We stopped for a real rest and had a Mars Bar and water etc. Then we set off over relatively flat ground running, or 'yomping' all the way. I can only run about two hundred yards normally before asthma takes over but in the state I was in I didn't care about anything else. Off we went through marshes, paths, rough grass etc. This went on and on and on ad infinitum, up and down with a brief respite every now and again. And then we went down the last hill to base camp. My headache was so intense that it was all I could do not to lie down on the ground. That doesn't actually help, being susceptible to hay fever, but anyway I just collapsed in a heap somewhere to contemplate whether life would be worth living or not. *Can I just die here, and be shoved into a ditch to be forgotten about?*

The last team came in and we were assembled to see who had won. To my utter amazement, and certainly to the doctor's, we came first! No we couldn't have – they must have got it wrong. But no, we had won and were cheered by the others. Then the prize: maybe a £10 token each, a couple of six packs of beer for us all, or something that no one else would get. But what we actually got as a 'prize' was

50p each off whatever we wanted to buy from the NAAFI! That really pissed me off. All that effort for nothing.

With hung heads and drooped shoulders we slouched back to our tent. It wasn't even worth going to the NAAFI for the sake of saving 50p. But winning had taught me one thing: TEAMWORK. Never give up. They did not give up on me and I didn't give up on them. I would never have completed it if it hadn't been for them, for which I will be forever grateful. The bastards – fancy putting me through all that! Also the point of winning is not what the prize is, but the fact that you have won. Do I agree with that? Hmm, not sure – it depends what the prize is!

We sorted out the last 'supper', and went straight to bed, as we were all totally exhausted. The next day we went home by train for a long hot bath and relaxing sleep in a bed. What joy! The following day, Mum managed to burn some fat in the kitchen and coat everything in the kitchen with a layer of grime, but that was inconsequential after what I had been through. Mum & Dad bought me a record for winning – *Don't Fear the Reaper* by Blue Oyster Cult, which was much appreciated. So ended my first experience of the real world.

CHAPTER 2

Into the world of work

Time for a bit of background. My name is Geoffrey Paris, or Geoff as I like to be called – Geoffrey sounds too sissy for my liking. I was born in London in 1959, and my father was killed in a car accident when I was about four, but my Mum remarried, so in 1964 my sister Robin, my parents and I moved to Beckbury in Shropshire and stayed there until 2002, after which they moved to Albrighton. My mother bore two other children in Shropshire, Judy and Bridget, giving me three younger sisters. My stepfather, hereafter referred to as my dad, became Finance Director for Tarmac and my mother occupied herself with Meals on Wheels and other charitable stuff. The Old Rectory where we lived was a lovely old seven-bedroomed house with ample gardens in which Dad eventually installed a tennis court and outside swimming pool. I went to prep school (The Old Hall) in Wellington, Shropshire and thence onto Wellington College in Crowthorne, Berkshire. I am not going to dwell on my childhood, which was difficult, because this book is really about my catering career.

Vague thoughts began to keep popping up from time to time with increasing regularity until finally I had to take notice of them. What was I going to do after my 'A' levels? How was I going to earn money? How was I going to aspire to the career level of my dad? These seemed impossible targets and I had no idea where to begin, but I had to. My tutor, Tony Pickering, was my mentor and friend; he understood some of my problems and helped me to grow up and gave me sensible advice. He was the only person I could talk to or confide in. It was expected at Wellington that you either went into the Armed Forces or to Oxford or Cambridge, Wellington being a very military-orientated establishment. At a push, another university was deemed acceptable, but anything else was considered inappropriate.

My 'A' level choices were English, Chemistry, and Physics with Maths. My epilepsy drugs at the time were basically sedatives, and were, I was told, used to put horses down. So my intellectual development was limited. I was permanently tired and found it a real struggle coping. English was a nightmare; I had no idea what to write about in an essay and hadn't even passed English Language 'O' level. Indeed I had been through every tutor and my grades had got worse and worse, ending in an F or fail before I actually passed it with a C a term before the 'A' level! After every essay I could see Sniffer getting more and more frustrated until one day he burst out 'Oh for heaven's sake forget about alliteration!'

'Well what do I write about then?' I replied in astonishment. He was totally at a loss, so he gave me some good essays to read from the class. This helped a lot and I then began to get the drift, but it was too late. Physics with Maths was the hardest; I could understand things like working out the half-lives of various radioactive elements, but for 'prep' or homework, I just couldn't get it, and in the end had to give it up, leaving two 'A' levels. Most of my colleagues were doing four 'A' levels and were expected to pass at A or B grade, such was the academic brilliance at Wellington, which I have to say, was outstanding. I was the exception and probably an embarrassment to the school.

Chemistry, however, was a doddle. To me it was mainly mathematical – the make-up of molecules, the interaction of electrons and protons in reactions, the periodic table, and so on, and I really enjoyed it. I did not enjoy one particular day in the lab, however. The labs were old fashioned with huge, long waxed wooden worktops with Bunsen burners, water taps, and sinks at the end. We had been doing experiments with basic alcohols like methanol and propanol to record the difference in flame colour, intensity, shape etc. The Kiwi teacher, Mr Carter, had left the lab to get something, so I thought I would do my own experiment. I poured some alcohol onto the wooden worktop to see what difference the wax burning with the alcohol would make to the flame colour, then lit it with my Bunsen burner. There were various splashes of water all along the worktop for about three feet to the sink at the end into which we had been pouring waste alcohols. However the splashes of 'water' ignited, being alcohol not water, along with the sink, and there were flames everywhere. Christ, I thought, what do I do now?

At that point Carter came back in and whilst sticking his arm through the flames to turn the tap on in the sink, bawled at me 'What the bloody hell are you doing? Get back!' He proceeded to put the rest of the flames out with an extinguisher whilst I was standing helplessly aside and then turned to me and snarled 'Well?' His face was contorted with anger. I knew this was bad, but I had to try and defuse the situation so replied as matter of factly as possible, 'It fell over and lit up…'

'Don't give me that! Get out! Go away and report to me at the common room at 4.45 pm. This will be detention at least! Now get lost!'

This was bad. I thought the best policy was to say nothing and slink off. I thought also that it would have provided the class with much-needed amusement! As I went out of the door with my work, I genuinely offered an apology but was ignored by Carter. I don't blame him. Here was the eldest schoolboy and a school prefect who had just done something really puerile! 'What does he think he's playing at?' he must have thought.

What actually concerned me more at the time was how to get out of detention. This was held on Saturday evenings for two hours and involved writing out lines non-stop or something equally tedious. Normally there were about half a dozen youngsters who have committed some minor misdemeanour. A prefect never went into detention, except to supervise it, which we occasionally did on a rotational basis – it had been my turn the week before. But this time I would not be sitting at the front watching them, I would be amongst them! It was a real mark of shame.

But that did not matter. What did matter was that it was Lynedoch's (my dormitory) dance that night. This involved 'farming' in an equal number of girls (to the boys going) from one of the local girls' school such as Luckley Oakfield and leaving us to it. It was known as a cattle market. You eyed a girl up and down, as they did to us, picked one, spoke briefly, had a quick dance, and proceeded to snog, and some no doubt had sex. It was as simple as that. Being in detention would mean that I would be late for the dance, so I would 'get' the least attractive girl, one that no boy had picked for the evening. But on the other hand, I was quite appreciative of being in detention because I wouldn't have to go through the ritual of approaching a girl, talking to her, dancing with her, and being spurned. How could I compete with my colleagues? They would just laugh at me, and supposing the girls did? What would I do?

So I had to do detention, much to my chagrin, and over the next week some 'community service', I suppose you could call it, which was an unusual form of punishment. I had to clean up some of the science labs both inside and out. That was OK, I could cope with that.

After the detention, I rushed down to the dance and found the last girl on her own, the one for me! She looked like the goalie for a lacrosse team, but it didn't matter, there was no question about it – we were for each other. We introduced each other, I apologised for being late, explaining what I had done to be in detention, which must have amused her, then had a quick dance and proceeded behind the curtain, where there was a room set up with a dim light for discreet 'activities'. We sat down on the bench against the wall together, and proceeded to snog. My arms could barely stretch around her she was so big, but she had all the requirements, which was what mattered! It was part of the ritual, expected, and it was great. No words were needed, it was automatic, and we both knew what we wanted. We carried on like that until the end, pausing only to catch a breath or get a drink. Conversation wasn't required, or at least not as far as I was concerned. So all in all a good night! We did not keep in touch after – it wasn't necessary. I certainly did not want to know, not that I knew how to go about keeping in touch anyway!

Reading back on my diaries, which I kept in those days and filled in on a daily basis, except in times of depression and being under the influence, I note that I did actually interact more than I can remember with that most revered species, the female. Most of this, being twenty-five years ago at the time of writing, has long vanished from my memory. Despite being so shy and withdrawn, I even briefly had a girlfriend, in Shropshire, whom I thought was lovely, but this relationship was difficult because I was disadvantaged from the start by not being able to drive, so couldn't really take her out.

It was now time to think about a career suitable for my qualifications. Brewing was an interesting subject of course, beer being an ever-increasing part of my life, and as I brewed beer and wine at home, a career in brewing would seem to be a natural extension of this. There was also the chemistry side of it, which was always interesting to me. I went to look around Wolverhampton & Dudley Breweries, but Dad put me off it as a career, much to my annoyance!

I went back to the Careers Room at Wellington to look at the Hotel and Catering section, which in those days meant going to college or university to do an HND or degree or joining an in-house training scheme such as the Savoy Hotel in London or Trust House Forte. But it was not considered to be a 'career' as far as a public school was concerned, so I did not get very far. I can remember, on Dad's instructions, writing to his old school friend Hugh Wilbraham, who was a fun, extrovert man who seemed to enjoy life to the full and had been general manager at the five-star Park Lane Hotel in London. I felt there was no way that I could aspire to his level of professionalism. He did the sensible thing and became a wine merchant, which was probably an extension of his own life! So I didn't achieve anything.

Our summer holidays in those days were spent in Aberdovey; we stayed for the first few years with some great family friends, the Tildesleys, who had a seafront house. Our days were spent sailing in a variety of boats from GPs, to a Drascum Lugger, to a yacht and then pottering about in Dad's little C-Craft – an inflatable dinghy with a Mercury outboard. Fishing for mackerel was high on the list, as was drinking at every opportunity.

At Dad's request I had written in advance to the various pubs in Aberdovey for a summer job. One of the Tildesley clan, Mary, was my age and as well as a great sailor with her brother John, she worked in the Dovey Arms for the summer. I held her in great esteem because she was also very pretty, lively and positive and had everything going for her, and it would have thrilled me to have the opportunity to work alongside her, but yet again I was also afraid; would she mock me for making mistakes or trying to hold a conversation?

This was the worst part of my life then; I did not know how to talk to people, how to hold a proper conversation, what to talk about, when to speak etc. The more I got to know people, the more withdrawn I became, because in my opinion they would have realised that I was a dead loss. I was also very serious; I didn't know when someone was joking or not, could never understand jokes, let alone tell any, and trying to understand what people meant when they said things was a nightmare; did their conversation have a hidden meaning or not? Consequently I could not keep up with a conversation and everything I said was a real effort and took courage. Nothing came naturally.

I don't know when this 'condition' started, but it was probably at school. Bearing in mind that the pupils were among the top 10% of the intellectual population of the UK, they always seemed to know the answers to my questions or thoughts. How come I didn't? I developed a conviction that they could read my thoughts, so I trained myself to think a certain way, which would not provoke someone into reading me the wrong way. Was it because I was a virgin? I assumed that no one else was at college. I thought perhaps something 'happened' to a bloke, like it does to a woman on losing their virginity. Sad isn't it? This was my life, which I reverted to more and more. It wasn't even my secret, because they could read my thoughts! And as they could read me, why bother to say anything?

It wasn't until I moved to Torquay fifteen years later that I started to get a life and realised that this was a load of crap. I should really have gone to a shrink to unscramble my brain, but I didn't realise it was a problem in those teenage years. Well, perhaps I did a little bit, but I didn't know what to do about it. Maybe there's a medical term for it? I have only ever told one person about this, and that was a year before I started to write this book, because he had personal problems at the time so felt it prudent to explain mine! But now I can look back on it, perhaps it will help somebody else?

Quite how I was going to cope in a pub or with the public at large was beyond me. I really wanted to be a chemist, so I could work on my own and get on with it. The thought of 'management' was incomprehensible; how could I tell someone what to do?

The Penhelig Arms accepted me as a barman for the two weeks of our holiday. This was my first real job – OK, I'd done gardening for local people at home and had two weeks' experience in the computer room of Tarmac's Head Office where Dad was Finance Director, but they didn't count – and it filled me with dread and excitement at the same time. Dread at the thought that I would inevitably cock it up and excitement at the fact that I had started my career, not that I knew it at the time.

The Penhelig Arms had a small bar, filled with the local Welsh and the odd tourist. It wasn't an exciting bar and was a bit out of the way even though it was on the main road. Duly kitted up in black trousers and shoes, white shirt and tie, in I went, very nervous. Would I be shown what to do? Would I have to talk to people? What would they think of me? What if I did something wrong? Would they laugh at me? All these and other thoughts kept popping up in my head and getting me into a state.

I gradually learned the job bit by bit and worked split shifts, 11.30 am to 2 pm and 7 pm to 11.30 pm. Food of some description was provided for the staff and I thought it great being allowed to drink Coke or lemonade, although I very rarely did in case I had done something wrong. I had to learn what drinks went in what, though I knew about beer, what to put ice and lemon with, what to ask etc. So it went on. Two diary entries were as follows: 'Made a bit of a balls in Penhelig' and 'Quite a bit more taxing on the brain'. It could have been trying to remember the prices, trying to add up mentally (which actually was one of my fortes), or dealing with the Welsh, or more likely a combination, but looking back on it now, it's laughable.

One particular evening in the first week, one of the locals said, 'I'll have a brandy.' A brandy? What would I serve that in?

'What do I serve that in?' I had to concede.

'That glass up there.' He pointed upwards.

'This one?' I replied, pointing up to a half-a-yard of ale glass fixed to the wall above the other glasses. 'That's right,' he said with a straight face. I duly reached up and fetched the half-a-yard down, dusted it off, poured a sixth of a gill of brandy into it and passed it over. The whole pub erupted into laughter, and I didn't know why. He knocked it back and told me that you serve it in a brandy glass. I went red with embarrassment and the next day it seemed that the whole town knew about it! That was another lesson for my naïve little self: even adults take the piss!

For those that are unsure as to what a 'half-a-yard' of ale is, it consists of a glass with a circular bottom like a ball which stretches into a thin neck which gets wider until half a yard in length is reached, with the top where you drink it from being about the width of a straight pint glass. Beer is normally drunk from them in one go and is quite an art. You will know if you've tried it!

So ended my first job. It was good to earn some money – I could now buy some records and drinks in the bar. No longer, at least not for a while, did I need to rely on an allowance from my dad.

CHAPTER 3

Geoff the chef

The rest of the summer was spent lazing around in Shropshire. I wrote to various organisations such as Grand Metropolitan, THF, Claridges and so on, as well as some catering colleges, including Ealing, Westminster, and Birmingham College of Food & Domestic Arts (BCFDA). Westminster rejected me due to poor 'A' level grades; I only got two 'E' grades as it happened, which as far as I was concerned classified as a fail. This meant that my chosen career of being a fighter pilot or submariner went out of the window, as did the next option of being a surgeon or chemist. Hotel and catering was, in those days, considered a career for those misfits who hadn't been able to decide on anything else or who were too idle for a proper career. It was a kind of last resort. Hence my 'choice'.

I wasn't keen on Ealing because its location in London left a lot to be desired, nor Birmingham, because Dad worked in Birmingham and he might be a pest and interfere, but the bonus was that it was closer to home so travel costs would be cheaper, free food being the motive! I went for various interviews in London and at Ealing and BCFDA, the latter of whom advised me to have a year out. That was what I decided to do, or rather, was decided for me. It was good advice, and I would recommend it to anyone following a similar career.

Our close friends Richard and Celia put me in touch with a friend of theirs, David Elliston, who, with his wife Pinkie, ran the Feathers Hotel in Ledbury. This was a traditional hotel with an Elizabethan front, antique furniture, and about twenty bedrooms, and it had a good reputation. I was to ring him and arrange an interview for a job, and a week later went down by train for my interview. I was nervous because this was uncharted territory in that this would be my first proper job and I hadn't a clue what to say. Partly I wasn't bothered because I had the feeling that the matter of my employment had already been arranged above my head, and that my 'interview' was merely a formality. It also bothered me that because it was an arranged job, I was still being looked after, and hadn't found employment on my own two feet. But anyway it was a start, and what did I have to lose?

And so I moved to the Feathers. The accommodation was attached to the hotel in which several staff lived. There were two Australian girls, an oldish couple who did the washing up, and me. The girls, in their mid-twenties, were fit and one was very pretty and sweet, but they were real women. And I was going to be sleeping in the room next to them and sharing a bathroom! I'd never slept next door to strange adult women before, except for friends and family members occasionally. What happens in these situations? Do we take it in turn having sex? Do we talk to each other off duty? Do I let them into my room? What if I see them naked – do I avert my eyes? What if they knock on my door at night? Do I knock on their door? Are Australians different? These were the sorts of questions that popped up. My room was small with a single bed and long window that stretched down to the floor overlooking the main street. I was horrified, as was my Mum, who had brought me down, by the bathroom; the floor was covered by odd spare pieces of carpet laid loosely, damp from the toilet which leaked slightly and smelled, and there was a steady trail of ants along the floor, up the toilet bowl, across the front rim, and down the other side! It didn't bother me, but I always wondered with amusement if the girls were bothered in case, when on the loo, the ants took a wrong turn! I don't blame them if they did.

That first evening I started work at 6 pm. I had never been in a hotel kitchen before and had heard all sorts of horror stories. The chefs were either mad or alcoholics or both, could be fat, shouted as if you were on another planet, and only had a basic command of the English language. What were they going to think about an ex-public schoolboy going into the kitchens? Would they take the piss? They might think I should be out front learning management, not mucking in with them.

So in I went, quietly and timidly. The head chef was thin as a rake and actually seemed to be quite pleasant. Perhaps this was a one-off to settle me in, I pondered? He showed me around, found some 'whites' for me – chefs' check trousers, a white jacket, and apron – and explained that they did bar snacks and a dinner menu for the residents. How was I going to remember all this? What if I got it wrong?

That first evening I just more or less watched what went on. I was even too afraid to ask for something to eat, so after service I went out for fish and chips. Later that evening I went into the main bar, the Prince Charles Lounge, for a drink. I stood there on my own and occasionally, as if to look as if I was being sociable and not just a nerd, I moved from one spot to another. On one such move a man holding his cigarette out at an angle brushed it against my tracksuit top, burning a hole in it. This was new and my pride and joy at the time. I just stood there and glared at him, and he at me. I was thinking, my god a confrontation, what do I say? He was an older man and certainly stronger than me. Should I cause a scene? He must have been thinking 'Well, what are you going to do about it?' As you can imagine I backed off and soon left the bar, feeling even more awkward and annoyed at myself for being a wimp.

The next morning Roy, the head chef, started to show me how to chop onions. This was complex: peel it, cut it in half across the root, slice it lengthways, slice it at an angle a couple of times, and then slice it the other way, at ninety degrees to the first direction, but leaving the root. Then he gave me half a sack of Spanish onions to peel and chop. Even to this day the one thing I hate about catering is onion skin. You can never get rid of those little pieces that flake off and get in the way, likewise those pieces of root. I duly peeled every one slowly and carefully, eyes streaming. Then he showed me how to make beef bourguignonne. He got down a massive saucepan, the likes of which I hadn't thought existed, melted a huge piece of lard, threw the meat in to brown it, then some of my chopped onions, then after a while he added some flour and stirred it a while to cook out the 'roux' and added a bottle of red wine or two, stirring it all the time. It looked disgusting. Then in went some chopped garlic, a couple of bay leaves, some chopped parsley, a few herbs, seasoning etc, and the heat was turned down and left to cook slowly. Later some fried chopped bacon, known as 'lardons', mushrooms and button onions were added. This was exciting – real cooking! But was he going to expect me to cook it next time?

That afternoon I went out to buy my first knife from a normal shop. I proudly came back with a carving knife. It was what someone at home might use to carve a turkey but in a professional kitchen it was totally inappropriate, because the blade was the wrong shape and not flexible enough, and therefore actually more dangerous than a catering knife. But I didn't know and tried my best with 'my' knife. I had to let them sharpen it on a steel every other day or so because I hadn't got a clue!

I settled down into my routine; split shifts over five days. Mornings were spent doing 'veg. prep' and getting ready for the lunchtime bar snacks, which were my responsibility. This involved preparing salad items including chopped parsley, which was the bane of my life. It took forever to do and caused my hands to come up in wheals, which itched and caused eczema, which I suffered from occasionally. But it had to be done; a kitchen isn't a kitchen without chopped parsley. Quite right!

One thing I found quite strange at first was that any leftover raw bits of vegetables from preparation, eg leek skins, onion skins and roots, old overripe tomatoes, mushroom trimmings, and so on were thrown into a large pan that was constantly simmering twenty-four hours a day. Basically anything that would normally have gone on a compost heap at home went into this massive saucepan that had its own separate gas ring. This became known to me as the stockpot, another essential requisite for kitchens in those days. It contained beef bones, even eggshells floating on top, which like onion skin, helped to clarify it. It is sad and pathetic that it is now considered to be too much of a health hazard to keep stockpots on the go for weeks on end. I really felt I was learning something.

In the evenings I would again do bar snacks and when the second chef, Tony, was off duty, I would 'do' the veg. When a main course was due to go out the chef would scream 'Two veg!' which meant that a dish containing the two potatoes of the day was required, along with another one with the two or three vegetables of the day. My veg could only be put out after his meat went out – never before, as it would go cold. I used to wait, cloth in hand, for my 'signal', and if it went well then I was pleased with myself. When there was a lull between orders, we used to perch our arses on the lower shelves of the worktops so that we were half crouching and half sitting – it gets tiring constantly standing on your feet in trainers. I never joined in any conversation because first I thought they had too much to think about, and second, I was a commis chef and therefore hardly worthy of being a human. Chefs were gods in their kitchen, and I was a servant to them. You only spoke if spoken to. After weeks of being silent in these situations I eventually forced myself with great determination to say to Tony 'I'm sorry I'm so quiet, it's just that I'm shy.'

'That's all right,' he replied, 'I used to be as well.' Whether he meant it or not is another matter, but right then I believed him, and after that we occasionally had brief conversations.

There was also a pastry chef whose ability was restricted to pastry and desserts and therefore was a bit slow and didn't offer much conversation, so in a way I felt on a par with him. There were three washing-up staff (referred to as KPs from now on – kitchen porters). They all wore long white coats as if they were laboratory assistants. Ronnie was a small creature who looked like a rat that had popped its nose up out of a sewer in a Dickens film, and he used to scurry around like a weasel with huge sideburns down to his lower jaw. Fred and Laura had come from the local 'open' institution and were husband and wife. They plodded around, were dreadfully slow, always looked dirty, but reliable.

Ronnie, to my amazement, bought me for Christmas that year two knives; a chef's knife and a little veg prep knife. Both were excellent and I still use the chef's knife to this day at home, as my primary knife! It really upset me years later when I lost the veg prep knife; it had just the right amount of flexibility on the blade. Thank you, Ronnie.

We also held functions in a room upstairs, which could hold about one hundred and fifty for a sit-down meal. This was a nightmare for the kitchen and nowadays would be a health and safety issue. We had to carry the food up steep narrow stairs and had to sometimes tilt whatever we were carrying to get through the narrow doorway. One such evening when it was time for the main course to go up, I grabbed the large tray of roast potatoes from the oven and proceeded towards the stairs. Suddenly something blocked my path and I tripped, but I managed to stay on my feet despite burning both sides of my arms along the tray. But I did not let go of it, and it was excruciating. To have dropped the tray and spilt the potatoes would have been a fate worse than death!

I regained my balance and to everyone's surprise, including my own, I shouted at the Head Chef, 'What the bloody hell are you doing there? You don't peel potatoes in a bloody doorway! Get out of my way!' He was so shocked at my outburst that he duly moved everything and laid cloths down on the ground where the water had spilt. This was like a private telling his general what to do! He had put a large saucepan in the doorway of all places and had just started to peel a sack of potatoes into it, and of course, having lifted my roasts out of the oven, I could not see this.

I carried on up the stairs with the potatoes and afterwards sat trembling in the staff room. How dare I shout at the Head Chef! Would he sack me? Would he hit me? Ronnie came in with a cup of tea, consoled me, and told me that I'd done well and not to worry about it. The chef and I didn't speak for several days after that, so I felt obliged to apologise for swearing at him, me being the lower form of life, which he duly accepted and things went back to normal after that, except I kept an eye out for stray pots and pans on the floor!

Eating there was great. I could help myself to more or less anything for my meals and used to raid the main back fridge. All the 'stew' items that were cooked, such as chicken à la king and beef bourguignonne, or beef bogy as it was called in the kitchen, were kept in large buckets with lids for about a week. I could help myself to any of these and the walk-in fridge had that lovely smell inside that is peculiar to catering kitchens which signifies that there is good food within, which is also regularly turned over.

Milk in those days was delivered in milk churns, large cylindrical metal containers about three feet tall with lids. You left a ladle in them and kept them in the fridge. Presumably it was pasteurised. Most catering establishments bought their milk this way.

My live-in wage in those days was about £19.50 a week, after a live-in deduction, which mainly went on beer, cigarettes, and the odd record. I cycled everywhere, so I had no motoring costs. I either drank in the Feathers Hotel or, after about six weeks, in a local pub I had gravitated to. I could escape there properly and relax at the bar and drink to my heart's content. There I met the proprietor's son, who eventually would take me out drinking. There are quite a few times when I found myself slumped on the floor somewhere in this pub, much to the consternation of his father. These were my most embarrassing days and ones I do not care to remember; he was an ex-SAS soldier. But one evening we came back to the pub after everyone had gone to bed and went into the pub kitchen. He grabbed a watermelon, cut a hole in it, and proceeded to abuse it, encouraging me to try it, saying it was like the real thing. I was dead embarrassed, wondering what would happen if his father came in, so I declined, not that I would ever do anything like that anyway! After he'd finished, he left it on the worktop. I have always wondered if it ever got served to someone, and even what the kitchen staff must have thought had happened to it overnight. Perhaps they were used to it! The mind boggles.

There were some good nights too in the Feathers. Quite often after time, the local police would come in for a brandy and sit by the fire. It was irrelevant whether some of the locals were still drinking or not, and so after the police had warmed up, presumably to get to the next pub, we would carry on, sometimes to 6 am!

One day Laura, one of the KPs, began to irritate me by gesticulating with her arms and shouting. She was dumpy with ponytails and this was totally irrational – perhaps it was the time of the month – so I had had enough and called her 'Gertrude', that being an appropriate name for a cow. Next thing I knew a knife was flying towards me, which I avoided with skill, and then she went off crying. The bitch! And now she was using that female get-out-of-jail-free card; crying! Still, you must go through the process, so I went up and apologised to her.

Not long after Christmas, the KPs had to leave. We had discussed for several weeks how their work had been deteriorating further (if that was possible), so the powers that be felt they had to move on. This meant going back to the 'home' that they had come from. They had been released to the hotel originally to see if they could cope with life, but after an average start, they had fallen back. We were a bit sad to see them go, me in particular because I would now be doing more washing up than anyone else, even if it was on a temporary basis.

The next day the maintenance man and I went up to their bedroom. The sheets hadn't been changed for months, if at all, and the centre of the bed had become a sort of pit in which various items that you might find in a waste paper basket had gathered including Christmas tree light bulbs! Just as well they didn't break in bed! It was so disgusting that we threw the whole mattress out of the window and burnt it in the car park, and I believe we got Rentokil in to de-bug the room, which included having a go at the ants in the bathroom. That was Fred and Laura, bless them.

On Christmas day the Ellistons cooked all the staff a six-course meal in their house nearby, which was excellent and included a 'Russian cigarette and vodka' course which I thought was a superb idea. I was really in awe of them – they were genuine employers and lovely people. Afterwards we went back to the Feathers for further drinks and I was coerced into cooking breakfast for us all at 4 am. I felt dreadful in the morning, but it was well worth it. The hotel in those days must have been shut over Christmas.

Shortly afterwards, in the New Year, we had our staff party. I had tried to invite two friends of mine, but not together – Debbie from home, and Caryn, who was the sister of a good friend of mine from school, Peter Churchill. I had met Caryn when she was visiting Wellington and had spent time with her and thought she was adorable! In the end neither could make it, but I don't know how I would have coped if they had; at least I had tried. So I got pissed instead.

As well as the food, which I had to prepare, there were party games. One was musical chairs; eventually it got down to me and a waiter who was a bit on the dim side, with one chair, so I cheated by pulling the chair around with me as we went around. That meant that whenever the music stopped there was the chair for me to sit on! I was quite proud of my ingenuity, but a bit ashamed of cheating!

Shortly afterwards I was introduced to cooking breakfasts for the guests, which was normally done by Ronnie, the KP. However, after three days of me doing breakfasts on my own, I came in to find the pastry chef doing them. Steve, the manager, had thought me disorganised, which was probably quite true. So I went back to my normal duties. I thought the manager was rude and arrogant to the kitchen staff, especially me, but he always appeared smart and in control, and I wondered if one day I could step in his shoes as a manager and command the respect and knowledge that he displayed. It seemed such a steep hill to climb.

Another time, my friend from the pub got me pissed on Polish spirit and lager and arranged for a girl to come over to his flat. She was probably a hooker, as he phoned her and over she came about forty minutes later. The deal was this; I would leave to go home, only to find that I had lost my key or couldn't get in, so I would return to his flat. He would let me stay the night with this woman in his bed and convince her that I would be OK. So this happened and we all ended up in bed together, which has been my one and only threesome.

I really began to feel that my drinking was getting out of hand and decided shortly after that I should leave. I went to discuss this with David Elliston, but not, of course, for the above reason of alcohol consumption! There were some work-related things that I felt were inferior for someone of my standing: when there was snow on the pavement outside it was my job, in chef's whites, to clear it up. Chefs do not stoop so low to do that sort of thing; KPs or some other lowlifes do, don't they? I had also worked a few times in their function bar (as the barman) and felt I should learn more in that side in the interests of my career. So at the beginning of February I gave two weeks' notice. I had applied and been approved for a job as a commis chef at the Hotel Hessischer Hof in Frankfurt, which was a five-star hotel. I was amazed that they had offered it to me – after all, my experience was limited to four months from scratch – but they must know what they're doing surely?

Amazingly, I popped back to the Feathers for the first time in February 2011 as my Mum had sadly just died and I was on my way back to Torquay. There was an old white-haired receptionist, Mary who, on my enquiry, informed me that the Ellistons still owned the hotel and she remembered me, or certainly my name as she had worked there since 1978. The two old barmaids who were talking to customers at the bar drinking coffee etc had been there since 1976, although I didn't recognise any of them. That's an incredible length of service for three members of staff and just goes to show what good employers David and Pinkie are.

When I left the Feathers I went back to my parents' house in Beckbury for a week, where I chilled out and tried to learn some technical German catering words. BCFDA also accepted me as a student, starting that September for an HND course in Hotel, Catering, and Institutional Management. Dad telexed the Hessischer Hof from work to confirm acceptance of my job and enquired about accommodation, the start date etc, and a reply came back a few days later confirming it all. So I organised £150 in Deutschmarks and Travellers' Cheques and booked the train.

This was going to be an adventure in itself, and I was looking forward to what lay ahead. Here I was, on my own, having got a job through my own merits and in a foreign country! But I was also a bit anxious, because I knew what pissheads the Germans were and that their bars stayed open far later than ours. My 'problem' was that being epileptic and on drugs, there was only a small amount of alcohol I could consume because it interacted with the drugs and could cause a fit (always the next day, if it happened). After three pints I had to stop or go on to Coke or soft drinks, but that was hard because it was not a manly thing to be seen drinking soft drinks. Men drank bitter. Men who drank lager were almost considered poufs in those days, but it was deemed acceptable overseas, where most of the beer was lager.

I had only been to Germany once before, for a week in Berlin when my cousin flew Sioux helicopters around West Berlin for the Army Air Corps. I could remember making a right prat of myself at the airport. I was intensely proud of my record collection of a dozen or so LPs and they were in pristine condition. There was no way they were going to be left in the hands of my three sisters, so I borrowed a little suitcase from Dad and packed them. I was walking up the steps to the plane when I dropped this case over the side, and it crashed onto the concrete apron below and burst open and all the records spilled out! I had to fight back down the stairs to get my precious records. Embarrassing or what! Some of the records spilled out of their cases onto the apron – oh my god – what if they had been scratched or cracked? Luckily, they seemed to be all right and I quickly wiped the dirt off and repacked them. I could inspect them properly later.

So off I set by train to Frankfurt via the ferry to Ostend. After a long journey I arrived at Frankfurt but without my luggage, which, for some reason had been sent separately. I looked at a map, found the street and walked to the hotel, practising what to say to the receptionist in German. I also had in my pocket the telex from the hotel, which could explain everything in case my German was that bad.

I walked up the steps and into a magnificent reception lounge bright with opulence and massive chandeliers. Tentatively, and when no one else was about, to avoid embarrassment, I approached the reception.

'Guten Tag!' I said. That was a start; so far so good. I proceeded in broken German to explain my predicament. With a dismissive sweep of her hand, the tall blonde receptionist ushered me to one of the luxurious sofas. 'Nehmen sie Platz!' she announced, in other words, 'get out of my sight and park your arse over there you bloody foreigner!'

So there I sat all excited. I'd managed the first part and had broken the ice. This was a good hotel, five stars, bright and efficient I thought. Then this official-looking man walked over to me and said, 'Herr Paris?'

'Ja,' I replied.

'Velcom!' he answered with enthusiasm, trying out his English but failing miserably. This had to be the manager, so I rose and offered my hand. He not only shook it but hugged me as if I was the world's saviour. This was a bit OTT I thought. He carried on in German, 'Welcome again Mr Paris. It's so good to see you. Did you have a pleasant journey? Let me show you to the kitchens!'

I was totally flummoxed – had he got the right person? A commis chef isn't worthy of being treated like this. Was it for show, being in the public areas? So he took me down along corridors and down some stairs to the kitchen. Wow! What a kitchen – it was massive. This is a mistake I thought, I couldn't work here. He introduced me to the head chef, saying that he had employed me, and the chef's body language gave it all away. That dumb arse manager hadn't even told the chef that he had employed me! The chef looked around the kitchen at the various departments and in despair waved me towards the 'meat and sauce' section. What? You're kidding!

In a hotel of this size there are various departments to a kitchen, which include pastry, larder (salads/starters/cold/preparation), vegetables, fish, meat and sauce, soup, stillroom (where tea, coffee, toast etc is made), and wash-up. I should have gone straight into the wash-up section and at a push onto salads, but to the 'meat and sauce'! This was the most important kitchen section and I had only cooked a steak a few times at The Feathers, mostly for myself when they were going out of date! And German food is all different – they don't eat roasts like we do – how was I going to manage? Would I be trained? Would I let the side down?

I moved into my room, which was at the top of the hotel where the staff accommodation was located, and an English chef took me into the city centre that afternoon to buy my 'whites'. Yes, I liked these, black checked trousers, not the customary blue as in the UK, and white jackets with little black plastic studs as buttons. This would be a pose back in England, I thought. They cost me about £45, which to me was quite a lot of money.

The next day I 'started'. First, I had to have a medical. Then to the kitchens, having got changed in the kitchen changing rooms where I was issued with a locker. They got me doing all those tedious little jobs that are beneath the dignity of a chef, such as chopping parsley, which seemed to be a twice-daily routine. And it had to be chopped perfectly – no bits of stalk and no pieces larger than the rest, and then you had to wring it out in a cloth to dry out the excess moisture; god, what a palaver! I hated this because the parsley juice reacted with my hands, making them itch with wheals; the only way to temporarily relieve this was to rub my hands under hot water to almost burn them, but I guess this in reality only intensified the itching. I used to suffer from eczema as a child.

At times I would stand by watching them all shouting in German and pan-frying all sorts of strange cuts of meats with or without various sauces, none of which I had a clue about. It was a fast environment, and they knew what they were at; when they told me to get something I hadn't a clue whether my actions were correct or not. I can remember making a massive amount of horseradish sauce. Daily. Why bother, I thought, when you could buy it in a jar? To make this I had to scrape the horseradish roots with the back of a knife until they had all been scraped away, then mix it with cream. The scrapings looked a dirty cream colour and had the appearance of something you had pulled out from the bin. Was this the correct way? Perhaps they hadn't heard of graters in Germany? My eyes were streaming from the horseradish; peeling and chopping a whole sack of onions would almost be preferable!

Evenings were spent in the Düsseldorfer, a bar just down the road. Most of the chefs went there and when it closed at about 4 am, one across the road opened, which was convenient. We usually all sat around a particular table and ordered beer after beer, racked up with little marks on your beer mat. This was a new situation for me and a bit of a learning curve. Here I was sitting amongst a group of men, real men, or so I thought; I had been accepted by them – as far as drinking went – and was part of a team and they were mostly Germans as well. I couldn't offer much in the way of conversation but was happy to be amongst them. But what did they think of me?

But in the kitchens I had a feeling that it wasn't going too well and I was way out of my depth. I didn't feel that I was contributing enough and couldn't think for myself. All the time I waited to be told what to do, which was monotonous but at the same time exciting.

One evening a week later I was handed an envelope in the kitchen. I knew exactly what it was even before I opened it. I'd got the sack! It was in German and although I couldn't read it word for word, I got the gist of it.

I stormed up to the manager's office and barged in. This idiot had made a mistake and employed someone who was totally unsuitable. He remained calmly in his seat and said in German, slowly and deliberately, as if immensely inconvenienced, 'If you want to speak to me Mr Paris, go out of the office and knock on the door.'

'You bastard!' I thought. I was fuming already, but that was the last straw. I don't know how I contained myself, especially as I was in 'kitchen' mode so was in that state of mentality that is peculiar to chefs and the insane. What a twat he was! And he didn't seem to care! I went out, shut the door, and knocked on it, this time harder as if to imply that I was getting my own back on him.

'Kommen Sie herein!' he called out. I walked back in as calmly as possible.

'What's this?' I demanded, brandishing his letter, 'You've wasted my time, you've wasted your time, you've wasted my money and you've wasted your money! Why did you employ me?' Even if he didn't speak English, he got the drift all right. He could tell I was pissed off.

'Es tut mir leid,' (I'm sorry) he replied.

'You're sorry? Is that it! Jesus Christ!' I ranted, and immediately stormed off before he had a chance to explain himself and get the upper hand. I went back to the kitchen and asked a Scottish chef if it really was my notice, which he confirmed. The chef told me that the head chef was trying to find me another job, but I was so mad I just flicked my hand at him as if to dismiss him and the entire German population! My wages had been paid the day before and they came to the equivalent of £43, which meant that my entire week's wages had been spent on my kitchen 'whites'! What a waste of time and money.

The next day I went to look for a job in the local Arbeitsamt (job centre) but soon gave up because I was still pissed off with the hotel, and therefore the entire German population, all of whom I assumed knew about my predicament. So I decided to go back to England. I had registered with the German police two days before, as required by law, so I had to de-register and buy my ticket from Transalpino, which is a sort of travel agent. The next day I went back to England by train. On arrival at Ostend at 9 pm I had all night to amuse myself before the ferry departed in the morning, so I went for some food and then to a pub next to the station. I was quite nervous, being in the rough area of a foreign port, and it took quite a bit of courage to go into this pub. I got talking to some local women, and a couple of men. This was going well I thought, and these women were nice. But gradually a stomach ache was manifesting itself. I had been trying to suppress it, due to the female company, but it eventually got so bad that I had to leave, even abandoning my pint of lager, which was sacrilege, and I spent the entire night curled up on a station bench in absolute agony, bent double, being sick, and sweating buckets despite the cold. Food poisoning or what! I was really pissed off at having missed a potentially good night.

Back at my parents' house in Shropshire, the routine started again; testing the swimming pool chemically, various bits of gardening – as there had been snow, this was thankfully reduced to a minimum – shopping with Mum in Wolverhampton, not forgetting my favourite banana milkshake at Beatties, wine and beer-making, decorating, feeding and occasionally cleaning my sister Judy's hens, and general dossing about. Oh, and I did sign on and apply for jobs by letter and phone.

As Dad worked in London once a week, I went down with him by train to various London agencies to look for a chef's position and back to Shropshire on the late afternoon train with him. On the second such trip I went to the Jubilee Catering Agency, who sent me to the Master Robert Motel in Hounslow and to the Preston Cross Hotel in Bookham in Surrey. In later years, the Master Robert Motel seemed to be one of those establishments that was always advertising for staff and therefore one to avoid. I had interviews at both, and then went to two more agencies in London before getting back to Wolverhampton by train at about 11.50 pm.

The next day I phoned the Preston Cross Hotel who had agreed to take me on as a commis chef on a live-in basis. I was to start the following Monday, which gave me four days' grace. On one of those days Robin, the eldest of my three younger sisters, drove me to Birmingham, where I bought a chef's hat and some chef's aprons. The latter I never really liked because they were partly synthetic, which meant that the knot you tied with the straps soon loosened, but at the time I was very proud of having my own 'uniform'. I also left my acceptance note with the Birmingham College of Food and Domestic Arts (BCFDA) where I was to start in the autumn to do an HND in Hotel, Catering, and Institutional Management – a mouthful if ever there was! So it seemed that my life was getting organised...

Some friends of my parents, the Slowes, were staying the weekend and as they lived in the south east, they dropped me off in Great Bookham by car on their return trip on the Sunday. I knew the way to the hotel, or so I thought, and didn't want to inconvenience them anymore. Besides, I didn't want them to drop me at the hotel in case there was a fuss, ie I didn't want friends of my parents coming in to check the place out and making sure I was ok. I could stand on my own two feet thank you very much.

So after thanking them, off I set. It was really pissing with rain and I was wearing trousers and a navy-blue jacket, as it was the done thing in those days for someone of my education, and my haversack contained all my stuff, with one small additional bag. As you would expect, I got lost and walked around for miles before eventually arriving soaked to the skin, cold, miserable, and in need of a beer.

I felt a right twat going into the hotel looking like a drowned rat – not the way to present yourself to your employer, is it!? They fed me; I unpacked, watched some TV, and went to bed, but froze all night because there were no blankets on the bed. The next morning I started at 10 am and worked till 3.15 pm, then 6 pm to 11.30. I got some blankets in the afternoon from the laundry room and caught up on much-needed sleep. I can't remember why we finished so late, but my diary records that I drank champagne with Chris and Eddy till 2 am, which was a good way to break the ice. However the next day I nearly had one of my epileptic fits, having drunk too much the night before.

There seemed to be a really bad atmosphere between the kitchen and the management, and I obviously sided with the boys in the kitchen. The general manager wasn't so bad, but the assistant manager was a right bastard and I didn't like him one bit, especially as one of his eyes looked away from the other. I hadn't met anyone before with this abnormality and it gave me the creeps. The job itself seemed to be OK with me doing much the same as before, which was bar snacks, cold preparation, and potatoes & vegetables (prep, cooking, and serving).

But something just wasn't right there in my humble opinion. The hours were OK, being split shifts of about 10 am till 3 pm and 6 pm till 11 pm, as was the job itself, but nobody seemed to be happy. As for myself I didn't go out at all but just watched TV; well we couldn't go out, what with working all through bar opening times. How long could I keep this up, I must have wondered? My diary entry for Thursday 5th April sums it up: 'Watched TV. Had bath. More TV. Evening TV. Great life isn't it!'

It was a busy hotel though; on the Saturday we cooked for two hundred people 'a la carte', which is quite good going anywhere. But on the Sunday afternoon I rang my parents to say that I was coming home and that I had had enough. I hadn't actually resigned or anything like that; before taking any action off my own back I felt it was an obligation and necessity in those days to get my parents' 'permission' for anything, so by pre-empting them as to my intentions, this 'permission' had, as far as I was concerned, been granted.

So I gave the manager two days' notice and took the train to Wolverhampton, where my Mum picked me up. That evening, as expected, I had a massive row with Dad, who obviously wondered what the hell I was doing. Two jobs in a month. His career path was from being a successful accountant up to Finance Director for Tarmac; mine was a comparative failure. I had to list career objectives and a short-term plan which I thought fairly pointless, but I agreed, if only to calm him down and humour him a little.

On the train up to Wolverhampton I had been talking to a very nice blonde woman who I guess was in her mid-thirties and she advised me to buy 'The Lady' magazine because catering jobs were advertised in it. I dismissed this magazine as being jobs for women – chefs look in a male orientated publication like 'The Caterer', or so I thought. I rang a few agencies and a couple of local hotels, all to no avail, so out of curiosity and near desperation, I bought a copy of 'The Lady', if only to prove to my father that I was doing something.

To my surprise there were jobs advertised for all sorts of catering staff, as well as for nannies, au pairs, and the like. One such advert appealed to me – The Rose Revived pub near Oxford was looking for a full-time barman, so I rang them and arranged an interview. As the pub was out in the country it would mean cycling from Oxford, which was the nearest railway station. So off I went by bike the following morning from Beckbury to Albrighton to catch the train to Oxford. A day's adventure! I had already bought a map of the area and had worked out the route to the pub, which meant about an hour cycling from Oxford to Standlake. I arrived hot and sweaty and was interviewed by Mr Howard, who was a nice chap in his early thirties with a long black beard which seemed to cover most of his face. What a lovely pub! Uneven stone flooring, an uneven polished wooden bar top, genuine old furniture, real ale (very interesting!), half a dozen bedrooms, an extensive bar snack menu, a restaurant, and outside, a lawn with wooden bench-style tables and chairs, which led down amongst willow trees to the river Isis, which flows into the Thames. I think there was some confusion at the time whether the river at the Rose was in fact the Thames or the Isis.

Across the bridge was a pub called the Maybush and the bridge itself lent its name to Newbridge, being the postal address. It couldn't be described as a village, not even a hamlet, being just two pubs, and I don't know what it would be called, but it's ironic that the bridge is one of the oldest in Oxfordshire, being a narrow humped stone bridge – really rustic and romantic I suppose. It really was a lovely site.

The interview went well and there was accommodation provided, which I had a look at, and it seemed the ideal job. To my amazement he offered it to me, and I accepted. The day was Thursday 19th April, and I was to start on the Sunday. Great!

After something to eat I cycled off to Steventon near Didcot where Peter Churchill, my school friend, lived with his three sisters and mother. His father had been a pilot in the RAF but had sadly lost his life due to a flying accident. I was knackered by this time but Pete, his sister Caryn (who I fancied the arse off) and I went out for a drink or two. I stayed with them that night and Pete took me and my bike back to Oxford station the next day. It had taken me a week to find a new job – Dad could stick that up his arse! At least

I could get away from the never-ending list of chores that had to be done in the garden. That pleased me as well; I also had friends quite close by to my new job.

On the Sunday Dad took me to Wolverhampton station to get the 8.59 train to Oxford. Quite why train timetables are 8.59 am and not say 9 am I'll never know. It's really irrelevant due to the lateness of trains and delays, but it's nothing like what it is these days. I'm just glad I don't have to rely on public transport now – it's shocking that the service can get so bad. I digress...

John (Howard) picked me up at Oxford and took me to the Rose, where I moved into my room. This was a specially built staff block in the car park containing about six rooms and a communal bathroom. I didn't have much time as I started at noon, working till 2.30 pm, and then back in the evening from 7 pm till 11.30 pm. I was extremely nervous, what with a job on the public side, but I had to take the bull by the horns so to speak – I had to make this job work.

John began to show me the bar, the types of beer, the menu and wine list, and the kitchens. All the staff seemed nice, especially the evening waitresses who all appeared to be aged nineteen or thereabouts. Although the Rose was a free house, the real ales (Morlands Bitter and Morlands Best Bitter) were supplied by a local brewer. Lovely beer as well I might add!

I went straight to bed that night because I was quite tired, but also it meant I could avoid any conversation with the staff, which is pathetic, I'm well aware! About a minute after going to my room, there was a knock on the door. Christ! What's that! I thought with alarm. Did someone want me – like a girl (get real Geoff!) – or is someone taking the piss? Should I open the door?

I waited without replying, holding my breath in alarm, because if it were important, they would knock again, or call out my name. But nothing happened so I assumed to my relief, that it was one of the first two options, and probably the second chef whose room was next to mine. The bastard!

The beer cellar was a large refrigerated room with a concrete floor with wooden planks raised off the floor along one side, called a stillage, I was to learn. There were massive barrels on this wooden contraption and smaller barrels of bitter, lager and Guinness elsewhere in the room. It was clean, tidy, and cold. As John and Eileen, his blonde and attractive wife, had gone to Sicily for a long weekend, the running of the pub was in the hands of John's father Ted, who was an enormous, frightening, bearded man who was an experienced publican and ran the White Hart in the nearby village of Fyfield, which was a traditional pub, a 15th century chantry house with oak beams and log fires which sold all the popular real ales. This eventually, as you will read, led to my downfall.

On John's return a few days later I was shown how to deal with the real ale, which would be my responsibility, being the only full-time barman, a thought that terrified me. The casks, which were thirty-six-gallon barrels (unless they were eighteen-gallon kilderkins), were lifted with difficulty onto the stillage and left to settle, making sure the hole for the 'spile', a wooden peg, faced upwards. After a while, a spile was hammered with a mallet into the top of the barrel to remove the plug. A porous spile can be used or a hard one, but if you are using a hard one, you will need to periodically pull it out to vent off any gases that have accumulated. When this has happened, the tap can be hammered in and when the beer is ready to be served a porous spile is inserted, and the pipe connected to the tap.

My morning routine, starting at 10 am, was first to make the obligatory cup of coffee to recover from the previous night's drinking, sort out the empty bottles from the skip, then to apply polish to the stone flooring with a rotary machine, then buff it up with a rotary polisher, clean and polish the bar counter, mop the cellar with boiling hot water, pull through say a pint of each beer line to make sure it was OK, get the ice, oranges and lemons and other bits like cucumber and mint leaves, open up the bar, put out bar cloths on the bar, get the till, put out the bar snack menus, ashtrays and coasters and ensure everything had been stocked up properly. The bar had metal shutters, or grates I suppose they would be called, which came across from one end horizontally, much like the way a London underground station used to be shut at night.

Mopping the cellar was a nightmare, because as the floor was concrete, any water applied by a mop immediately soaked into the concrete, so it had to be done quickly and efficiently. No chemical like bleach was ever used in case the smell tainted the beer. I liked doing all this because I could take pride in my work and kept it clean. All too often in badly run pubs, the beer lines aren't cleaned regularly enough, nor is any pulled off to start with. Beer that has been sitting in the pipes between the cooler or refrigerated area becomes warmer, so the yeast multiplies and gives it an 'off' flavour, which is very irritating if you go into a pub early and get the first pint which hasn't directly come from the cooler.

Eventually, as polishing the bar counter by hand was a chore, I started to use the rotary polisher by holding it at the base and running it along the bar. I thought this was very clever of me and did just as good a job. Once a week I would do the bar order, and initially I would check with John that it was more or less correct until I was confident enough to do it alone. When the brewery delivered, I would open the cellar and check it all off. This was the only establishment I have worked in whereby the draymen were looked after. After the delivery they would be supplied with sandwiches and either tea, coffee, coke/lemonade or as was the case more often than not, a pint. They were good people and they really appreciated the way they were looked after.

It was a busy bar, based on bar snacks but with the usual locals drinking. As well as serving at the bar I would take food orders into the kitchen and distribute that food once ready, having first put on the tables the appropriate cutlery and condiments. I had to have my wits about me, and I enjoyed it. My confidence soon rose, and I even started to have conversations, although I never really could offer much, only comment on a particular subject. I'm also one of a rare breed who isn't interested in football, rugby or cricket, although I used to go and watch Wolverhampton Wanderers in Wolverhampton from time to time with my best teenage friend Henry Carver, who was later to take over the family firm Carvers (builders merchants) and transform it into the 21st century, increasing turnover substantially. His has been a real success story as well as to the benefit of Wolverhampton, and he has put his whole life into it. Well done him.

When the weather was hot, and especially at weekends, we used to frequently serve litre jugs of Pimm's outside. As well as the Pimm's, lemonade and ice, in went chopped lemons, oranges, apple, cucumber, and perhaps chopped strawberries, with a couple of mint leaves. It is sad that these days a Pimm's is frequently served with just ice. It's part of the modern trend for everything to be simplified, perhaps due to the cost and effort.

In the afternoons I either caught up on my sleep or went for a quick cycle to the nearby village of Standlake. Most evenings after work we sat drinking with the staff and locals till late or early morning, so I frequently had hangovers. Of the waitresses and bar staff I remember Tina, Vicky, Hazel, and Rose. We used to chat but they all realised how shy I was so they sometimes tested me to see what I would or would not do to them.

Once a week we all took it in turns to do the washing up. There was one KP, called Frank I think, who occasionally did a couple of evenings a week and perhaps some at the Maybush, but he was an odd character wearing a long raincoat who looked like a tramp. I think he was homeless, and I believe he used to sleep in one of the sheds at the back. The wash-up room contained two large industrial sinks in front of a window that looked out to the side car park, a plate rack on the left-hand side, and a more or less triangular shelf on the right for the dirty plates and kitchen equipment. This shelf measured about two foot by three foot and was nowhere near adequate for the covers we did, say fifty in the restaurant and probably about the same for bar snacks.

It was an unwritten rule that the waitresses, as in most catering establishments, when bringing in dirty plates and cutlery, would stack them neatly, but as the session progressed, it became an untidy wobbly stack with the overflow stack being on the floor. Jeans, T-shirt, and trainers were the required clothes, and one sink was for washing, the other for rinsing. The former had to be hot obviously, but the latter even hotter so that plates could drip dry from the heat. Gloves were available, but I hated wearing them because with my small fingers the glove was not skin-tight, making it difficult to pick things up. Besides, they used to get punctured from the cutlery. I rarely used them.

Plates were washed in the first sink and dropped into the next one with hot water. Once the latter had filled up you had to get them out, which had to be a pre-planned job, immersing your hands and arms for as little time as possible to keep the burning heat on your skin to a minimum. As the session progressed, the room would get into more and more of a shambles, because it was impossible to keep up, I would be sweating buckets, whilst my temper gradually began to get the better of me. I frequently swore at the waitresses, who understood and just glared back, but mainly I swore at the window or thumped or kicked something. As my temper gradually rose in crescendo, I would flip, grab a main course plate, and throw it out of the open window like a Frisbee. Woe betide anyone walking by or having parked their car in the way! At this point I would realise it was time to calm down and tell the next waitress to get me a fucking pint. God it was a battle getting through all that, and then you had the kitchen pots and pans to do. I would always have to retrieve the broken plate afterwards from outside and bin it without the boss seeing it.

On days off I used to go cycling and exploring, usually to Witney, the nearest town. At other times I would catch the bus to Oxford and occasionally go out with two of the locals with whom I had become friendly, Rob and Sue Sheasby. He was a traditional rocker, with long unkempt hair and old denim jeans and jacket. She was small, blonde and quite nice, and they were local people with hearts of gold and very considerate. They did not have a motorbike but a three-wheeler car, which they used to drive at its top speed of 40 mph or so. I felt really embarrassed being driven by them because although it was their pride and joy, they drove so slowly. My parents would have been horrified at the thought of me associating myself with a rocker. Rob frightened me a bit, even though he was soft spoken with a nice character. It's always assumed by the middle to upper classes that rockers will cause a riot, but for the most part, they are genuine people and would help anyone out in difficulty. I can't say the same for other trends like Mods, not that I've ever associated with them.

When we used to go to Oxford there was a rockers' bar, the name of which I forget, which was in a basement, with frequent entertainment, and you just ordered a bottle of 'steam'. In those days, before it was presumably copied by the Newquay Steam Company, I seem to remember that 'steam' was Carlsberg Export. I felt privileged at being able to 'join' this group and it took quite a lot of guts for me to go in there, especially as I didn't have the correct dress code – denim all over – but I tried as much as possible to comply.

On one day off I went to see Vicky, who worked as a secretary on a site in the country on the way to Witney. I'm unsure whether it was a building site or something like a quarry, but she worked in a Portakabin. She had a lovely personality as well as being fit, and I really liked her company. Off I cycled, having had directions, but at the entrance I thought, how can I cycle into private property? Are the men going to tell me to piss off? I cycled back and forth along the road, trying to pluck up courage. On the one hand I was afraid of provoking a confrontation with a stranger, but on the other it was a chance to see Vicky, which as you can imagine, seemed the preferable option. So I eventually cycled up the muddy track and found her Portakabin. To my amazement, no one had stopped or questioned me. She was as glad to see me as I was to see her. She was lovely. She made me a coffee. The sort of things that would have been going round in my mind would have been, *am I allowed to have a coffee? Will I have to pay for it? Should I say yes or no?* In those days I could still rarely pluck up the courage to speak to a girl and quite often I had to plan what I was going to ask, having previously considered the pros and cons. I was terrified of being made to feel even more inadequate than I already was. Likewise in certain ways I was still like a kid, not knowing whether something is allowed or not and often feeling the need to ask 'permission' to do something.

There was a spare chair in the Portakabin, and I asked her if it was all right to sit there. She looked at me in exasperation and said in bewilderment, 'Yes of course'. I went red with embarrassment, realising what a futile and irrelevant question I had asked. There was no way she would go for me now I thought. She proceeded to tell me about her job, and we had a brief chat and then I made my excuses, thanking her profusely for the coffee. It's always stuck in my mind what a prat I must have appeared.

I enjoyed cleaning the pipes, which was performed at least once a week, and testing the beer. When it was busy and a cask ale needed changing, I would go into the cellar with a pint glass, loosen the spile on the new cask and pour out about two thirds of a pint. This first bit was normally cloudy, so it had to be pulled off before being connected to the pipes. But before connecting up, I would pull a clear pint off, because the bar was busy and I was hot, and drink it in the cellar in one go in about five seconds flat; by God it was good. Then I would connect the pipe up and carry on in the bar. I loved that beer.

I also started to go and see Caryn, either in Abingdon, where she attended Abingdon Girls' School, or at her mother's house in Steventon. On one of the first occasions at her house, we were both seated on a sofa and her mother left us to it. It felt as if it was some sort of initiation ceremony whereby her mother had given 'permission' for us to do whatever, almost as if I'd been accepted by both Caryn and her mother as being a suitable boyfriend. Once alone, I sat there rigid, terrified as to what might happen or what was expected of me. Do I start or does she? I couldn't pluck up the courage to say anything and I think she felt the same, so we both sat there in silence.

After half an hour or so, her mother walked back in to see how we were getting on! I'll never forgive myself for not making the appropriate advances on Caryn or chatting her up. She had this lovely personality, and her words were short and clipped which I found endearing. But I tried to see her as much as possible on my days off.

Usually when I met her at her school we would walk around town or perhaps have a coffee somewhere, but one time she took me up to her dormitory, something that was obviously against the rules. She sneaked me in and told me that I was the first boy she had taken upstairs. Wow! What a privilege! Yet again I was terrified. What if we're caught? What will happen in her dormitory? Will we have sex? Will the other girls want me as well? A thought which was a real turn on, this being uncharted territory – will I be gang raped, so to speak? Or worse still, will they just laugh at me? Once in her room, what now? Who makes the first move? I was so in love with her that, despite being shy, I didn't want to make the wrong move and so lose her.

The tension was electric and we both wanted it, Caryn presumably for the first time, but after a few minutes of staring into each other's eyes, I bottled out and said that we ought to go downstairs. I was really happy just to be in her company and loved everything about her. Yet again I had to kick myself for not making a move.

But I was happy in Oxfordshire. I had a job which I enjoyed, I had met some new friends who I would go out drinking with, normally to the Maybush opposite or to a nearby pub, the Blue Boar, or the White Hart, or occasionally in Witney, and I had a girlfriend, and all the time my confidence was growing. I was also getting on quite well with the staff and began to socialise with them.

In those days when the roads were safe from perverts, one could hitch lifts. It was the Speech Day at Wellington, my old school, and I had arranged to meet some old friends there. I hitched various lifts, and on one of them I met a girl doing the same, and we managed to get picked up together by an old Italian couple. He then managed to crash his car, so we legged it and left them to it! I'm not sure if we even thanked them for the lift or not, but we were not hurt, thankfully, and to this day I'm not sure if they were injured, or what state their car was in.

One morning in June I sensed something wasn't quite right in the pub. Hazel, one of the girls, lived in our block and it was her birthday that day. I had to ask Mike the chef what was happening, especially as I had seen Hazel packing up her belongings. It transpired that John, the landlord, had been caught by Eileen shagging Hazel in the bar, either the night before or early in the morning, presumably as a 'birthday' present! Needless to say Eileen sacked her, and from that day on John and Eileen's relationship seemed to deteriorate a bit.

The food was good. Mike the chef would often cook us something not on the menu, for instance homemade burgers, which were seemingly about one pound in weight and size and topped with a fried egg. It is sad that some chefs do not give a shit about staff meals and have the mentality that it is preferable to give food to pigs rather than staff. In those days we had pig bins; these were large metal rubbish bins just for waste food. Farmers collected these and gave them to their pigs, along with plaster (building plaster) – but not from catering outlets I might add! – which was mixed in to stiffen up the joints of animals, perhaps veal especially, thereby enabling them to be slaughtered earlier. Another food substitute for pigs in those days was fish meal (I think), which you could sometimes smell on cheaper bacon. An initiation ceremony, equally if you were leaving a job, was to be put in the pig bin!

The 17th July was a day off, so in the evening, I cycled for a beer first at the White Hart, then to the Crown at Marcham and on to the Nag's Head at Abingdon where I met Caryn and Pete, her brother. After leaving Abingdon I revisited the above pubs on the way back, ending up at the White Hart for a quick last beer. Old Speckled Hen was a favourite, and, as it turned out to be the chef's birthday there, one quick beer led to several and so on until about 1 am. By this time I was totally legless and unable to walk, and Ted the landlord offered to put me up for the night, but as is too often the case when under the influence, I declined aggressively, implying that I could manage. I cannot remember being in the bar at all, or who I was with I was that far gone. When I eventually left, I staggered and crawled outside to my bicycle. I can remember getting on it and cycling off – God only knows how. A bit later I found myself being driven in a red car back to the Rose. On reaching the car park I thanked the driver profusely and tried, unsuccessfully, to get out of the car. The locals, who were still drinking in the Rose at the time, came out to see what the commotion was. One of them was a drug rep so he knew a bit about medicine and said to me 'You're going straight to hospital.'

'No, I just want to crash,' I managed to slur. Ironic words, seeing that unknown to me that's precisely what had happened!

'No, take him to hospital can you,' he replied to the driver, and with that I must have passed out. So he took me to the John Radcliffe Hospital in Oxford. I had no idea what was going on and was so drunk that I had not realised I had been in an accident. It turned out afterwards, when out of hospital, that my bicycle, which was still at the side of the road where the accident had occurred, was mangled and a bike mechanic informed me that I hadn't just fallen off or hit a tree, but a vehicle had crashed into me, or me into a vehicle – more likely the latter. I presumed it was the same car that had picked me up.

When I next awoke, I was lying on my back strapped to a bed in some corridor, unable to move, unable to speak, and not knowing what the hell was going on. I lay there in and out of consciousness or sleep for what seemed like for ever. Eventually I woke up groggily to find myself in a ward, and again, I couldn't move but was aware that something was different.

When I eventually came to, a nurse came over and asked how I was feeling. Like shit! She told me that I had been in an accident and that my glasses had smashed up my face and I had been given plastic surgery. They had operated on the afternoon after my accident, presumably to allow time for the alcohol to dissipate. They had extracted glass from my face and eyelids, though thankfully there was none in my eye, stitched up my upper eyebrow and the skin between my nose and upper lip, performed a 'cheek rotation' in which they cut the skin along the side of your face towards the ear and pull it round to join up where skin was missing, below my eye and upper cheek in my case. I also had a skin graft taken from my upper arm, which went onto my upper eyelid, or what was left of it. Blood and guts have always interested me, and this was really exciting. I could not open my mouth due to the swelling and bruising, could not see out of one eye and was told to lie flat on my back due to the injuries. It was also quite painful so I must have been on drugs to ease the pain. Food had to be absorbed through a straw, called a maxillary diet, as I was to find out a year later when I trained as a hospital chef.

My pillow was dirty with bits of grit, mud, and dirt that had been picked up from the road and these were falling onto the pillow, and after three days of the nurses refusing to wash my hair, because my face had to be kept dry, I created such a scene that they complied, and so came my first venture out of bed since the accident. They had even refused to give me a mirror to look at my face, so I realised it must have been quite bad, so bad in fact that when my Mum and oldest sister Robin came to visit, they walked straight past me. I feebly waved a hand and uttered something, and they came over in obvious shock. My Mum had to sit on my 'good' side. She must have been really anxious because my real father had been killed in a car crash (not his fault) when I was about four years old, which, at the time, devastated us all, and she didn't want to lose another member of her family.

I wasn't a pretty sight. My right eyelid had begun to open a bit and the eyeball was red, or rather the fluid inside was. I had scratches, bruises and stitches on my face, and it didn't seem that the person looking back at me from the mirror was the one looking into it. They brought me some cans of lager, which was a godsend, but I was not allowed to drink them!

It was really strange that on the night of the accident I had been wearing trainers, T-shirt and shorts, being the summer, but there wasn't a scratch, bruise or mark anywhere else on my body from the accident; my face had taken the brunt of it. Maybe I had hit the windscreen of a car face first out on the main road.

I had a visitor each day. John, my employer, broke it to me gently that 'We'll have to see whether you can work afterwards or not', and I apologised for having let him down. I think in reality he was furious that I had 'let the side down' and to this day I regret the way I left the Rose. Rosemary, one of the live-in staff, brought me some grapes and strawberries, which was sweet of her. The nurses, that wonderful breed, were fabulous and really helped me through that difficult time. I will be forever grateful to them.

On the bed opposite was Dave, who had broken his ankle on a building site, so once I was allowed up I would move over to his bed to play cards. He was one of those people who could crack a joke a minute at the nurses and he was very funny, but it caused me absolute agony. Anything remotely like a smile on my face stretched my scars and I would have to clench my fists trying not to laugh or smile. It's extremely hard, I can tell you!

After six days the surgeon gave me the all-clear, had my wounds redressed and discharged me. What, after only six days? I was flabbergasted. I thought I would be in for at least a few weeks and had not really prepared myself yet to face the outside world. John picked me up and took me back to the Rose, where it was formally decided that my face was too horrific to be in public view, so my employment terminated. I would like to thank you both now, John and Eileen, for a wonderful time. A few days later my sister Robin came to collect me, and I went back to Shropshire.

A few weeks later it had occurred to me that I hadn't phoned Caryn, nor had it occurred to me to phone her whilst in hospital. Her mother was upset, saying 'Why didn't you call, are you all right? You could have stayed with us afterwards,' which would almost have been preferable than going to Shropshire! I missed out on a good one there and to this day I could kick myself for not pursuing my interest in her. I saw her only once after that, at Peter's wedding to Jeanette, by which time Caryn was happily married.

CHAPTER 4

Birmingham – the college years

And so ended an enjoyable few months. My convalescent period lasted a few months, giving me a legitimate reason for doing as little as possible, which pleased me immensely. I had to visit the surgeon in Oxford a couple of times to see how the scars were healing and see my local GP for check-ups, but otherwise that was that. I also had to get some new glasses and had my eyes tested by our family friend Tony Blackham to check the physical state of my eye. I could not make up my mind whether it was cool to have a 'war wound' or whether girls would now look at me as an ugly bastard. If it was the latter more probable option, then I had nothing to lose, because I thought of myself as being quite unattractive anyway!

The whole family went to Aberdovey for the summer holidays to spend time with the Tildesley family. Dad, due to a golden handshake from Tarmac, had been able to buy a cottage in Aberdovey – Heather Cottage. He had changed jobs to become a Director of BZW, which was the merchant banking side of Barclays Bank. He also became a Director of Barclays Bank itself. We normally sailed in Richard's Drascum Lugger, which was a nice little boat with a mizzen mast, occasionally in his father's yacht, or pottering about in Dad's C-craft, which was a little inflatable with an outboard engine. There was also a lot of mackerel fishing; the fish used to collect near the sand bar at the mouth of the river, and sometimes you could haul them out as fast as the line went in. It was a bit foolish of me to go sailing, which I did on a daily basis, because I was supposed to keep my face and right arm and skin graft dry. It also enabled me to avoid the daily ritual of swimming in the river Dovey before lunch or supper. The water was invariably cold, and swimming against the current was a complete waste of time and a pointless exercise, but one had to suffer in those days. They were good days, with a very enjoyable social life.

Back at home I decided to get a part-time job, if only to partially avoid doing housework and equally menial chores at home. Robin worked as a waitress at a local hotel called Hack Cottage. This was part of the Patshull estate, and Hack Cottage had been converted into a small hotel. I was to help in the kitchens. This was an unusual professional kitchen; domestic cookers and female chefs! In those days women chefs, or cooks, were usually confined to pastry or starters, not being deemed by the men to have the stamina or experience to being in charge! Apologies to all you excellent female chefs. There were three of them as well!

The one and only fridge was just a domestic one. Next to the kitchen was a large room, still, it seemed, in the process of being built, for it contained newly erected plain pine wooden shelving using 3" x 2", but no actual glass in the window space. Each evening three or four different joints of meat were cooked. These shelves contained cooked meats from previous evenings, most of which were in various states of decay including some that had gone mouldy. After being used for the evening they were just left there and what with the heat of the summer, they deteriorated fairly rapidly. The vegetables were all fresh with perhaps the exception of peas and chips, and were all grown on the estate. Again these items were either cooked or uncooked and in various stages of decay on the shelves. Any local animals such as foxes could easily have jumped through the window at night and had a field day gobbling up scrumptious foods. I had never seen anything like it. It was strange in those days being told what to do by a female chef, but I assisted as best I could given my physical condition. I think I just did veg and salads – nothing too demanding.

After the evening service finished, we invariably went up to the bar for a drink. Most evenings, and I only really worked there for ten days or so, Chris the manager let us buy discounted drinks and sometimes gave us hotel bedrooms to use for the night, in case we were too drunk to drive, I guess. Very generous I must say. I don't think I really contributed much because I was trying to protect my face and help out where needed.

Another reason for only working temporarily was that I had arranged my own holiday, which was a week in Christchurch with my old school friend Richard Allen, a few days with my Granny in Exmouth, followed by a party near Bayford with the Wilbrahams, who were family friends, and then back to Shropshire.

For my first year at the Birmingham College of Food I was going to be residing at Cambrian Hall, student halls of residence near the college, so I had to go through the process of applying, being accepted, enrolling at college, and buying a set of Sabatier knives, a set of chef's whites, a white laboratory coat and a waiting outfit of white jacket, bow tie etc. As I already possessed my German chef's whites, I had a heated argument with the lecturer concerned who said that everyone had to wear the same uniform. I won this argument, and this made me stand out from the rest of them because my German trousers were black check whereas English ones in those days were just blue check. Nothing fancy like modern multicoloured chefs' trousers, so I was able to pose wearing my chef's whites.

When I moved into Cambrian Hall, each unit contained ten bedrooms with each pair of bedrooms sharing an interconnecting bathroom with shower only, and a central area consisting of a lounge with TV and kitchen. The sexes were segregated amongst four blocks, each block containing four units. I soon made friends. Everyone seemed to be very friendly, and it was especially helpful to meet some of the third year HND students who were doing my course. Cambrian Hall also accommodated students attending other colleges or Universities locally.

I soon settled down to college life and made quite a few friends, which was quite easy because we were all in the same boat. Life revolved around lectures Monday to Friday 9 am to 5 pm with Wednesdays and Fridays being half days. Lunchtime was either spent in the college refectory, more often than not at the 'Kiss' pinball machine, or in the Shakespeare Pub, which was 'home' for three years and just across the road from the college. The fact that it was a rough run-down pub seemed irrelevant at the time, as long as it served beer, which was all that mattered.

Subjects, in order of preference, included Food Science (mainly because the lecturer was an attractive blonde), Microbiology, Material Science, Cookery, Food & Beverage Operations, Front of House/Reception, French, Building Management, Management, Housekeeping, Work Study, Economics, Accounting, Law, and Social Studies. With all these subjects and subsequent homework, it was quite a tough course. During the evenings, after having eaten, I normally tried to work until about 10 pm when it was time to go to the college bar, which for one term was shut down due to a riot and fight, or would go out with friends to other pubs, perhaps to listen to a band, or go for a curry which cost about £3.50 in those days.

I am not going to dwell too much on life at BCFDA because I could go on forever. The lecturers were all very professional, for which I will be forever grateful, even if one or two did have their idiosyncrasies, such as Ben Eshelby who 'taught' us cookery. His favourite phrase was 'Essence of Anchovy' and it seemed that everything we cooked had to have a splash. Yes, well, enough said! I quite enjoyed cookery, mainly because I had a head start on all my colleagues from my previous – if limited – experience. One cookery chef was a fifty-year-old Frenchman, Mr Piotet, who, on day one, showed us how to peel a carrot, which was to peel half of it away from you, then turn the carrot round to peel the other half. I peeled carrots by holding them lengthways in my hand and peeling the whole length towards me, rotating the carrot with my fingers.

'You're not doing it right,' he told me.

'Well, I've always done it like this!' I exclaimed as he looked at me with incredulity. He must have thought, 'A little nineteen-year-old telling me how to peel a carrot! Who does he think he is?' I realised the crassness of what I'd said to him. I had to do it his way, even though my way was far more efficient!

The worst subject, and one that we considered to be totally irrelevant to our course, was Social Studies. It was so boring, but, as one finds out in the real world after college, surprisingly relevant. Who wants to know about people and their problems, we all thought? Housekeeping was equally tedious, with a timid old woman teaching us how to change a bed in thirteen steps. How is one going to do that in practise we thought – what a waste of time. Housekeeping became more interesting in the subsequent years when 'Mama' Webb became our lecturer, a huge black woman with an equally huge personality. I must mention Val Barker, who was responsible for the Front of House side. With her vast expertise, although tedious and monotonous, she was very valuable in our education. Madame Callow was invaluable in our French lessons with her homemade book of French culinary and catering translations.

On Monday mornings our lecturer 'Shortarse' (real name Shorthouse I think) went through food and beverage service in one part of the industry or another, such as trains, cruise liners, hospitals and then prepared us for lunch service. We had to wear our white waiters' jackets and serve lunch in the restaurant, which was open to the public. Stress or what! We each had one or two tables and the food was cooked by other students in the kitchen. We were on show and had to perform 100% professionally. In reality it was a farce because everyone queued up at the same time to collect the main course 'meats', silver served them, and then went back for the vegetables; by the time they were served the main course had gone quite cold! And then when you get out into the real world, you may have fifteen to twenty tables (shock horror!) not just two! Shortarse took an instant dislike to one of my friends, Nick Pearson, who started college on the second Monday and arrived late for the lecture. In he walked with a crash helmet and bike leathers, like a rocker. Shortarse went silent in disbelief at this unshaven longhaired 'lout'.

'Who the hell are you?' he demanded.

'Nick Pearson, I'm starting the HND.'

'Not like that you're not!' Shortarse retorted. 'Go and get your hair cut, shave yourself and then we'll see!'

'You can't make me cut my hair,' Nick replied, eyes narrowing.

'If you're going to be serving the public and attending my lectures then you will. Sit down for now and you can go when we start lunch.' Nick quietly sat down, not sure whether he had won the argument or not. He duly had his hair cut a bit and shaved to oblige Shortarse. He became a good friend of mine and eventually went into hospital catering.

Money was always an issue. I was unable to get a proper college grant due to the level of earnings of my father, so my entire spending money relied on his allowance to me. Ever since I was sixteen and had my first pocket money, I had had to prepare 'accounts' for him of my spending, which pissed me off immensely. I recorded all daily spending in my diaries of things like food, basics like toothpaste, travelling etc, but these had always been falsified (whether he knew it or not was irrelevant) with the majority of my spending on alcohol and cigarettes allocated to other departments such as food, clothes, stationery and domestic items like toothpaste etc. But it was getting to the stage where I needed more cash to fund my social life, so I had to look for a part-time job.

I scoured the local paper and found a job as a barman at Samantha's nightclub above Silver Blades Ice Rink. The bars I had worked in before had all been relatively quiet, but this was a nightclub where everyone got pissed. How would I manage? At least I was familiar with Samantha's as we all went there more or less weekly anyway on student night, and it would help knowing that some of the people I would be serving would be recognisable.

Work started at 9 pm and finished about 2 am. The other bar staff were lovely – Penny, Carol, Anne, and Theresa. I need not have worried because it was quite easy to serve in the bar, and the evening gradually built up into a crescendo of activity and I felt mature enough to deal with everything. Yes, some people were abusive and nasty due to the effects of overindulging, and others cantankerous; women could be bitchy, but overall, I enjoyed it. Being a half hour walk from my digs, I used to get home between 2.30 am and 3 am and frequently began to miss the following morning's lectures. Even though I only worked a couple of nights a week, it was a huge effort to get up in the morning. Attendance at college counted as part of the course, and you could be failed for poor attendance.

One Saturday night three fights broke out almost simultaneously, one of which was between two women. I leapt over the bar and approached them. By God, the claws were out! I hadn't the faintest idea what to do or say, so I just watched them with mild amusement whilst they scratched each other to pieces and slagged one another off. When the bouncer came over, he gave me a right bollocking, as did the manager Paul later, saying that that was his job; mine was to look after the bar, cash and alcohol being the obvious concern. Oops! My mistake, but it was instinct, I explained. Also it hadn't occurred to me that I had never been in a 'grown up' fight or that my glasses would get smashed, never mind my face, which was still a bit tender from my accident earlier in the year. Then there was the insurance angle. Bar staff were not insured for that sort of thing. That was a lesson.

During the Christmas holidays I alternated between Shropshire and Birmingham as far as working at Samantha's and socialising with friends was concerned. I was due to work at Sam's on Xmas Eve and had a massive row with Dad at home. His head turned purple.

'You can't work on Xmas Eve! It's our family time! Tell them you can't work!' he ranted.

'Fuck off you bastard!' was what I wanted to say, but he did have a valid point in that public services on Xmas Day would be severely limited. But I did not want to let my employer down because it was an important night for them and difficult to get staff. I was in a real quandary – how to please both sets of people?

The first thing was to get away from Dad, so I went to Birmingham and found out when the last train was back to Wolverhampton. Then I gingerly went into Samantha's and explained to the manager, Paul, that I had to leave early because of the transport, something that had not occurred to me until today! We had a massive row and I apologised profusely but offered to work a short time, but he let me go so I caught a train back to Wolverhampton and went to the Tildesleys' house, from which someone took me to Beckbury. I had survived the day intact, even though I got a further bollocking from Dad for being 'moronic'! As an appeasement I offered to work New Year's Eve at Sam's, which made up for letting him down at Christmas I suppose...

Reading back on my diary of 1980 it is apparent that the entries were pretty similar; fell asleep, did homework, went to pub(s), did more work, with more intermittent items such as went with so and so to a film or band, went to see Wolves play, missed a lecture (normally economics), got pissed, went to a party etc etc – you get the drift! I was constantly knackered, and often hung over, but they were good times and this was the start of me growing up a bit.

The summer term of our first year was spent on Industrial Practice, which meant two sets of six weeks in a catering establishment, be it hotel, hospital, contract catering, pubs, restaurants, industrial catering and so on. My first one was at Stoke Mandeville Hospital and the second at the Worcestershire Hotel in Droitwich. The thought of the former really excited me – all those rampant nurses! I arrived via a complex route; train to Oxford, bus to Aylesbury, and taxi to Stoke Mandeville (SMH). The living quarters were very strange, long buildings, all ground floor only, six of which spread out at angles from a central point. Each building contained about twenty single bedrooms I would guess, with a central corridor. They were old, dilapidated, and looked damp, and reminded me of Nissen huts. I was shown the staff cafeteria, and more interestingly, the social club which was close to our bedrooms and in the evening met some of the staff. I felt I had a USP (unique selling point), so to speak, in that having recently undergone plastic surgery, I had inside knowledge of hospitals and was not just some green student, and I assumed they would be fascinated by my facial scars. Yes, I know, a bit juvenile of me to think this way, but what the hell!

My function was to be trained in the operation of the kitchen. I also had to write a report on my experiences for college, the following of which was the introduction to that report:

INTRODUCTION

Stoke Mandeville Hospital in Buckinghamshire is a large general hospital, which has become world famous because of its specialised unit for the treatment of spinal injuries. It has also gained valuable publicity and funds through the efforts of the TV personality Jimmy Savile, who also has a part time job at the hospital.

In order to attract suitably qualified staff from all over the world to work at the hospital, an attractive working environment needs to be provided. A good salary, recreational and social facilities, and good food are probably the three main aspects which will attract someone to work there.

Appetising food is also essential to the patient, especially if they have undergone major surgery or will be confined to a wheelchair for the rest of their life, or are expecting a long stay in hospital, for the patient relies very much on the friendliness, help, and psychological support of the nurses before they leave hospital and go back to the 'outside world'. Similarly, appetising, nourishing and varied food plays an important part in the patient's psychological struggle in adapting himself to his new condition.

This project shows how the kitchens operate, showing the type of food given, and some of the problems that occur.

My first day was spent with one of the four ward clerks who go around the wards getting the next day's food orders.

The clerk collects today's supper, tomorrow's breakfast and tomorrow's lunch and start at 9 am and finish at 1.30 pm. 'Normal' patients, ie those who are not on a special diet or a private patient, have three lunch/supper choices, 'A' for a normal meal, 'B' for a light meal, and 'C' for a (weight) reducing diet. They are asked on the spot for their choices, taking into account special fancies whether for taste, religion, vegetarians etc, and these are taken back to the office where the staff collate them to work out the food required for each ward, and in total.

There was a blackboard in the main kitchen on which these entries were written so the kitchen staff were able to work out what to put where. I think there were about thirty wards in all. Each ward had a 'trolley', which was plugged electrically into the wall so as to maintain a hot cabinet and a cold cabinet. At the appropriate time, a four-wheeled vehicle connected them up like a train and trundled off, dropping the appropriate one off at each ward. Each ward also had a small kitchen in which eggs (for scrambled eggs – one of the evening choices), ice-cream, rolls, tea/coffee etc were kept. Private Patient orders were given to the Private Patient chef, and special diets and/or likes/dislikes to the diet kitchen.

The next two days were spent in the 'Provisions' or Store Room, and here is my report for that department:

PROVISIONS (STORE ROOM)

Function: To supply Stoke Mandeville Hospital and thirteen other local hospitals with food components.
Staff levels: 1 storekeeper, 1 storeman, 1 assistant.

The first two work more or less on the same level of

responsibility except that the storekeeper is in charge. They receive incoming goods and deliver requests. The assistant mainly does the heavy work and odd jobs.

A bin card system is in use for all the dry goods on the shelves, whereby when an item is issued out it is marked on the card, which is beside the item concerned. The same applies when goods are received. This method ensures an up-to-date stock record, and instead of having a regular stock-take, random checks are applied to see if the card agrees with the quantity.

There is a freezer for meats and frozen vegetables, and a fridge room, theoretically for defrosting meats before being sent to the kitchens. (This, however, did not always apply.) Meats and vegetables are delivered each morning (however not until 10.15 – 10.30 sometimes) whilst dry goods are delivered on Tuesday to the main kitchen, diet kitchen, (and presumably the new wing kitchen). Milk is delivered on a standing order basis to the main kitchen and the wards. Each ward can present an order any day for dry goods eg tea, coffee, bread, and these orders are delivered the next morning from the day the requisition is received. The milk delivered to the wards varies from day to day according to the number of patients in each ward.

Food not consumed or used by the kitchen is not 'issued back to the stores' but is used up for something else, eg old stew to mince. The only way that waste food can be used up is through the cafeteria. Otherwise it has to be thrown away and this was often the case. Ice-cream and fish are kept separate from the rest of the food orders as they are frozen.

Each month the kitchen can make a profit or loss through food, even though the staff cafeteria aims at a

30% profit. This can arise from:

a. Money not being received until the month after
b. Bad food control
c. Wastage of food
d. Overspending of monthly budget

The monthly profit (or loss) does not take into account any overheads eg wages, lighting, heating, contract cleaning etc.

My opinion of the storemen is that they work according to their own time and not to that of the kitchen staff. They frequently deliver late, ie frozen chickens arrive in the morning; there is not enough time to defrost them so they have to be put in the oven frozen. Whilst I was in charge of the diet kitchen several times I had to 'ask' for a particular food item which had not been delivered on time. Although I eventually got the item, they proved to be argumentative, and several times I collected the whole week's order myself, just to be certain that I had it ready for use.

The store-keeper himself has worked in the stores for 39 years and will have a routine to suit himself first. I can only see the system being improved when he retires.

Both of the above extracts are from my report, and whilst the terminology may be a bit studentish, I think the caterers amongst you who are reading this can see that something isn't quite right! The hospital catered for about one thousand patients for lunch and perhaps a few hundred less for supper and breakfast, with about eighty special diet lunches, as well as the staff canteen.

I spent a day or two with the Private Patient (PP) chef and my god, what horrors arose there! On one of the days, a patient's lunch was roast chicken, which is easy enough, but due to the ordering system with the stores, the chicken would arrive at about 10 am and in this instance, was completely frozen with the giblets inside the chicken wrapped in the usual plastic. The chef just opened the oven door and lobbed this frozen chicken inside and left it to cook on its own. No de-frosting first and no basting with oil or fat. No roasting tray. I was aghast, being a student, and wondered whether this sort of practice was commonplace in the trade – I can assure you that it is not! So this frozen chicken, after being cooked in the oven, was duly cut up for the patient, plated, and put in the appropriate trolley.

The kitchen staff always had a break after the lunch had gone out and work resumed about 2.15 pm to prepare for supper. One private patient had ordered an omelette for his supper, served at approx. 6 pm, so the chef cooked it off at about 3 pm, plated it with a lid, which every plate had to help keep the food hot, and put it in the hot section of the trolley. This meant that a private patient, who was paying to stay, was going to be served an omelette that had been cooked and 'standing' for over three and a half hours! It must have been horrible. No wonder people were ill!

I mentioned this practice to the Catering Manager, in the guise of it being part of my college report, and he duly bollocked the PP chef and told me that he shouldn't do it. However, the chef did not really have much of a choice with the chicken, unless the ordering/supply system was changed.

After that experience, I went into the main kitchen, which was all part of the same area as the private patient section, and helped the chefs. It terrified me that I might be responsible for cooking, or more likely cocking up, mashed potato for a thousand people! There would normally be five chefs cooking the lunch, excluding the private patient, pastry, and diet sections. Graham, the supervisor, who was a real queen, would write on a board the particular duties for the day for each chef. Most of the equipment was steam based – something I had never come across before – so you can imagine my interest. Soup and vegetables were cooked in massive steam boilers whilst potatoes and some vegetables like carrots were cooked in steamers. There was also a Collins rotary oven with eight carriers, which was impressive! There were four KPs for the washing up, and one woman who just seemed to walk around cleaning work surfaces with a dirty cloth – it seemed that if this cloth had passed across a table, then the table was deemed to be clean, which of course was totally the opposite. This was all so exciting for me – a large operation with some good organisation but appalling hygiene. In those days government departments were covered by 'Crown Immunity', meaning that they were exempt from visits by health inspectors. Thank god, for the sake of the UK population, that that is no longer the case!

What did become apparent was the lack of enthusiasm in the kitchen amongst the staff, with the KPs virtually ignoring instructions from chefs or the supervisor. Perhaps in the case of the gay supervisor, this was because he would just mince along gesturing flamboyantly with his arms and hands, with his instructions seeming to be more like genteel requests than orders. Also, leftover food was put in one of several fridges, but there seemed to be no demarcation between salads, raw meat and cooked meat, which were all mixed up. Dreadful really. There was not much incentive for the chefs because the menus were rotated, so no room for personal flamboyance, and although one chef might cook the soup on a Monday and the vegetables on a Tuesday, the food was pretty dreary and bland.

Then there were the cockroaches. Where do I begin on this one? These little beasts like steam, or the heat it generates, and as the kitchen was fairly old, it contained lots of little cracks and crevices for these little bastards. Every six weeks the pest control company came in and painted a clear substance across every skirting board, every floor edge, across doorways, along door edges etc so that wherever a cockroach went, it would walk over this poison which would kill it. They do not like light, so they come out at night, and on the morning after a visit by the pest control people there would be about fifty to sixty dead ones on the floor. The following morning you would find about thirty and so on with these numbers gradually decreasing each day, but never below a dozen or so. At first I avoided them like the plague, but eventually they were so commonplace that I just walked over them, squelching them to put them out of their misery in case they hadn't quite died. They also had that particular smell which is peculiar to cockroaches and one I will never forget! They are virtually impossible to eradicate, or were in those days, and the building of the new kitchen, which was imminent, would be a godsend in several ways. I have only ever come across them in one other hotel, and that was just the one cockroach.

Evenings were often spent in the social club where I soon mixed with the nurses and other staff, all of whom liked alcohol as much as me, and I had the occasional night out with someone in Aylesbury.

After a brief visit to Mum and Dad I returned to be hit with a bombshell.

THEY WANTED ME TO RUN THE DIET KITCHEN!

I had only been working in the hospital for a week and they wanted me, a snivelling little student, to run a department? Had they got the right person? Were they out of their minds? Despite my protestations, I knew that this was a real challenge and make or break time as far as my career to date went. I did not have the faintest idea how to go about it, never mind the cooking, and as for the diet aspect I might as well have been on a different planet! So I braced myself and once over the initial shock, I did my best to tackle it with enthusiasm and intelligence. Better lay off the old alcohol for a bit Geoff, I said to myself; this is serious stuff. I was to be trained for a week and then take it over.

The diet kitchen, which was a separate kitchen adjoining the main kitchen, normally had three staff with two working the shift. There was a head chef, an assistant, and a trainee. The responsibility of the head chef was to do the cooking, dishing up the food, making maxillary soups and sweets, making weekly food requisitions, and supervising the assistants. Maxillary diets were liquid diets for those unable to eat solids. The assistant did the washing up and made tube feeds and nutrient drinks, mise-en-place, and helping the organisation of lunch service and labelling of foods.

The head chef was about to go on holiday whilst the assistant was ill, leaving just the trainee and me. Incredible I thought – talk about being thrown in at the deep end! The dietitian, who was responsible for deciding the type and quantity of food that a patient might require, gave me a crash course in diets over the first two days, which I frantically scribbled down parrot fashion in the hope of digesting it later. Each patient had a colour-coded card to denote the type of diet, with his name and ward number and diet written at the top with three columns, one each for lunch, supper, and comments. On each of the meal sections, lines were drawn to specify the quantity (in ounces) of meat, vegetables, potatoes and sweet. Then there were separate sheets of paper for tube feeds, nutrient drinks, maxillary diets and sandwich fillings (for some reason). Most of the diets were diabetic, but others included weight reducing, low cholesterol, low protein, high protein, low fat, low fibre, high fibre, milk free, gluten free, and low sodium and/or potassium.

On starting at 9 am, I would collate all the cards for the lunch, which was normally for about eighty people of which say sixty would be resident and twenty from the Geriatric Day Unit, and put milk on for the hot milk pudding, of which there was always one each day. Then I would dish up all the cold sweets such as tinned fruit, jelly, or fresh fruit. I would collect all the raw meats needed for cooking the lunch from the main kitchen and start these off. Then I would make the milk pudding. At about 10 am any remaining meats like lamb chops were cooked off and fresh vegetables cooked in one of the steamers. Frozen vegetables were cooked in saucepans. Potatoes and the soup were obtained from the main kitchen. In between all this I had to do the maxillary diets. These were liquidised diets taken through a straw and had to be pureed and strained so as to avoid any lumps, so the soup was easy, but the sweets were a little more complex. Often, in fact most of the time, I took a sweet from the main kitchen – say trifle – and liquidised it. It might look horrible, like the contents of someone who has just had liposuction, but as far as I was concerned, it was nutritionally correct. Otherwise we would liquidise and strain tinned fruit in water, or blancmange with flavourings and milk or water to dilute it. Some of the maxillary soups were given additives, eg 15g Casilan to ½ pint soup, which still had to be strained into plastic cups with straws, and labelled. Casilan in itself is pretty disgusting, but we did not really have time to improve the flavour.

At 10.30 am all meats, potatoes, and vegetables were set out and 'tinned up', which meant that if a particular ward required six portions of diabetic food, six portions of the meat dish were put into a tin, six portions of potatoes into another tin etc. Individual diets eg one low sodium was plated, and the metal cover labelled accordingly. Then all these were placed in the hot compartments of the ward trolleys and any cold items in the cold sections.

Let's say the main meat dish was mince based. On the stove would be 'normal' mince (ie oil/mince/salt/pepper/onion etc) for say fifty diabetics, a small saucepan with oil and mince for four low sodium diets and a small one with water and mince for a low fat diet; in all there might be six saucepans all with different ingredients according to the diet and it required some intelligence, and a clear head, to keep mental control of things and which pan contained what.

Everything was normally finished by 11.30 am, the assistant having done the tube feeds and supplements and distributed them accordingly. It was, and had to be, a highly organised system, but it certainly didn't leave any room for error, what with having just an hour and a half to cook everything off and an hour to dish it up. What did hold up the system, to our utter frustration, was if the main kitchen was late in making the soup or potatoes; we were all under time constraints, but none more so than the diet kitchen. Quite how some of the meat dishes such as a stew could be cooked off properly in an hour and a half seemed to be irrelevant!

After a quick coffee break, we would sort out the supper cards, make the sweets, have a half-hour lunch break, then sort out and cook the supper food, with it being dished up in the same fashion as lunch from 4.30 pm onwards with us finishing about 5.30 pm.

Tube feeds were made up of various ingredients. For example a full-strength feed, which would be 200 calories and contain 70g protein, would contain 600 ml milk, 200g Complan, 125g Maxijoule, 50 ml Prosparol, one Ketovite tablet, three salt tablets (300mg) and diluted to 2160 ml with water. Supplements were either taken in addition to a normal or prescribed diet, or as a diet in itself and as well as the above ingredients they included products such as Build Up, Clinifeed, Vivonex (a meal in tablet form also used by Astronauts), Hycal, Rise and Shine, Coffee Mate etc. All these were ordered from the hospital pharmacy.

We also prepared pureed meals for people who had progressed from maxillary diets to pureed ones. All in all, the responsibilities were quite comprehensive.

Occasionally I would be late with the maxillary diets and would miss the train which would set out from the kitchen at midday, dropping a trolley at the appropriate ward, so I would take various feeds to the ward myself and pass them to the nurses. On one particular day I gave a maxillary soup to a nurse. 'Hi, this is for Joe

Bloggs!' I announced, proud of the fact that I had made it myself and brought it personally to the ward.

'Oh, we don't need that, we give him the normal soup,' she replied, dismissing the interruption I had caused to her routine.

'You can't do that,' I retorted with authority, 'He's on a maxillary diet!'

'This soup's disgusting – no one can drink it,' she replied with finality. I went bright red as this was an affront to my cooking skills and then my temper hit red as well.

'I've worked my arse off making this soup and you just chuck it away! What do you think I am? You're not the dietitian, you can't change a diet without authority!' and shoved the soup into her hands and stormed off. I was furious, absolutely mind-bogglingly 'mental', and swore profusely all the way back to the kitchen.

I normally went somewhere on my days off, either with hospital friends to Aylesbury or to see old friends from my Rose Revived days. One day I hitched to the Rose Revived to see everyone. During the evening Eileen, who had split from John by now, enquired where I was going to stay the night, so offered to let me stay in her room, which I gratefully accepted. 'Sleeping' with an ex boss! Yes please, I thought, I could do with a bit of that! Later in the evening, after a meal of chicken liver pâté followed by a steak, Ted, Eileen's father-in-law, and a huge, bearded man, asked where I was staying the night.

'With Eileen,' I beamed, in total ignorance of the implications.

'No, you're bloody well not,' he retorted, face full of anger, 'you can sleep out the back!' So, not soon after and feeling a bit sheepish, I made a quiet exit to the sheds at the back and settled down somewhere rough where I thought I could sleep. Not that I did, as I was racked with pain, was sick all night and had got food poisoning, presumably from the pâté. I imagined it was that bastard Ted's way of getting back at me!

My last ten days at the hospital were spent in the pastry section and when I had finished my six weeks training, I went back to my parents in Shropshire. Two days later it was my next six weeks training, at the Worcestershire Hotel in Droitwich, and my sister Robin kindly drove me down. My hospital reference given to the college stated that my main weaknesses were 'Failure to understand some of the principles of NHS catering. Lacked self-confidence with other people', whilst the strengths were 'determination to carry tasks through to the end. Adaptable. Able to work unsupervised', which I thought was quite an insult after all the effort I'd put in.

The Worcestershire Hotel was a traditional Victorian stately looking four-star hotel, with at least two bars. The main one was called the Sovereign Bar and the other the Gents Bar. The former had all the action, the latter for men only. Nick Pearson, a friend of mine from college, was also doing his training there. It was just my luck, being introverted and quiet, to be allocated the Gents Bar. Thank God these places are virtually non-existent now. This bar was for men only and had that decades-old smell of stale tobacco, along with a brown ceiling and equally morbid looking centuries-old décor. Each lunchtime, just one old fart came in, ordered the same half-pint of bitter and smoked his pipe like it was going out of fashion. Conversation between us was stilted and rare, as we had nothing in the world to talk about. It would have been better having no customers at all. It was mind-numbingly boring. I worked split shifts, 10.45 am to 2.45 pm and 5.45 pm to 11.45 pm. The evenings were equally monotonous. Quite why they did not turn it into a bistro or something else that could generate income was beyond me.

After closing the bar at night I would proceed to the Sovereign bar to help serve and/or clear up. This was such a relief! Real people and some action. I do not remember much about the bar staff, except for one barmaid, Cynthia, who ticked all the boxes.

After two weeks of the bars, it was time for two weeks in the kitchen. I duly presented myself in whites and knives at the ready, and they just left me. There was no training, they never asked me to do anything and I was astounded. When the kitchen was busy and in the proverbial, I would offer to do something, only for one of the chefs to exclaim in amazement, on viewing the result, 'How did you know how to do that?' They obviously thought I was 'green' like most students. So those two weeks were a waste of time.

The voluptuous housekeeper, Caroline, also lived in the hotel, as well as Nick, me, and maybe one or two others. We would often drink and socialise in her bedroom and Nick regularly took great pleasure in jumping up and down on her bed with her. I am not sure to this day whether he was trying to break the bed or shag her – if the latter, good luck to him. But it was all a good laugh. The staff were all ok and our personal social side with the live-in staff was cool, inevitably so with lots of drinking.

The last two weeks were spent in the restaurant, which was traditional silver service. Quite frightening really, as this was my first test of working in a proper restaurant.

The shifts involved a 7.30 am start to 10 am for breakfast, 11.45 to 2.45 for lunch, and 6.30 to 9.30 for dinner. Not much to say here except that I missed breakfast one morning after a party in one of the staff bedrooms the previous night, and when I did make it down, by God I was bad. Alcohol makes my epileptic drugs ineffective, and coupled with the inevitable brain dehydration it is, and always will be, a nightmare for me. I suffer from immense hangovers, and any sudden movement or noise which could cause the brain to 'start' is enough to trigger an epileptic fit, so I have to be quiet, keep as cool as possible temperature-wise, move slowly and deliberately and eat some food, which seems to help – maybe something to do with blood sugar levels? I did not have an actual fit that morning, but they started on several occasions, and each time I managed to overcome them. When these start, you have a 'hungry' feeling in your stomach, you can smell something that isn't there – always the same smell – and what you are looking at starts to flash like an old film reel jumping. You can stop this by putting your head between your legs, which presumably increases the blood flow to the brain, but if you are too late then the fit starts and you lose consciousness and do whatever you do. It is remarkable that some epileptics, including me, can sometimes subconsciously 'delay' or prevent the onset of a fit until they are out of danger or in my case, out of public view. I dread these days when I am 'bad' and just plod through on autopilot until I can get some sleep.

It had been arranged via my college that for the summer I was to go and work in Germany, not for official training, but general experience, so I had been to the college to sign a contract and bought things like a haversack in Birmingham and ordered some Deutschmarks. I only had two days between finishing in Droitwich before leaving for Germany, so I had to be organised.

CHAPTER 5

More European adventures

Germany here I come! I'll get you this time you bastards! I'm not taking any shit like I did in Frankfurt!

I was determined to get my revenge on the entire German population for my previous demise at the Hessischer Hof. Quite what this might have involved was beyond me, but terrorist tactics were certainly not on the agenda! I was equally apprehensive of the fact that a repeat of my previous time – ie being sacked – would really drive me mad and demoralise me. It had never occurred to me that I might not be a good employee!

So off I went by train to London, where my diary records that I met Caryl, who I guess was also a student at college doing the same thing as me somewhere else. We took the evening boat to Ostend and the night train to Munich, arriving at 9 am the following morning.

This was a huge railway station, a bit like Euston or St. Pancras, and the sight of fat German men in their lederhosen drinking lager at the tall beer-barrel-style tables at the railway bars and throwing up at 9 am filled me with dread. What had I walked into now? Was this what they did here? I hoped these beer-swilling German pigs who were about to be my colleagues weren't going to get me too pissed! Actually, believe it or not, I like the Germans as a people as well as their country, which I always had to play down to back in England, there still being at that time the German/English thing, much as there still is today with the French and English.

Anyway I took public transport to the nearby town of Oberau, where I was to work in a hotel. However, the manager, who obviously did not want me, had arranged for me to work elsewhere, so he duly took me to the pretty little village of Oberammergau. These towns and villages are situated at the start of the Alps and if you climbed up the local mountain, you could see where the Alps ended and the plains began. What a beautiful fairy-tale village! Every house seemed to be painted with quaint decorations and it was rather like going back a century in time. There were murals of daily life, for instance the local landowner on horseback, a woman baking bread, pictures of dogs, social gatherings etc, mostly in shades of blue and brown. Another might depict a religious scene from the time of Christ. Lots of window frames and surrounding walls were elaborately painted. Some houses sported wooden balconies, and most were fronted with hanging baskets. There were no gardens as such in the town centre, and outside the main square houses were dotted around randomly, with their surrounding land being mostly rough grass, where you might find the odd goat or horse. Lovely and rustic, and ideal to live in as there would be no garden to worry about!

I located the Wienerwald Restaurant, which was in what I assume was the main square, and the dray was outside, this being a beer delivery vehicle, except this was a horse and cart! I was to work in the kitchens. The Wienerwald was part of a German restaurant chain, a bit like the Berni Inns in England. My accommodation was provided and meant sharing a room with a Scottish lad called David, who was a waiter at the Wienerwald. He was probably a bit annoyed that I had to share with him, especially when it came to the evenings vis-a-vis his girlfriend. As there was only one key to the room, he laid down the law with regards to me entering 'his' bedroom. I would have to throw a stone up to his window, whereupon he would give me the signal that it was OK to come in and he would come down to let me in. The only difficulty was that the window was behind the restaurant and access to it meant climbing a gate and going across some waste land. This gate was a military style vehicle double-sized gate with three rows of barbed wire angled at forty-five degrees on the top, ie about ten feet high, to prevent entry. I was incredulous; what were people going to say? Would I be arrested or deported? Was I allowed climb this (obviously not!) and walk on this land? Was this for real?

Anyway, I could manage it quite easily because I could just fit the four fingers of one hand between the sections of barbed wire and get over. And then I had to get back over again the other way. It also meant that I had to stay out if he was out, or otherwise 'occupied' in his room! Not the most ideal of domestic arrangements I can tell you.

For the rest of the first evening I walked around the village, and the one thing that struck me as being odd was that most of the locals sported long beards. Perhaps it was a peculiarity to the area or a religious sect, like the Orthodox Greeks or the Belgians who seem to sport beards and unusual hair designs, or the druids even! The outskirts of the village contained a massive coach park with hundreds of coaches. What was going on? Where were all these people? It turned out that it was the year of the Passion Play, which is a world-renowned event held every ten years in the village, involving most of the town's population for which the men grow long beards to look the part. It was fortunate for me that I was able to witness this, even though I did not go to see the play. Amazing really. They all wore lederhosen with wide colourful braces, and it felt like belonging to part of a bygone era.

The best seller in the restaurant was spit-roasted chickens, for which they were renowned, and they were sold on a daily basis by the hundreds. One of my jobs was to prepare and roast the chickens. The parson's nose would be cut off (god knows why), and I think we cut off the feet and wing ends and after seasoning with their special mixture with a paprika tang, they were skewered on a metal spit with five chickens to a spit. About eight spits would fill up a metal tray, and these trays were stacked up. They had a rotary spit roaster, so a spit was slotted in and left to turn in the roaster. They were sold fast enough to warrant constant replenishment. I soon became sick of the smell of raw chickens, as well as fed up with constantly having to wash my hands to get rid of that slimy coating you get from handling them, but the smell of them roasted soon compensated, and they were lovely and succulent. They were cut in half with scissors that resembled secateurs more than anything else and sold as a half portion.

Most of the salads were tinned, as they are in Europe, these being julienne of cucumber with a slight minted flavour, sliced beetroot, sauerkraut, which is pretty gross at the best of times, and julienne of carrot or crinkle sliced carrots. All these products were limp and soggy as if they had spent the afternoon in the pot wash water and been recycled – they might have had more flavour! They were pretty bland and tasteless but were the norm, much as in England we used the ubiquitous lettuce, tomato and cucumber. Various types of lettuce and tomatoes were fresh and I can't remember whether boiled eggs were cooked fresh or whether they were that awful product that resembles a tube whereby the proportion of yolk to white remains the same throughout the whole length, and that was that.

I enjoyed it there and felt I was doing a responsible job. It was simple enough for me and after two days I had got the hang of it. The manager treated me as an equal, ie someone with a modicum of intelligence, and showed me as much as possible, including, after a few days' work, how to use the take-away section. This was a small hatch where the customers could order takeaways direct with the kitchen with a till. One of us would take an order, take the money, prepare and wrap the food and give it to the customer. As most of the orders were chicken and chips, this was fairly easy, and I felt terribly important being able to operate a German till and felt that I was contributing to the well-being of the German population. If I could, I would try to avoid the takeaway in case I made a fool of myself in terms of language difficulties, and being shy, it took double the effort.

One problem which occurred daily was wrapping the takeaway chickens. We would lay them on a thick tin foil, which was about half the thickness of cardboard, bring the two ends up around the food and smooth them out between our first two fingers so as to be able to fold or roll the top of the foil down neatly. I was constantly slicing the foil into the skin in between the two fingers in use – a bit like a paper cut – so I had to start again because of the blood. This was a constant annoyance to me, being time wasting, and one that I could not avoid, despite trying my best.

One day two young lads came to the takeaway and ordered something which I didn't understand. 'Wass?' I said – 'what' in German. That is not particularly polite German, 'Wie bitte?' being more appropriate, meaning 'yes please', but, as I was a chef and not bothered with the delicacies of life, it was entirely appropriate! Especially as I was busy and not keen on doing the till, so anything to piss a German off and to let them know that I wasn't amused at being disturbed without being obvious seemed in order to me.

'Oh, erm, two... chicken... and chips... please,' one of them replied.

'Oh, we've got a right pair here,' I thought, so again I asked 'Wass?' with the intention of winding them up, now that I had realised they were Brits. They began to look exasperated at each other and me, and again the request came.

'Chicken ...... chips?' as if I was an idiot.

'Ich verstehe nicht!' (I don't understand) I replied as ignorantly as possible, shaking my head.

'How are we going to ask this fucking guy for food, let alone where we can find a garage to fix our tyre,' one said in desperation to the other.

'Wass wollen Sie?' (What do you want?) I offered as if to show concern, as they stood there in silence and at a loss as to what to do. I could see they were on the point of leaving, so I felt sorry for them and said with a sarcastic grin 'So it's two chicken and chips then lads?'

'Er...Yes, thank God, you speak English!' one gasped in relief. Moron, of course, I am bloody English.

'Yes, I am, that's xx Deutschmarks and if you're looking for a garage, take that road up there and there's one two hundred yards on the left!' I beamed.

'Oh thanks mate, thank you very much, we don't know what we'd have done without you. Cheers, thanks then,' they grovelled to me during their exit as if I was their lord and master. 'Ha! Got you! Sucker!' I thought, and that tickled me for the rest of the week.

The assistant manager however, treated me more like a second-class citizen or like one of the Yugoslavians. In those days, as sad as it was, Germany had a lot of Yugoslavian employees, much as in the UK we had coloured people, and they were treated with contempt and often held basic jobs like being a KP. This assistant manager obviously felt that anyone who did not have pure German blood was a lower order of life, and he made me do demeaning jobs for a chef, like sweeping and mopping the floor, and this began to irritate me.

Most evenings after work were spent in the nearby disco, Maxim's, until 1 or 2 am. One night on my own I was talking to a British soldier on leave at the bar and having a normal conversation. Eventually I bade him goodbye and left. Outside I was suddenly punched in the face, and reeling, fell over the edge of the pavement onto my back in the road. This bloke had followed me out and punched me for no apparent reason and now he was kicking the shit out of me as I tried to protect myself. All I could do was to try and fend off his kicks. Then suddenly someone else came up, karate chopped this guy, which laid him out cold, and helped me to my feet.

'Thanks,' I offered.

'No problem. I'm his officer and I'm sorry he's done this to you.'

'He just attacked me for no reason!'

'Well, it's alcohol that does it. If I were you, I'd beat it, because his mates aren't going to be too amused with you when they find out what I've done to him,' he stated matter of factly.

'Oh, OK then, bye.' I staggered off, tail between my legs so to speak. I was shaking from the adrenalin and climbed up the double gate near my room, but when I got to the top, I slipped and fell off, gashing my arms on the barbed wire. 'Christ Geoff, what a mess you're in', I thought, as blood was pouring from my arms. I climbed back up, got over, signalled to David to let me in, climbed back over the other way, and once inside, tried to clean myself up. I had to sleep on my back with my forearms up off the bedding because they were bleeding so much. I should really have gone to a doctor and had stitches, but I was afraid to, and didn't want to cause a fuss, being British. Stiff upper lip and all that crap! I probably should have had dressings applied and taken antibiotics or whatever, but in the morning I just applied quite a few plasters on them in the kitchen. I still have two scars to this day.

I had decided to leave because of the attitude of the assistant manager, so I phoned the agency in Frankfurt that my College had booked this job through. They advised me to go to the Arbeitsamt (job centre) in the nearby town of Garmisch-Partenkirchen. The next day, my day off, I did this by bus. A local hotel in Mittenwald was looking for a salad chef, so I applied and so went to the Hotel Wetterstein for an interview, for which I had to wait four hours! The following day I phoned the proprietor, Frau Monika Lorenz-Rechthaler, a small fat woman whose grandiose name implied a high standing in the Bavarian state, and she offered me the job. Great I thought, and with that phoned Herr Schmidt in Oberau and broke my contract with him (my original contract was with him even though I was working elsewhere). The next day, 16th July, I moved to the Hotel Wetterstein which I would describe as of a three-star standard with nicely decorated outside walls with pictures with a nightclub in the basement called 'Zur Holle' or 'To hell'.

I was led around the back of the hotel through large double gates into a stable yard and in through an old barn style door and up some old stairs to the staff quarters, which were above the stables. The room was pretty dingy but adequate with a bathroom and shower at the end of the corridor. My window looked out onto the yard, where there was a huge pile of horse manure! I became very anxious, because I'm allergic to horses and anything or anyone with a horsey smell can set me off, but I had to start work at once so I unpacked my chef's clothes, changed into them and went downstairs, through the yard and stables to the kitchen, where I presented myself to the head chef, a fat greasy, sweaty ugly man in his forties, to say the least.

Detlef, a twenty-one-year-old German, was the second chef and he proceeded to show me to my area, this being the salad section. There was also Roland, a tall good-looking aristocratic-type German catering student much like me who worked in the main kitchen. The salad section was a small room with a window which looked out onto the stables and the horse manure, which was directly outside my window. On the windowsill were our salads, namely lettuce, tomato, grated carrot, julienne of cucumber (may have been tinned), Bavarian potato salad, and so on along with cold fish like roll-mop herrings (matjesfillet), salami etc; in all about a dozen square plastic containers put out along the windowsill. My job was to plate up salad-style starters to order, along with garnishing other dishes. The Bavarian potato salad, made with stock, oil, vinegar, seasoning and finely chopped onion was out of this world. The rest were relatively ordinary salad items and in a day or two I had picked up the routine, including the orders in German. The heat was intense and there did not seem to be any air conditioning. It became a kind of mental torture as to how long I could put up with the heat before opening the window; this then meant that a collection of flies, mostly the German variant of bluebottles looking for an alternative to manure, or their next course, flew in and settled on the salads and proceeded to do what flies do. I hate flies with a passion, so I could only put up with this for a couple of minutes before having to close the window again. It was dreadful to think (at least in my college times when you assume that everything should be clinically clean!) that people were eating food that had come into indirect contact with horse manure! I'm not talking about one or two flies but probably a dozen at any one time.

Shifts were split, normally 8 am to 2 pm and 5 pm to 9.30/10 pm, after which the live-in staff normally went to one of the pubs, the Alt Mittenwald or Blakey's. The kitchens themselves were quite small and from memory, rather dirty. It was awful to think that you could legitimately have stables and manure outside, but there you are. You live and learn. Nearest to me in the main kitchen was the vegetable section where Roland or Detlef worked. Opposite him the head chef worked, calling out the orders and what was to go 'away'. The vegetables were finished off in frying pans with butter and seemed really fresh and appetising. There was a huge pot constantly on a very low simmer, and the contents, a grey-green pulp that perhaps could be used as rat poison, smelt like the after-effects of eating a ton of baked beans with cauliflower! This gruesome substance turned out to be sauerkraut, made with green cabbage, and it seemed to be gently simmered for days and days, much like a stockpot. It was constantly in use but was pretty revolting to taste. The only other ingredient worthy of mention was caraway seeds. Cafés and takeaways use tinned sauerkraut normally, as we did in the Wienerwald Restaurant, and I can only make a comparison with the tinned and 'freshly made' sauerkraut with freshly made coleslaw in England to the pre-made variety in plastic containers which is always overloaded with mayonnaise and bland. We occasionally made rotkohl, which is similar but is made with red cabbage, apples, onion and wine and had a sweeter taste. I have always found sauerkraut to be tasteless and therefore pointless to eat, much like Iceberg lettuce in England. Being English I suppose, I was never allowed to do the vegetable section, but I made such a fuss one day that they let me do it, with Roland doing my salads. I was horrified afterwards that he put lemonade in my grated carrots to keep them fresh, and the next day I threw them out as they had fermented!

So, here we go, the first order. No problem. I have done this in England, I can cope with this... And then they started coming in and I began to get mixed up with whether he wanted the veg 'away' or 'on order'. Or whether he had repeated the same order twice. I got in such a shambles that I had to admit defeat and let Roland back in. That was the only time in my life that I felt out of my depth during service. I was really embarrassed that the British side had been let down by me, as well as the kitchen. They were right; I couldn't do it and was acutely embarrassed. I had felt competitive with Roland, German student versus English student, so wanted to outperform him, which ended disastrously for me.

We weren't allowed into the public rooms of the hotel at all, but we did once manage to go down to the nightclub, which was decked out with murals of people, scenery and buildings in mainly blue and brown and variants of them, similar to the outside walls of the buildings in all of Bavaria.

The scenery was beautiful locally and quite often I went walking in the hills and forests. There were lovely little lakes, like the Lautersee in the hills with small, almost individual beaches where we could sunbathe and swim. There was also a cable car, which went up to the Karwendelgebirge, the local mountain, which was quite a sight. Another day, some of us went up the Zugspitze. There were two Irish chambermaids, one of whom was called Cora, whose only claim to fame was her entry in my address book, which included, as well as her address, an entry 'Land of Queers and Piss Heads!' I didn't particularly get on with them; they were pale skinned, anaemic-looking alkies who swore a lot and were too loud for my liking – not their fault but mine, because I preferred quieter people.

I also worked one day a week as the KP and helped with general chores like putting stock away, moving beer barrels etc. Less than two weeks into my job I was lifting up a new beer barrel which was sitting horizontally on top of another when my left hand slipped, being greasy from cooking, and the barrel fell onto my fingers between the rim of the bottom barrel and the other on top. Christ, it was agony! My third left finger went black, as did the nail, and tears were streaming down my face from the pain. Frau Lorenz-Rechthaler offered some kind of sympathy, but I didn't know what to expect anyone to do. Besides, my secret opinion of Germans, never mind a German chef, was that they were superhuman and things like that would not bother them, so after ten minutes or so, I carried on working. Again stiff upper lip and all that! I couldn't let the British side down, now could I? It was busy and work had to be done!

I was the KP that day, which was the worst possible thing to do in this situation – the slightest touch on my finger produced horrendous pain, and to clean the large pots and pans, I had to lift them with thumb and first finger! Not an easy task I can assure you, especially when you are trying to keep the injured finger out of the way! It was a mammoth task getting through the day and wore me out.

The next day, coincidentally, was my day off, so I went to a doctor who took an X-ray for which I had to pay and informed me that I had chipped the bone. He gave me ten days' sick leave, which to me confirmed that my injury was serious enough to warrant time off. But what would the head chef say? Would he beat me up? Would he smack me in the face? In the event, he just swore blindly at me for ten minutes in that chef fashion. Oops! I thought it prudent to get out of the way, so I went sunbathing on the Lautersee and in the evening I went to the cinema to see 'Atlantik'. The following day Roland and I went to Grubsee, which was a car ride away, and went in a boat – god knows why – but I got asthma and bronchitis so I had to go back to the doctor in the morning. I also had to get a sick note from the hotel and register at the town hall.

A couple of days later David and I got up at 6 am to go to Austria, where he did some skiing on a glacier near the Italian border. He had a car, so he drove, and the scenery was fantastic. As you drove through Seefeld, which was a small town on the valley floor near Mittenwald, a whole new valley opened up beneath you, the views of which were quite staggering. Obviously I couldn't ski because of my finger – not that I could anyway – so I wandered about the mountain.

Later in the afternoon back in Mittenwald, I went to see the doctor because I was getting bored from not working, as you can imagine. I was getting fed up with drinking all the time and could not really afford it. Frau Lorenz-Rechthaler sacked me and told me to leave, but at lunchtime the manageress (Frau Lieb in my diary) told the boss she couldn't sack me, so I stayed but was moved into Dave's room for some unknown reason. Perhaps she wanted my room for someone else? So the days went on; I went sunbathing a lot at Lautersee, and one day I walked to the nearby town of Welmau and hitched back. Leutaschklamm, the local waterfall, was a good place to visit. However when I went back to work, it did not feel right and as I could not function properly, not being able to use my hand effectively, I gave the boss two weeks' notice. The rest of my time seemed to be spent getting pissed, but I did go to Innsbruck one day by train and hitched back. It was good in those days that you could do this without any trouble.

I left on Saturday 23rd August, and I wasn't really sad to go. It was an ordinary job in an ordinary kitchen. The only memorable girl I had met was Penny Frith, a history student at Durham University. The rest I couldn't have cared less about, except Roland because he was a catering student and had taught me some things.

I hitched to Oberammergau to say farewell to the town and the staff at the Wienerwald and then hitched to Munich, left my luggage in the station whilst looking around the city, and then, after collecting my luggage, went to look for the youth hostel. Upon arrival, they directed me to 'the tent', presumably an overflow youth hostel, which I think was somewhere on the way to Schloss Nymphenburg. This was a huge marquee on the outskirts of Munich where you paid three Deutschmarks for a space and a blanket.

When I went into the marquee, where were the beds? There was nothing, not even camp beds. A bit bizarre I thought. There were various backpacks/rucksacks/haversacks/sleeping bags littered around, maybe a couple of dozen, some seemingly abandoned, and some with people around and about. I was in a real dilemma as to where to camp. Against the edge out of the way? But the grass might give me asthma. In the middle, where I might be in people's way? Should orderly rows be formed? Should I pitch away from everyone else or would the rest of the world think me abnormal? Was there a section to separate the sexes? Fuck it, I thought. I dropped everything where I was and went outside to see what was what. A pretty Austrian girl came up to me and introduced herself which was great. Her name was Metina and she was a dentistry student. What was a stunner like her doing talking to me? Was she right in the head? I couldn't believe my luck, so as the time was about 5 pm off we went together for a walk and something to eat and drink and returned about 11 pm.

Amazing! The marquee was jam packed solid. Every imaginable space was occupied by bodies in rows either in sleeping bags or in blankets with luggage at one end. I hadn't a clue where my belongings were – or even if they were still there – and clambered over countless bodies before finding it. There wasn't a lot of space left for me but, as quietly and unobtrusively as possible, I managed to bed down for the night. I couldn't believe the number of people there; it was quite staggering.

There was so much activity early in the morning that you felt obliged to get up at the ungodly hour of 7.30 am and boy, was it cold for August. You were presented with a cup of a hot insipid-looking liquid in a plastic cup which I can only imagine was an attempt at black tea: were we worthless lost souls being offered the cheap equivalent of a soup kitchen or what? But at that time, it was just about the best tea I had ever had and although it gave me spasms of hunger, as tea does to me, it was most welcome.

That was our breakfast! No food, not even a stale roll. No wonder everyone was packing up and moving off. There were showers and washing facilities, along with benches and seats to drink the tea on and to recover from hangovers. You were only allowed to stay three nights, couldn't pre-book and had to take everything with you in the morning.

I dumped my belongings in the main railway station and wandered down to Marienplatz and the rest of the city centre. What a lovely city – clean with attractive buildings and tourist features. In the evening the plan was to return to the tent, and for some unknown reason I took a train, presumably the underground, which I have to say was the cleanest and most efficient I had ever had the pleasure of using, but it didn't stop where I had hoped it would, so I had to travel on to the first place it stopped at. It may have been a normal train, above ground, which I thought would stop at all the local stops, but as it didn't I ended up god knows where and got lost. I walked for miles and miles that evening, navigating by road signs back to Munich, and eventually ended up at the tent exhausted, hungry and thirsty. I had to go without food and beer that night, never to be repeated! Bad move Geoff, but at least I was at my destination.

The following day I went to the Olympic Stadium, which my parents had been to for the Olympic Games back in 1972. Very impressive, as were the Botanical Gardens and Schloss Nymphenburg, which I also visited.

The day after that I had to move on, so after a final look around town, I walked to the motorway to hitch a lift north. On the slip road there was a queue of about twenty people, all waiting in turn to hitch hike. Bollocks to this I thought, I'll start walking along the motorway, thumb out. Fortunately after a hundred yards or so, a businessman stopped and offered me a lift to Bonn. Brilliant! Off he sped at a hundred miles per hour or so, and duly dropped me off in Bonn, where I stayed the night in the Youth Hostel. After looking around Bonn in the morning I hitched to Cologne where I met three English guys and we went up the Dom cathedral with its magnificent and intricate spires before having a few beers beside the river. The next day was spent looking at the Tutankhamen exhibition and the Romanisch-Deutsche Museum and generally wandering about. I had a German pen friend, Petra, so I phoned her and arranged to meet up in Essen in a couple of days' time. I took the train to Essen and after finding the youth hostel I was met by Petra and went out for a meal with her and a friend and then went back to her flat. As they were talking German non-stop, my conversation was limited. She was a nice enough girl, but her friend Karyn was much more attractive.

The next day we drove to a nearby lake, Werden, and did the tourist stuff before they took me back to the station, where I caught a train to the north coast and the night ferry to Harwich, and then by train to Wolverhampton. In those days, my father expected me to start walking from the nearest town with public transport, Albrighton, and this time they did not collect me, so I walked to Beckbury. That was a good experience; I had worked the summer abroad, had a week travelling – had achieved something, so I felt entitled to do nothing for the next two weeks before going back to college.

I had previously arranged with Chris Sykes to live in 'digs' for the second year of college and we had found rooms with the Hemmings in Small Heath, one of the more salubrious parts of Birmingham. This was in St. Oswald's Road, which is off the Coventry Road, one of the main roads into Birmingham. The other student living there, Jon, was studying to be an optician. The Hemmings had their own private lounge and further back a smaller lounge which was mainly where their Labrador slept, and through that, the kitchen, which we could use. Upstairs we each had our own bedroom with a communal bathroom for us three, but our toilet was outside the back door, via the kitchen, in a converted coal shed. They were nice enough people, but the dog was a pain in the arse because if you wanted to go to the toilet at night, it meant passing through the dog's 'room', which woke it up and hence was followed by incessant barking. The toilet was not heated so in winter we froze our bollocks off!

We had to take the bus into the city centre and then it was a short walk through the shops to the college. It was good to be back with old friends and soon some of the new first year HNDs became our friends too – mostly those that frequented the same bars as us, these, as always, being the Shakespeare, the Longboat and the college bar. There was the occasional party, either in Shropshire with friends from home, or somewhere in Birmingham at students digs. And so life went on; they were good times, but the work was hard, or rather it was hard with the hangovers.

The Lent term was going to be spent on Industrial training, so Nick Herman and I had been selected to work at the Novotel in Nottingham; actually it's at Long Eaton, which is a nondescript town off the M1 between Nottingham and Derby, so mid-December Nick drove us up for our interview, which was really a formality. It was a French-owned company and the management were French, as were some of the staff. The hotel had about one hundred rooms, along with conference and banqueting facilities and an outdoor pool. Fixtures and fittings were plain and modern. A practical hotel. We had a look at our digs, which were a ten-minute walk down the road in a house owned by the hotel where various staff lived. That was that. Job done. I was actually looking forward to it; I had this idea that working for a hotel group meant that certain standards and systems were in place.

We went up to the Novotel on Sunday 4th January (1981) but it had been arranged for me to go to Wordsley Hospital in Kingswinford to have another operation to my face, which meant two weeks away, so I only actually worked two days before leaving again! They cut out the previous scar on my face and stitched it up and also gave me a skin graft from behind my right ear onto my lower right eyelid, resulting in a total of thirty stitches. No problem. It was a bit boring in the ward, except that I was frightened by one of the patients. I only glanced at him the once out of the side of my eye because his injuries were too horrific to look at. It was as if someone in a horror film had gone up to his mouth and pulled out his lips, teeth and tongue. There was just a void where a mouth should have been. It looked that grotesque that I couldn't even find the courage to ask the nurses!

The general manager was a portly French gentleman in his forties called Michel Dubois. He seemed to do nothing but sit in his office and reminded me of the Fat Controller in Thomas the Tank Engine. The deputy manager was a professional Frenchman in his early thirties called Pascal Naneix, whom I came to admire in every respect. He was everywhere, knew exactly what was happening in every department and never seemed to lose his cool.

I started off doing the morning room services. This meant getting up at the ungodly hour of 5.15 am, ready to start work at 6 am. If room services had been booked for earlier, then we had to start earlier. We had to prepare each room service on trays and then put the trays on a trolley and proceed via the lift, around the floors to each room. This was all very well and a good system, except that four trays would not fit across a shelf of the trolley! Two of them would have to be at a slight angle. Wheeling the trolley was fine, yes that could be managed without too much hardship, but at the lift, the gap between the lift and the floor meant that the trolley wheels jolted, causing the fruit juice to spill. This happened every time. Combine this with a hangover and general malaise at being at work at a ridiculous hour and you can see our predicament! Such is life. Why we did not use our brains and carry the fruit juice in a jug on the trolley and pour it at the last minute God only knows, but they had systems, and they had to be followed.

The food was OK and most of the breakfasts were continental with croissants etc. On this shift you would continue with portering in the morning and help with lunch, whether for conference delegates or normal guests, before finishing about 3 pm. It was quite a busy hotel with conferences and training sessions, the most notable of which were by Boots Ltd, who held residential staff training sessions, and some of their staff were babes and a half, and always a hot topic amongst us blokes. The porters had to prepare the function rooms, making sure things like paper and Novotel pens were out, iced water and glasses, audio-visual equipment, mints, tea/coffee and biscuits etc. I enjoyed this part, having a target to achieve which, although routine, was easy to complete. Getting delegates in and doing their beverages was very satisfying. It was methodical work. We had function sheets for each day, so we knew what to expect.

'Mr Paris!' announced Mr Naneix one morning at just after 9 am.

'Yes, Mr Naneix?' I answered nervously.

'I need room 107 set for a boardroom meeting in five minutes.'

'Yes, but that's a bedroom, I can't do that?' I offered, as a feeble excuse to get out of doing it.

'Take the bed and mattress out, move the other furniture around and set up a trestle table. Quick! They wanted this room five minutes ago!'

'Oh OK,' I submitted. I wasn't one for letting an employer down, so even though there had been a cock-up somewhere along the line, I set to it and turned the room around in record time. What annoyed me was that I had now got into a sweat, which meant I would smell later, which was most inconvenient. Sad isn't it! I generally prided myself on my appearance and hated to have a single hair out of place, I couldn't stand getting my glasses dirty, and was forever washing my hands, but this was unacceptable.

Then I moved to the bar, which meant mainly split shifts. Finishing at night could be early if you weren't the 'late' member of staff so it could be 10 pm or, if you were late, 1 am, 2 am, 3 am etc, whenever the guests had finished. The hotel had one of its 'Café de Paris' nights, which was a dinner/dance affair and for that one night

I worked 6 pm to 6 am! That was different; I had never worked like that before and it was hard work. The staff were all very friendly, but there were one or two of the lazy ones you get everywhere, and they were probably French! The main bar was small but functional and there was also another bar called the Tickler Bar which I guess was more like a function bar. I seem to vaguely remember one member of the bar staff leaving a bitchy letter for another over what had or hadn't been done the shift before. Basically, the unwritten rule is to leave the bar or any area in the way you'd expect to find it, or certainly clean and tidy, glasses washed, the sides wiped down, ice/lemon/beer nozzles etc dealt with, and so on.

One day I was asked to prepare a bedroom for a stag do. This room was a suite, so the lounge was set up leaving just four easy chairs and a couple of little tables for their drinks. I had to set up a 'mobile' bar, ie spirits, mixers, bottled beer/lager, wine, coke/lemonade etc with ice and lemon and an appropriate supply of glasses. There were four men attending what turned out to be a strip show, of which I had no advance knowledge.

Mr Naneix had said I could do the bar, which I thought would be a real bore stuck with four men. How wrong I was! Their topless waitress took orders from the men whilst I served her, and she took the drinks over. Quite nice really! Then there were five strippers who changed in the bedroom and did their stuff, including lesbian acts, in front of the men. And it was explicit to say the least! That was my first strip show and most enjoyable... After a couple of hours it was all over, and a couple of the men were talking to the girls. Oh yes, I know what they want... One of the girls looked at me, sauntered over and with eyelids flashing, asked matter-of-factly 'We need another room to change in.'

'Oh no, I can't do that,' I replied, with alarm. Still in those days if an adult told me to do something, I would probably do it because

I was still so immature and didn't feel like a proper adult so I was never really sure of myself.

'We really need another room,' she continued, and with that I definitely knew what she wanted it for.

'No,' I replied with renewed enthusiasm, and I certainly was not going to go to reception to find out, hence leaving 'my' bar unattended. All the men were pissed. One of them, realising that they weren't going to get an extra bedroom, and therefore a shag, came over.

'And what about him, he's seen all this for free!' he shouted. I think they had each paid about £60 for the show, with the drinks on a cash basis.

'Well, erm, I'm just doing my job, I can't help that,' I offered with alarm at the thought that they might hit me or try to get money out of me.

'Yea, he's right,' one of the others replied, to my relief. 'Come on, let's get going, and thanks mate. Did you enjoy it?' he continued. Phew! Off the hook!

'Yes thank you, very nice,' I replied, not trying to sound too over the top. I did not want to tell them that that was my first show or how much I had really enjoyed it! With that, they left, the girls packed up, I closed down my bar, tidied up the room and finished about 4 pm. A good day.

I also worked in the restaurant, which involved split shifts starting at 6 am (or sometimes 5 am if I also had to do the room services) till 11.30 am, then about 6 pm till the end, which could be midnight. Sometimes, depending on conference or banqueting business, I would do a straight, say 3 pm till midnight. The restaurant was clean, basic and functional and the kitchen was modern and well lit, with a long 'pass', and it functioned like a well-oiled machine. From memory there never seemed to be any problem with the food. Whenever there was a flat of chips, sorry pommes frites, waiting to be taken out, I always used to nick one. Maybe because I had previously worked in kitchens, I felt I had a God-given right to help myself. Deep down I knew it wasn't right and very unprofessional, but it was a habit I couldn't break. One day, as I went to nick a chip, I sensed that something was wrong and snatched my hand away just in time before the chips went flying with an almighty crash and clang. I stared with amazement at the chef who had brought his meat cleaver down onto the flat of chips with all his force!! If I had left my hand there, my fingers would have been chopped off! When this dawned on me, words failed me, as I just could not believe what he had done.

'DON'T YOU EVER FUCKING DO THAT AGAIN!' he bawled. Words still failed me. I slowly backed out of the kitchen, staring at him, not really knowing whether my stare was one of shock, defiance, incredulity, or something else beyond normal reasoning. I had to go and sit down in the restaurant for a few minutes to gather myself together. I was also amazed that my sixth sense had warned me in a flash that something bad was about to happen, even though I had not seen his cleaver! To this day I have never taken food like that again, except in an instance where a chip is going to fall off or from a managerial point of view whereby I would be testing the temperature and quality of something going out. That really shook me up, and being a student, it was a valuable lesson.

Evenings out were spent with the staff, mainly the live-in ones, in local pubs called Donovan's or the Sportsman's. My diary also records that we played pool until 3.30-4 am, and I can only guess that that was in the Novotel, because I don't think clubs would have been open until then. I used to cycle everywhere, and I can remember a couple of times nearly falling off on the left-handed curve with a down-gradient outside the hotel or just along Bostock Lane when pissed. Sometimes I'd leave my bike at the hotel and walk home. Wages in those days were about £50 per week net and tips could be £10 per week.

There was a nature reserve nearby with a lake or pond, I seem to remember, and one day with Nick and some of the staff I went for a walk, something I didn't really regard as an essential part of life. Nick was, along with the others, taking the mick out of one of the girls, but I hadn't a clue what was going on so I went to her defence and said something to back her up.

'Geoff, you always back the winner, don't you?' Nick retorted.

'Do I?' I replied, not knowing whether I did or didn't or whether it was right or wrong. 'Yes, Geoff you do, and it gets a bit boring,' he stated, matter-of-factly.

'Oh, sorry,' was all I could muster. That upset me and for the rest of the walk I was in a sulk, my mind churning this latest revelation over and over. What did he mean? Did he mean I was always a goody-goody? Should I change? How? What did people think of me? A snotty nosed four-eyed twat? There was no one I could talk to about these sorts of things and I have remembered his comment to this day.

The restaurant also had an à la carte menu, which included flambé dishes. The latter terrified me; cooking in front of the customer! What if I got it wrong? What if they didn't like it? What if I cooked the wrong item for the wrong person or table? But my dad always drilled into me, 'Do a proper job!' I also realised that I was representing my college and that as I had had previous chefing experience, I didn't have a leg to stand on. It was actually quite easy. Crepes Suzettes were a doddle and I soon realised that the majority of customers hadn't got a clue anyway, so it didn't matter if something wasn't quite cooked by the textbook. Then for main courses we cooked items like Steak Diane and Fillet of Beef Stroganoff.

I can't remember exactly what was on the menu, but there were several dishes. Basically, there was a trolley with a few bottles of spirits like rum, cognac, Cointreau or Grand Marnier, perhaps vodka, and maybe some red and white wine. The trolley also had a gas burner and several copper pans. A copper pan is officially called a sauteuse, and they were always the favourite because, apart from being a nice colour, they were thicker and, added to the way in which copper conducts heat, they allowed the heat underneath to be more evenly distributed than conventional pans, and hence not burn the sauce. There might also be a section on the trolley with little containers for the various ingredients.

Whether you could cook or not, the main criteria for doing flambé work is 'mise-en-place'. If you don't have everything ready from the start, you'll ruin the food. And it isn't just the food: the customer perceives a flambé dish as being an experience, so you must be seen to be in control from start to finish. The kitchen prepared the ingredients and put them in little dishes, and the waiter prepared the hot plates and any cutlery needed for the cooking. In the kitchen you would use your fingers to add an ingredient to a sauce, but in the restaurant you had to use teaspoons – a bit tiresome really.

The best part was adding the alcohol. When it was added it was best to let it warm up for a bit and let it add its flavour to the meat before tilting the sauteuse to ignite it on the flames. The flaming had to be done right at the end so that the dish was more or less ready to serve. The last ingredient on any dish, however, was cream, which shouldn't be overheated or overworked as it could spoil. It was really up to the person cooking the flambé how they did it, and it was always satisfying to see customers congratulating you on nicely cooked, tasty food. We also filleted whole Dover sole in front of the guests which, again, was something I enjoyed doing.

In the middle of February Val Barker, one of the main lecturers at the College of Food, came along for our assessments. I thought I was an excellent student, so I was very upset to receive the following:

Did the appearance of the student ever let him/her down?
NO

Was his/her timekeeping good?
YES

Was he/she ever lacking initiative?
YES

Was the student able to cope without supervision?
YES

Was he/she cooperative?
YES

How did the student get on with your staff?
GOOD

How did you rate his/her relationship with customers?
AVERAGE

What was the overall standard of his/her performance?
GOOD

Main weakness: In the clouds, tends to dream a bit. Walks like a zombie (sic). Tends to panic under stress. Very nervous.

Main strength: Easiness with figures and polite. More inclined to office work than manual work.

'Walks like a zomby'! Whatever next? What the hell did he mean by that? Maybe I did walk in a strange way – I did have rather skinny legs although my calf muscles have always been strong, from cycling. Or perhaps 'zomby' in French means something else? 'Tends to dream a bit' – well, I'll put that down to a combination of my anti-epileptic drugs combined with hangovers. Nothing unusual there, or at least not to me! 'Tends to panic under stress' –

What a nerve! No comment on that.....

Sometime later the dance group Hot Gossip arrived to use a small function room near the reception as a 'chill out' room before their evening bash. They ordered a couple of large flats of sandwiches along with some soft drinks. I knocked on the door and was answered by a girl in underwear with a superb figure who said 'Oh, come on in; leave them over there,' and as I walked into the room, there they all were, about a dozen I suppose all dressed in just their underwear, and without make-up. I did not know where to look! My face flushed and I hastily put down the sandwiches before beating a hasty retreat. I had to go through the same performance a few times more to finish off their order. They all had good figures. I wonder if Sarah Brightman was amongst them? Hot Gossip were one of the first girl dance groups and were all the rage at the time. What a privilege!

At the beginning of March I moved into the reception. This was good fun: I could sit down and work straight shifts. I had risen up the ranks, at least as far as receptionists perceived themselves. Hotel receptionists have always had this notion that they are superior to the customer, possibly on a par with management, and of a higher caste than other staff of any level. They think they have a God-given right to be looked after by other hotel departments. Receptionists never make mistakes, instead the customer has changed his mind, and the customer is always right isn't he? What they do have, more often than not, is more intelligence than staff of other departments. They look smart, are usually pretty, young and attractive, and are professional in their job. Do I have a thing against hotel receptionists? Not at all, the opposite in fact, just over twenty years of observation!

A couple of times I worked the night shift, which was about 11 pm to 8 am. I can't remember whether the night porter did this or whether it was a member of reception, but all the day's takings from each department, including reception, along with occupancy levels, number of covers in the restaurant for breakfast and dinner etc etc, were entered on a standardised form on the computer and left for the manager to see in the morning before being faxed off to Head Office. It was quite an important role and not really one for your average night porter, at least not in Devon, where I ended up.

Our stint at the Novotel finished on the 10th April and Mum collected me and took me home. Then I had to write a project for college on my experiences.

The summer term in Birmingham continued as usual, with lots of work getting ready for exams. There was only one memorable event, as follows. Chris and I had stopped on the way back one night for an Indian curry in the Coventry Road in Small Heath. We both ordered chicken dishes, but the meat was strangely dark. We both looked at each other and complained to the owner who confirmed that yes, it was chicken. Well, we grudgingly ate it and, in the morning, told Mrs Hemmings our Landlady of our experience. The following evening she was waiting at the door for us to return, waving the local paper. That same restaurant had only been 'done' for serving dog meat! Chris laughed at my comment 'As long as it's reached core temperature!' We hadn't had any side effects apart from the usual shits maybe!

I had decided to go to Germany for the summer to find work. I chose Munich because I had been there before, it was a clean and vibrant city, and I knew where the Youth Hostel tent was. So off I set on the 19th July, leaving Wolverhampton at 9 am and arriving in Munich via Ostend exactly 24 hours later. I dumped my luggage in the station and went straight to the Job Centre or Arbeitsamt. They packed me off to the Café am See at Tegernsee and then the Hotel Bachmair am See, but neither employed me. I stayed at the tent that night and the next day fixed an interview at the Sheraton Hotel, who were looking for a KP or *Spüler*, as they are called in Germany. The tent was full that night, so I had to stay at another Youth Hostel near the Olympic Stadium.

My interview at the Sheraton was unsuccessful because I could only work the summer and they required a longer period of employment. After another night in the tent I went to Garmisch-Partenkirchen and enquired at their Job Centre. They had no work going because the weather was bad and therefore so was the tourism. That night back at the tent would have been my last night, because you could only stay three nights and I had managed to stay four, even though one was somewhere else. I would *have* to get a job tomorrow.

In the morning the Job Centre fixed me an interview at a restaurant in the centre of Munich called Schwarzwälders in Hartmannstrasse (No.8) and it turned out that the manager was also a lecturer at the local catering college, so I guess he took pity on me! I was to be a barman, I suppose you could call it. He gave me the address of a flat for which they would deduct a weekly amount, and I moved in there and then. My wage was 1200 Deutschmarks monthly. That would do. The flat was in a suburb and required a U-Bahn ride for about ten minutes to the centre. I loved it! I had keys to a property in a foreign city. Wonderful! I really felt that life was taking a turn for the better.

It was either near Sendlinger-Tor-Platz or Goetheplatz and the U-Bahn would have taken me to Marienplatz in the centre, then it was a short walk behind the Frauenkirche, the main church. My flat was in an old building and once you went in through the front door, you were greeted by a marble-style floor with a wide ornate staircase with marble-style steps, and a high ceiling with any noise echoing off the walls. My flat was on the first floor. I have a total blank as to what it was like inside except that there was a view of the street and a large roundabout and intersection at the end. The flat may only have been a bedsit with bedroom and bathroom, but that was irrelevant.

Restaurant/Weinhaus Schwarzwälder, to give it its proper name, was a high-class restaurant with chandeliers, woodwork, light brown walls that had mellowed with years of nicotine stains, oil paintings, shelves with ornate plates, vases, other crockery items, tankards etc. All very traditional, with that atmosphere that tells you you're about to spend a lot of money! The restaurant was founded by Richard Schwarzwälder, who was a pioneer of Pfalzer wine, Father of the wine renaissance and passionate about his work. He came to Munich in 1912 and opened the Wine Restaurant, which was a novelty to the beer-loving people of Munich. Maria, presumably his wife, was an expert cook and she introduced a high-class menu, which included fish and was highly regarded in Munich. The vast cellars underground held about 63,000 litres of wine in about 81 barrels, as well as thousands of bottles. There were all sorts of German wines, and maybe some other European wines as a gesture, young, old, red, white, some with just one or two bottles, some with hundreds and so on. Utterly amazing.

How do I remember all this? Well, there was an A4 brochure around then, when I was in Munich, called 'Munchens feine Adressen' that advertised all the high-quality shops, restaurants, hotels etc with a picture and short description. I think I've translated the German accurately enough! The restaurant and vineyard were actually owned by the Wienerwald group, for whom I had worked the year before in Oberammergau briefly.

My job was to get the bar ready and serve the waiters. I wore black and white. They would give me a chit for an order of drinks, which I had to prepare for them or fetch a bottle of wine. Meals came down a tiny lift and my other job was to inspect the food and make sure it was the correct order. Similarly, dirty plates went up in the lift. My hours were 8.30 am to 4.30 pm. A piece of piss!

Why I started at that time I've no idea, because all I had to do was to stock up, tidy the cellar, and get ready for lunchtime. The wine list was enormous with a lot of wines available by the glass. The waiters were friendly people but all middle aged, which presumably reflected the experience required for this style of restaurant. They were always trying to con a glass of wine out of me and it was hard to refuse, bearing in mind their experience and age against mine. 'Habe die Ehre!' was my morning greeting from one short fat waiter with hair colour that matched the nicotine stained wallpaper. 'Habe die Ehre!' I would reply, not really knowing what it meant, but assumed it to be a local Bavarian way of saying good morning. I think literally it means 'It's an honour'. That's what it sounded like, but it is not a general form of German greeting these days.

After work, I would go home, have a rest and then wander around the city centre in the evening. There were a lot of buskers around Marienplatz and the pedestrian area that went up towards Karlsplatz and the railway station. These buskers had groups of students and teenagers sitting around in semi-circles on the pavement with others standing, and I soon joined in. I did not relish the thought of sitting on a pavement. How could I mix with people of unknown background; what about the buskers – were they homeless and therefore vermin? If I sat on the pavement, I would get dirty with nowhere to wash my hands. So I stood up to begin with.

I met Tom and Lyndsey and went for a drink with them; I think from memory he was an Irish busker. A couple of evenings later I met Lyndsey and went for a drink with her. This was looking good. A social life starting already.

On my first day off I went to have a look at the Englischer Garten, which is a large park with a stream running through it. Families walk their children, dogs run around with endless energy, couples stroll hand in hand without a care in the world, and it seemed a place to forget everything. Then there were people sunbathing naked! Wow!

I looked around as if I had somehow entered a separate area, but no, it was all part of the park and no one batted an eyelid. I found a spot and changed into my trunks, using a towel to hide my private parts. They must have thought me a right prude.

Later that evening I went out for a drink with someone called Matthew down near where they hold the Oktoberfest and got pissed. When we split, I knew roughly how to get home, and passed a sign that said 'Nachtklub', so I thought I would have a quick beer.

I knew at once that it was a mistake. 'Nachtklub' literally means nightclub or disco, and as this would be my first visit to a disco in Munich, it seemed a brilliant idea. I was led downstairs by a meatloaf of a bouncer into a bar and lounge. As I looked around at the soft warm lighting, the various sofas, the several blue movies being played on screens, the topless girls, and a few men, I realised at once that it was a brothel. What the hell, I thought, I will just a have a beer and be on my way.

A topless waitress came over and escorted me to the bar. 'Waitress' would be an unfair description really – one expects a waitress to be young and attractive, but she was in her mid-forties and far from attractive. The bar was good: it was modern, curved and stylish with a see-through ceramic top, with small tea-light style candles dotted around, but the barmaid was even better. She was oriental and extremely pretty, in her mid-twenties, again topless with nice breasts on show.

My 'woman', or maybe 'Frau' would be more appropriate, offered me a substantial drinks menu. I was pissed and just wanted a beer, so I did not bother to read it but just ordered a small lager. My Frau, who had by now sat down on the next bar stool, asked if I would buy her a drink. Oh, fuck me I thought, I suppose I'll have to, so she duly ordered the German equivalent of a Babycham, served in a cocktail glass. *You don't want to be here Geoff*, was all I could think...

She started talking to me, asking me where I was from, what I was doing, about my family etc, and I replied in German in as basic a form as possible without any interest whatsoever. My mind was racing – what are they going to do? Will she take me somewhere and shag me? Will other people be watching? Will it be recorded? What will it cost? Do I have to make the first move?

Everyone else in the room seemed quite at ease and casually enjoying themselves. I cannot be doing with this I thought and asked for the bill. The oriental girl smiled sweetly at me and gave me the bill. God, she was a honey. What? That can't be right? 60 DM? The exchange rate in those days was about 4.5 DM's to one pound so this worked out at about £13. It does not sound a lot today, but to me as a student in 1981, it was the equivalent of I guess £45 to £50 in today's money for two drinks. Maybe a girl was included in the price? I certainly had not got 60 DMs on me so asked to see the drinks menu, which I read word for word, which also gave me time to work out my plan of action. And there it was, the first drink was 40 DMs, whatever it was. And hers was 20 DMs. Fair enough, my mistake. I decided that my only course of action was to pretend to be ignorant and act British, I'm sorry to say. First, I told the girl in German that I didn't know about the first drink and that I hadn't enough money to pay. She again asked for the money, whilst beckoning the bouncers over. I knew there was going to be trouble, so I slammed my hand down on one of the candles to extinguish it, which was meant to signify that I meant business, and I wasn't a softy, got out all the money I had, which was about 30 DMs, and mouthed off in English that I was English, didn't know etc. In other words I pretended to be ignorant and stupid.

The bouncers grabbed me, searched me for any more money, then carried me, one each side and threw me out onto the street, shouting obscenities. I retrieved my glasses, picked myself up, checked myself for any injuries – just a few grazes – looked around in case anyone was watching, and went sheepishly off down the street. Phew!

After about thirty yards, the street suddenly seemed familiar and with dismay as well as relief, I realised that my flat was right in front of me. *I cannot live in the same street as this nightclub, oh please no!* I had never turned left before out of my flat, I had always walked to the right, so I'd had no idea the nightclub was there. So that was that, one of life's little experiences!

The most popular buskers were 'Mark and Simon' who played and sang mostly Beatles music and had a large following, including a good set of female 'groupies'. I soon joined this set, sitting amongst the others, and afterwards we would all go for a drink or a meal, say half a dozen or so. Sometimes some tourists would join us, maybe a few English girls or some Yanks. It was great. I was meeting all sorts of nice people, mostly student types, and it was casual and fun. We might go to the Hofbrauhaus, a massive hall with long wooden tables and benches with much excited conversation, frivolity and laughter. A remarkable place. Buxom German women in traditional costume marched down the aisles with maybe four steins of lager brimming with froth in each hand, dishing them out where required. There might be a jazz band playing. You didn't order anything else really – you just drank the lager. And it was good, probably Löwenbraü, the locally brewed lager, for which I developed a lifelong affection. Or we might go to Schwabing, the popular student quarter, and visit Scisso's, a relaxing underground pub with arches – a bit like a cellar, or to the Oasis Bar. The main set included Declan, Jenny, Jamie, Sylvia, Tony, and a stunning dark-haired girl from Romania who was living in Munich illegally, but I didn't really talk to her as I couldn't quite decide whether she was from the 'other' commie side, or not.

I regularly walked to the Englischer Garten on one of my days off to sunbathe. I had plucked up the courage to sunbathe nude, but only lying face down so as not to expose my small parts to the entire German population! I usually chose a spot near the stream because one section had a weir, which meant that you could use it as a small swimming pool, if you kept away from the edge. And yes, guess who fell over the edge! As I reached the point of no return where I knew the water would take me over the edge, I was gone. I fell a short distance onto the rocks below and bounced along them, carried by the water until the current fell away into a pool. I was all right, just a few scrapes and bruises, but I had lost my glasses and frantically searched for them to no avail. They were my only pair, so I had to phone home and get Tony Blackham, a family friend and optician, to send me out a new pair. I was so embarrassed. I can't see a thing without glasses.

The job itself went along fine; my main shifts were the daytime ones, but occasionally I worked the evening, being 4.30 pm to midnight. I nearly got a severe bollocking because one morning I had nothing to do, so I thought I would clean all the bottles in the cellar, which were covered in dust. Just as well I didn't, as those who are in the trade will realise. The laundry was cleaned in-house on the first floor, and the 'housekeeper' had tried to set me up with one of her staff, a Yugoslavian girl, who was slim and pretty, but I just didn't think it was the done thing to involve oneself with people from the former communist bloc countries. There are two girls' names in capital letters in my diary, and capitals usually mean something important. They are Maria Schaubeck and Vera Golvbovic. And no, I haven't a clue!

My flat was not too far away from where the Oktoberfest took place, in a park called "Wies'n" by the locals, and I could see them beginning to get ready for this beer festival of beer festivals. It actually starts in the last week of September and I was eagerly awaiting its approach. Unfortunately, to my dismay, I had failed my Economics exam, so my college was holding the re-take on the

14th September, and they had only just informed me. I rang them and explained that I was working in Germany blah blah, getting experience blah blah, but they were having none of it: if I wasn't in college on the 14th, I would fail the course. The bastards! So I had to cut short my employment and duly left on the 7th September by train. I don't think my employer Herr Schaber was too amused, but he gave me a good reference. Here is an English translation by Mrs Kaye, who taught us German at college:

RESTAURANT WEINHAUS SCHWARZWÄLDER
Hartmannstrasse 8
MÜNCHEN 2

TESTIMONIAL

Mr Geoffrey Paris, born 26.4.1959, worked as a volunteer in our Specialities Restaurant from 25th July till 6th September.

Mr Paris was an extremely capable and hard-working colleague. He showed great interest in all his work and carried it out to our complete satisfaction.

There were no problems working with him, because of his friendly and open manner. He was valued by both his superiors and fellow workers. He was always punctual as a matter of course.

Munich 6.9.1981   Siegfried Schaber.

To sum up the summer, I fell in love with Munich and everything about it: the BMW factory, the Deutsches Museum, the river Isar, Schloss Nymphenburg, the Olympic Stadium, the brass statue of a hog in the city centre, the clean streets, the clean Underground and trams, the lack of litter, the welcome absence of British yobbism, the clean high-quality lager, the design and colour of the buildings, the parks, and last but not least, the German people. Thank you from all my heart to all the residents of Munich for providing and maintaining such a lovely city. If there was anywhere else I would like to live, Munich would win without fail. God bless you all.

It was not until August 2014 that I managed to return to Munich, which was tremendously exciting. I went with a friend, Rob, who had booked an average hotel near the railway station. After dumping our bags we headed straight to the city centre – my patch, so to speak. Oh boy was I disappointed. How time, approx. thirty-five years in this case, can change your perception of a city. It was full of coloured foreigners – no disrespect to any of them, they have just as much right to be there as I do. Actual white Europeans seemed to be a minority, let alone any Germans.

We sat down outside a café in Marienplatz and ordered two steins of lager. I would almost have felt uncomfortable, if it hadn't been for the fact that I regarded Munich as my haven. We finished our beers quickly and moved off to a restaurant. My old place of work now seemed to be offices, which really upset me, even though the wälder sign still hung above the street, or maybe it was a lantern, and on the street corner there was an off licence, but it was closed. Yet again I visited the site of the Oktoberfest, currently being set up, and walked to my old bedsit nearby, which had obviously been renovated. We did the tourist things like the Deutsches Museum, the BMW Museum and the Olympic Park, the Hofbrauhaus and the Englischer Garten and so on. Although we had a good time, ate some nice food and met some nice people, it just did not seem the same.

CHAPTER 6

Lovely Lucerne

And so began the final year at college. I passed my economics exam the same day that I retook it, but what really pissed me off was that I had revised everything except questions related to the original exam, so what did the sods do? Yes, you've guessed it, it was exactly the same paper! I was not amused and felt failure to be imminent. So it was with relief that I passed.

I was staying at Cambrian Hall and my diary entries seem to revolve around drinking in one bar or another, more often than not at the college bar, the good old Shakespeare, or the Opposite Lock, parties in one of the units at Cambrian, parties at someone's house or flat around Birmingham, parties in Shropshire, Vindaloo curries at the Padma Restaurant, the odd concert or two like Blondie and ELO, who I saw in Birmingham and so on. Lots of late nights and quite a few morning lectures missed seemed to be the trend! Quite an enjoyable life. The way it should be.

One such party was an official Cambrian Hall party, held in a room on site with a disco. I had met a girl and we really hit it off at this disco, which was excellent as far as I was concerned as she was beautiful. We were dancing away and had connected – life was roses etc etc and I was revelling in the fact that I had pulled a babe when all of a sudden my hair was pulled down from behind me with such force that I had to fall over backwards.

'WHAT THE FUCK!' I shouted, more to myself than anyone else. I looked up to find Noel standing over me. He was a case and a half. Noel was a student in Cambrian, black with short black wiry hair and an amateur boxer to boot. He took great pleasure in bullying and invariably called me 'Spak' – short for spastic I presume? Not nice. I constantly avoided him and certainly would never speak to him. He was obviously jealous about the girl I was with. I leapt up in fury and demanded to know what the hell he was playing at.

'Outside, Spak!' he shouted, above the music.

'Right, let's go,' I retaliated, blind with fury. As he was about to set on me outside, which filled me with absolute terror, Tim stepped in and challenged him. 'Pick on someone your own size!' he shouted, with which the two started fighting. I was aghast that someone who was a distant acquaintance of mine had stepped in for me, and his face was beaten to a pulp. That was the end of what *was* going to be a most excellent night!

A college visit to the vineyards of France had been organised and my parents had mercifully allowed me to go on this trip – aka piss up! There were a couple of dozen students and several lecturers and two or three mini-buses. So, on Friday 26 March 1982, off we set to Southampton to catch the overnight ferry to Le Havre. The next afternoon we arrived at our first stop, Amboise, where the youth hostel stood on an island in the middle of the river Loire. This was cool.

Our bedroom window looked out over the end of the island, of which the concrete walkway was pointed like the bow of a ship. It felt as if we had occupied this little fortress on an island which we would defend against the French invaders! Unfortunately I had the flu and the shits, so much so that I crapped myself in the evening! Fortunately, we were out on a pub crawl, so I didn't have far to walk to sort myself out. I had this awful affliction whereby you want to fart but can't tell if it is wind or something worse. Something was playing merry hell with my insides and it was not a pleasant or comfortable situation to be in!

Breakfast consisted of croissants with jam and coffee served in cereal-sized bowls, and we made packed lunches most of the time, consisting of baguettes with pâté or cheese. The next day everyone else went to Château de Chenonceau and in the afternoon to the Cointreau production plant near Angers, where they saw miniatures being bottled, but I stayed in bed due to feeling so rough. In the afternoon I did manage to look around Château Amboise, which lay the other end of our little island. Lovely.

The following day we moved off to stay at a motel in or near Gujan-Mestras near Arcachon, below the Bordeaux coast. We ended up at a little wooden hut on what I assume was a river inlet or creek where the oyster farm lay. We were to have oysters and champagne. The thought of eating something that had come out of what I assumed were dirty muddy waters, uncooked, unprocessed, and with our fingers, which we could not wash in advance, filled me with dread! I was awfully fussy about what I ate, its age, where it had been etc, and this to me was akin to one of those insect-eating challenges from 'I'm A Celebrity, Get Me Out Of Here'. Still, you only live once.

We were herded into a ramshackle hut, where a small old Frenchman with a tanned wrinkly weatherbeaten face proceeded to hand out oyster shells to each of us. He showed us how to 'eat' them, which is to slip the oyster into your mouth and swallow it complete without chewing. WHAT!? What's the point of that? And they call it an aphrodisiac? Hardly, if it goes straight down. Perhaps French couples use them as a sex toy? I thought the whole idea of chewing was to enjoy the flavour?

So we took these drab grey shells, which had previously been opened, and the oyster separated from its base, and tentatively slipped this horrible cold wet lump into our mouths and swallowed. Yuk! Thank god for the champagne, which we downed almost in one gulp. Never again thank you very much!

At the hotel dinner that night I couldn't believe it when oysters were served as a starter. They were equally disgusting, but the rest of the food was OK and was washed down with wine. Many people who'd eaten those hotel oysters had the shits – we were told to drink white wine because red wine would react with the oysters for some reason – but Chris and Nigel had drunk so much red wine that the oysters stood no chance!

Later that evening, we went by minibus to Arcachon and Nigel remembers that when we went into one bar, which was full of French locals, it fell silent, but we soon had them on our side drinking Ricard and smoking Gauloise cigarettes!

On the way back, around midnight, Dale Lyons, who was one of our lecturers, got off the minibus and went for one of his runs. He arrived back at the hotel two hours later dripping buckets! We were also late getting back to the hotel and were locked out, so we had to wake up the owner, which did not amuse him! Several times at random points during the week, Dale would get off the minibus and go for a run, meeting us at our destination.

We went to stay somewhere else for two nights in Bordeaux, because one afternoon, early evening actually, we played the Bordeaux football team (although some of their players were not 'A' team players). This attracted the local press and a fair few spectators. We won (of course!) in the last few minutes due to a suspect penalty. My diary is blank for five days of this trip. I have had valued contributions from Chris Sykes and Nigel Pike, but some dates or times may be inaccurate.

Back at the hotel that night we sat on two long rows of tables and benches for our dinner. The chef had baked a cake, as it was someone's birthday, so we stayed in the restaurant and got totally hammered. There was cheap plonk on the table to start us off and if you took five empty bottles back, you got another free. That was a great game! It was quite cheap anyway. I was absolutely smashed and the next morning I awoke in someone else's bed with a hangover from hell and was duly informed that I had been a real source of amusement the night before by running around the car park naked like a headless chicken!

I felt so rough that I feared I was close to having an epileptic fit, so I had to stay in bed yet again and miss the trip. Chris and Nigel had overslept and had to run out to catch the minibus. God, I felt bad. I managed to get up mid-afternoon and venture downstairs for a coffee, after which I had a quiet alcohol-free early night.

We also went to stay in the town of Cognac and got lost. When we eventually found the hotel, it turned out to be in the red-light district! But it was a nice hotel on a street corner, with dimly lit ornate chandeliers and red patterned carpets.

I remember being really embarrassed in some of the French toilets, because you do not have a proper door but more of a stable door so that you could look over and under. And just a hole in the ground. How primitive is that! And with my farts, chronic diarrhoea, and accompanying vile smells, it was not the most comfortable of situations. We obviously got smashed again because the next day we went to Château de Cognac, which is where they make Otard Cognac. This château was steeped in royal history, and founded originally by Baron Otard, of Nordic descent but living in Scotland, who followed King James into exile, bought the château and started making cognac. The château was marvellous, and the barrels were stored in underground cellars. The smell of the cognac in the air was superb and I was amazed at the number of wooden barrels, but as I had the most awful hangover, I started to feel unwell and dizzy, and could not walk properly, so much so that I had to retreat outside and sit down for twenty minutes or so in the fresh air. I guess the alcohol in the air had hit me!

In the afternoon we went to a Martell distillery but got lost and were late, but they stayed open for us, which was much appreciated. Back in the 1980s Martell was always considered in the trade to be slightly inferior to Courvoisier, so it was a shame that we were going to the poorer cousin, so to speak. However at the end of our tour, the manager gave each of us a boxed and wrapped half-bottle of Martell Cognac to take home. What a good marketing ploy! From that day on I have always served Martell in preference to Courvoisier.

We viewed the copper stills where the Charentes wine is distilled twice and put into French oak barrels. At this stage it is a colourless liquid at about 70% proof, and it is the oak that mellows and colours the liquid over the years. It is kept at ground level or below, in the dark. It also loses strength and volume into the atmosphere and this is known as the 'angels' share'. At the time of our visit, this was the equivalent to two million bottles per year! And the number of barrels was staggering – thousands of them, and this was just one of about fifty Martell distilleries. Even by 1728 the French were exporting 27,000 barrels of Cognac each year from the Atlantic ports! Chris and Nigel found an old barrel with '1800' chalked on it with some words from the Napoleonic times, and they were not well received by the tour guide when they asked if they could taste it!

We were on our way back to Le Havre, but I was determined to stay in France because I wanted to contact Cathy (da Silva), one of my friends from Munich the previous summer. She was lovely, tall, and slim with long dark hair and I was infatuated with her. She lived at Villeneuve la Garenne, wherever that was, and I was desperately trying to find her phone number in the French phone directory, but it was impossible, because they were categorised by towns or districts and it was a fruitless search, much to my irritation. I was even tempted to stay in Le Havre overnight and ask someone in the morning maybe at the post office. So I got on the ferry with great reluctance.

We arrived back in England at 7 am sporting berets and drinking neat Martini, and stopped at Stratford-on-Avon for a tea break. I went to a red phone box and phoned Mum and Dad to let them know where I would be to be collected, and whilst speaking to them, horror of horrors, I filled my pants. Oh my God! And it reeked! What to do Geoff, what to do? I bade my parents a quick goodbye, tied my anorak around my waist to hide any evidence and looked for the public toilets, where I cleaned myself up as best as possible. What a nightmare! And I had to sit in a minibus with my friends for another hour or so…

Anyway, after we disembarked at the college, Mike Bates, who was one of the cookery lecturers, drove me to a pub near Wolverhampton, from which I could get a lift home from my parents. But I could only find French currency on me so could not make a call. I begged the landlord to lend me a coin to make a phone call and much to my annoyance he refused. I searched my pockets and my luggage time and time again, but no, I had no English money. I was about to give up, bearing in mind that I'd been at this pub unable to buy a drink, and begin a long arduous trek home – ten miles or so – and with soiled pants, when I actually found some money in my pocket to my utter amazement, so I phoned a friend, Dave Clubb, who collected me and took me home. Thank God for a shower!

So now I was in my final term at college, summer 1982. It consisted of the usual revision, exams, drinking and parties in or around Birmingham. One such instance was particularly memorable; it was a Saturday evening and several of us had settled down for a night's drinking in the college bar when Nick Pearson, obviously the worse for wear, staggered in and announced that he was going to a party in Northfield and would we like to come? So off I went with him, along with a law student.

Nick was driving, and obviously pissed, when he ran into a van.

'Fuck it!' he announced after it had hit home what had happened.

'Pull over down that side road,' I shouted, which he duly did, as it was seemingly the only option. We all got out of the car and I suggested that we should get rid of the booze in it, cans of lager and bottles of wines and spirits.

'Quick, shove it in the hedge!' the law student said, so we quickly bundled the offending items into the hedge.

'Christ,' I said, looking over the hedge to the building beyond, 'Is that a cop shop?' Just our luck, it was. This was getting worse and worse. What next?

Then three or four men stormed over from the van.

'What the bloody hell are you playing at?' one shouted.

'Well, erm...' Nick decided to offer as an explanation – the best he could do in his state.

'Look, I'm a lawyer and I'll sue you for slander and for driving incorrectly,' the law student stated, 'and there's a police station over there, I'll call them over if you carry on!'

'No, there's no need for that,' came the reply, 'but if we see you again, you're dead!' And with that they retreated. Phew, that was close! We had been shit scared that we were going to be beaten up, being outnumbered and in the wrong, so with that we hurriedly got into the car and drove off to the party, having abandoned the offending alcohol.

The party itself was good and we all continued to get more pissed, but later the atmosphere changed. Someone had crashed the party, which was quite a normal occurrence, but this person was not welcome by the host, and we could not get rid of him. Suddenly, he grabbed a bottle, smashed the neck off and slashed Jim, who was trying to get him to leave. The jagged edge went through his leather jacket and slashed his upper arm with blood pouring out, and the gatecrasher continued to punch Jim until we overpowered him. The culprit then decided he had done his bit and had made his point so he fled, shouting obscenities.

We stopped the music and called 999 for the police and an ambulance. The ambulance service said that they would do the best they could, but all their vehicles were out on calls, being a Saturday night. The police were not much better. After our previous car incident we certainly did not want to drive, but no one else had a car and Nick was in no state to attempt this, so we laid the injured chap out and bandaged him as best we could. Two hours later, a cop appeared on foot and confirmed that there were no ambulances and that one of us had to take him to hospital. Being students, we didn't take taxis due to the cost, and it hadn't occurred to us as an option, but as the cop had suggested, it was a simple answer. So that's what we did and the hospital sorted him out. Quite a night for us!

Looking at my hand now reminds of a stupid thing I did to myself whilst under the influence. A so-called friend of mine called Pierre Shirley got me to try a trick. He placed a crisp £5 note around the back of my hand, tight to the skin, and said I could have it if I could burn a hole in it with a cigarette. Easy, I thought. It was excruciating and I tried three times, each time making my eyes water from the pain but to no avail; the note was untouched. It transpired that banknote paper is stronger than skin! I had three massive burns or blisters which I had to protect, but every week or so by mistake I would put my hand into the back pocket of my jeans and scrape the scabs off, so the healing had to start again! It took months for the skin to grow over, and I still have three scars.

Our final exams came and went with relief, and that summer six of us had been selected to work in Lucerne, Switzerland, on the paddle steamers, three boys and three girls, which kind of evened things up. We all had to have a knowledge of German and mine was far superior to any of the others, whilst Liz, it transpired, had no knowledge at all. My friends were Andy Ross, Martin Greensitt, Grace McColl, Liz Turner, and Marilyn Hall. Marilyn was a lovely girl, blonde with a buzzing personality, and she pursued a career in hotel management, ending up at the Belfry Hotel in Sutton Coldfield. Liz was pretty, blonde, slim and about five foot three, and really nice. Grace was Scottish, stocky but not fat, and liked her drink. Andy was a friend, with a pockmarked face at the time. Martin was a big Yorkshireman with a deep voice and kind personality who pursued a career in McDonalds and was an Area Manager last time I heard. We were all friends anyway. I eventually lost touch completely with Liz, Andy, Martin, Grace and even Marilyn with whom we had exchanged Christmas cards for years and even met on the odd occasion.

My plan was to spend a few days in Munich before going on to Lucerne. On Monday 28 June off I set by train to Munich, except that there was a train strike so I had to take a bus to Dover. On arrival at 8 pm the following day I phoned Mark and Simon, my Munich busker friends from the year before, and asked if I could stay with them a couple of days. It did not matter if they declined because I could always stay in the youth hostel 'tent'. They said I could stay in their hippy-style VW van, which was a bit bizarre, so each night I kipped in the back with my sleeping bag, which was an essential item in those days of European travel!

After a few days of re-acquainting myself with that wonderful city, doing touristy stuff, drinking with Mark & Simon and other friends, I took a train to Lucerne via St. Margrethen. I had this mystical and magical image of Switzerland – that it was a place of wonder, almost cut off from the rest of the world, so much so that I thought you had to be special to be allowed to go in. What wonders lay the other side were beyond me.

I had to get off at St. Margrethen, which was on the Swiss/ German border, for a medical, and was kept waiting for hours. I thought they were deciding whether or not to admit me to their magical country! Eventually I caught another train, but it was the wrong one and stopped at St. Gallen. This was a small side station with a little hut for sitting in but no catering arrangements. I had to wait several hours there too, so eventually arrived in Lucerne at 9 pm, found my employer's shore-based office, which was nearby, was shown to my digs, had a quick drink with Andy and went to bed. It's amazing now that in those days we used to find new people we were looking for, find new buildings in unfamiliar places, and conduct our lives normally without mobile phones, which now, like chewing gum, seem to be the most essential part of normal life.

Part of the deal for working for 'Schiffs Restauration', loosely translated as 'Ships Catering', was that we were provided with accommodation, so Andy and I were housed in a small dingy room with twin beds in a row of low-grade apartment blocks in a back street called Neustadtstrasse behind the railway station. We could hear trains, whistles, and other railway-related noises through the curtains. But what did concern us was that in the next room, which I might add was only accessible through ours, were two Yugoslavian workers, who traipsed in and out with their pals, clutching bottles of vodka or Slivovitz. We wanted to get some sleep, but this was impossible. Also there was nowhere else for us to safely stow our passports, money, cameras etc. This was not part of my vision of Switzerland and I soon realised that it was just like any other country.

In the morning I gazed out of the window with awe. Our bedroom window looked straight down onto countless railway tracks: the main half a dozen lines for passenger trains then up to a dozen sidings for freight trains, trucks etc. It was amazing watching them and would be orgasmic to a train spotter. A shunting engine might pull one or two trucks along and across various lines, stop and uncouple the trucks, wait for the tracks to change and then reverse, pushing the trucks. Then the engine would stop, leaving the trucks to freewheel to their destination, which would be to join existing trucks so as to make up a train. They were really clever with this and most of the time judged it to perfection. It was mesmerizing! The engines went backwards and forwards all day, sorting out the trucks. Heaven knows what was in them.

We went to meet our boss, Herr Schmidli, who was a well-suited middle-aged man with all the trimmings: a belly that signified a lifelong rich diet, a large bald patch, a suntanned face, and an air of authority that was beyond our imagination. He explained where we were to work, what to do, how everything worked etc etc. We were given two company T-shirts, which were part of our uniform, and told to buy a 'portmonnaie'. This was a full-length black wallet which fitted into a holster around your waist. We felt especially important!

We had the next two days free, so we looked around Lucerne, which was extremely pretty with its old wooden bridge across the river, complete with centuries-old cobwebs. We also visited each other's accommodation and sunbathed on the Lido, which was just along the lake about thirty minutes' walk from the town centre and had a beach, lawns for sunbathing and picnicking, a small catering outlet and an outdoors life-sized chessboard on the ground. The pieces were plastic, about three feet high and it was great fun for me as a chess player to play while walking amongst the pieces.

Nearby there was a jetty, which was the last stop for some of the boats before reaching Lucerne. We were told by a fellow English worker how we were expected to behave – we could be fined for littering, ie cigarette ends or bottles, we could be fined for crossing the street in the wrong place, and we could be fined for not carrying enough money. These were all on-the-spot fines, so quite how they were going to achieve the last one was beyond me, but we heeded this advice. The old town itself was lovely, with cobbled streets, elegant four-storey buildings, decorative walls and general cleanliness and a feeling of well-being. The Kapellbrücke or wooden footbridge, which sadly got burned down about twenty years later but was thankfully rebuilt, was an iconic tourist feature.

The scenery around the lake was fabulous in the summer: vast green meadows rising from the shoreline to the tops of gentler slopes. The occasional wooden bungalow dotted around the slopes contrasted with the greenery. Forests of various types of trees also led from the shoreline up to the higher slopes and finally to the mountain tops. Little beaches dotted the lake in places, whereas in other parts the trees gave way to a rocky ledge. Small villages or towns dotted the flatter shoreline areas. Mountains were visible in the background. The views were fantastic.

The company SGV owned the boats and the catering was franchised, which is where we came in. Of the paddle steamers, all of which were majestic old ladies, the DS *Stadt Luzern* was the largest and the flagship of the fleet and was built in 1928, DS standing for Dampfschiff or steamship. Others were the DS *Uri* (1901), *Unterwalden* (1902), *Gallia* (1913), and *Schiller* (1906). They looked marvellous – the sports car equivalent of their day. They were white with two decks both fore and aft and both open and closed, and polished brasswork, wooden decking, wooden bench seating on the open decks, and portholes below the main decks. Funnels rose proudly at the top above the back awning and their horns gave off a deep bellow that rumbled around the mountains. The paddles gave off a 'swish swish swish' as they effortlessly rotated in the water. The engines were visible to everyone inside along with little glass oil containers to keep various parts well oiled. Everything was spotless and the brass work shiny. Absolutely marvellous.

In fact, I've been spending a lot of time looking at their website which is www.lakelucerne.ch, and reminiscing. There were also Motorschiffe or motor boats, amongst them the *Gotthard* (1970), *Winkelried* (1963) and *Schwyz* (1959) along with a few smaller vessels, I think. All these boats travelled around Lake Lucerne stopping at various stops on the way to the other end at Flüelen, which would take about three hours. Then it would be the same on the way back. Some boats had different routes, much like a town's bus service. There were tourists, locals travelling to see friends or go shopping, groups of schoolchildren and so on. I dreaded the schoolchildren because if they asked for a Coke (it was something like 'Eis Goggi' in the Swiss German dialect whereas in high German it is 'Ein Cola'), I could understand, and serve them. If they asked me a question like 'how much does a Coke cost?', I would be unable to understand the dialect, so they, being children, think you are thick! Every word had to be learned as if a new language, despite being spelled the same as German, so you can see how hard it was. The boats could also be hired privately and once or twice a week there was the 'Nightboat', which people booked to go out in the evening around the lake with singing and dancing provided by local entertainers in Swiss costumes and a three-course dinner with wine. In the middle of the lake they blew the Swiss horn, which echoed around the mountains. On my first Nightboat I took three hundred Swiss Francs in alcohol sales (about £80 at the time), which amazed my Yugoslavian waiter colleagues. Although I had worked hard, it did not seem out of the ordinary to me, so I played it down. One up to the Brits!

Marilyn and I were rota'd to work on the Gotthard, but I was jealous of my friends who were working on the paddle steamers, as they were the cream of the fleet. All the ships were moored at night near the offices and kitchens on land. The shift for the Gotthard started at 9 am, whereupon you did the mise-en-place. This was to get the essential coffee on, prepare the tables, crockery and cutlery, take provisions on board, and clean the windows. WHAT? Clean the windows? Don't be silly! I thought maybe this was a once-a-week job but no, every day two of you cleaned them inside and out, one washing whilst the other rinsed and dried them with a rubber squeegee thing, not forgetting the edges and windowsills. I soon became an expert!

I was amazed at the appearance of the ship, with flowers above the brass-like lion's head adorning the bow, flowers at the front of the upper deck, bunting from bow to stern, and a large Swiss flag sticking out of the stern at an angle. The boat was celebrating seventy-five years of something. At about 9.45 am the ship would move around to the embarkation point for the passengers and let them on, ready for sailing at 10.30 am. We had nothing to do with the sailing, just the catering. Both decks between them could seat about two hundred and seventy people, I would imagine.

I was extremely apprehensive, as this was uncharted territory. People piled in. Some just sat down, others ordered coffee or cold drinks and you could have one hundred and fifty people to serve! We worked either as a 'buffet worker', which meant you served the waiters from the bar, in which case you wore the company T-shirts, or if you worked as a waiter you wore a white shirt and bowtie whereas the girls wore a blue blouse. As a waiter you would take someone's order at the table, go to the till and insert your card and put the order through, take the receipt and leave it on the customer's table with the drinks. Each person had a paper place setting, which was a coloured map drawing of Lake Lucerne.

The kitchens were on the lower deck and food came up a little lift to the buffet bar. The waiters then distributed the food to the table. The first fifty minutes were often manic; coffee after coffee, drink after drink – it was relentless, and you had to ask the customer for payment before they left. We carried about £100 of our own money in Swiss Francs in our portmonnaie, some as notes, but mostly as change as this was our 'float'. At the end of the day, the supervisor would 'read' the till, which would tell us how much we each owed it, whereupon we would pay our own amount. On a busy day we would take up to SFr 900. Our portmonnaies would be stuffed with notes. Any money left in my portmonnaie would be my float and tips. If something cost ninety rappen (100 rappen = 1 Swiss Franc) then we would be left a franc so that ten rappen would be a tip. All our tips were normally made up of small amounts like this and I was amazed that on average we would make £30 per day. Well it might have been 30 Swiss Francs, or more, but even so it was good and enabled us to live off our tips.

So we settled into a routine. Start work at 9 am, rush around to get everything ready, pick up the passengers, travel to Flüelen, have an hour's break, travel back to Lucerne, tidy up, and go to the land kitchens at about 6 pm to get something to eat, followed by the nearest pub, which I think was called the Radi. It was more or less across the road, and it became the most important part of everyday life. The staff meals in the canteen consisted of salads, mostly tinned, along with cold meats and salamis. Not what we Brits call a meal. Also we were hot, tired, and thirsty, so we only picked at the food. It did not seem to vary, but at least we also ate on the ships during our lunchtime break.

The ships tended to finish within the same hour so normally we waited for our friends in the canteen before heading for the pub. This was just over the road, Werftstrasse, and looking on Google Earth, it still has an orange awning outside! When it rained though, it rained

– big heavy drops that lashed down like there was no tomorrow. We would get a black plastic bag, cut a hole in the bottom for our head, and two small ones at the corners for our arms, pull it over our heads and 'wear' it like a Mac and run for it – to the pub of course! We still got soaked and looked right idiots, but it was the best we could do!

Andy and I complained to Herr Schmidli about our accommodation, so he arranged for us to move to Eichhof. This was a dream come true. We were housed in a bed-sit, which was part of the nearby hospital's staff block – ie nurses! It was clean, comfortable and even had a communal laundry room. We were well impressed, but it meant that we had to take the tram to Kriens from Lucerne, which was a twenty-minute ride. On the first morning we awoke to the whiff of hops as it turned out that the Eichhof brewery was close by – this was the local lager and our basic commodity. We were in seventh heaven! I became even more impressed with the Swiss because a few days later they resurfaced the curved road outside the block and the new tarmac was smooth and neatly adjoined the pavement edges; there were no bits missing, so it was a perfectly-laid road. We used to catch the 8.30 am tram to go to work followed by a few minutes' walk, so that we would be on time to start at 9 am. If we missed the tram, the next would be in twenty minutes' time, meaning we would be twenty minutes late for work. This did not matter so much because you could rush to get ready and catch up. If we missed the last tram at night, which I guess was around midnight, then we had to walk, and this took us the best part of an hour depending on our ability to walk in a straight line! Andy and I also developed our own language which we used when we had to walk back at night, which would be a basic German phrase spoken in an English dialect followed by an English swear word, normally beginning with 'c' and ending with 't', because no one would understand…

In our local pub we mixed with our Yugoslavian staff, some of whom worked as waiters and some as buffet workers, whilst others did more menial kitchen tasks on land. Liz, who had a boyfriend in England, soon became friendly with one of the Yugoslavians, but Liz could not speak German and he could not speak English! I soon became their translator in the pub, which became kind of weird as they could only gaze at each other, hold hands and wait for my reply. More than once, out of jealousy, I was tempted to misinterpret the translation to ruin their courtship. In those days Yugoslavians were regarded by us as almost third-class citizens and she was going out with one! We all thought it a bit strange, but good luck to the guy, she was a pretty girl.

One week I was to work on the Winkelried, and this started from Flüelen, which meant getting up at 6.30 am in order to catch the 7.15 am bus to Flüelen in order to start work at 8 am, then the bus back afterwards, so it meant getting back to Lucerne about 7.30 pm. One day's diary entry goes as follows: '8–4 Winkelried. Boring as ever. Tadia let me off before last trip. Had a few drinks at our place ie got pissed'. If the weather was bad or indeed raining, then there were fewer tourists and two of my days' work on the Uri were cancelled because of rain. And so it went on, work and drinking and hangovers. We also frequented the Pickwick, the Braukeller, the Kuche Kashli and the Bonanza, to name but a few.

The first few times I worked on one of the paddle steamers I was filled with alarm when we approached a jetty. They approached at seemingly full speed, and if coming up to moor sideways, would approach head on, but at the last minute we would turn the rudder and reverse one of the paddles and the boat would turn on a sixpence and stop. Their accuracy was amazing. Likewise, when approaching the night-time berth, which meant paddling into a mooring slot with decking either side, they would approach at full speed, so fast that you would think the Captain had lost the plot, but with ten seconds to go before hitting dry land, they would put the paddles into neutral and in the last few seconds, full reverse. They would stop more or less instantly. My eyes would be wide open in fright!

One day Debbie and Janet came down from Mt. Pilatus to meet us. There was a hotel at the top of this local mountain where a few Brit friends worked. You could travel up by cable car or by a funicular railway, which at the time was the steepest in the world. You could do a round trip, a popular tourist attraction, which was to travel by boat to Alpnachstadt, take the funicular railway up, the cable car back down to Kriens, and then the local bus or tram to Lucerne. On the terrace of the hotel's bar, you could feed the ravens, which would settle on the railings and eat out of your hand. There was also a secret military hospital up there along with a nuclear bunker for the rich and famous.

So off we went for the usual, drinks, film, more drinks, and so on. They would stay with one of us for the night and once or twice some of us stayed the night when we visited them at Pilatus-Kulm. I arranged once to meet one of them the following week and I will never forget walking down beside the river past the bars and shops with people enjoying drinks on chairs and tables outside to find a beautiful blonde sitting on the railings waiting for me. It seemed that everyone was staring at her beauty and figure, and why was she on her own? Who was she waiting for? And yes, it was me! As we blokes all know, it is a huge ego boost to have a pretty girl on your arm. I was so happy that she had decided to meet me, an introverted boring old fart. So we had a good day.

Quite often there were American and Japanese tourists on the boats, the majority of whom could not speak any German. We used to take American dollars as payment and would have a rough idea of the currency value, but we would ensure that we ripped them off. Likewise we took sterling but did not rip the Brits off quite so much! Most English-speaking people naturally assumed we were Swiss, so they spoke to us in pidgin English or attempted some German. One particular man, Miles Jervis, was so relieved that I was English that he invited me to his cinema in the Midlands and left me his card. When back in England I took him up on his offer and he showed me around and I watched a film from the projection room – in those days films were on large spools through which a light shone to project the images – and he gave me a full-size poster of the film 'The World according to GARP' which I still have to this day; this was special for me as GARP are my initials!

One morning I arrived my 'acceptable' twenty minutes late to find my boat for the day (Winkelried) motoring off up the lake. I hadn't a clue what was going on so I enquired at the office. It had been booked privately and was going to Flüelen to pick up the guests. I apologised profusely because I had no idea about this, so they told me to take a bus to Flüelen and pick up the boat along with the guests. My colleagues were not impressed with me when I arrived, having had to do my preparation job as well as their other work.

Once the boat set off with the party there was a champagne drinks reception. You had to allow for the gentle swaying of the boat whilst filling the glasses and it was a bit tricky; what was even trickier was re-filling their glasses, because you had no idea how the people were going to sway, once they had drunk a glass or two! Then there would be a buffet or sit-down lunch.

Our wages, which worked out at about £60 per week, were paid into a bank account, but we did not have chequebooks or bank cards. One day I went to withdraw some money from my Swiss Bank account, the first occasion of two, because we virtually lived off our tips, and what a palaver! I had never seen a bank like it: large, majestic rooms with high ceilings along with ornate decorations and furniture which alone made the ordinary mortal such as myself feel intimidated. I was ushered into one of these large rooms, which seemingly contained just a desk and two chairs in a corner, and waited for a member of staff. I had to fill out a form, giving place of work, passport details, bank account number, and probably the reason for withdrawing money. All I withdrew was SFr 200 – anyone would think I was about to withdraw two million for the time it took! Then after what seemed like about twenty minutes the person just brought the money along and gave it to me; no going to a bank teller at a counter. Very unusual.

One night we went to a party at someone's flat in the centre of Lucerne which was going well, with the usual loud music, lots of alcohol and laughter, a rough equal mix of boys and girls along with low lighting. Time: about 2 am. Whooooosh!! Immediately and all of a sudden the room had clouded up. Shit! What the fuck was that!? We started spluttering and blinking and, in the confusion, not knowing what to do, I noticed that the hair and clothes of the girl next to me were covered in a white powder. We could not see more than a couple of feet in front of us, but I remembered that there was a window in a particular direction so made for it and opened it. Gradually the room began to clear a bit and then the sirens started and became louder and louder. Oh shit, this does not sound good, I thought. Everyone was standing around looking at each other, almost in shock, and in total bemusement as to what was going on. As the dust settled so to speak, everything, including us, was covered in a layer of white powder.

RAP! RAP! RAP! on the door. When it was opened, the police and fire brigade came in and ordered us downstairs and outside, which of course we did to the best of our drunken ability. I thought there must be a fire in the block, which was exciting, as all three emergency services were present, but then why was no one else from other apartments outside? It was all happening too fast for our fuddled brains to comprehend, but we did work out that a powder extinguisher had been let off in the apartment.

The police took our names and details, and once the fire brigade had finished checking the apartment, they let us go. Once back in the apartment, Debs, the girl who lived there, burst into tears due to the mess. The electrical equipment was probably ruined due to the powder inside and everything had to be taken out of the apartment to be cleaned. We did a bit there and then, but this was going to be a long job, not something you do at 3 am in a country in which you are supposed to behave!

It transpired that someone had let off this extinguisher for a laugh, but obviously never admitted to it, so the powder had gone into the corridor of the block and under someone else's door and they had called the services, thinking there was a fire. You can be fined for wasting police time in Switzerland, so for the next week went around a bit sheepish, expecting the worst.

We frequently went to the Lido on our days off and Andy, Martin and I got into the habit of swimming out to the jetty to meet the *Stadt Luzern* boat; the Lido stop was the last one before Lucerne itself and Andy worked on the *Stadt Luzern*. The catering supervisor would get a bottle of Pils for each of us, open them, and then drop them over the side for us to catch. Most of the time we caught them, in which case we felt really cool, and proceeded to drink them whilst treading water. If we missed or dropped them, we left them to sink to the bottom of the lake and hoped we would be dropped another bottle.

Pete was an English worker, and we went out on the 22nd August for his last night and got wrecked, to say the least. I was thrown in the lake and lost my glasses so I trudged home, furious, cold and miserable. I felt awful the next day at work but fortunately Marilyn found my glasses in the lake! Over the next few days I got worse and worse and had got flu and even spent my day off in bed and went to a doctor who gave me something and a day off work. Gradually I got better.

Just over a week later I was supposed to start on the *Uri* at 7.30 am but got there at 7.45 to find it moving off. Oh shit! Not again! Rather embarrassed, I went to the office to ask what to do and Herr Schmidli shouted at me, warning at me that if I missed another boat I would be dismissed. Oops! It was pointed out that there was a rota on the wall – no one had ever told me. I had to take a bus to Vitznau to catch the boat. When I got to the boat the boss informed me that I was to work as a chef. What? The kitchens on the paddle steamers were below decks just above the water level with a couple of portholes, which were always open to let out the heat. On a normal trip, the chef – always only one – used to finish about thirty minutes before getting to Lucerne so he would sit at the 'Stammtisch' or staff table, which in the case of the boats was normally the one nearest the tills. If we had a food request after the chef had finished, he would let us do it ourselves, but it would often be something simple like goulash soup, which was tinned and just required heating, but anything more than a ripple in the water, or a sharp turn, caused water to cascade in, so I frequently had to leap out of the way as lake water poured in through the open port holes. But today was a banquet, and sometimes these went to seven courses. Although my diary says I was the chef, I cannot believe that I was the only one! Later that night my diary records that I got smashed – I must have been proud of my work that day despite being late!

The other area below decks was the store for crates of beer etc, so as well as bringing the food on board, there was the alcohol side. The steps down below were steep with only a narrow step, so this was quite a hazardous operation. Andy would stand at the bottom of the steps with his forearms extended, hands facing up, a bit like a forklift truck. I would drop a crate of beer onto his forearms from the deck above and he would catch it. Quite a novel way...

There was a Swiss girl called Gabi, a supervisor on the boats, who I guess was in her mid-twenties, very pretty with an excellent figure along with a tanned skin. She deserves a mention, but I cannot recall why. We used to end up at her flat sometimes at different times of the day and I really can't remember whether one or all of us blokes were involved with her sexually, or platonically, but she would cavort around in knickers and bra quite frequently. Wednesday 8th September reads, in capital letters, I might add, 'BEST BREAKFAST I'VE EVER HAD' so she must have made a mark somewhere!

It was getting towards the middle of September and we had all passed our final exams at Birmingham except Andy, who had given up after a couple of exams. It occurred to us that we were now in the big wide world and had a career to think about. Hmmm... We viewed working in Switzerland as our honeymoon, so to speak, but now we had to get serious with our careers. So Marilyn, Mark and I went to Davos, a ski resort, to find a winter job. We trawled all the hotels, bars and restaurants looking for work but to no avail, which disappointed us, but at least it was a scenic train journey! We didn't bother after that...

We had our staff party at the end of the season on one of the boats, and it was a buffet affair with wine on the table and a disco. Everyone was in good spirits and getting fairly well intoxicated. We had all chipped in and bought Herr Schmidli and his wife a picture, which we duly presented, and he gave a speech and maybe a prize or two for the best employee etc. All was good, Herr Schmidli was happy, and now that the formal stuff was over, we could get on with the party. I wanted to put my bit in on behalf of the Brits, so I went up to him and beamed 'And so how have us Brits done then?'

'And as for you!' he thundered back. Oops, this isn't going right I thought. This is totally wrong. I thought we had worked really hard.

'Er, what?' I stammered back, lost for words.

'Because of YOU I can no longer send anyone to Eichof. I give you a nice flat and you leave it in a mess, so bad that the cleaner will not go in, and they will not take anyone else from us!'

'Oh, I'm sorry, I didn't realise, and it wasn't just me. I'm sorry,' was all I could manage. I was expecting praise and all I got was one of the worst bollockings of my life! And in public. I proffered another apology and slunk back to my chair, red as a beetroot. Andy and I had no idea that there had ever been a cleaner in our flat, but we were quite messy, what with beds unmade, clothes everywhere, unwashed coffee mugs perhaps with mould in the bottom, maybe a bad smell, and so on – typical student room. If we'd known it was serviced, I'm sure we would have been tidier. Oh dear...

Swiss, Brits, and Yugoslavians were all getting along fine that night even though we did not totally trust the Yugoslavians, and we Brits were all taking pictures when Marilyn's expensive camera disappeared. She was in tears. Someone accused the Yugoslavians of nicking it, and suddenly there was racial tension with lots of shouting and swearing, so much so that we had to leave. A sad end for Marilyn, who had scored with one of them.

Because eating out was relatively expensive, we only ate bratwurst and chips or the like or maybe Gulaschsuppe (Goulash soup), which I adore, even the more common tinned variety. But for our last night we arranged and booked a table for six at the Old Swiss Haus, which was a nice restaurant. Andy and I arrived and waited at the table for the others... and waited and waited. The waiters were giving increasingly frantic looks at us as they desperately wanted to know what was going on. We were also getting embarrassed because our friends had not turned up, and we knew why – it was too expensive. So after thirty minutes or so, we apologised and left, went for a meal at the Möwenpick Restaurant and later found the others in our local. We were NOT amused!

Later that night, on our way back to Zürichstrasse where

Marilyn lived, to go to a party, they tried to throw me in the river, but I resisted, and they failed. It was only later that I realised I had lost my gold watch. The next day we packed up, took our luggage to the railway station, left it in lockers, withdrew our wages from the bank and bought some things for the family, all of which we left in the lockers. We then had until 8.14 pm to mess around. My next concern was my watch, so I retraced my steps from the previous evening, and lo and behold, I saw it glinting in the river! I looked up and down the walkway at the tourists ambling along thinking what shall I do, what shall I do? Bollocks to it I thought, and with that I stripped to my underpants, went through the chain railings and jumped in. I dived for my watch, put it on, and swam back to the edge, where fortunately I found a ladder which went up the walled embankment. Someone helped me up, so I shook off the water, put my clothes back on and walked off, much to the astonishment of the tourists!

That evening Martin and I caught the train to Ostend and I finally got back to Shropshire about 10 pm the following evening. And so ended a fabulous summer. Marilyn stayed in Lucerne and worked the winter and then the boats again in the summer. My reference was more of a certificate, stating more or less that they were satisfied with me in every respect. I don't think they actually meant it!

CHAPTER 7

On the job market

My three years at college had ended on a positive note, I had had some fun in Switzerland, so now it was time to think about a career in the hotel industry. Because I had now worked abroad four times it only seemed appropriate to continue in that vein, so started to apply to chain hotels such as Sheraton, Southern Sun, Hilton, various foreign embassies and so on. Most of these interviews were in London, so I invariably stayed with my sister Robin.

It soon became apparent that I was hitting a brick wall; all my applications and interviews were in vain, so I reluctantly started to look locally in Wolverhampton and other local towns, not just for a management job but anything. The Lea Manor Hotel offered me a job as a general assistant, working as a waiter and barman. The Lea Manor is more of a motel, situated on the main road between Shifnal and Wolverhampton and a convenient four miles from Beckbury. It is your average place with that ubiquitous red patterned pub carpet, well-worn of course, with equally naff but practical dark wooden chairs and tables and complete with that stale beer and cigarette ash lingering odour and nicotine-stained paint. Ghastly really when you've come out of college! The bar was average, complete with a good set of locals, and there were about a dozen bedrooms upstairs, including a jacuzzi, which could be hired out, and a function room with large tarmac car park. It was seedy and grubby and just the style of establishment that I did not want to work in. But sweeping leaves in Beckbury was not going to 'earn my keep!' The hotel was owned by Bob Eaton, who had a lovely house on the outskirts of Albrighton; his daughter Carol had been to primary school with me and she was an absolute honey.

After last orders had been called and the bar shut at the end of the evening, we would carry on serving the locals till about 1 am. The most famous of these was Garth, a middle-aged, slightly overweight man in his fifties I guess who was diabetic and so drank bottled Holsten Pils lager. They always sat at the bar and his wife invariably fell asleep on the bar but would still manage to demand 'Give me another brandy!' more often than not when Garth wanted to buy another drink for himself. He was hilarious.

I would normally get a lift home from June, the manageress, or one of the staff. My parents owned a Citroen 2CV which was used as a spare car for us children, so I quite often used this to go to work. In those days you could more or less drink drive and not worry about it, especially in the country, so I used to have a drink or two, to say the least.

One night when I was a bit the worse for wear, I discovered a flat tyre, so in the dark, at about 1 am, I undid the nuts, jacked up the car and yanked the tyre off. But I could not get the spare tyre on. The jack was at its furthest reach, so I could only assume that I'd jacked it at the wrong place. I couldn't even get the punctured one back on. Oh my God, what was I going to do!? So I left it jacked up and staggered home, which was about three or four miles away. It was dark, no moonlight and it was a case of four steps forward, two back and one sideways into the hedge! I eventually got home about 3.30 am. In the morning I had a chronic hangover, felt like death and knew I had to do the inevitable.... I had to tell Dad. He went ballistic! Absolutely and totally. Purple with rage. Fortunately, it was a weekend, so he was able, to his complete frustration and annoyance, to take me to the 2CV, where we sorted it out. I kept quiet and obedient for the rest of the day, if only to appease my hangover.

It turned out that the relief chef was Mike Bates, a cookery lecturer at my college. It was a real surprise and a bit of a shock to find that the 'them and us' of lecturers to students attitude was now different, and he was one of the boys. We had a good laugh, especially when I did the odd shift in the kitchens!

I hated the restaurant. It was dimly lit, probably deliberately to avoid the customers seeing how dirty the room was, and the carpet had degenerated into a solid black grease patch near the kitchen door. The furniture consisted of spindly wooden chairs, the type that make you want to cringe, and the menus and wine lists were tacky. The wine list, if that's what you could call it, consisted of a few red and white wines, including the most popular naff ones of the time eg Bulls Blood, Blue Nun and the ubiquitous Mouton Cadet or Côtes du Rhone. Bog standard wine lists in those days were mainly French, with one or two German (Blue Nun and a Moselle, like Piesporter), a Spanish Red (Rioja) and possibly a couple of Italian wines. The only rosé was Mateus Rosé, which was enough to make you want to cringe. New world wines were unheard of. The menu was equally boring – again the ubiquitous prawn cocktail, packet soup and bought in pâté. Sweets were invariably sherry trifle, fruit salad, Black Forest gateau or cheese. And the cream was that horrible bland spray stuff.

We did the usual Christmas parties, catering for over a hundred in the main function room, so we were busy then. January was quiet so I became a casual, but they made me the restaurant supervisor. One night I was called in to run the restaurant as no other staff had come in, only to find that nothing had been prepared and it was almost service time. I was furious as the place was a mess and instead of half a dozen guests, there were about twenty. I had to rush around, but I never caught up.

After a few months of fruitless applications, I realised that I was not going to get a management position overseas so I started to look in the UK. Interviews I went to included the Hydro Hotel in Eastbourne, the Royal Overseas League in London and the Blakeney Hotel near Norwich. My college friend Nick Pearson worked at the Norwich Post House so I went for a drink with him and two girls and got to bed at 6 am. Must have been good! Also the White House Hotel, Watford, Durrants Hotel in London, the Kensington Hilton, Novotel Coventry, the Dormy Hotel near Bournemouth, the Hotel Riviera, Newquay and P & O cruises.

This last one fascinated me, and I was on best behaviour. I had applied to be a deputy (or trainee) assistant purser and passed the first interview, and a few weeks later I went for a second interview which I also passed. They informed me that the third and final interview involved three candidates in front of a panel of interviewers who would select one candidate. I was well pleased. But on leaving, I mentioned casually about my epilepsy – and that was the end. They could not employ me on medical grounds; in the event of an emergency I would be required to do several things, which might be to organise an emergency boat and if I had a fit, this could jeopardise people's lives. I was absolutely gutted because I would have been sailing around the world having a great time, and it would have been the start of a career. I actually cried when I was alone.

I was getting a bit despondent. But I remember reading 'The Mayor of Casterbridge' at school, in which the successful Mayor Henchard's life goes pear shaped, and all is doom and gloom for him. But somewhere in the book he realises that, maybe on a bright sunny day, life will turn out all right in the end. I cannot, being so long ago, remember the actual section, indeed it could be from 'War and Peace', which I also read. I realised from this that my life would turn out all right in the end. It would probably involve a lot of hard graft and toil along the way, but if I persevered, I would come out on top.

And then on the first of March the Riviera Hotel in Newquay, Cornwall offered me a job as a trainee manager. I was thrilled, as this was the start of my career. The hotel is situated on the cliff on the outskirts of Newquay with rough grass lawns called Barrowfields outside the hotel grounds stretching along the cliff to the town centre. I loved walking along Barrowfields, complete with rabbit warrens and collections of droppings. The hotel itself offered nicely tended lawns and a neat tarmacked drive with about nine flagpoles displaying European and the American flags on the hotel roof. It had superb sea views. The hotel had just under fifty bedrooms, all rather average, was three star and as well as the table d'hôte restaurant for the guests, it had an à la carte one called 'La Corniche' which served things like lobster thermidor and had been awarded some AA rosettes, and 'La Piazza' for dancing. It had a function room, a meeting room, with outdoor pool, sauna, squash court with viewing gallery, table tennis and kids' games room, and snooker table. It also had a hairdressing salon (I don't remember this but it is in a 1989 brochure) and laundrette, which was available for the guests to use. It all looked clean and well run, so it was an appropriate place to start my career.

David Nixon was the man who had interviewed me, and he was a jovial character despite dressing in undertakers' clothes, ie a black suit with greyish tie and striped black trousers. Very odd I thought at the time, but this was the management dress along with 'Black Tie' for the evening. So, back in Birmingham I had to buy two morning suits which cost me a fortune!

At the hotel I moved into room 127, which was a small dingy single room. All hotels have one or two of these 'bedrooms', or more accurately small storage rooms big enough to hold a single bed, a wardrobe, a bedside table and chair, a small TV and maybe a bathroom with a shower but no bath. They were usually next to lifts or air conditioning systems or boilers, ie noisy, and invariably would not be decorated to the same standard as other bedrooms and were used as a last resort or for people that didn't matter so much, like coach drivers (sorry!). The carpet would be tatty and there wouldn't necessarily be pictures on the walls which, along with bits of woodwork, would need painting. The wallpaper might be an off-yellow flock, the bathroom suite might be yellow or pink. In other words, grim.

The pub across the road was called the King Mark, and it immediately became my local – it had a pool table, which meant it was not far to stagger home to the hotel!

Newquay is world famous for its surfing on Fistral beach, surrounded by the Atlantic and Headland Hotels on the cliff top, a zoo, a railway station, a nearby RAF base at St. Mawgan, numerous other hotels, B&Bs and self-catering properties, caravan parks, tourist attractions and so on. Most of the pubs were pubs in their own right, but since the 1980s the surfing has become much more of an international event, with the pubs now being pub-discos, with many more restaurants, so the town has lost some of its old seaside atmosphere.

I was to work in all departments to learn the ropes with another trainee manager who started at the same time called Paul, but with different rotas. On my first day I started in the bar – the Swiss Bar, so called because the owners' business partners were Danny and Sylvia Moret (who were divorced or separated) and Danny was a Swiss national, as well as being the pastry chef for the hotel. He kept out of the running of the hotel. Mr Nixon was the Managing Director and General Manager. The bar was not that big, but the back was 100% mirrored with lots of glass shelves. I can't recall there being any optics, so I think every drink was poured by measure. The bar also led into the function bar; the room was called 'La Piazza' and it held a dinner dance every Saturday evening and nightly discos in the summer, and doubled as a coffee shop during the day. Behind the bar there was a servery where the restaurant staff could get drinks and wine from the bar staff. Everything had to be done properly, which was good, and we had to be attentive. Glasses were polished, the correct fruit added to drinks and cocktails, ashtrays regularly cleared and cleaned, tables polished etc and the middle-aged barmaid, Ann, showed me the ropes.

That evening I started with the restaurant orders and cashiering. Being a bank holiday La Piazza would have been open for a dinner/dance, as these were extremely popular. I think we'd take and serve the wine orders and later do the bills. This meant sitting at the restaurant desk at the entrance and collating all the charges and eventually presenting a bill and taking payment. I loved doing this because I'm an organised sort of person and it meant I could sit down; more to the point, I felt important!

The wine list was something else, with I guess 40 bin numbers. It had a major German section with all grades including Eiswein, all supplied by a German wine distributor called Deinhard, the best seller being Deinhard Green Label. I came to learn that German wine comes in either a brown or green bottle – brown for Hock, which includes things like Liebfraumilch, and green for Moselle, being Piesporter and so on. We also used hock or moselle glasses, brown or green with a long stem and short bowl for the wine and matching the colour for that wine bottle. I was impressed by the standards of wine service and I've never used them anywhere else, and it is a shame that German wine bottles in the 21st century are no longer restricted to those two colours. It is also a shame that the British do not appreciate the lovely wines that Germany produces, most of which the British have never heard of, let alone tasted.

The next morning I was sent up to work in housekeeping – not my favourite – and the following day to reception. I was a bit apprehensive here but also excited – this was uncharted territory for me. And I would be working with some lovely girls: Heather, Sue (who I'm still friends with to this day), Sylvia with hairy legs, Sharon (nicknamed the Rottweiler, for being scary), Gail, and someone with the nickname Ethel. They had the strangest telephone contraption called a PMBX or Private Manual Branch Exchange. The telephonist would sit in front of a panel, which consisted of maybe ten pairs of cords (cables with a coloured sheath) with metal jacks on the ends, which were spring loaded so that only the jacks protruded. Each pair of cords had a colour, eg one was yellow, the next green, the next blue, and the next might be green and so on. The hotel had about four outside lines, each of which was indicated by a jack hole and a light. The telephonist wore a headset. If a call came in from outside, a light would light up for that line so you would insert a jack into the hole which enabled you to speak. To transfer the call to a department or room number you would insert the corresponding jack into the room number's hole and its light would light up. Similarly internal calls could be transferred in this way. When a call had finished, the light would go out so you could pull the two cords out and let them wind back to their resting places. At busy times you could have the cords all over the place and criss-crossing, so you had to have your wits about you to insert or pull the right ones, especially as you could have cords with the same colour in use. The telephonist could also dial out with the circular dialler – now an antique! There must also have been switches which would have enabled you to speak and cut yourself off from calls.

It was a busy job, and you could not just get up and go for a pee or get a coffee – you could be quite in need of a drink by the end of a day shift. Evenings were a lot easier, with the phone being busiest during business hours – to book a meeting or dinner, suppliers calling, orders to make, people booking accommodation or meals, etc. I was shown how to take bookings for meals, reserve bedrooms, check guests in and out, and type letters and menus, the latter being in French. Having done a typing course at college and knowing a bit about food, the correct French spelling of the menus became one of my daily rituals, and I frequently corrected the receptionists on incorrect French wording.

What was soon to become another of my rituals was the weekly cleaning of the outdoor pool. The 'sunbathing terraces' as they were called then, warranted a daily inspection to be tidied up and loungers put back neatly, although we didn't bring these out until the end of April. The pool terrace had to be periodically scrubbed and hosed down. Rick was the main porter and a lovely chap in his forties, so this was one of his jobs. I was trained how to test the swimming pool for chlorine and pH levels. The Riviera's pool was a lovely blue sparkly colour, just as it should be. As a rough guide, if the pool looks slightly effervescent, then you can assume that the chlorine levels are in line.

The bottom of the pool kept getting dirty, and it took months for me to discover why. It might happen only a day after the pool had been vacuumed and the terrace cleaned, so I knew it wasn't the sand from the filter, and I knew it wasn't from guests' feet. It was actually red sand being blown over from the Sahara desert! Amazing. It just had to be vacuumed and that was that. I relished this part of the job because I could work outside and get away from the mundane jobs like serving tea. It was more of a man's job dealing with mechanical things – stopping the filter pump, changing it to 'vacuum', connecting the vacuum hose, having previously filled it with water, turning on the pump and so on. I enjoyed 'backwashing' the pool and topping it up with fresh water. I also tested it at weekends when the maintenance man was off duty.

On Saturday evenings the hotel held its popular dinner dance; guests would first eat in La Corniche and then proceed to La Piazza for the disco, where our resident DJ would do his stuff. It was geared for couples and we had to be on our best behaviour. My role was to take the wine orders and get them ready at the table. I think Mike, the restaurant manager, took the food orders. Once all were greeted and seated, and wines distributed, I would sit at the desk and get the bills ready and take payment. A nice easy job – an important one but a pleasant change from running around getting sweaty!

So what of the staff? Mike, or Mick as he was called, was in his thirties and his wife Gail worked in Reception, although she had to leave soon after I started due to cancer and sadly died some years later. He did a good job, was conscientious, rushed around, looked the part, and was a strong member of the team. He also liked his beer, so he regularly asked for the drip trays to drink, if he didn't have any money on him to pay for a pint. Drip trays are little square plastic containers that collect the drips from draught lager and bitter taps, so we'd collect them all up, lager, bitter, mild, Guinness, and pour them into a pint glass for him – resulting in a brown warm stagnant looking liquid which he'd consume with relish!

We played squash occasionally in the hotel's squash court. Two of the waitresses were called Sylvia and Yvonne. The kitchen comprised John Brightling, the head chef, Danny in pastry and after he retired, Bruno Coeur. Bruno found me on Facebook in 2010 and I upset him because I didn't initially remember him! He has done well and become a world-famous chocolatier and has his pâtisserie in Burgundy, France. The sous-chef was Chris Hopkins, a tall good-looking bronzed lad to which any girl would gladly succumb. Lucky sod! There was another Chris – surname Taylor?

John was quite a character, again very professional but occasionally you would find him crying during a busy service.

'John, are you all right?' I'd say, with the utmost concern.

'No, I just can't take it anymore!' he'd reply, sobbing.

'Can I get you anything?'

'A large gin & tonic!'

So off I'd trot to get him his G & T, and every time it did the trick. He would be fine after a drink and resume work.

Housekeeping: I can't remember the housekeeper's name, but Paul's girlfriend Sherrie worked as a chambermaid. There was an old scouse night porter as well as Nigel, who was a part-time night porter but was not quite all there. He did a good enough job and put his best into it, but one night Paul reduced him to tears by bullying him and I took an instant dislike to Paul from then on. As for the management, David Nixon had an office, Sylvia Moret had an office, although I was never really sure what she did, Heather Stevens was the assistant manager and had a desk, and then Phillipa the secretary had a desk. Heather never really seemed to do much, but this was probably because she did not need to. I was young, keen and fresh out of college: everything was black or white; it was either right or wrong and anything that did not conform to these standards irritated me beyond imagination. To me a grey area didn't exist, an attitude you don't begin to change to until you get older, like Heather.

We used to frequent the Central Inn, the Newquay Arms, Bertie's, and Tall Trees, a nightclub near the railway station. The first two pubs are now pub discos and have contributed to the transformation of Newquay to what it is today.

My next challenge was to look after the stationery side of things. I reorganised the stationery cupboard, and listed all the items required, from pencils to till rolls, headed paper to brochures. The printed stuff came from somewhere in Truro I think, whereas small items were purchased from a stationery shop, Penver's around the corner in Chester Road, which was still there in 2011. This was now my baby; no one was going to mess with my organisation. I relished being able to order things and keep to a pre-determined stock level. I loved proof-reading new printed items and began to feel that I belonged at the hotel and that my life had a sense of purpose.

The winds in the winter could be awesome, indeed just along the street near the Bristol Hotel, the wind could howl around the corner so much that even as a fit young man, I would have to cling onto the railings to drag myself along the pavement. The Riviera's driveway contained half a dozen or so of old-fashioned street lamps, each of which had four glass panes at the top. To replace a light bulb, you had to lean a ladder against the lamp, climb up and unscrew one of the four sides, which were effectively hinged glass windows, and change the bulb. On a normal day it was easy, but one winter's evening Nixon (we addressed each other with surnames on a day to day basis) made me change one. It was blowing a gale and the rain lashed almost horizontally, yet he wanted me to go up a long ladder on my own, with only the circular stem of the lamp as a leverage point for the top end of the ladder. How I didn't fall off God only knows, and I was absolutely terrified! One of the standards of the hotel was that ALL lights must be on and working – and to this day you can instantly judge a hotel or restaurant by this maxim, similar to the state of the toilets. If the toilets are clean, tidy, and smell fresh, then you can more or less assume that everything else will be.

The thought of being a duty manager terrified me. How would I know if a decision I made was right or wrong? Where should I be in the hotel? What if my co-workers disagreed with me? I sweated buckets in those first few weeks, but it gradually dawned on me that you didn't need to do much; if all the staff were there and they were all doing their jobs, then things ticked along nicely. Just make yourself visible, make sure staff get breaks, make sure they are all right, and check around the customers. Not so bad after all.

The worst part was that I had to speak to every table in the restaurant during dinner. It was rather futile for me because I was still really shy, so making conversation was not my forte. I would ask the first table 'Is everything all right?', and if they said yes, I would proceed to the next table and ask exactly the same. God forbid if they said 'No,' or said something that required further comment or action. It became really obvious that I was not doing this properly, so I gradually developed a set of questions, to be asked in rotation: 'Have you had a good day?' or 'How's your dinner?' or for arrivals, 'Did you have a good journey down?' Occasionally one had a genuine conversation, but from my part it was normally me answering questions, not the other way around. I only had something positive to contribute if I had been somewhere or done something constructive on my day off.

We regularly had a daily lunchtime 'management meeting' in the bar, which was really an excuse to have a cocktail, which was invariably an Americano, consisting of Campari, sweet Martini, soda water, an orange slice and ice. Lovely, but they used to go straight to my head! One of Nixon's favourites. The management ate in the restaurant all the time and were served by the staff, so we sat once the busiest part of service was over. Our dinner menu always contained, as an extra if you like, an omelette of the day and a cold meat salad as main course options. The food was good, I have to say.

The staff could use the snooker room in the evening if available, for which permission was required from the duty manager, and Mike and I took advantage of this occasionally when off duty. One such

Friday evening, not long after I had started as duty manager, whilst I was looking after the bar, Mike asked me for a game of snooker, so I asked him if he thought it would be all right for me to play whilst leaving the bar open and he said it was fine, as all guests had gone to bed and the night porter was around. So down we went along with Sue and a waitress to play snooker. I couldn't be bothered to walk back upstairs to get drinks when required, so I told them to get their own and put the money in the till. We finished about 3.30 am and I was slightly the worse for wear the next morning, something that became all too frequent!

The following Monday morning I was summoned to David Nixon's office. Oh dear this can't be good, I thought.

'Were you playing snooker on Friday night?'

'Yes.'

'Were you in charge of the bar?'

'Yes.'

'Did you leave the bar unattended?'

'Yes.'

Did you tell the staff to get their own drinks?'

'Yes.'

'Well Mr Paris, if you had answered any of these questions incorrectly, because I know what went on, you would have been out of the door by now,' he stated matter-of-factly. Christ, I thought, that was a close shave. I apologised profusely and offered to pay for any drinks that weren't accounted for and said it wouldn't happen again. I guess the night porter, quite rightly, had reported me to the boss. I didn't put a foot wrong for the next few weeks! David Nixon was quite hot on keeping the brass polished, so I took it upon myself to ensure the door handles, the bar brass, and the copper heat deflector above the fireplace in our conference room were spotless and extra shiny.

Nixon began, over the next few weeks, to show me how the monthly liquor stocktaking operation was performed, which I found very exciting. I soon started to be involved with the liquor ordering and after a short time I took it over completely. The stationery side of things soon became a tedious affair, and it was the same at every hotel I have worked in since. Bottled mixers like tonic water, fruit juices, bottled beers etc all came in plastic crates and the breweries charged a £1 refundable deposit for each crate delivered. We therefore did stocktaking for the crates as well as the liquor, so we had to count crates whether full or empty due to their value. Empty bottles, being returnable in those days, were also counted. I was fastidious in making sure that the empty crates were stacked exactly on top of each other and ensured that the partially filled crate was on the top, and the entire area had to be kept neat and tidy. Wherever you worked in those days, staff often left this area in a mess. New stock was always rotated so that the oldest was on top or at the front. Wines and spirits were stored in a separate cellar on metal racking with the bin numbers labelled and the wine on its side to keep the cork moist. Amazingly the beers and wines were sometimes delivered by horse and cart! The stocktaking results were fed into a primitive computer, which was DOS based and the paper was printed onto a printer with tractor-feed paper which had wide green and white lines – I've never really understood why. It was a bit of an operation in those days and would take days to complete; these days it is easy to set up a Microsoft Excel program for stocktaking.

When working a split shift, most afternoons involved a quick sleep for an hour or so, but as the summer approached I took these naps down on Lusty Glaze Beach, which was a stone's throw from the hotel. I virtually lived there in the summer and would bound up the steps two at a time all the way to the top of the cliff. I was fit in those days.

Nixon had a yacht somewhere up the Fowey estuary in South Cornwall and occasionally he would take guests out for the day, which was chargeable. He invited me to crew for him, which thrilled me. I would invariably be on split shifts for these days, being breakfast and then the evening in the Corniche restaurant, so after the breakfast shift, he would drive me down to his yacht, *Treyona*. The guests had to make their own way there. I was also responsible for the catering, being cake and tea. We would sail off around the coast and moor somewhere suitable with a pub at hand where we would have lunch, and afterwards sail back. Cake and making tea were one of my jobs on the way back. It was great fun crewing, and using the galley, but boy would I be knackered by the evening back at work!

Life began to get into an all too familiar routine: sleep or sunbathe or go for a cycle in the afternoons, go out to pubs or discos or play pool/snooker in the evenings, but it was great. I was really enjoying life. I started to have driving lessons. I subsequently failed my first test because I had worked out, being good at maths, that there was a formula for the distance required to stop at a given speed, except I forgot the formula on the day of the test!

We did the odd wedding at the hotel, so we kept the bar open late on occasion. One such time was when Bob Potter from the Lakeside Club stayed and made me keep the bar open till 7.30 am. I didn't go to sleep afterwards because I was to open the bar at 10 am! I just had breakfast, a shower and change of clothes, so I was knackered. One late-night celebrity was James Last of orchestral fame, who only drank Brandy Alexander.

One day both Chrises from the kitchen, Sue and I went deep sea fishing. This involved bringing a cool box filled with cold lager cans and a knife. Off we went on a charter boat along with some other people for a good day out. We caught nothing but mackerel, which was kind of frustrating, so on the way back we decided to gut them, chucking the guts overboard. Seagulls were screeching overhead, and the other fishing guests were steadily throwing up over the side, not helped at all by our fish-gutting, whilst we laughed, made merry and drank cans of lager.

Amazingly, I was allowed to have a holiday at the end of August, so I went off with my old college friends Chris Sykes and Shirish Patel back to Lucerne, where Marilyn and half a dozen of the current final year Birmingham HND students were working for the summer. We had a brilliant time.

One day in the summer, Mike and I were asked to take some kids staying at the hotel to Newquay Zoo. This terrified me: never in my life had I been put in charge of a strange kid, let alone a whole bunch of them. Especially as I don't particularly have the time for them! So off we trotted to the zoo, which was about a thirty-minute walk from the hotel. Once we'd paid for them and got them inside, Mike said 'Right then, off you all go, there's some money for ice-creams, and meet back here in an hour.' I was aghast! Leaving kids to their own devices? Mike said it would be all right, and as he had children himself, what could I say? So, a little nervously, I followed him to the nearest bar, where we remained for an hour. Not so bad after all. When we met the kids, who amazingly had all collected themselves at the allotted time and place, they seemed oblivious to the fact that we had been drinking!

The staff house, Clarendon, next to the hotel had several bedrooms with a communal bathroom, which consisted of the middle floor. I believe the top and ground floor were rented out as holiday accommodation. I eventually moved into one of these bedrooms, which delighted me because it meant I would be living in the same house as Sue the receptionist, who I had a real crush on. Her boyfriend was a hunk who worked in the haulage business, so

I knew there was no hope for me and we were simply good friends. I was so glad to get out of that dingy little hotel room which stank to high heaven; dirty smelly socks and pants, white shirts with BO, no air flow as I never opened the window, a few dead flies around, maybe a few small flies collectively flying around in a circle, with the curtains always drawn shut, mainly to prevent other guests looking in, but also to save having to draw them every five minutes.

As autumn approached, I joined the pool team at the King Mark and soon progressed to the 'A' team. I virtually lived at the King Mark and being in the pool team gave me a real sense of purpose and occupied what would have otherwise been dull evenings. I enjoyed visiting other pubs for matches and bought my own cue, which was my pride and joy.

Ironically, the hotel closed at Christmas, so Sally's father drove both of us back to the Midlands on Christmas Eve night, arriving at 3 am, and Robin collected me the following morning from Sally's place for Christmas at home, which involved all the usual 'adult' drinks parties, dinner at various people's houses and a party or two. Sally and Kevin duly drove me back to Newquay on the morning of the 29th December and I worked the evening. New Year's Eve was a great night, with David Nixon doing the washing up in the kitchen. I must have drunk too much as I got to bed at 4 am, and the following day I felt awful. In the evening I must have had a fit in the wine cellar, because I had collapsed and woke up a short time later, and Nixon asked me if I'd had a fit because I was walking around with a dazed look, so I must have, so he let me go early – to bed, and Sue remembers that I had cut my face and it was bleeding. Then on the 2nd January we had the staff party, which was in fancy dress and held in La Piazza, with a buffet and disco. I was dressed as an Indian and thankfully was off the next day, so I had time to recover.

Friday 27th January 1984 was a good day as I finally passed my driving test, and that evening I went with some friends to see Tina Turner in concert at Carlyon Bay. Soon after, I had a week's holiday, so I was able to borrow my parents' 2CV and drive around England visiting friends, which was great. Freedom at long last!

There was a training course held at the hotel, the HCITB Trainer Skills One, and each of us had to perform a training session as part of the exam. As alcohol seemed to play a large part in my life, I decided to 'train' someone how to make an Irish coffee. Each person had their various props ready in advance, but when it came to my turn, the cream had turned a bit due to the warm temperature in the room, so it wouldn't float, so I got in a fluster and didn't know what to do and failed! I was so embarrassed. A few days later the trainer returned, and I performed the same operation and passed with flying colours.

One of the duty manager's winter jobs is to light the fire in the lobby, a real fire with logs. If it wouldn't light, one trick was to hold a large sheet of newspaper open in front of the fire so as to block off the air supply, so that the air flow has to come from underneath and 'draws' the fire. This was quite a regular system, but one particular night the newspaper I was holding caught fire, so I stuffed it into the fire, but it went up the chimney alight. I put my ear to the fireplace, and it sounded like a jet engine in the chimney, so guessed it was on fire. Christ! I am going to burn the hotel down! Would I be sacked? Would I have to pay for it? I ran down to Nixon who was having dinner in the restaurant and screamed at him 'Mr Nixon, the hotel's on fire!'

He slowly placed his knife and fork down on the plate, looked up and said matter-of-factly 'Mr Paris, if you would like to talk to me, go out of the restaurant and come back in in an orderly fashion.' I was aghast at this casual response and thought 'You bastard!' but without further ado, I turned on my heel, walked out of the restaurant, and turned around and walked slowly back up to him.

'Mr Nixon, the hotel is on....'

'Where is the fire?' he interrupted.

'The chimney is alight! Some newspaper went up it alight!' I replied, terrified.

'Come with me,' he said in a resigned apathetic manner, as if to imply he had seen it all before and was annoyed to have his dinner interrupted. He strode off with me following sheepishly to the top floor, undid a fire hose reel, climbed out of a window onto the roof, and instructed me to put some old blankets around the fireplace and wait there. I duly did so and waited at the fire with blankets around. *Quick, quick, quick, come on turn the water on you idiot! Get on with it! I don't want the hotel to burn down... what are you doing?? Come on, come on come on...* I was getting exasperated as the minutes went by and nothing happened. Eventually, to my intense relief, water began to trickle down the chimney and the fire was out. He must have had the hose on for fifteen minutes or so down the chimney before anything happened. I was so relieved! That also taught me one of my main lessons in life: don't panic!

Sometimes, in the summer, when down on Lusty Glaze beach, instead of bounding back up the steps, I would climb the cliffs up to the top without any safety equipment, which was relatively easy and enjoyable. One day, having sunbathed in a different location and subsequently become cut off by the incoming tide, the choices were to either swim around to the beach or climb the cliffs. No sweat. As I had my wallet, watch, towel, and other personal items, swimming was not the best option, so started to climb. Near the top, the rocks slowly gave way to a combination of sand, tufts of long grass and other small plants. I was at this point facing the cliff but every time I tried to find purchase with my hands up above, the grass gave way, so it was impossible to grip anything. I couldn't move to the left, right, up or down. I was stuck.

I looked out to sea in case there was a small fishing boat passing so that I could shout for help, but it was empty of vessels. Shit! I knew that above me was the coastal path, so I shouted for help... and waited and waited and waited and waited. HELP! HELP! Nothing happened. What was I going to do?

I tried to move yet again but couldn't. I just couldn't move in any direction. I was beginning to wonder what the hell I could do. Wait for a boat to pass? Obviously no one could hear me, so I resorted to the last but one option, jumping to my death below, and said out loud to the world in general, 'Oh Lord, I know I don't go to church and I know I don't pray as much as I should, and I know I could be a better person, but I could really do with your help! And if you do help me, I will give some money to the church and promote Christianity.' And with that I seemed to just walk up along the cliff edge and up out of danger to the footpath.

I stood on the footpath, absolutely staggered at what had just happened. Wow! I couldn't believe it. Was there something in God after all? I thanked him out loud and promised to do something, but I am ashamed to say I did nothing except to recount this occurrence verbally to various people during my life. I still find it incredible.

And so life went on. I was happy with my job, had a good set of friends and a reasonable social life, and things were going in the right direction. But all this was about to change. There was a general staff meeting called in June and it was announced that David Nixon was selling the hotel to a Fred Rolfe, who was a retired estate agent. How could this possibly be? How could you do this to us? Nixon was a professional; and had taught me a lot, and all that was going to change.

All my conditions of employment were the same. One of the first things Mr Rolfe spoke to me about was organising the change in printed stationery. The Rolfes moved into the bungalow adjacent to the hotel. He didn't say much, but his wife, an elegant blonde lady whose first name was Liz, busied herself with non-operational things like flower arranging and gardening, and was someone you could talk to. Fred did what he wanted and got us to do likewise with no arguments. He didn't seem concerned with the hotel at all. If we protested, it was to no avail. A hotel should have a resident's lounge, which is an AA guide requirement for residents to sit quietly in a room to read the paper or book, or have a quiet chat, with no radio, TV or background music. There had never been a TV in the Riviera's lounge, but Mr Rolfe installed one, much to our horror and disgust, and not only that, proceeded to adopt it as his personal TV room! The guests had no say in anything, or the choice of channel, and he made anyone sitting in this lounge feel uneasy in 'his' room, which we really couldn't tolerate. But what could we do? Oh, and our daily lunchtime cocktail ritual finished. Hmm...

I bought my first car from Danny the chef, a silvery Mitsubishi Colt Celeste sports car, for £350, and it would nip around the Cornish country roads. The only problem was that it was rusty as shit, so much so that there were several holes, and as Danny had taken out the speakers, which were in the doors, I could put my hand right through the driver's door to the outside! But I could visit Cornish towns on days off like Truro, Bodmin, Penzance, Liskeard, Launceston, as well as smaller coastal ones, either on my own or with friends, which was great.

One evening about six weeks later, I drove Graeme, one of the porters, and his father to the Plymouth Novotel as they were going on holiday, but my car broke down on the A30 on the way back. Oh my God! Remember readers, mobile phones did not exist then. It was pissing with rain and I walked for hours before coming across a house and begging them to let me use their phone. Mrs Rolfe duly collected me by car, for which I was forever grateful. As I had walked for so long in the rain, I got a stinking cold to boot! Also I had to work as the night porter that night, which started at about

10.30 pm, so I was already past my start time when I phoned Mrs Rolfe. It transpired that I had blown the head gasket, which was my fault because I hadn't realised that cars needed water and oil, so the garage charged me £230, far more than the car was worth, but hey ho....

Fred changed the policy on the liquor ordering. He wanted everything ordering by the case or cases in order to achieve the best price, even drinks like Galliano, of which a bottle would last a year or two in the average hotel. This was ridiculous. Then items like tonic water and fruit juices were to be bought by say a dozen cases, again to achieve a better rate. Before long the cellar was overflowing, so I had to have more space, and he gave me a bedroom! And then another! My diary entry for October states that I unpacked a delivery of sixty-three cases of wine into room 117. It's unheard of to reduce your bedroom selling capacity. The amount saved by purchasing in this way would easily be lost by reducing the number of available bedrooms, especially in the summer! It went against everything I had been trained to do.

I kept him informed of our massive stock levels on a monthly basis, once the stocktaking had been done by me. Then one day out of the blue he asked why I had got so much stock and then ordered me to send it back!

'What planet are you ON?' I thought. Some items, like tomato juice, were beginning to go out of date; those at least could be used by the kitchen as a base for a sauce or soup, and bottles like grapefruit juice could be used for the breakfast buffet, but generally I was in a bit of a dilemma. I had a good relationship with our brewery supplier, Courage, but in a way, I was glad when they refused to take much back, and handed it over to Mr Rolfe to deal with. I believe more was taken back in the end because he threatened not to pay his account or would change suppliers etc – typical cowboy behaviour.

Another shock to the system was the Rolfe family itself. Rex and Pauline arrived and moved into the bungalow. Pauline was Fred's daughter from before Liz's time and Rex, her husband, was from New Zealand. Both were lovely people, and gave up their life in New Zealand to work at the hotel, but Mr Rolfe ostracized them both, even though Rex was employed as a trainee manager under my wing. I don't think this was really his thing and career wise was just a stop gap. They were hardly spoken to by Mr Rolfe, which made for an uncomfortable atmosphere. Then there was Mr Rolfe's own daughter, whose name I've forgotten, who swanned around like Lady Muck. She would sunbathe and swim by the outdoor pool, which reduced space for the hotel guests. She was a blonde in her twenties with not a bad figure. What we did have to complain about to Mr Rolfe, very reluctantly I might add, was that she frequently sunbathed topless. Not the done thing in an English hotel in those days.

As time passed, it became obvious that that Mr Rolfe had started an affair with the housekeeper, with his wife virtually under the same roof! All very strange. It became more and more apparent that the hotel had effectively become Mr Rolfe's personal retirement home. My initial contract with David Nixon was for eighteen months, expiring at the end of January 1985. I decided not to renew it, and started applying for management jobs elsewhere. I went for various interviews at four or five-star London hotels, also the Norbreck Castle Hotel in Blackpool, the Queens Hotel in Hastings, the Moat House at Southend-on Sea, the Mendip Lodge in Frome, all coinciding with overnight stays with friends along with pub crawls etc. Two other reasons for leaving was that I had had to move back into room 127, I think because our apartment in Clarendon was not included in the sale to the Rolfes, and secondly Sue, who had become Head Receptionist after Heather had left, had handed in her notice to become an air hostess with British Airways – a very successful move, as she ultimately became a Cabin Director on Concorde. Things were not the same without her jovial character.

My leaving do was arranged in the local disco, Tall Trees, but because I had been working the evening, I arrived late – and was refused entrance as it was after midnight! To my own leaving party! Ironic – so I missed my leaving do. And so ended a good period of my life.

During Nixon's time we regarded the Riviera as the second best, if not the best, hotel in Newquay, the best possibly being the Bristol Hotel. The Headland, and to a lesser degree the Atlantic, were not far behind. There were various smaller hotels that probably provided a far better holiday experience. Over the years all these hotels had their ups and downs, but sadly the Riviera hotel went downhill. It became a coaching hotel, then a bed & breakfast, then they built a training facility in the car park, and then it was abandoned and finally there was a fire. It was really sad to see such a good hotel go down the pan.

As for Nixon, he went on to start a management company. Much later, in 2007 when I was working at the Riverview Hotel, we used a company called DCN to process our wages, and DCN was Nixon's initials - it was his business, although by then he had retired.

Further interviews during February and March included one at the Mollington Banastre Hotel in Chester, and the return journey nearly ended in disaster. Only one lane was open on the main roads, due to snow and ice, and on the way back it was on the other side, so you drove along it and just moved over to your own side when an oncoming vehicle approached. My side consisted of compacted ice and snow about six inches thick, and everyone managed this reasonably safely – except me! Previous snow and ice had been shoved to the side of the road by a snowplough, forming a huge bank. I veered on to my side of the road, but went up the bank and the car nearly tilted over. Fortunately, it stalled, and therefore as forward momentum had ceased, it dropped back down upright. That was a close one!

When I had recovered my senses, I got out, looked at the tyres and car to make sure it was in one piece, and drove back home very very gingerly!

Other interviews were at the Bedford Swan Hotel at Bedford, the Eccleston Hotel in London, the County Hotel in Canterbury, the Strathallan Hotel in Birmingham, the Ship Hotel in Weybridge, the Kings Head Hotel in Cirencester, the Ruthin Castle in North Wales, the Ariel Hotel at Heathrow, and another grim-looking London Hotel which I never went into, and the most interesting of all, the Gleneagles Hotel in Scotland. I took the train and stayed the night in the staff block at the Gleneagles. This was my first time to Scotland, and boy what fantastic scenery. During my interview the following morning, the fire alarms went off for a fire drill, but the chefs just ignored it – they often think they're on a level beyond normal human etiquette; but I was just the same – whenever I put on my chef's whites, my character would change – kind of Jekyll and Hyde, and woe betide anyone who got in my way.

I also arranged an interview at Crest Hotels' head office in Banbury but got lost due to the fog (young readers: nothing like sat nav in those days!) and so was two hours late. It was re-scheduled the following day, but I had such a hangover that I had to cancel. I had met Nick Pearson (old college friend) that night in Belbroughton and gone on a pub crawl and a curry of course and crashed at his house. Otherwise I worked a few shifts at the Lea Manor, helped Dad with his garden projects and went out drinking. I sold my car at auction for £150 and then used the 2CV to visit Newquay and collect my bike, which I had left with my granny in Exmouth. I rode it to the Ariel Hotel as they had offered me the position of restaurant manager, which I reluctantly accepted. My interview had been for a junior assistant manager, but they were worried about my epileptic history, as were most of my interviewers, especially corporate companies. I always mention it because by chance I had omitted this fact when I started at the Riviera, and this had concerned David Nixon for a while.

I subsequently drove down to the Ariel on Sunday 7th April and moved into a staff room on site. The Ariel was the first hotel to be built at Heathrow Airport. The company, J Lyons, which ran tea shops, restaurants and hotels in London amongst other things, decided that as air travel was taking off (no pun intended!), and car ownership was increasing, motel-style hotels should be built near major roads outside cities. The first was on the busy A4 or Bath Road, but as it was near an ever-increasing airport – Heathrow – they actually decided to make it the first airport hotel, so it was right at the end of the main runway, which was across the road. The design was modernistic for the day, being circular in design with a black band around the edge of the roof and above the first floor, so as to give the appearance that the hotel was floating, maybe like a UFO. The company was eventually bought by Trust House Forte (THF) in 1978.

As you walked through the sliding glass doors onto a marble floor, the reception was on the left with the lifts nearby and the Willow Restaurant on the right, with the bar towards the rear of the hotel I think, and in the middle of it all, a curving staircase. There was a circular central courtyard, so that the hotel was effectively doughnut-shaped. There were also several meeting rooms on the ground floor. Of the 185 original bedrooms on three floors, singles were on the inside, with doubles or twins on the outside. In the 1980s an extra outside wall was added with sound insulation to help combat the ever-increasing noise of the passenger jets. The car park surrounded the hotel. Sheratons,

Hiltons, Ramadas, Thistles, Post Houses and numerous other hotels littered the surrounding land.

The management consisted of Jerry Lawless, the general manager, a man in his fifties who looked the part, a food & beverage manager, a front of house manager and a human resources manageress, all of whom took turns with duty management. This style of hotel and this kind of company were all new to me. Apart from my six weeks at Novotel, this was my first employment with a chain hotel group, and there were company rules and regulations to follow, something I found a bit difficult to comprehend.

The restaurant contained a central oval cold buffet station, a hot carved meat section, an à la carte menu and a desk at the entrance. The self-service buffet was the centrepiece, with dishes of starters or hors d'oeuvres, cold meats, fish, crustaceans, potatoes, salads, etc – you name it, it was there, and it all fitted in metal containers over ice and was angled outwards. Bright lights shone down on all the food with maybe decorative displays of jars and coffee beans or bottles on the central top surface. I still have two menus from 1985, which were A2 in size, colourful and laminated. The menu was ordinary; for instance whitebait cost £1.95, lemon sole £6.30, a lamb steak £6.65, a dessert £1.75, a pot of coffee 90p. These were probably quite expensive for the time. But the 'Huntsman's Table' was the breadwinner; a two-course lunch with coffee cost £7.50, consisting of either soup of the day or hors d'oeuvres from the buffet, then either roast beef or one of the hot dishes of the day with potatoes or vegetables, or a cold buffet selection, followed by coffee with a selection of chocolates. A similar dinner, including a dessert or cheese from the trolley, cost £8.95.

So it should have been fairly straightforward, you might think. But oh no! Airport hotels automatically overbook their rooms so that each day they might be running theoretically at 110% occupancy, but each day there are delayed flights, passengers cancelling due to illness or other circumstances and some guests arrive and depart at odd times, so it's possible to re-let the room so that at the end of the day you end up with as near as 100% occupancy as possible, or marginally over, if re-letting rooms after they've been serviced. It doesn't matter if you're full and there are arrivals – they are transferred to other hotels nearby, a bit like herding sheep. All airport hotels do it, every single day, all over the world, as do city hotels. Rooms are not actually allocated until you speak to the check-in person. Concern for the wellbeing of the customer didn't seem to be of any relevance. If you were a regular guest, there was a chance you might be looked after.

So take the Ariel, with 185 bedrooms. Half of the rooms will be single occupancy, the other half double. Not everyone will want to eat in the restaurant in the evening – they might go out to eat, or might be sleeping, or arriving or departing. So let's say we have one hundred guests wanting to eat in the evening in the Willows restaurant. The restaurant had ninety covers, so if, for argument's sake, all the tables were for two, we could sit 45 couples, but if most guests were singles, as they usually were, then very soon all the tables were occupied with not many people in the room. We also took bookings from outside guests, so tables had to be reserved for them. During my time there, queues developed in the evenings with guests waiting for a table, which were automatically re-laid ASAP. They might be in a strop – tired from a long haul flight, pissed off from a delayed flight, even more pissed off from being accommodated overnight by a cancelled flight. Or they might be business travellers who haven't got time to mess about in queues, or people who normally bypass queues due to their status in the world. To me they were bodies to occupy vacant tables. Next!

The food and beverage manager was on holiday when I started, so one of the other management just pointed me towards the restaurant and left me to it. I was terrified; I was now a restaurant manager in a prestigious chain hotel at one of the busiest airports in the world, and I would be dealing predominantly with international businessmen who expect things at a flick of a switch. Not like your bucket & spade hotel, which would be more laid back, and where the customer almost expects Fawlty Towers-style service, and being British, accepts it. That's the way it was.

They ordered business cards for me – my first ever – so I was extremely excited. Nice ones too, with an embossed typeface. 'Geoffrey Paris/Restaurant Manager'. I still have one to this day, as does my father, who has a display cabinet full of hotel business cards from his time travelling world-wide as a company director.

The restaurant was busy all the time. To begin with I probably ran around like a headless chicken, being reactive to situations, not pro-active as I should have been. One major problem was that we were so busy that we frequently ran out of crockery, whether cups and saucers or plates. They just could not be washed fast enough in the pot wash system, so often we had to wash things in the hand basin with plain water. Strictly against company rules!

People came in, ate and went. Tables were re-laid at once. The flow was never ending. The buffet, which always looked brilliant, had to be regularly topped up by the chefs, who were professional in everything they did. Bits of fish, salad, meat etc would spill between the metal containers onto the ice below, which slowly melted into a slush, so that when the buffet was cleared at the end of the evening, the stench was minging and one wondered how it could start smelling so quickly. But the buffet console was cleared and cleaned so that it sparkled. And it was relentless.

After a few days the food and beverage manager returned from his holiday and as he was my immediate superior, I decided to make a good impression. So I knocked on his office door, went in and introduced myself as Geoff Paris, the new restaurant manager.

'Hi,' he said, not shaking my hand, not giving me some guidelines or asking me to sit down for a chat, not even looking up at me. He just carried on working. I was flabbergasted at his disregard for a colleague, and from that day on from my point of view he was a marked man.

The rotas had to be done weekly for the restaurant. Some staff were full-time, some were part-time, and were some casuals, some of whom could work just say a Wednesday and a Friday, or just so many hours. It was a nightmare doing the rota and when it was eventually done and out, boy what a relief! But if one waitress said she couldn't work a shift it caused the whole rota to be virtually re-written. I hated it. The staff were lovely with lots of Filipino waitresses, some of whom I became friends with. My shifts were mostly split shifts, and I would mainly catch up on sleep in the afternoon. Otherwise my shifts were midday to midnight, or 3 pm to midnight, midnight being the approximate finish time after everything had been cleared up. The breakfast shift started at 6 am and I know I worked some of these, but I guess a normal split shift day would start at 9 am. I could sleep through all the noise of the jets taking off in the afternoon, as they started their take-off near the hotel. Concorde, which I believe took off about 5 pm, rattled all the windows and was immensely loud, but I could sleep through that too. What did wake me up every time was the Royal Mail helicopter which landed nearby around about 5 pm each weekday. It was so annoying!

Working six or seven days per week, I became tired and fractious. I managed to order masses of crockery which was delivered into the back corridor. It stayed there in boxes. No one in authority in any department told me it had arrived; it could have been for the function side of the hotel which had its own separate crockery sets. I left it for three days in the corridor before finally asking the food and beverage manager if it was for the restaurant, to which he just replied 'Yes'. This was an example of the dire communication by the management. It soon became clear that the three duty managers regarded me as an inferior, whereas in my opinion I should have been an equal, and this gradually rankled more and more. I had to adhere to hotel policy by the book. Suppose I was standing at the front of the restaurant waiting for guests, and someone walked in through the front door, struggling with luggage and looking around for the check-in desk for assistance. My natural reaction was to go over, greet them, and offer assistance. But no, I was the restaurant manager and could only look after the restaurant. I would be neglecting my own post. Unbelievable! So after that bollocking, if guests came through the front door, I would turn on my heel and walk into the restaurant on the pretext of doing something. I could not just stand there and watch them.

Arguments happened occasionally at the desk between guests with reservations and the front desk staff or the front-of-house manager, because the hotel was full, even though a guest might have a legitimate reservation. It was normally sorted out by moving them to another hotel, but one day a guest kicked off so much about his reservation that this manager picked up his luggage, walked outside across the car park, and threw the luggage onto the pavement of the A4! I was gobsmacked! You can't do that to a guest! It was something you expected Basil Fawlty to do. The guest looked around for sympathy from anyone, then in a state of complete shock, he stormed out of the hotel, never to be seen again!

The Monday Club was the most important weekly event. This involved all the airline executives, about twenty of them, who came for lunch every Monday. Their service had to be prompt and efficient, as their time was limited. We looked after them. They sat at a block table and had a two-course lunch with coffee.

One day we were about to do the desserts. I regularly arranged it so that while the staff plated the desserts, I would prepare any ice-cream orders, timing it so that both would go out together. But the bitch of a personnel manager saw this and told me to throw them away as they were being 'pre-prepared'. For a start it wasn't her department – remember how I had to stick to my own department – secondly the ice-creams were about to go out, thirdly it was going to cost the hotel money through wastage, and fourthly I was not used at the time to being reprimanded by someone in another department! So I threw them away, glared at her and immediately started to make some more as by now the other desserts were ready. So frustrating, almost as if they thought I was a member of staff not management...

I mainly worked and slept, worked and slept, worked and slept, sometimes seven days per week. If I had to go out it was just to the local shop for toothpaste or similar basic items. It was boring. To brighten up my life I would drive to the airport and park outside the main entrance on double yellow lines and nip into the airport shops. I felt important, as if I was travelling somewhere. But the airport police were quick, all credit to them. I could get a parking ticket after only a few minutes. Sometimes I would get away with it, but after a couple of tickets I had to abandon this expensive escapade, sadly.

If I had the odd night off or day off, invariably I would travel to London to see my sister Robin or friends and stay the night there. Occasionally I met Sue from the Riviera, who was by now an air hostess with British Airways. That was always a high point. She was way out of my league, sadly, but we were good friends.

After a month at the hotel we broke the record for the number of dinners served per week, then a week later we broke it again, with a record of 861!

My diary soon became blank due to the workload and my gradual decline in my regard for the duty managers, especially at the weekly management meetings, and it was clear that this was only going to go one way, so my employment ceased on the 17th June. I think this was a mutual decision and I was immensely relieved; I was not enjoying the work, I was constantly knackered, and the management didn't want to know about the restaurant. It is one of those areas in hotels which sometime scare managers because they must go into unfamiliar territory, so to speak, and get involved with the nitty gritty of it. They might get their hands dirty, in more ways than one. And this is an area where management may have to confront a guest about a complaint, and so deal with something that takes them out of their comfort zone. I knew exactly where the Ariel's management were coming from. And I was past caring. Most of the restaurant staff were sad to see me go as we had a good working relationship, which extended, against company rules, to friendship with some of them. Back I went to Shropshire.

In 2011 I went on holiday to Thailand, my first venture to the Far East. As my mother had sadly passed away recently and left me a nice bequest, thank you very much, this was to be a blast for me, staying in whichever hotels I fancied, and doing whatever. Cost wasn't an issue. Part of the plan was to stay at the Ariel both the night before flying and the night of my return. It all seemed to be in the same place, if a little difficult to drive into. Check-in was efficient – at least I wasn't going to be transferred! The room was bog-standard and nothing to write home about.

So I had to eat in the restaurant, didn't I? There were just a few businessmen on their own in the bar and a few old couples and that was about it. Nothing happening there. No totty. So after a pint I moved to the restaurant. To my complete shock and disbelief, half the restaurant had been roped off as shut, and only two other tables were occupied. Oh my god! The central buffet station was missing! I was so looking forward to stuffing myself with the buffet. It was so sad to see this once thriving restaurant now looking like a morgue.

I would have gone elsewhere to eat straight away if I hadn't done a deal at check-in which included a discount off the dinner.

After studying the menu thoroughly I realised that due to the lack of custom I would have to choose something 'safe'. I am a fussy eater, and if restaurants aren't busy, I would rather not eat at all in case the products are old or going off. I didn't want food poisoning BEFORE a holiday! So I chose a steak, cooked medium rare. When it eventually arrived it was burnt to a crisp, black and solid, but as it had taken so long, I persevered. I could hardly cut it, let alone chew it. It was dire. It looked like it had been found after a week on the floor of the kitchen left behind an oven or something.

The next table – and it seemed strange that with a virtually empty restaurant, two table bookings had been put side by side – were also grumbling about their food, so I had to tell them what it was like in 1985! I ate what I could and left. It was crap. No wonder they had no business.

Breakfast was OK, but continental as my flight was an early one. I always eat at airports anyway, as I like to stock up on the old grub before flying – just in case no food is provided.

On my return stay at the Ariel I thought I would try the Sheraton Skyline next door for a meal. We used to love going in there for a drink after service in 1985. I was ushered into their Sports Bar and Grill. Wow, this was more like it! It was full, it had character, attractive waitresses, things happening – ideal. The menu offered a good range of curries, pizzas, burgers etc, just right, as being shattered from my flight, I just wanted a couple of beers and something simple, so I had a curry. It was lovely. I would recommend this to anyone, and if in a similar situation, I would certainly return. This really rounded off my holiday.

The following morning, before driving home, I walked around the hotel inside and out. I found cigarette-filled ashtrays left outside from the previous night, litter around the car park and dirty windows

– not dirt from the London air, but greasy fingerprint marks. There was dust inside here and there. A genuine lack of attention to detail.

A few weeks later I emailed the Ariel to complain about my steak, and they refunded it, with a standard apology. In May 2014 I emailed the general manager at the Ariel with what I had written about my time at the Ariel, but obviously omitted the part above when I was an unsatisfied customer!

CHAPTER 8

Brend Hotels: Saunton Sands and Sidmouth

After quite a few interviews around the country, all of which were combined with catching up with a friend or two, I was offered a job at the Dolphin Hotel in Swansea as a food & beverage manager. So on 28 July 1985 I drove to Swansea in my new red Renault 16, which I had bought second-hand from a garage in Bridgnorth.

The Dolphin was a city centre hotel with an entrance that looked like a shop front. The hotel was located upstairs on the first floor. Downstairs next door, as part of the hotel, was a coffee shop with its own manager and staffing. The owner and manager was Indian and called Ninja, I think. The management set up also consisted of Mr Whitehead (?), a man in his sixties who ironically had been the previous owner of the hotel. He was working as the assistant manager. The hotel marketed itself as a three-star business hotel, with the opposition being the far classier Dragon Hotel belonging to THF.

My diary records my shifts as being either 9 -12 or 9-1. There's no way these can have just been the morning, so shifts must have been 9 am to midnight or 1 am. Thinking about it, out of all my shifts, there is only one diary entry, recording that I went to a nightclub, met a couple of girls and got to bed at 3 am. I seem to remember the job mainly being office based, so I started to review all the food & beverage operations, costing out menus etc. Highly tedious, but I was keen to improve the menus, and 'prove' myself. All my ideas seem to be counteracted by Mr Whitehead, who dismissed each one by saying 'That won't work'. Maybe he was right. But I was trying, and this constant rebuffing became an issue. Was he wrong? Maybe he was, or he would not have needed to sell his hotel. I didn't know what to think, but my patience was beginning to wear a bit thin because I wanted to achieve something and make my mark. The hotel didn't have particularly high standards in my opinion, nor did I like the way it was operated.

I didn't have any days off the first week, and the second week I had just a Saturday off so I drove home to Shropshire for a couple of hours, then back to Swansea.

I can still remember one of the weddings I supervised. The groom's bar tab had been miscalculated by £1 or so and Ninja made me get the money from him. I was aghast and sorely tempted to pay it myself, but I went apologetically to the groom to ask him for a measly £1. Everything had to be paid for on the day. I was so incensed that when it came to announcing the bride & groom in for the wedding breakfast, instead of the usual 'Ladies and gentlemen, please be upstanding to receive your bride and groom,' I said 'Ladies and gentlemen, please stand up to receive your bride and groom.' Looks of horror came from the guests as they stared at me for breaching protocol, but I was past caring.

There were double yellow lines outside the hotel, but when I had to buy items for the hotel or maybe do the banking, I used to park there for a minute or two. One day whilst parked outside, I was held up inside by a customer for a few minutes, and by the time I went back to my car I had received a parking ticket. I asked the staff in the coffee shop, who told me that some Welsh person had 'shopped' me to the traffic warden, who had only just put the ticket on the windscreen. With that, I looked down the street, saw the parking attendant and went up to him to complain. I made a mental note of the number on his epaulette and explained the situation, to which he replied that he could not retract it, but he said he would make a note, and I should disregard the fine, so I did. Some time later, months or years, when living in Torquay, I received a court summons to a court in Swansea regarding this unpaid parking ticket. I was absolutely incensed! I wrote a stroppy letter back explaining what the traffic warden (I quoted his number) had told me and said I was not paying the fine, and that in any case I would rather pay it than waste my time driving to Swansea for a poxy court case over a parking fine! I never went to court. Job done!

On my second day off, August 18, I drove around the Mumbles and surrounding area, and then the following day I was sacked. I had complained to Ninja about my office situation with Mr Whitehead, and this was the outcome. Oh not again! Sacked twice in a row, what the hell were my parents going to say? I had mixed emotions. I was happy to leave a hotel that was abusing my working time, but sad to not to have found my niche career wise.

Back in Shropshire I felt terrible and really pissed off. As a family we all went to Aberdovey for a few days, and then I stayed with Mick and Gail in Newquay for a week, which was great except that they lived in St. Columb Minor, which meant a long walk if I missed the last bus. Mick, bless him, was always after the girls, which was sad as he had a lovely wife, but he could and would drink and occasionally drink-drive. Once a couple of us were trying to find him by car, and I drove, despite being over the limit myself, to the car park, where we found him driving around and around in circles in a cloud of dust. We couldn't stop him; he seemed absolutely deranged. There were some bad demons in his head, and we were quite worried. This went on for an eternity until eventually he sped off down the road. We didn't know what he was going to do, so I think we left him to it. I don't think Gail was aware of any of his demon driving episodes.

The usual routine continued; a few shifts at the Lea Manor, frequent interviews around the country, including London, drinking, partying etc. On the way to the Ware Moat House interview, my car's head gasket blew, so it had to be towed back. A few days later I bought a manual and proceeded to dismantle the head to see what had happened. I had no idea how to proceed but thought I would just unscrew a few bolts and see what came off, boys being boys! I tinkered about, and I remember the cylinder head being very heavy to lift off. Once I had moved that I was at a loss, so had to ask our mechanic, Ian Waye, to sort it out.

My next interview was at the Queens Hotel in London for the post of assistant manager, and I had to travel by train as my car was out of action. The train was flying along when suddenly there was a loud bang followed by another and another and then a window smashed. Glass flew everywhere, there was pandemonium in the carriage, and then I could see the cause as the next bang shattered the peace. Somehow the pantograph was catching the overhead electric cable and slamming it down the side of the train against our windows, and this happened repeatedly until the train stopped. Either someone pulled the alarm cord, or the cable broke so as to break the current which stopped the train, the latter being more likely. Someone had a minor cut from the glass but otherwise we were all OK.

We had to wait ages for a relief train, which had to be a diesel, because the electric cable was down. Eventually we were rescued, but I went back home because I had missed my interview. A few days later, my car now having been fixed, I drove to the Queens Hotel for my rescheduled interview, which went well, and I accepted the position a day later. It was a pleasure to cancel two forthcoming interviews, one of which was at the Ware Moat House. One interview I did not cancel was at the Saunton Sands Hotel in North Devon, which is a Brend Hotel, so I packed my car with the usual luggage, hifi system, records, cassettes, bicycle etc and drove to the Saunton Sands, where I was interviewed by Peter Brend and the manager. After staying the night, I met Granny in Exmouth and took her for lunch before moving to the Queens in London, where I moved all my belongings into a hotel room, which I found highly embarrassing.

The management asked me to join them for dinner and they all seemed a nice bunch. As the general manager was on holiday, my rota had not been finalised, so I had the following day or two off. I duly phoned the Saunton Sands, who offered me a position as assistant manager. I accepted at once; this was what I was after – a four-star seaside hotel. I had a day out in London visiting friends, then went back to the Queens to tell the manager, who was now on duty. 'GET OUT!' he yelled at me. I felt terrible and offered to pay for my accommodation, not that I could afford it. 'Just get out of my sight!' he shouted, and with that he waved his hand at me as if to dismiss me and glared at me as I left his office. Sheepishly I spent the next hour reloading my car, then found a B&B for the night in Croydon. The next day I drove home to Shropshire and two days later I left for the Saunton Sands. This had to be it now. This was my ultimate test. I could not afford to be sacked again. No one would employ me ever again. And I was excited.

The Saunton Sands was one of half a dozen two to four-star hotels in Devon and Cornwall owned by the Brend family. Florence, a dear old lady, lived permanently in a suite in the hotel, whilst her three sons ran the businesses; Peter and John the hotels, and Richard their Taw garage and petrol station in Barnstaple along with the North Devon motel (now the Park hotel) next door, and the head offices. The Saunton Sands boasted 90 well-appointed bedrooms, an indoor and outdoor pool, sauna, jacuzzi, games room, film room or cinema, a clothes shop, and a hairdresser. There was a function room and bar called the Saunton Suite, a large restaurant and several lounges, along with twenty or so self-catering apartments in a separate building. The hotel stood on the cliff looking out along the several miles-long golden beach of Saunton Sands, behind which were Braunton Burrows, or sand dunes. It was a magnificent setting, close to Braunton, Croyde and Barnstaple.

My position as assistant manager paid £130 per week live in, whereas at the Riviera I was being paid £310 per month live in, so this was a definite improvement in terms of salary. The general manager, Tony Bruce, was approximately my age or possibly younger, and tall and lanky. The deputy manager was known simply as Baptiste because that was his surname, his Spanish Christian name being too complex to pronounce. There was another assistant manager who had not worked there that long called Simon Portet, whose father was Captain of the QE2. Simon was a bit dithery and hesitant, but meant well. There was Paul Gist, who was an assistant manager, and Matthew Raistrick soon joined as a trainee manager. There were two restaurant managers, which initially seemed a bit odd to me, one being Greek whose surname was Kyriakou or something similar, the other being Bryan someone, a Brummie with a partially pock-marked face. We all wore morning suits, which I approved of; however the management wore short jackets whilst the restaurant management wore morning coats. All of us wore DJs in the evenings.

I set off early from Shropshire, arriving at 12.30 pm, and started work at 1 pm with a meeting. My shift finished at ten. Shifts were either 8 am to 6 pm, midday to 10 pm, or 3 pm until 'LU' or lock-up. It seemed that after work we would drive to the Aggi or Agricultural Inn in Braunton, which quickly became my local. The staff, management, and owners were all charming, and Peter Brend was very approachable and was referred to as Mr Peter. I can't remember having any specific responsibilities, but our duties involved day-to-day management; this would involve helping at breakfast, stocking up the bar, checking some bedrooms for cleanliness, helping with lunch service and/or bar snacks, assisting with afternoon tea, and helping in the restaurant for dinner, whether for wines or food. As the hotel employed porters and a doorman, with John Belchamber being the head porter, there was not much need to help with luggage.

And then I saw the pictures.

Oh My God! On the wall near the reception was a collection of half a dozen A4 frames which contained photos of when Pink Floyd had stayed at the Saunton Sands when they were filming the WW2 scenes of 'The Wall' album on Braunton Burrows and the beach. I had missed my heroes by only a few weeks! Nevertheless I felt honoured in the knowledge that THEY had been present in the hotel.

Famous people stayed regularly; so many that you tried to give them special treatment, yet always remain unobtrusive. I do not want to mention anyone because I'm not sure that some of the guests' partners (not staying) knew what they were up to. Most were friendly enough but in the end you treated them as normal people, which is what they wanted – to be left alone, or not made a fuss of.

One such person though I could not make head or tail of: Dave Stewart from the Eurythmics and Annie Lennox were popping in for a coffee. In the end it was just Dave Stewart who arrived wearing jeans, T-shirt, leather jacket I think, but certainly dark glasses, so I ushered him down to the first lounge at the bottom of the main stairs. As the hotel is built on a hill, you go down the 'main' stairs to the lounges, bars and restaurant. He sat facing the stairs but didn't say a word. Nothing. He didn't want a coffee, nothing, not even water. He just sat there for hours, motionless. I didn't know if he was asleep, or for all I know he could have died. Maybe he had a hangover? He just sat there with a glum face – he could have been a dummy out of Madam Tussauds for all I know! Then after an hour or two he left, which was a bit annoying because I had wanted to serve him, or at least have a conversation of sorts. I felt that I hadn't been of service. Not that I ever liked his music, never mind the fact that his dress may have been deemed inappropriate!

The afternoon tea service was all part of the show. The waitresses operated from a small still room where the likes of clotted cream and strawberry jam were prepared in little bowls, along with appropriate crockery and cutlery and silver tea and coffee pots. Everything was washed by hand in a little sink and dried with tea towels. It could get quite busy so we would help, but my main priority was to dive into the still room, first to be out of sight of the customers, second so I could nick a scone or get a cuppa, third to chill out, and fourth to roll up my sleeves and do the washing up, as we frequently ran out of cups and saucers. I always remember Simon as dithering and wringing his hands as if he was debating a plan of action which never seemed to happen. Not the sort of person to have in charge of a battle! But he had a charming personality. I believe Paul Gist still works on the management to this day.

Peter Brend had two girlfriends. During the day Adrienne floated in and out of the hotel, dealing with flowers, decorations etc. She was stunning with a lovely personality, real eye candy. She may have 'worked' 9 am to 5 pm, but she didn't involve herself with the trivialities of dealing with customers. Sometimes Vicky (I think) arrived in the evenings; she was the other girlfriend. They must have known about each other, but they never seemed to meet to my knowledge. Vicky was also a stunner, but with mousy blonde hair as opposed to Adrienne's dark hair. Adrienne was a red rose amongst the flowers she tended; always cheerful, always gorgeous, and was always a breath of fresh air wherever she walked. To me she appeared to be a goddess, me being the lowest of the low, unworthy of looking her in the eye, let alone speaking to her!

The management offices were behind the reception, not that we spent much time there, and beyond that was the wages office. Wages were paid in cash and had to be collected between 1 pm and 2 pm only on each Friday, regimentally via a hatchway, or you had to wait until the following week!

I was well impressed with the standards of the hotel. The white bedroom towels all had the Brend Hotel logo stitched on, the bathroom toiletries had the Brend logo printed on them, and strangely enough I still have a bath towel which I borrowed at the time to clean my bicycle, along with a half-used miniature bottle of Brend's Eau de Cologne made by Gilchrist & Soames. I now use the towel as a bed for my cat's basket when he has to go to the vet! And I don't use the eau-de-cologne; it's a historical item, I guess.

In my first month or so there were some late nights; after a busy night on duty, shutting the Saunton Suite at 5 am, on another night playing snooker until 5 am. There was a staff party for us at the Royal Duchy Hotel in Falmouth and Mike Bennett came down for it to join me. That was a late one, getting to sleep at 7.15 am. Needless to say I felt awful the next day and could do nothing except lie down quietly until the coach took us back to the Saunton Sands. Then I had to work 6 pm until midnight, and I can tell you that not a lot would have been accomplished!

Then on December 19th Paul and I were roped in to serve the Christmas OAP presentation at one of their Barnstaple hotels. Quite why we had to do this was another matter, but we felt important. It looked like a cushy little number away from work where we might have to help serve a few cups of tea.

How wrong I was! Upon entry the pensioners were offered a complimentary glass of sherry; sweet, medium or dry. Fair enough. The sherry and glasses were all laid out on several trestle tables ready for us to serve. Not too bad; we could cope with that. And without help from the hotel staff – just us two from the Saunton Sands. Then we were to serve them a cup of tea. All the teacups were laid out on separate trestle tables. OK then... but the tea could only be served in normal large sized teapots, enough for say just seven or eight cups each, so we frantically had to go back to the still room and refill the teapots with new tea bags and hot water, which meant breaking through the line of the bloody pensioners who did not, under any circumstances, want to compromise their place in the queue. Back and forth, back and forth. 'Oh no, that's far too weak', 'not so much milk', 'black for me', 'do you have peppermint tea?' and so on until we had served seven hundred and twenty cups of tea to 720 pensioners! I was sick of the smell of tea and vowed never to drink it again!

The pensioners then went on into the ballroom which was set up with boxed trestle tables with joints of meat, poultry, bottles of wines and spirits, boxes of chocolates, boxes of fruit and vegetables, tinned items I guess, all manner of food and beverage items stacked around the edges. The directors stood at the front and wished each person a Happy Christmas and gave them a large plastic bag for them to fill up with whatever they wished from the room. I was astounded and deeply touched by the generosity of the Brend family to the local pensioners. And they took it all. Some could hardly carry their bags they were so full. Amazing.

Our staff meals were plated and left for us and the management ate the same as the staff. Throughout December, with all the Christmas parties, turkey became the only meal and you were lucky to get something else. I would complain bitterly, as having been eating in the restaurant at the Riviera this was, in effect, slumming it! The head chef, for whom I had a lot of respect, started calling me 'Turkey Geoff'!

I had moved into the staff cottage, which was an old white cottage about a mile down the road from the hotel. It had a small kitchen, a lounge with a real fireplace, a few bedrooms and a couple of bathrooms, I think. My room was the best, on the first floor along with a bathroom. A Greek waiter lived there also, but I soon fell out with him due to his slovenly way of living. We had to use the fireplace in the winter with logs or coal because I don't think there was any central heating, or if there was it was minimal. It was basic, but functional. I could walk to the hotel in about twenty minutes, cycle, or drive, which I would do if it was raining or I was working a midday to 10 pm shift, meaning that a quick exit to the pub was needed! The small garden became my concern, only because no one else bothered. Gardening tools were non-existent, so I used a silver main course fork from the hotel restaurant for the weeding and had to cut the small lawn with a pair of scissors!

Christmas came and went with late nights until 3 am or 4 am. My New Year's Eve diary entry was 'good night, in fact excellent, bed approx. 4 am' whatever that means; maybe a snog or two with a waitress, but I had professional ethics in those days, amongst other things! You also find that some guests offer you a glass of their champagne during the evening, which was always appreciated!

In January, the hotel closed for a couple of weeks, being the quietest time of the year, which meant that the staff could all have a holiday, and essential maintenance could be carried out. Even Florence moved out. She never appeared in public and only had room service anyway, so because the hotel was closed, she could not be served. The reception was manned for incoming phone calls and the management covered the hotel over twenty-four hours. This was a piece of cake, and the night shift hours were 11 pm to 7.30 am. You were the only member of staff on the premises, which filled me with dread. There wasn't much to do except regular patrols of the public areas behind the scenes, and the bedroom corridors. The staff entrance door lock had broken, so anyone could gain access to the hotel that way. All the reception and office safe keys, about five in total, were locked in one safe, and the key for this was kept in a place accessible to all, but hidden. Obviously, I shan't disclose this! An amazing lack of security really.

At night there were no other sounds, just the creaking and groaning of the hotel in the wind; swing doors would move and creak, and you really had no idea whether someone else was on the premises or not. Was it a member of staff or an intruder or thief? Think of the film 'The Shining' starring Jack Nicholson, and you will get the picture! I used to creep around, stay stock still for a couple of minutes listening to the sound of 'movement', and then an extra minute in case my 'adversary' was trying to outwit me, and then I would leap around a corner with my arm held high ready to karate chop whoever was in the way. Sadly, an adversary never appeared, but I became quite paranoid about it all.

So life went on. I normally worked six days per week, and regularly played squash at the Riverside Club, the Cedars in Barnstaple, or the Leisure Centre. If I was on a middle shift, 12 noon to 10 pm, Tony would let us go when everything had quietened down; 'OK Geoff you can skedaddle,' which was a terminology I hated, presumably used up North. Then off to the Aggi. I worked the odd shift at the North Devon motel to help when they were holding a busy function such as a dinner/dance.

The hotel did not accept coach tours, except private ones such as a gardening society or ramblers' club, but one such tour company regularly arrived from Bristol with their private group. The tour rep was a dark-haired German girl, maybe in her late twenties, who wore a short skirt which revealed superb legs and a trim body. Wow! She just oozed charm and sex. Polite, efficient, crisp, like her white blouse, and my knees just folded whenever I saw her. She was a German goddess.

As far as the customers were concerned, there was a hierarchy in the restaurant, which was long and narrow. Those considering themselves more important than others felt the need to sit closest to the entrance doors, and the restaurant management allocated the tables accordingly. Repeat guests and VIP's were sat closer to the entrance. Dinner was a formal affair with silver cutlery, sparkling glasses, crisp clean white linen, attentive and good-looking staff with clean uniforms, and the show had to run like clockwork. The menus were printed daily, and the wine lists looked clean and informative. All the lights worked, the staff appeared happy, and guests could expect an enjoyable evening. Invariably we would do the wines and take half the restaurant each. The kitchen ran the entire length of the restaurant, with two sets of swing doors between the two areas, along which a corridor ran in the kitchen, being the 'pass' area. One end was for dumping dirty crockery and cutlery, other parts of the corridor being for collecting the food items. At one end Chris Farnsworth dispensed the wine via a hatchway. We would give him one copy of our triplicate pad wine order, signed by the customer, and Chris would give us the wine to serve to the customers.

It was hard work carrying several bottles of wine at once to various tables, along with ice buckets and white napkins placed on them for serving the wine, in order to avoid drips on the table or wet hands. Bottles were presented to the person who had ordered the wine, invariably a man in those days. Upon approval, we would virtually bow deference and acknowledgment, slice the cap off the bottle, and uncork it with a corkscrew. A taste was offered to the same person. Upon approval, ladies were offered wine first, followed by the men, the last one being the man who had ordered it. For expensive reds or most Bordeaux bottles, served in a wicker basket, it was customary to leave the cork on the table for the customer to inspect. Glasses had to be topped up, more wine fetched if required, and service had to be unobtrusive yet attentive.

In the morning we had to polish the glasses, maybe a couple of hundred, which is one of the most boring tasks ever. We would hold each glass over a tea or coffeepot full of boiling water to steam the inside, which was then polished with a tea towel, or napkin. In later years synthetic napkins appeared which are no good for polishing because they do not absorb the moisture. We tolerated the occasional arrogant customer; some were downright rude, but most were average in behaviour, some even nice. People in those days occasionally clicked their fingers in the air for IMMEDIATE service! To me it's the height of ignorance.

This happened one particular evening. I happened to be close to the restaurant entrance when Bryan suddenly got down on his hands and knees and started walking dog-like along the floor. Had he lost his mind? To my horror and amazement he proceeded most of the way along the floor to a particular table and barked 'WOOF, WOOF!' Then he stood up and walked away. I was aghast. It turned out that the customer had clicked his fingers at Bryan! That would teach him.

The bar had a particularly good centrepiece on the back shelf containing some fine brandies such as Armagnac, Remy Martin VSOP, Hine VSOP, Martell Cordon Bleu, Hennessy XO, and Remy Martin Louis XIII. The latter cost about £70 for a measure, being a sixth of a gill in those days, and the cognac was at least a hundred years old. Most people had never seen a Louis XIII bottle before, which was shaped like a Mateus Rosé bottle, but this was made of clear crystal glass with intricate bits and a gold top. We tried desperately to sell this, and if not the next one down the list in terms of price, and sometimes, say there was a group of men on a business lunch or dinner, we would get them going on it, because their bill was being paid by their company, and they would be wanting to impress their business colleagues. Yeah!

One evening, a VIP was attending, Charles Spencer, known as Viscount Althorp in those days. Now he is Earl Spencer, someone who is EXTREMELY high up in the pecking order. He had been for dinner, and once his guests had retired for the night, we started on him. As he was a few years younger than me, I felt I could talk to him, so we plied him with cognac, on the house of course, and asked him about his sister Princess Diana, and other family matters. What he told us was mind boggling. He was saying this will happen, that won't happen, their marriage will last, theirs won't etc. We fed him drink after drink till he was pretty well pissed. To have such 'inside' knowledge about 'the other family' was awe inspiring and jaw dropping! Don't worry, I can't remember anything, as I may have had the odd brandy myself! He was also a charming person.

During my daily tours of the hotel, the bedroom corridors and bedrooms were a must; one of the chambermaids was a real piece of totty. Fit and the right shape in every respect. She always smiled at me in that 'come on' way, so I always made a point of calling in on her to see how she was getting on. I had a real crush on her, and we would have a quick chat, gazing into each other's eyes. For professional reasons I never made a move, but I was convinced (mistakenly probably) that she would have gone further... oh well. The other girl I took a shine to was the girl that operated the boutique. Same as above. An absolute honey.

I noticed a block booking coming up under the name of Carver which caught my eye. My best childhood friend in Shropshire was called Henry Carver, and sure enough that weekend along came Henry with his brothers, father, uncles, cousins etc.

'Oh hello Henry! What are you doing here?' I said excitedly.

'It's the Carver Cup,' he replied matter-of-factly, as if I should have known, and after a brief chat moved on. It was a weekend squash tournament for his family. Henry always used to annoy me when we played squash as adolescents because he could play equally well with his right or left hand, so he would not have to move quite so much to return the ball. Grrr.

One morning I was getting a breath of air outside the front door of the hotel when a man came running up and shouted, 'Get an ambulance!'

'Yeah right,' I replied nonchalantly, as if he was taking the piss.

'Get one NOW!' he screamed in my face. Shit, I thought, he means it, so I rushed into reception, called an ambulance, and then went outside to see what was going on. There was a man lying in the road wearing black leather biker's gear, and nearby a mangled motorbike and a helmet. His head was bloody and dirty from the road dirt, and a liquid, more akin to a partially set strawberry jelly, was oozing from one ear. That's not right, I thought. That's bad. I knew it was more or less over for him, because that was his brain fluid draining, not that I had any inkling what brain fluid looked like. One just knew.

I rushed back to the hotel and grabbed a couple of blankets from housekeeping and covered his body with them, with one under his head for support. The next priority was the traffic. As one lane of a busy main road was effectively blocked, I stood down the road, controlling the traffic, stopping one direction to let the other through, and vice versa. However one fucker of a driver refused to stop, and I had to leap out of the way, shaking my fists at him and shouting the usual expletive in total astonishment, the bastard!

After twenty minutes the ambulance arrived. The biker was drifting in and out of consciousness but had not moved. The crew attended to him and stretchered him into the ambulance. It was then that a hundred yards down the road I noticed a woman wandering around aimlessly in a daze, and she turned out to be the pillion passenger. Someone else had been comforting the car driver; a guest at the hotel had pulled out into the road and the biker had driven straight into her side. The entrance to the hotel car park was between two buildings which lay directly at the road's edge, meaning that to drive out, the front of your car had to stick out into the road in order for you to look both ways before pulling out. She was totally distraught, understandably, but in all honesty, there was nothing she could have done. The ambulance took both the biker and his girlfriend to hospital, but he died on the way. I cleared up as much as I could, and the police, who I think had arrived by then, dealt with the bike and other debris. A sad day.

On a brighter note, we were looking forward to Tony Bruce's stag night on the 1st May. Peter Brend, we management, some HODs, and as an exception to the rule, the German tour girl who happened to be staying, all set off to Barnstaple for a night out. We had decided that she was worthy of joining the lads! The meal was courtesy of Peter, which was good of him. Various pubs later we were paralytic, at least I was, so we rolled back to the Saunton Sands after the pubs had closed, to continue the festivities. We piled into the indoor swimming pool starkers, along with the German girl, whom I'm told Bryan ended up shagging in the shallow end. Lucky boy!

Several of us were in the jacuzzi enjoying ourselves, so I decided to get some towels. I staggered off to reception, totally starkers, and shouted for the night porter, who was the Cornish salt-of-the-earth type, tall, in his sixties with a rugged complexion and long straggly grey beard, like Moses. Just looking at him made you cower. And there I was, totally starkers with my small pinkie and balls in full view of this mammoth man, demanding towels. He just stood there, stony faced, hands on hips, and stared at me. He didn't need to say anything. I knew this was futile, so I turned tail, blustering that I would 'get him', staggered back to the jacuzzi lost for words, and promptly fell in. I was so hung over the next day that I had to do a sickie.

When I next returned to work, Peter Brend laughed at me because of my actions. It transpired that in my drunken stupor I had pulled a three-foot plant pot into the jacuzzi, which had put it out of action the next day, because the earth had got into the filter, so they had to change the filter sand and clean it out as well as the jacuzzi itself. Not that I can remember any of this. He just laughed when I apologised profusely. He was great like that – money didn't come into it. It was all just a bit of fun!

Tony began to talk about the 'Harrison weekend' at this time, and it came to be known as something that was beyond a VIP event, so I wondered with trepidation what it was all about. In fact Mr Harrison was the Managing Director of Racal, the big electronics group. As it approached, we were all on edge. Our suits were clean and we were on best form as we waited for the arrivals. I thought I recognised one of the sons, so when he went down to the bar, I said to him that he looked familiar and it turned out he was Mike Harrison who I knew from Wellington, so he bought me a drink. The other management were in awe that a mortal like me could be casually talking to the most prominent of VIPs! The weekend went fine – I was off the hook, I could chill out and to a certain extent I joined in.

And so the summer approached. Life went on; work, drinking in the local pubs, playing squash, cycling around, going for walks along the beach, and generally enjoying life. We didn't drink-drive that much, but we could get away with a lot because of who our employers were – they were big in the area. My car at the time was a Renault and quite often I took staff home. There was a staff van which collected us and returned us from Braunton and various local pick-up points, but I could drop people like Bryan back home from the pub.

One night I was stopped by the police. What? Unheard of for us lot. The cop breathalysed me and thankfully I had only drunk a bottle of Becks or similar, so I was under the limit. What a relief! I was that shaken up that I had to go back to Bryan's house and have a stiff brandy before driving off home.

Another time Chris and I had a session in the pubs in Braunton and it seemed to be a good idea at the time to drive back along the beach. There was a track that ran through the Braunton Burrows dunes, so you could drive along the gorgeous mile-long beach and come out near to the hotel and turn back onto the main road. It seemed like a marvellous idea, not to avoid the police, but to have some fun! This track was rough, embedded bricks here and there jutting out at angles, random rubble, huge potholes, and then shit – I had beached the car! So to speak. The track ruts were so deep that the car was sitting on its belly and the wheels were spinning off the ground.

We staggered out of the car to try and find something solid to put under the tyres to give them purchase. This was futile in the middle of a sand dune, so we soon gave up and opted to sleep the night in the car. In the morning, feeling like death warmed up, we set off on foot. It was overcast, we were surrounded by dunes and we hadn't the foggiest in which direction to go. He set off towards the hotel whilst I walked towards Braunton, to arrange a pick-up truck to move my car.

After what seemed like an interminable struggle, I came to a feature from which I could get my bearings and realised to my dismay that I'd been walking in the wrong direction. I felt like shit and just wanted to curl up and sleep, but I had to get my car rescued. So off I set, and eventually I found a garage with a pick-up that could tow my car. Sitting in his front seat I directed him and once on the track, he put his vehicle, which may have been a Land Rover, into four-wheel drive and edged slowly forward. His vehicle was bumping along slowly, avoiding any hazards and he was amazed that I had driven along there as if it was a normal road in a normal car. I was a bit embarrassed, to say the least. He duly hitched up my car and towed it off its perch and I drove sheepishly back home, having paid him his fee. He was rather bemused by my situation, to say the least!

The Saunton Sands hotel was pretty much the way I had envisaged a four-star hotel should be. Good food, an efficient restaurant, various lounges, a patio area with superb views in an idyllic location, young and old well-dressed professional staff, an excellent boss (Peter Brend), the use of silver tea and coffee pots, which to me is a prerequisite in standards, towels/robes/toiletries all bearing the Brend logo, outside activities for children (which was not my preferred activity if I was put in charge of their games for an afternoon), also leisure facilities, a couple of shops, and a hairdressers. I was enjoying it. Whether I did a good job or not is hard to tell being so long ago, but I didn't want my lifestyle to change. The hours were long, but that's what you did in those days without question. Most of the guests were charming and it was a pleasure to work there. There was no hassle.

One day out of the blue, Peter asked if I would like to move to the Victoria Hotel in Sidmouth as senior assistant manager. This was promotion! How could I refuse? He wanted me to keep an eye on it for him, whatever that meant. So with sadness to be leaving the Saunton Sands, but equally with excitement at a new venture, I set off for Sidmouth with all my luggage.

The Victoria was an imposing red-brick Victorian hotel built on a slight rise at one end of the seafront and the staff house was the other side of the seafront, up a hill. The house was for the management, the other occupants being Michelle, a tall slim girl in her early twenties with a charming personality, and someone else. It was basic but functional, with a few bedrooms. Walking to work down the steep footpath to the river and along the seafront took about twenty minutes. That was doable, no problem. I only drove to work if the weather was bad or too cold, or if I needed my car for work reasons, such as going to the florist in Newton Poppleford and filling my car with flowers for the hotel, which I hated doing not only because they gave me hay fever, but also it seemed such a cissy thing to do!

The hotel itself looked the part; a brick-built covered entrance so you could get out of your car without getting wet, well-tended gardens, a uniformed porter in attendance, as at the Saunton Sands, gleaming brasswork, a heavy revolving turnstile door, and inside everything spick and span, huge arrangements of flowers, gleaming chandeliers, attentive staff, and so on. *Oh, this is nice,* I thought, *I'm going to like it here.*

Roy Smith was the general manager and appeared to be in his forties, so he was the oldest manager in the group. For this reason, the directors tended to leave him alone and not visit so much. He looked fit, well dressed and professional. His wife, who seemed to appear here and there, did the flowers and messed about, but don't think she was a member of staff in the normal sense, certainly not management, and she soon became an irritant, telling us to do this and that, which was none of her business. I soon took a dislike to her, especially as she was overweight and had a miserable disposition.

We had to call the manager 'Mr Smith', which seemed a bit over the top, but hey ho if that's what he wants, so be it. He seemed a fairly pleasant chap with a positive attitude.

I think there were three assistant managers – Michelle, someone else, and me, and we each had an area to look after. Mine were the lounges. Great! How exciting... Basically I had to ensure the lounge staff did their job and ensure everything was in order. Boring or what! I would move each sofa or armchair an inch this way or that to ensure they were exactly where they should be. Oh my God, how long do I have to do this for? This is not like the Saunton Sands. Chalk and cheese.

Mr Smith casually invited me for a drink at 7 pm at the bar, which I accepted. There might have been some of the other management present. It soon became apparent that we were not going to get on. I had been sent down by the directors, meaning that he had not employed me directly and this showed, almost as if he thought I was a spy. I don't recall having a bar drink that frequently, partly because I was on duty and partly because I hated his guts, and the fact that I didn't join him regularly only served to fuel our mutual dislike.

This manager would frequently drink at the bar in the evening, followed by a bottle of wine at dinner in the restaurant. We lower echelons of management had to eat behind the scenes in a staff room without chairs, so we ate standing up with plates on a windowsill. Lovely. Then he would return to the bar or play snooker downstairs with someone. Maybe he was doing the PR bit for the hotel. All his drinks were undoubtedly on the house. His wife never ventured into the hotel in the evenings. Occasionally we would have to half-carry or escort him back to his flat around the corner, he was so drunk, but he was always back on duty at 8 am, positive, alert, and seemingly without a hangover. I don't know how he did it!?

He barked orders and sometimes swore at us in public, which was so disrespectful. Soon, like the others, I became terrified of him and became despondent under his spell, so to speak. They were not happy days. We loved it when he had a day off, but then his wife might fuss around the flowers or tell us what to do. Come on! Really?

We had a permanent resident, who had been knighted and had two suites permanently booked, one for his wife, one for him. She had died some time previously, but he still paid for the second suite, in her memory. Nice enough though he was, we also suspected that he was a spy for Mr Smith, so we grew to resent him a bit. But he was a nice chap and harmless enough, and we could sometimes ask his advice on personal matters.

We were all well and truly under the autocratic spell of Mr Smith. No one ever dared contradict him. He was older than us, more experienced, wasn't he?

There was a young French lounge waitress who was lovely with a sweet, charming personality. One of Mr Smith's routines was to order a bottle of Pils lager in the late afternoon, which she duly brought him up on a silver tray. Mr Smith's office was on the first floor, just off the grand central staircase, so you could see his office door, with its small window above the door. She would take in his drink, the door would shut, and the light would go off. Dreadful, and I can't imagine what went on. I imagined the worst. I certainly don't think it was consensual on her part. This was a regular occurrence, and we were appalled, but the consequences of speaking out were unimaginable. Again, nothing could be proved. Maybe she wanted it?

I needed to drink more than ever when off duty, so we frequented a couple of pubs, mostly on or near the seafront, being on the way home. I liked the town which was and is very picturesque and quaint, but full of 'old' people who I hadn't much time for at my age then. I can't remember there being a nightclub or disco as they were called then. But the beer was good, and we could forget about the nightmare at work.

The work was steady but so, so tedious, old dears coming in for morning coffee or afternoon tea, some lunches in the restaurant, and dinner for the residents and outsiders. The food was good as were the standards. It ticked all the boxes. There was the odd function, all running smoothly.

Then a major function loomed, the staff party for Racal Electronics, who were to take over the entire hotel. Even our permanent resident had to vacate the premises for this one. I had met the managing director of Racal, Mr Harrison, at the Saunton Sands, as referred to earlier, and knew his son Mike from Wellington. They took all the bedrooms, had a disco, maybe a band also, and a three-course buffet for a hundred people, I guess. Anyway it was a success and their total bill for the weekend was eye-watering, thank you very much!

I don't want to dwell on the Victoria because my time there was so unhappy.

The Carlyon Bay hotel, which was also a Brend hotel, was to hold the staff party for the Saunton Sands, the Victoria, and maybe some of their other hotels. So down we went on Sunday 11 January and I checked into my room. It was brill, involving a drinks reception, three-course buffet, maybe some speeches/prizes, a disco etc. It was a great night and I got smashed. Can't remember most of it, but I know it was memorable. What a hangover – I couldn't move I was that bad. So close to having an epileptic fit.

At about 9 am the chambermaid came in to kick me out. Yes, but I'm a manager, you should give me some extra time was all I could think of, but no, I had to vacate. I quickly washed and packed, then lay down in the corridor to rest, as I really wasn't good. I was driven back with Bryan and someone and we stopped at the Devon motel for lunch. Nice lunch, especially as we walked out without paying. I was horrified, but they knew who we were and could always charge us, being a Brend hotel. We never heard any more, so we just assumed it had been written off!

Later that day I caught a bus and train from Sidmouth to Shropshire. I was going on my first ski holiday, so in Wolverhampton I bought all the ski kit, jacket, trousers, gloves etc. I was going on my own and was actually quite frightened. I had no idea what to expect and thought they just pushed you off the top of a mountain, and if you survived you were lucky!

The day before, I went to stay with my sister Robin in London, stayed up all night, then caught a taxi to Gatwick followed by a flight to Munich, then by coach to St. Johann (in Tyrol). There was a sweet family staying called David and Amy with two kids, all of whom became my main friends for the week. I did all the requisite boozing/partying with the ski company and had a good time, although it was a quiet resort. I think I came third in the whole ski school race that week so I was very chuffed, thanks to Toni the long-haired instructor. So ended my first skiing holiday, which I really enjoyed.

My diary entry for 30 January 1987 reads: 'Started 3 pm work. Didn't want to go back'. That says it all.

One day in February I had an epileptic fit, so I had to surrender my driving licence. That was a real pain and really moved the goalposts. What to do with my poor Renault?

One day Mr Smith sacked the second chef and gave him a week's notice. Everyone was flabbergasted. He was a nice chap and did his job well, and we could not see why this had happened. An hour or so later Mr Smith called me into his office and sacked me. WHAT? WHY? He didn't offer an explanation, just glared at me and gave me a letter to read which gave me a week's notice. I went straight to the second chef and said, 'Guess what! I've just been sacked too.' Everyone was mortified, but having thought about it, I had mixed feelings. Then Mr Smith demanded my keys from me, safe keys etc... he obviously didn't trust me. Unbelievable. So I couldn't perform my job properly for my last few days.

Dad arranged for Ian Waye to collect my car on my last day and take it and me to Shropshire and eventually for auction. It cost me £80 to get him to drive it up, and after the auction in April and costs it only made £50 so my net loss was about £30. I should have just had it driven to a scrapyard!

So ended my time at the Victoria. I missed the staff and fellow assistant managers, but not the hotel and certainly not Roy Smith. For decades afterwards, if I saw him in the street, my first instinct would have been to punch him in the face.

A year later I booked a two-night break on my own at the Saunton Sands, but as the hotel was full, I suggested one of the apartments, which they gave me at a good rate. I treated myself in the hotel, eating dinner in the restaurant then drinking with the staff. It transpired from talking to the staff that the directors had no idea what was going on at the Victoria in terms of the antics of Roy Smith, and eventually they had physically thrown him out of the hotel, telling him to never set foot in the place again. Just desserts! I spoke to Peter Brend, who apologised and explained that the second chef was getting better than the head chef, and with me, I was a scapegoat – they knew something was wrong but didn't know what. He said he would give me a good reference. That made me feel a lot better, truthful or not. I proceeded to tell all about Mr Smith, and Peter was amazed, saying how he wished they had known, but I did explain that we were terrified to speak out against him. Upon checkout, Peter waived my accommodation costs, which was genuinely nice of him, seeing as I had stayed in an apartment with something like three bedrooms and two bathrooms and a balcony, just for myself! I only had to pay my drinks tab. Thank you Mr Peter!

I asked Peter Brend for a reference, which he gave me, as follows: however it is dated March 1987, so maybe he backdated it.

TO WHOM IT MAY CONCERN

Mr G Paris was employed at the Saunton Sands Hotel as an Assistant Manager from 1985 through to 1986. During his time at Saunton I found Mr Paris to be a reliable member of the Management Team who carried out his duties in a professional manner. I am pleased to recommend him to any future employer.

P. A. Brend
Director

Matthew Raistrick (nicknamed racetrack) was regarded by us older management as a young upstart of a trainee manager at the Saunton Sands, as well as an irritant, due to his above average common sense and intelligence, but he went on to become general manager at the Victoria after the demise of Roy Smith, and has since become an area manager for Brend hotels. Well done him! He's enjoyed a solid career with Brend hotels for I imagine his entire life, and that's admirable.

It was back to the routine in Shropshire, applying for jobs and going all over England for interviews, or going for a drink with my old school friend Henry Carver to play chess – he usually won. Peter Churchill, another school friend, became based in RAF Shawbury where he was training to become a helicopter pilot. After his RAF career he went on to become a British Airways pilot, and we met a few times.

Helping in the garden, going to supper with friends, a brief visit or two to Aberdovey, lazing about, cycling about, and so on, but applying for jobs was quite an effort. All job listings came from the 'Caterer and Hotelkeeper' magazine, and maybe 'The Lady' because remember this was all before the internet and mobile phones were invented. One interview was a screening interview at Knutsford for Berni Inns, which went quite well. A week later I went for an interview at the Albany, a Berni Inn in Liverpool, and was offered the position of assistant manager. Yeah!

It's amazing how I travelled around in those days. For instance I went by train to Liverpool again to find the staff house I would be living in with Berni Inns, then back to Longbridge (near Birmingham) to stay with Nick Pearson, who was a catering college friend, so obviously we went for an Indian and a pub crawl, then the next day to London to stay with Chris Sykes, and along with Tim Humpidge, and another college friend we went for, yes, an Indian and a pub crawl. Before taking the train back to Wolverhampton the next day, I popped in to see Robin, who lived near Madam Tussaud's.

Amazingly, it took me a week to accept this position. Maybe I thought a chain restaurant, in terms of standards, was below par for me? Was I going down market and would it affect my future career? And it meant living in Liverpool, home to scousers. They have such a reputation outside Liverpool that I was quite anxious about living and working there. I imagined snobbishly that they would beat up this ex public schoolboy almost daily.

My parents drove me to the house, which was in Shirley Road, Allerton, and I was relieved to find that it was a perfectly good house in a nice suburb, and the tube (overground) station was nearby. The Albany was in Old Hall Street in the city, and you could see the iconic Liver Birds on top of the building near the river. Shifts were split, so sometimes I would go back home to Allerton, and sometimes if busy it would be more of a straight shift. My frequent watering hole became Sam's, a nightclub or wine bar just up the road from the Albany on the corner. What amazed me was how beautiful the women were. They all seemed to be blonde and pretty, but with a scouse accent. In every bar or nightclub the women looked fabulous. There didn't seem to be any rough scouse men about so very soon, I came to like Liverpool and its people. It hadn't occurred to me that they could be so nice.

Berni Inns were basically steak houses, and menus were standardised throughout the group. In 1987, looking at the menus I kept, an 8oz sirloin sold for £6.95, an 8 oz. fillet steak £9.35, a whole Dover Sole £8.99, half a roast chicken £5.60 and so on, with all main courses including a potato option, peas or carrots, roll and butter, and a visit to the salad bar. An avocado and prawn starter sold for £1.75, sherry trifle £1.10. The 'new' Berni Health Range stated: 'As an alternative to our standard range of accompaniments this restaurant now offers Sunflower margarine, decaffeinated coffee, skimmed milk and Canderel sweetener'. All steaks were individually vacuum packed, as I guess everything else was, and all were labelled with their use-by date. These were stock rotated in the fridge and one of the daily management tasks was to check this after service. This was quite impressive.

The food tasted good, and complaints were few. Once served and finished, empty tables were re-laid for the next customers. I was in charge on the floor. Guests were seated, waitresses served drinks and food, they paid, and tables were re-laid. Our target was a hundred meals per day or evening, which we achieved regularly. One week we achieved a record, of a thousand covers for the week. The work was monotonous, with not much interaction with customers, so it was like a factory production line, much as modern chain restaurants operate. As a manager, we could eat anything from the menu at a table and be served, which was great, but I actually got fed up with eating steaks!

The manager was fine and I think my performance was OK, but what really pissed me off several times was that his wife, who must have been a former employee, would come in during the middle of service and take over, issuing me with instructions. How dare she! During service you keep a mental overview of the restaurant situation, which table is at what stage of the meal and so on. For her to destroy this by giving me instructions, treating me like a skivvy, not only ruined my mental map, but pissed me right off.

My pride and joy was a new cocktail book which had been given to me for my birthday. I lent it to the manager at the wine bar up the road, but when I asked for it back he professed to having lost it. I was quite upset as it was a brilliant book. My opinion of Liverpudlians was tarnished. He had not lost it, he just wanted to keep it. After a month at the Albany I resigned and gave one week's notice. It wasn't my thing working there.

My parents were quite frustrated with me and Dad told me to get out of the house and go and find a job, again, so I moved temporarily to London, going back to Shropshire maybe at weekends or for occasions. First, I stayed with my sister Robin, thank you Robin, but I found her dietary restrictions difficult; no meat could be brought into the flat because she was a vegetarian. Then I moved to a backpacker's called the Quest Hotel. This was embarrassing, sleeping in a dormitory with mainly student backpackers. I was the only person arriving daily in a suit and hanging it up. Everyone else wore jeans, T-shirts and trainers. I was so out of place. I think you could only stay three nights in a row, but I begged the manager to let me stay.

Sometimes I had to move on and stay with a friend in London or close by. Sometimes I had to stay in a cheap B&B. It was costing me dearly, especially having to eat out all the time. I had no money to spare. Interviews came and went around the country. This was a low point for me, wandering around London wearing a suit but not belonging anywhere. I almost felt homeless, certainly destitute. I had signed up with a catering agency, so I 'waited on' at various locations in London on a temporary basis.

One day we had to go to Oxford. We were all collected at the agreed pick-up point by a coach, maybe six or seven of us. We had no idea where we were going or what for. We were dropped off at a village hall in the Oxford area, and that was that. No one to greet us, no one to explain what to do, just a pile of trestle tables, cutlery, glasses and crockery. We were dumbfounded and looked around to find someone in charge, or just wait around. This was fruitless and ridiculous, so I eventually took charge and arranged the tables as I thought best. It was for a wedding, that much we had ascertained, so there may have been a table plan, so we set the tables and organised the room as we thought fit.

It turned out to be a Caribbean wedding and the caterers arrived with the food, which they set up with appropriate cooking equipment. The wedding cake was very strange, three or four tiers with white icing, but complete with a liquid fountain with appropriate plastic tubing to enable this liquid to recycle. How smart I thought...until they turned it on, and this horrible yellow coloured liquid shot out of the fountain, the colour of Galliano. How revolting!

The wedding breakfast itself went according to plan with the main course being a lovely lamb or goat curry of sorts. I'm not sure if I ran the wedding or not, but I sure was glad when it was over. I'd got talking to one of the waiters, so when the coach dropped us off in London, we went for a drink. We went to a big bar and sat at a vacant table which still had a tea service uncleared from the previous occupants. To my horror, this tea service, comprising cups, saucers, milk jug, water pot and tea pot, sugar holder, slowly disappeared into the waiter's holdall on the floor, which contained his waiter's clothes. He had nicked the whole lot. I was aghast!

We moved on to a gay bar. Oh no, I wasn't going in there. This was 1987, when things like this were almost unmentionable. Anyway he dragged me in and we got a pint each, but I sat at the back of the room well out of the way, and watched what went on, along with the entertainment. I was terrified of a gay person, let alone a stranger, talking to me so after downing my pint rapidly, we beat a hasty retreat.

On the 29th July I went for an interview in Torquay and stayed at the Kistor hotel. And so began my Torquay career.

A month after my bicycle accident whilst working at The Rose Revived

Off duty on one of the ships on Lake Lucerne.

With my mother outside Maxton Lodge in Torquay

At the Quayside Hotel holding my ceramic seagull

My ship MS Gotthard on Lake Lucerne

Hotel Riviera, Newquay

In my element!

Part of the former Palm Court Hotel, Torquay

A much-needed rest

Happy about something...

CHAPTER 9

Torquay: the Red House Hotel

Jonathan Hassell collected me from Torquay railway station in his open-top sports car, which was a thrill in itself, and gave me a quick tour of Torquay, which was very thoughtful. He was tall, tanned, slim, smart, very well spoken with a sense of humour. Someone who was noticed. Then he deposited me at the Kistor Hotel, which he also owned, where I stayed the night. All genuinely nice with pleasant staff. I was in a good mood.

Torquay was bright and sunny, with palm trees, hotels and bed & breakfasts everywhere, along with hordes of people strolling along the seafront, with families with buckets and spades, eating ice cream and so on, all enjoying their holidays. There were a seemingly equal number of seagulls. He invited me for a drink at Lauderdale in the evening where I met his wife Susan, after which

I went out into Torquay for a look around. I was collected in the morning for my interview. This was to be for general manager at the Red House Hotel in Chelston, which comprised a ten-bedroomed two-star hotel, along with Maxton Lodge, being 24 self-catering apartments, and a health and leisure club. He gave me a tour of the hotel, then I met the management, all female, then off to where he and his wife lived, at Lauderdale Holiday Apartments on Torquay seafront, which comprised three holiday apartments. His wife Susan was equally slim, smart, and well dressed. They talked about themselves, their group of businesses, and questioned me about my life, ambitions, and so on. I was prepared, relaxed, feeling positive, and the interview went well, and I liked the Hassells.

After the interview, I left for London by train and stayed at the Paddington Hotel, which cost me £20. The following day I went to Chris's flat and played a couple of games of squash over the next day or two before returning to Shropshire, to meet my parents back from their holiday in South Africa. To my utter delight, along with an equal amount of anxiety, I was offered the job at the Red House Hotel, so I moved down by train on the 3rd August. I was actually thrilled – my first job as a general manager. Now it was up to me to prove to my parents that I was capable of what lay ahead. That was what worried me the most – what my parents thought of me or might think of me.

I moved temporarily into Room 8, the only single room, above the boiler. It was HOT in that room, stifling hot, and due to its location at the back of the hotel, its window did not offer much in the way of ventilation. I was ultimately to move into the staff house, but they were waiting for someone to leave, so in the meantime I moved to the Westgate Hotel, a B&B on Falkland Road. I had visions of moth-eaten worn-out bedding, being a hotel snob who was used to four-star hotels, but it was OK and there was a tiny bar so was able to get a drink, much to my relief!

I started off doing splits, being 9 am to 4 pm, and 6.30 pm to 9 pm, mainly to get accustomed to how the management operated the hotel. I expect my attitude was a bit snobbish or superior, having come from four-star hotels, and the dinner menu was basic, as was the restaurant, which was the size of a Victorian house lounge. The original building was Victorian, so had six en-suite bedrooms, the restaurant, a small bar, a quiet lounge for residents, an office, the kitchen, and the 'sleep-over' room with bathroom for the management. At the back, an extension had been built which looked into the pool area comprising four bedrooms, the leisure complex, and a fairly characterless but practical lounge where people could have a coffee, bar snacks etc. The leisure complex comprised an indoor pool, sauna, and Jacuzzi, with an outdoor pool in the grounds of Maxton Lodge.

The management either worked an early or a late shift, with the late shift person sleeping over, followed by an early shift. This person cooked dinner, and in the morning, breakfast. No problem, I thought. A late shift could start at 3.30 pm, finishing 11 pm or midnight, depending on who was drinking at the bar, with an early shift being 7 am until 4 pm, I think. The late manager tidied everything up and locked the hotel before going to bed.

There was no chef, so the management cooked everything, hardly ever a KP, and one waitress at a time – they were called general assistants. Their shifts were either 8 am to 2 pm, 2 pm to 6 pm, or 6 pm to 10 pm, serving the customers, signing club members in and out, dealing with leisure club subscriptions, answering the telephone and taking bookings, serving tea and coffees, and so on. We would have an evening waitress if the numbers justified it, but it was a nightmare if you were on your own because it meant you cooked, served, answered the phone, dealt with club members, all on your own. There was also the maintenance man, Geoff, replaced by Don after a few years, and the housekeeping staff, which thankfully was a department I didn't have to worry about too much, which was just as well, because I detest anything to do with making beds.

After a week or so I was on my first late shift when it suddenly dawned on me that there was no one to cook dinner. Of course, it was me today. Idiot! The first thing the late manager did was to organise dinner, in your head if nothing else, so it was mid to late afternoon before it dawned on me. I cobbled together a menu, which would have been a soup (powdered) – yes, I know, ghastly – and maybe prawn cocktail. Main course could be frozen chicken Kiev or maybe I would make a beef bourguignonne. No, not enough time for the beef. Something else then. Desserts… I would make a gateau, eg Black Forest, using pre-made cake sponge, or something like fresh fruit salad. All fairly basic.

All went OK, and it was my first sleep in. Our room comprised two single beds, a bedside set of drawers, and a cupboard, with bathroom next door. The small window on the inside was at a normal height, but the outside was at ground level, because there was a steep incline outside to the car park, which was a bit unnerving, I'm not sure why. Maybe because you were effectively sleeping below ground level. I did not sleep at all the first night. In the morning I opened up, and cooked breakfast. All fine.

When I was exploring the area around the hotel on foot, I came across the Island Inn. I was looking for a pub to be my local. Not that I realised it at the time, but the Island Inn was a gay bar. However at one corner of the bar I met a group of straight people, and this was their spot. It was years before I told anyone that I occasionally drank there. I became friends with Graham and his wife, who was a drayman for Carlsberg, and I saw him from time to time on his deliveries over the next thirty years or so.

I joined the Riviera Centre's gym and started weight training.

Who were the management? In charge was Sue, a Yorkshire lass, who I found a bit scary, then Suzanne, followed by Rachel as a trainee. They were all good in their own right and had the business wrapped up, so they did not need a 'manager' interfering! A week after I had started, Mr Hassell informed me that Yorkshire Sue was leaving to go to work at the Derwent Hotel, which was a blow to me, but she had resigned before I started; they hadn't told me so as to not scare me off. So the other two went up a notch. They were happy about that.

I moved into the staff house in Goshen Road, which was only a short walk from the hotel. Andrew lived there, the assistant manager at the Kistor Hotel. He had a cat and a beat-up old Nissan car. We had our own bedrooms with communal lounge/diner and kitchen. Val, the neighbour, was a nice lady, but she would occasionally get upset over something we did and complain to the Hassells, who would have to buy her a plant as a gesture.

I began to settle in. I became friends with some of the club members, the staff accepted me, and the Hassells were redirecting me if I strayed from the path. They were both extremely helpful, Susan dealing with the day-to-day operations and Jonathan the financial side. They were both very experienced, as well as being fair employers.

What was involved on the managerial side? All paperwork was manual and on paper; a computer was non-existent, not even a calculator. Club member records had to be updated and membership cards issued. The late shift prepared the next day's arrivals. Friday night was the hardest in the summer season because Saturday was a BIG day; you could have twenty-four apartments departing and arriving, along with ten bedrooms. Everything in those days, certainly on the self-catering side, was strictly Saturday to Saturday. Everything had to be checked, and a registration form made ready, along with a little temporary club membership card. Phone calls could be for bookings, for which confirmations were handwritten on a headed template letter. Since there was no reception desk as such, the bar doubled as a reception area for arrivals. There were no receptionists so banking had to be done, which was collected by Mrs Hassell.

Wages were done by me weekly and given to Mrs Hassell for processing, along with a weekly and monthly wet and dry purchasing breakdown, done manually in a large accounts book. This had to be cross balanced, so down the page would be the days of the month and across the top the various departments, eg meat/veg/dry and so on. At the end of the month you would add up each line across, and down, with the two figures matching. If they didn't, you would have to start again. All this done in your head without a calculator! Stationery had to be ordered. We did not normally have a KP, so it was shared by the chef, aka duty manager, and the waitress. Staff were treated like humans, without any apparent hierarchy. Food had to be ordered nightly by the duty manager. Wet stock had to be ordered weekly. Bar snacks were cooked and served. The swimming pool and jacuzzi had to be tested regularly, recorded, and chemical action taken if necessary. When the club closed at 10 pm, the sauna, pool area and changing rooms had to be cleaned, which meant a mop and bucket with hot soapy or bleached water. The latter was a nightmare, being the last job, because the humidity in the pool area made me sweat. It dripped off me, and I hated doing it but had to be done. So we were kept quite busy in our own little way.

In November Rory Bremner, along with Jessica Martin, performed at the Riviera Centre, so after the show I went backstage and met up with him – we knew each other from Wellington – and went for a curry with his groupies. Although he is very funny and brilliant at what he does, he talked non-stop, seemingly about himself, which didn't impress me that much.

And so the months went by. It was a big learning curve for me, being my first general manager position, and there is only so much on which you can ask an employer for guidance. There was a fantastic set of staff and management, all female, mostly young and attractive, and all with nice personalities. Geoff the maintenance man was the only male. We all got along. They all did their job extremely well and from my point of view it was great.

Except for one thing. I did not really have a brilliant rapport with Suzanne and Rachel, and I don't know why. They both did their jobs properly, so what was it? Maybe I didn't step up to the mark from their point of view? Perhaps they did not like my style of management? If you ever read this Rachel, I would really like to know! Maybe they didn't like a man sleeping in the staff bedroom? But then, there had been a male manager previously. That room was also used as a changing room, so obviously you didn't go into the room if you knew someone was changing, but on one particular day I went in to get something, to find a blonde member of staff with sparkly blue eyes sitting on my bed in her underwear.

Later that day the fire alarms went off in Maxton Lodge, and the master keys were kept in the bedroom. I burst into the room, not realising that Rachel was there in her underwear, but I had to carry on, to collect the emergency keys. Later that day I told them I would get a lock put on the door for their benefit. It had happened from time to time, to me also. Maybe it was that?

My diary entries for 1987 became fewer and fewer to the point of none at all, but in February 1988 I did record that Suzanne's job finished suddenly. I cannot remember why. Rachel went up to deputy manager and I employed a new assistant manager, Nicky, who I believe had connections to the fishing industry. She was lovely and I fell for her totally. On the occasions when there were two members of management on duty in the evening, we would invariably sit in the bar together and eat our dinner, around about 10 pm, once we had cleared up. Anyway I told her one night how much I liked her, on a personal level, and after my two-week skiing holiday the following week, I returned to find she had resigned.

Well, I knew why and told Mr Hassell. That taught me a lesson and I was highly embarrassed.

Rachel was becoming a pain; our conversations had become stilted and anyway were always only work related. She could not look at me, but stared out of the window, even replying to the window. Maybe I was a bit lecherous? It is hard to know how the female mind works.

This was becoming unbearable, and I pleaded with Mr Hassell to transfer her to the Kistor Hotel. I cannot remember if that happened or not, but she left soon after, much to my relief. It was a pity because she was very efficient, liked by all, and a solid member of the team. However this meant I was the only member of management, so I had to work split shifts, seven days a week, sleeping in seven times instead of three. This was hard, and morale-wise I was at rock bottom. In the space of months I had lost all my management team. Was I such a failure that I couldn't manage a team? What was I doing wrong, could someone tell me? Would the Hassells get rid of me? What would my parents think?

But the Hassells supported me, which was encouraging. I am a fighter and do not give up. I certainly had a challenge, and that's something I thrive on. On a positive note, any new management could be trained to my way of working, whatever that was! After a few weeks of hell, Simon was employed as the assistant manager, much to my relief, so my trips to the Island Inn could resume!

I think Simon had been to South Devon Tech and passed an OND in hotel management. He soon picked it up, and after a week's training, he managed everything and could be relied upon. I think it was at this stage that I persuaded the Hassells to get a chef, to work five days whilst the management did the other two. They agreed, which was great because they could see that the membership was increasing, so bar snack sales were up. So John joined the fort, the son of a charming couple who ran the Walnut Tea Rooms around the corner. John himself was a baby-faced, tall fat lad who would not hurt a fly. He was a really nice chap. He soon settled in, and his cooking was adequate for this hotel. There was Mandine, who worked 2 pm to 6 pm in the afternoon and was charming, Barbara, who worked in the evenings and was the mother of Yorkshire Sue, and Val, who worked 8 am to 2 pm. Val was a lady in her fifties I guess. Apart from being obsessed with cleaning, she didn't take any nonsense and would openly criticise guests to their face, which I admired her for in a way. Her husband ran Torquay Mayor's parlour and they lived in an enviable house at the gates of Torre Abbey.

So my new team was in place and all was well. Only one problem – we still needed a third member of management, so we employed Fiona who did a good job and stayed for maybe a year or two. I cannot remember much about her except she could get in a strop and she bought her wedding dress whilst still single and unattached! She moved on eventually up the career ladder somewhere else. She was replaced by Jenny Dawes, who had recently finished an HND in Hotel Management at South Devon Tech. It was not until she had actually started that I realised how beautiful she was, and she told me she liked to be referred to as Jen. Her mother originated from Hong Kong, so she had a fabulous Asian face and jaw line and a superb figure. Her smile melted your knees. And her writing was so neat and tidy! An 'O' would be oval and perfectly joined, with a slight positive slant, and it summed her up... neat, tidy and beautiful. I could have married her just for her handwriting, that's how much I thought of her. She was brilliant at her job, so I gave her the club memberships to deal with which I think she enjoyed doing. Nothing was too much trouble, she was always positive.

So there I was with a full team in place, everyone getting along and doing a good job, and I was happy. Incredibly happy. My dire situation had been turned around. But there was one little irritant. I can't remember the exact dates or months of who was employed when, but certainly when Jen started, Val made her life a misery, scolding her publicly for every minor thing done wrong, which exasperated her, as well as me. A member of staff does not normally tell a member of management what to do. OK Val may have been right, she may have been wrong, but did it matter? When you are young you see everything as black and white; it is only with age that you realise grey areas are acceptable. But Val did not have that grey area.

It was a very tricky situation, because Val would snort at me if I had a quiet word with her, like a bull preparing to charge, while Jen understandably got quite upset, and I tried to appease her by saying I'd have a word with Val. So it was a game of cat and mouse. I even had to try to rota them separately. Was Val jealous of Jen's good looks and youth? But I did not want to lose Val because she performed her job well, people liked her, she was brilliant with customers, never went sick, and was always punctual. And I certainly did not want to lose Jen. She was perfect.

It was with great relief in a way, that when I replaced a member of staff, or maybe it was one of the new foreign students, Val turned her 'training method' if that's what you call it, onto that new member of staff, so Jen overnight became a long lost friend. It was extremely devious the way Val's attitude to a member of staff could change overnight, and it was the same with everybody. They had to undergo the ritual of being 'trained' by Val. This was a constant irritation to me, never mind what her current 'victim' thought, up until the day Val retired.

I enjoyed going to the Island Inn, but times have changed now. Two lads ran the pub, financed, I was told, by one set of parents, but it only lasted a few years after I stopped going there. It was quite enjoyable standing at the 'straight' corner with my friends watching the others, and amazing who you would see in there. The boys would often hire drag acts, starting quite late, so if you hung around they would give you free tickets to it, which we all found great, so we had a few late nights there. Some of the staff at the Island Inn confided in me as to what was really going on behind the scenes, and what the boys got up to. All remarkably interesting!

We would also hold 'swim saunas' at the hotel, but not in the summer. A group of people, up to about twenty, would all go for a swim in the evening, followed by a two-course supper in the restaurant, typically serving lasagne with peas, followed by a dessert. They were quite popular. One time when I was chefing for one of these, it was service time, so I pulled the tray of lasagne out of the oven, only to find that the glass bowl of peas in the side of the oven, came out as well and smashed on the floor. Grrr! I had to cook more peas ASAP! Only a minor crisis....

I had heard about the Saxon Bar also known as Jim's Inn, which was a local pub in Chelston, and I had cycled all over Chelston trying to find it several times without success, but eventually I found it, in the basement of the Courtlands Hotel. So I went in, and virtually lived there for the next fifteen years. Years later my friends told me that to begin with I bought them all rounds of drinks, as if to buy my way into their group. Well, it worked! The locals ranged from local businessmen to those who had brushed with the law. These were the good days, especially when operated by George Cooper and his wife Helen, who did the cooking, along with son Danny who was just a teenager, training. There were frequent lock-ins, which the police did not really object to provided there was no trouble, frequent parties around and about, and we were frequently pissed. That was how life went on, and it was good.

I joined the pool team, as a star player of course, playing on Sunday evenings in Rusty's Pool League. Having Sunday nights off often meant that I had to work Saturday nights, but if I did get a Saturday night off then it was invariably spent watching the band 'Prime Time' at the Fiesta bar on Paignton seafront. We knew some of the band and sat at the front, right in front of them. They were a fabulous band playing all the good songs by Pink Floyd, U2, Simple Minds, etc. Invariably John, the lead singer, would stand on our drinks table, which was low enough for him to stand on easily, or give us the mike to sing a chorus. They were great nights, always followed by a curry, and if we were the only guests in the Indian in Preston, we could play our own music on their CD system, normally Pink Floyd. It was the boys' night out. A little skivvy of a seventeen-year-old called Rupert used to set up and dismantle the PA system for the band, and gradually he became one of our gang, and is now a good friend. He ended up marrying Helen, who he first met when she worked at the Red House, whilst Rupert became a member. Sadly, the band finished playing there as the venue went bust, so that was the end of that.

In the winter we took winter lets at Maxton Lodge. They could rent an apartment for as little as £60 per week and we had all sorts of people, from people moving to a new house to single people working away from home, people on long-term holiday, and so on. One particular retired lady on her own was memorable to say the least; her hair was always plaited so she looked like an Indian squaw, her eyes popped out of her face as if on stalks, and worst of all, she ate raw garlic. Her breath was minging; when she entered a room, everyone could smell the garlic, which lingered for hours after she had gone, as if absorbed into the carpet. It was horrible.

I set up a Christmas drinks party for the residents at Maxton Lodge, except I forgot to tell anyone. Moron or what! The only person to turn up was this lady, who knew about the party because I had seen her and told her earlier that day. I had to talk to her and no one else. Sheer torture. Then there was the Swedish man who used the payphone every day to trade in the stock market; sometimes we would get a fax for him confirming this or that.

One year we had a fire company which booked several apartments for several weeks, which was a nice booking. But the occupants were all young chavs, both male and female, making a racket during the night, sometimes resulting in noisy complaints. When the first apartment gave me the apartment key back on their departure day, I thought I had better check this out, so I went over to have a look at the vacated apartment. I found empty vodka bottles, full ashtrays, jeans and other clothes, and a general mess. They must have earned enough money not to have to bother with trifling matters like clothes. I don't know what prompted me, but I ran my hand over the top of a wardrobe only to find a whole collection of opened letters with local addresses. These people had been going around the local suburbs trying to sell fire alarm systems, apparently by shouting 'FIRE FIRE FIRE!' through the letterbox to frighten elderly people. I guess when installing a fire alarm system in a property they had nicked their mail and opened it, looking for cash or whatever. I rang the police who came over, and as the occupants of one of their flats were still on site they took them away, along with the letters. Yeah!

I cycled or walked everywhere because I had to wait three years before I could get my driving licence back. I was fit in those days and weighed nine and a half stone at thirty. I played squash a lot. I could eat and drink anything without weight gain. I would ride to a meeting at the Hassells at Lauderdale in my suit, or to the Kistor Hotel, where I worked the occasional shift if they were short of management, maybe once a year.

Now is probably the right time to talk about my insecurity, if that is what it is called. I had always been shy, to the point that it took a great effort for me to do something out of the ordinary. I would weigh the pros and cons up in my head for maybe weeks before plucking up the courage to do it. It could be something as trivial as cycling somewhere different or going into a different shop or buying something different. Or even something normal. I was or had been very naïve, to the extent that if someone told me blue was green, I would have believed them. Working at the Red House gave me confidence, so very slowly I began to come out of my shell, and realised that my adolescent notions that people knew what I was talking about before I said it were a load of rubbish!

I slowly began to question, in my head at first, but later face to face, some things people would tell me, so that I could begin to debate a situation or event with them. It was almost a revelation to find that 'people' did not know everything, as I had for years and years presumed. Looking back on it, I think I was pretty fucked up, but I hid it well. Maybe it was a side effect of my epilepsy drugs.

My asthma was another issue. I used a Ventolin Inhaler to relieve it if I started wheezing, and a preventive inhaler morning and evening. Except I was not particularly good at using the preventative inhaler, which involved placing a capsule in a contraption, twisting the device so as to break the capsule, then breathing in the enclosed powder. All too much of a bother. Since my teenage years I had become addicted to my Ventolin Inhaler; I would use it whether or not I had asthma. For instance, on getting up, before going out anywhere, whilst going to the loo, before doing something else, so much so that if I did become asthmatic, it wouldn't really work. You are only supposed to use it say six times daily whereas I was using it maybe fifteen times. Ventolin is not good for you in excess. Ironically smoking helped a bit, by relaxing the body. So I plucked up the courage to sort it out with the doctor, started using the preventative one properly, and gradually weaned myself off Ventolin, to the stage where I only needed to use it if I mowed a lawn or actually became asthmatic, which is very rare now. The preventative one changed to a spray design similar to the Ventolin, so much more user-friendly, which helped.

Because Simon worked opposite shifts to me at the hotel, we never had time for a catch up to talk about work, and certainly management meetings between the three of us were hardly ever held. Simon and I held our 'meetings' at the hotel at the end of the evening and drank into the night. Many a time I have woken up either slumped in a chair or asleep on the floor, very occasionally not having laid the restaurant for breakfast, much to Val's irritation. Quite regularly I must have stunk of stale beer and cigarettes.

Another person who stayed Monday to Friday in the hotel was Dave Grey, who lived in Suffolk but was a sales rep for Safemaster Remoulds in Newton Abbot. Quite often I would have a few drinks with him, or with Vic, who owned the self-catering flats across the road. I really pushed it to the limit in those days – remember I wasn't supposed to drink because my epilepsy drugs become ineffective – but I did, and there's many a time when while I was the breakfast chef, having opened up and got everything ready for breakfast, I would have to sit in the chair in the kitchen with my head in my hands trying not to have a fit. After breakfast I would have to go and lie down in the bedroom to sleep it off, telling the staff to call me if Mrs Hassell came in. I suppose this was the sign of an alcoholic. But it only takes one extra pint for the difference in me from being fine the next day, to feeling very tender, hence taking slow deliberate actions to avoid triggering a fit.

That reminds me of a guest who stayed one night. He had booked maybe a day or two in advance, as a single person. On arrival he asked for some wine to be taken to the room. 'Sure, what would you like?' I asked. He ordered five Litres of the house red and a litre of lemonade! Wow! So I took it up in two trips and he paid for it. Our house wine bought via Carlsberg was something horrible called Maison des Bretons, whether red or white. In those days if you couldn't afford a bottle of 'proper' wine, you had to put up with something more akin to vinegar, and we used litre bottles of lemonade, our operation being too small at the time for draught Coke or lemonade. Anyway I never saw him again until I opened up at 7.30 the following morning, whereupon he walked through the front door, announcing matter-of-factly that he had been arrested the previous evening for being drunk, and had spent the night at the nick! He had not touched his bedroom wine, and I think he had even left a few bottles unopened on departure. Amazing!

Jen and I would go swimming together at the Red House if we both had the same evening off; we enjoyed each other's company, but I always wondered why she never asked her boyfriend to swim. However, desperate as I was, I could never ask her out. I tried indirectly to make a social acquaintance with her, which she quite rightly calmly refused, since as her boss I could not cross the line, and under no circumstances would I want to jeopardise her job, or mine, or our friendship. I hope I didn't make her feel uncomfortable, but I was in love with her. This was a very tortuous time for me.

I remember once we were both swimming towards each other, and quite without thinking about it, I deliberately splashed water into her face. I got it all back, along with a verbal tirade, followed by the inevitable stony silence! That's how frustrated I was. Obviously, I had to apologise. She was an alpha female, whereas I was far down the pecking order! I regarded myself as a good catch; however I was older, short, shy, and not particularly good looking. Such is life...

My aunt had died in Canada, so with my cut of her will, I was able to put a sizeable deposit down on a house, which was a two-bedroomed starter home in Ellacombe, on top of a hill with views over the town and, over the horizon to Haytor Rock on Dartmoor. Mr Hassell made a deal with me which I agreed to, which was that whilst I couldn't drive, I wouldn't live in my house. Fair enough. I rented it out, using an agency in Torquay which turned out to be useless. The first tenants seemed nice enough, the husband being a local councillor, the wife working in a shop in Torquay. But either the agent would not collect the rent, or the tenant was not paying.

I became so furious one day, at the agent's office, a dingy smoke-filled cupboard-sized room, that I stormed down to the shop and demanded the money from the wife, who was serving on the tills, and rather embarrassed, she paid me. I then showed this to the agent and shouted at him for being pathetic. When those residents moved on, so did the agent!

I then took on a lovely retired couple, Reg and Joyce Benstead, who had been regular visitors to the Red House and had moved down to Torquay from somewhere like Eastbourne. I regularly went over for a cup of tea, and we went out for the odd meal, and that carried on for years until they had to move into a retirement home. I acquired most of their furniture, which helped me when I eventually moved in. I was raking in the money whilst renting; this was the first time in my life I had 'spare' money, which was great and enabled me to go on my annual fortnightly ski trip to Mayrhofen, always on my own. Sad maybe, but none of my Torquay friends could ski then.

Most weeks out there were brilliant. I either took skiing lessons, both to brush up on technique and to meet people, or went with the guide, so I always met people. Some weeks I made two sets of friends, those in the hotel, normally the Strass, and those on the slopes. I came back to work for a rest, absolutely shattered! Even hotel staff and ski instructors got to know me.

This was the time when I started my coin collection. John the chef collected coins, which to him meant that he had been to the flea market and bought a little pile of coins, enough to fit in your hand, for maybe £5, if that. So I started to do the same. Most were pre-decimal circulated coinage like pennies or halfpennies, maybe a shilling. I started this, then went on to silver proof collections or random silver proof coins, and even a set of gold proof coins. I have thousands of coins, including international ones, collected over the years from holidays or at work, which have all been catalogued except for a few Middle Eastern and Far Eastern ones, or some which are too old or worn to accurately verify by an amateur like myself. None of the circulated coinage is worth that much.

One afternoon Mandine, the afternoon assistant, received an emergency phone call from her boyfriend. It transpired that there had been an accident with his lawn mower, so I drove her over there to see what was going on, for moral support if nothing else. It was quite bad actually, and interesting from a medical point of view to be privileged to view an injury of this sort. He had re-wired his electric mower and taken a shock through his arm whilst mowing. You could see the bone of his forearm, whilst along the length of it the skin and flesh had peeled back and melted into a pinky yellowy colour. A bit gruesome to be honest, and Mandine was in tears, bless her. An ambulance took him away and that was that.

Some of the summers were scorching, and that year there was a heatwave. Hoses, car washing, topping up of swimming pools etc had all been banned. We rigged up a system whereby we could transfer water from the outdoor pool to the indoor, so that the indoor one was always functioning, and closed off the outdoor one. We arranged with another local pool owner to 'buy' half a tanker each of water from up country, where restrictions were not enforced. A milk tanker duly turned up one day. 'Er, excuse me, no we don't need milk thank you very much, just water,' I thought to myself. Then the tanker manoeuvred into the car park and began to pump its water into the outdoor swimming pool.

'Well at least you don't have to clean it out, seeing as it's only water,' I said to the driver.

'We still have to clean it,' he said 'and by the time we've finished, we almost use a whole tank load of water each time.' I was gobsmacked at the amount of water being wasted, but at least we had our water for the pool.

We provided cots in Maxton Lodge and the hotel, so one year Mr Hassell bought some more. They looked smart, being wooden, and strong. The room attendants dealt with allocating the cots in the morning, but if a family arrived and we had forgotten to put up the cot, or they told us they wanted one, it really annoyed us because they were a nut and bolt affair, designed to be erected once and once only, and could take about forty minutes to put up properly, along with the bedding. They were not designed to be erected and dismantled every week. This was time which we could not spare on a busy Saturday afternoon in the summer, what with all the check-ins.

'Extra beds' or Z-beds are another matter altogether. In your average hotel or self-catering property, these are flimsy affairs that fold in two and can be wheeled along a corridor. Invariably the metal springs are worn out or stretched and with the flimsy mattress they afford no real comfort, with the occupant sleeping in a dip in the middle of the bed. They were terrible! And every hotel had the same design, so the same problem. They were designed for little children, so if the occupant was too big, it could cause issues.

Normal beds are another issue. Mattresses go soft, to the point that when enough people complain about not sleeping or getting a backache, you do something about it. I might say that in the decades to follow, hotels have become more proactive in keeping bed quality to a more professional standard. What I am writing here has nothing to do with the Red House Hotel, it is just the point in time when it warrants a mention.

I hate hotel pillows with a passion. Quite often they are cheap synthetic ones which afford no real support for the head or neck. Indeed when sleeping in hotels as part of a work sleep-over shift, I would bring my own feather one.

That reminds me of a couple from America who stayed a few days. They had booked a double room. She was large, but he was twice the size, both vertically and horizontally. I have never seen anyone like it. And they were both sleeping in a standard four-foot-six bed!? I wondered whether the floor could take their combined weight, let alone the bed! I didn't quite know how he would sit on one of our restaurant chairs, whether the chair would support his weight, indeed he might have needed two, one for each buttock.

Now the bread rolls were offered from a basket, containing about eight rolls, one per person. He had the whole basket! And he had to have extra portions of food. After the first night we had to put an extra mattress on the floor in the bedroom for one of them to sleep on.

Some families will do anything to stay in accommodation 'on the cheap'. They do not understand that we have tourist board and AA/RAC regulations that only permit a certain number of occupants according to the size of bedroom. So a double room only takes two people. If that room has the 'official' capacity to take an extra bed or cot, then the total for that room is three people. Some families think that two little children are the equivalent of one adult, but from our point of view, each child is a person. If a family has to take two rooms, then the first two occupants of each room are charged at the adult rate, bumping up the cost considerably for the family. The worst I encountered was a family of seven who arrived late at night, not having booked. As it happened I could offer them a family room consisting of a double and single bed, with an extra Z-bed, into which they 'top and tailed'. They would not have found anywhere else at that time of night. It just staggers me how some adults expect rooms to be available without having booked in advance, or even expect you to find another hotel for them!

Hotel chains offer rooms with two double or king size beds and charge for the room, which is fine, and makes it affordable for families, but classic privately-owned accommodation offers rates per person, with discounts for children according to their age. Sometimes a couple might arrive, having booked a double room. They would be checked in, and then a bit later on they would sneak in a child, hoping no one would notice. An occasional game of cat and mouse!

But I was committed to my job. I enjoyed every aspect, especially preparing the Saturday arrivals for Maxton Lodge. I had developed a knack of falling asleep at the desk with my head on the table, but as soon as I heard the floor creak around the corner, I would sit upright as if working normally. No one would know. I had it down to a T.

Once the first year had passed, you could look at work-related matters objectively; I had proposed new tariffs as requested, for both the hotel and Maxton Lodge, and what we called Aparthotel, whereby you could stay in an apartment on BB or DBB terms. Mr Hassell and I agreed between us and dealt with costings for the year, targets, budgeting, new projects etc. So I really felt that I had landed on my feet, being involved with annual financial matters. I learnt a lot more about looking after swimming pools, not just the basic chemicals and cleaning the scum line, backwashing etc, but also where not to put the chemicals, water hardness, alkalinity, bleaching out, how to tell if the baffles in the filter had broken: it was fascinating. I had purchased a wet rotary scrubber for the floor area in the pool, along with a wet vacuum. It was one of those machines which when turned on, shot off to the left. By raising the handle, it would stay still, and by raising it further it went to the right. Quite tricky to get the hang of. So I only let Simon, Jen and myself use it. It was a brilliant machine which made the main footfall area much cleaner, similarly the sauna floor, but as it took longer to complete, due to the vacuuming afterwards, it made you sweat even more!

I was only weeks away from getting my driving licence back, but shortly before this I actually had an epileptic fit. So I informed my doctor, as I always do. Hence my licence application was rejected for another year. WHAT? I had it out with the doctor, who told me that he was obliged to tell the DVLA. Grrr... I was furious and really upset.

When the year had passed, I went out and bought a new Renault 19, Ferrari red in colour. That was the only brand-new car I ever purchased. The next one will have to wait until I win the lottery! I moved into my house, which was great, finally in my mid-thirties living in my own property. All of my life so far, I had lived in hotel accommodation or staff houses, or at my parents' house.

However my house was the other side of Torquay from the hotel. No problem there, but the same applied to the Saxon Bar. This meant either staying at home in the evening, which now became the main option, or getting taxis to and from the Saxon Bar. A bit costly, especially as my source of rental income had dried up. I now had to watch the pennies. So that was the first lifestyle change. The bubble had burst!

We decided to take on students at the hotel, one at a time for six months or so, from Oxford Poly. They gave us their foreign students, those doing a degree in hotel management, because it was assumed that the training I gave them would be more personal, which it was. I devised a training programme for all departments. The first student was a girl from China or Hong Kong called Lin (name changed). She was all right and did everything very satisfactorily. Maybe a year later I went to see her in Oxford, without knowing what the outcome would be in the evening. Nothing happened, unfortunately, so I had to find a hotel quick. I knew of the Randolph, a four-star hotel, so I checked in there. It was awful. The old-fashioned single bed was convex, so you could only sleep on your back in the middle of the bed, but breakfast was the worst. The restaurant didn't know about me – late arrival, so my details were probably not on the A&D sheet for the restaurant. No one brought the cereal trolley to me, coffee took forever to arrive, the small individual glass marmalade and jam jars were already part used – it was just a shambles (this was 1990). So it was not a good start.

I packed and went downstairs to check out and asked for my car to be brought round from the hotel's garage. I told the receptionist that I would be in the lounge reading my paper. I read the whole paper, some parts twice. I guess forty minutes had elapsed, so I enquired at reception, when I saw my car outside on the double yellow lines. What! I asked for the keys, by now fuming, and became even more incredulous when the receptionist said they were in the car! Unbelievable! Anyone could have driven off in it. God knows how long my car had been there. I almost wish my car *had* been given a parking ticket because I would have given it straight to the manager! I drove off in a foul temper, which not even a visit to the Rose Revived could help. Woe betide anyone winding me up that day!

The second student was a man from Africa who was lazy and uninterested in anything. He irritated me; he refused to do some jobs like cleaning the pool scum line – maybe he couldn't swim. One of the more elderly club members, a man seemingly from the days of the Raj or suchlike, ordered a sandwich one day which the African took out. The customer refused to eat it, once he had ascertained that the African had made it. I was furious and nearly threw this racist member out of the club, but to keep the peace I made another, took it out to him and glared at him. Some people's notion of life is utterly amazing.

That reminds me of one genuinely nice customer. He was Arab, from Bahrain I believe, and took several apartments for several weeks in the summer. He also had to have a seven-seater automatic vehicle, this being for his wife, two children, a maid/cook, a relative, another wife/girlfriend, and himself. It was a good booking, but he never really rewarded me appropriately, as in a tip for procuring each time his hard-to-find hire car. But he was a gentleman, spoke brilliant English, and it was always nice to welcome him back, as it was with all the regular customers, most of whom booked their particular apartment for the same week or fortnight each year.

We had upgraded the apartments to four-key Commended, which is similar to AA four star for a hotel, but this was the WCTB (West Country Tourist Board) classification for self-catering. A contractor was set up for the work, which mainly involved replacing all the kitchens and bathrooms. This was a frustrating time; they were supposed to have a foreman on site but frequently I would find the labourers sitting about. It was none of my business but I could find that the plumber couldn't do his job because the sparky hadn't done his, and so on. I would have to ring up the contractor. Not my job! And the longer they took to complete, the longer the income was reduced.

The next project was to expand the leisure club. Basically, the waste land at the edge of the hotel outside the swimming pool became a corridor, accessed from the club eating area, with new changing rooms and a small gym, along with access to the outdoor pool with an external shower. It was thrilling watching this being built and finally opening. However, even though the ladies changing room had a dog-leg as you walked in, you could look through from the lounge area, which was a major planning mistake! So we swiftly erected swing doors like those you get if you go into a bar in a Western film. One of the old changing rooms became a hairdresser's, and the other a storeroom or massage parlour (can't remember). The club was almost becoming a victim of its own success. The membership built up to over 300 members, so it became overcrowded, which was counterproductive. Members then stayed away. You had the usual surge of members in October and January, but we had to restrict new members.

I even had to take the drastic step of issuing a questionnaire to the members concerning any issues and whether to continue with swimming lessons or not. Children must learn to swim, but they take up valuable space. Following this survey, which was a radical approach, it was with much reluctance that to her irritation I had to cancel our very own Baywatch babe, Rachel, who always wore a red swimming costume, just like the Baywatch lifeguards. She was another blonde with a fabulous figure, and she had a nice personality, with the added bonus that she controlled the pool when teaching, so preventing jumping and diving from other swimmers. But I was going to dry up her income stream, so she was not amused. Most of the actual members were friendly people who I knew on first name terms. They came from all walks of life. However, some would moan if the swimming pool dropped just one degree. Others, if the sauna became too crowded, would flush out those who did not 'belong' there by throwing so much water on the stones that the humidity and apparent temperature rise became unbearable, for the uninitiated!

The years progressed. In 1993 the housing market had crashed, so it was time to move to a new house, an upgrade in size and to a better location. I showed my mother, who came down to visit, some alternatives, which horrified her; one was in a council estate opposite the cemetery in Hele, so I looked in Livermead, where I had always wanted to live. The property in question was ideal, on a quiet residential street, with sea views, along with views of the front gardens of the cul-de-sac opposite. I lost about £30,000 on my old house with negative equity, so I offered about £30,000 less on the one in question, which was accepted, to my amazement. So my mortgage went up, but I would take in lodgers. I'm still there to this day.

I had an enquiry one day to provide a pre-match meal for a football club, Leyton Orient, who at the time I had never heard of. They would have a swim, followed by a hot buffet style meal before going off to play against Torquay United. The Red House was not really geared for this sort of thing, but we used trestle tables in the games room, where the players could collect their buffet style meal and eat it downstairs. Lots of pasta-based dishes, fruit, squash and so on from memory. I don't think we actually supplied sufficient food or of a good enough quality. Maybe they came back for a swim after the match, because I can remember the men's changing rooms ending up filthy, with dirty towels left lying around and mud and dirt everywhere.

Christmas and New Year were a doddle. The hotel did not offer packages, just a slightly higher tariff. Our marketing angle was that we offered a stay without any trimmings or fuss. After a few years it became quite tedious. I always volunteered to work the late shift on New Year's Eve, being the senior member of management, and once dinner had finished and the pool shut, the bar was normally empty, so I would spend the rest of the evening on my own. I would buy a bottle of champagne at 11 pm and slowly drink it until after midnight. Sometimes people came back and had a drink, but mostly I sat on my own wondering what the hell I was doing. Ho hum.

I made a real hash one New Years' Eve for dinner. I had planned a roast venison dish, but the venison was frozen. No problem, so I placed it straight in the fridge to give it two days to thaw. The chef cooked the joint, but it was still raw in the middle, so I panicked and told him to fry them like a steak, and guess what, the venison was tough. I was gutted, having planned something above budget and special for our guests, and acutely embarrassed. On another New Year's Eve a huge storm blew up, with the result that our maintenance shed roof flew off. This was no little garden shed, it was big. It was pissing with rain, I felt awful with 'man flu', but we had to deal with it. We gathered up all the men we could find, the Hassells, Simon and whoever, and between us with ladders and ropes attached to the roof, we managed to get the ridged roof back on and secure it with the ropes. We were drenched and knackered, but glad to have achieved our goal. Best of all, after a shower, I realised I had sweated out my cold!

I remember one strange thing Mr Hassell and I had to do occasionally when there was a problem with the water at Maxton Lodge, being a tank on the flat roof, or a leak from the flat roof. Although from the top floor there was a skylight, it could not be accessed unless you brought up stepladders. So, as some of the apartments were on a split level, we climbed out of the window of one apartment where the flat roof was maybe four feet above at right angles to the window. It's crazy now to think that one false move would mean falling to your death three floors down onto the concrete below. We managed to climb partially out of the window, lean across to grab the edge of the roof and climb up onto the flat roof, but to get back in, we opened the skylight, lowered ourselves down, and either jumped down to the floor or balanced on the bannisters. In terms of modern Health & Safety, this practice would be banned!

Every April the regional Ladies Hockey Championship was held in Dawlish, and a team from Bristol stayed with us. One year it was my birthday on the Saturday, so wisely I had rota'd myself off for the next two days. They invited me up to the hotel for a drink on the Saturday night, so I was well 'prepared'; I had eaten, was hydrated, and ready for a drink and a good time with a dozen or so women. They had actually won the tournament, so they were in high spirits.

We drank and chatted away, and after Simon had shut the hotel for the evening we piled into the sauna, jacuzzi and pool, all starkers. One of the team was a babe, so I thought she would be my birthday treat so to speak, but it was not to be, we just drank all night. I think I more or less drank a bottle of scotch that night after tiring of beer. In the morning Val came in at 7.30 am to find me sitting on the floor leaning against the bar wearing a towel, and maybe some of 'my' ladies were still there. She was disgusted, but I couldn't move. Eric

Roberts, one of the regular visitors to the apartments, came over for his paper, so I tried to buy him a drink, which he refused. He was always trying to buy me a drink during the daytime, which I always had to refuse, so this was payback time!

I next woke up in bed at home, and it transpired that Simon Scott, who was the KP that morning, had driven me home and taken me upstairs to my room. I had no idea. The next day was spent entirely in bed; even a sip of water would not stay down. I could not eat or drink anything. My hangover was extreme, to say the least. My cat had to go without food that day! The second day I managed to get up but take it easy. That was my worst hangover to this day, but it was a thoroughly good night!

We would employ a KP in the holidays, weekends, and at half term etc, so we used Simon Scott, the son of Rosalind, one of the room attendants. We also used Richard Hassell, the younger of the two Hassell sons. I felt slightly uneasy when he was around, because I felt that whatever we spoke about got back to his parents, and I would have to be on good form. But they were both valued for what they did and were always treated as equals.

Geoff the maintenance man was a funny one. He did a good job and I have no doubt as to his work ethics, character or performance. One day he walked through the kitchen with an empty cardboard box, paused at a fridge door, opened it, and put something in the box. I only saw him closing the fridge door, so I asked him outside what was in the box. He instantly moved it behind his back.

'What's in the box Geoff?'

'Nothing,' he replied. He was obviously hiding something.

'Come on, why are you hiding that box then? I saw you in the fridge!' I said, beginning to get mildly irritated.

'It's just some old lettuces,' he pleaded.

'That's not the point, they don't belong to you,' I replied. 'Give them back.'

'You're only going to throw them away,' he stated.

'That's for me to decide, not you!'

So he gave them back. He was right in a way, they were Iceberg lettuces beginning to go brown on the outside so we probably would have thrown them out, but that wasn't the point! I binned them later after he had gone home.

Geoff always parked his car in the same place, which was in a no parking area where one corner was blocked off by a wall, but you could just squeeze a car in there. One day a club member reported that someone had hit her car in the car park, so we went to investigate. Sure enough, she was parked next to Geoff's 'space', with a dent and scratch down her side, but Geoff's car was nowhere to be seen. I told her I would investigate the matter. He was on duty, so where was his car? Hmmm... I walked up the road looking at the parked cars, and sure enough, there was Geoff's car, oh and with a scratch along the side, matching the paintwork of the other car.

'Why've you parked up the road Geoff?' I asked him back at the hotel.

'Just for a change,' he replied.

'I see you've got a scratch on it,' I said.

'Have I?' he replied all innocently.

'Geoff, you've hit Mrs Smith in the car park, so you've parked out of the way to avoid suspicion,' I said matter-of-factly.

'No I haven't,' he replied.

'Don't give me that shit, go and sort it out with her and apologise!'

'No, why should I?' he replied, which was almost an admission of guilt.

'DO IT NOW GEOFF!' I shouted with finality, and he slunk off to find Mrs Smith.

John the chef's job was relatively easy, so he would help out front occasionally, things like giving out locker keys, maybe serving at the bar etc, but not bookings. He would frequently go and talk to restaurant customers after his part of dinner was finished, but his appearance was a sight. His apron, which at the beginning of the shift started above his fat belly, gradually moved under it, exposing part of his belly below his chef's jacket, so people in the restaurant had a more or less level eye view. Gross as this was, people liked chatting to him. That was John, and guests became used to his demeanour and friendliness. He never put enough salt in his vegetables, so we had a meeting in the office about it once, which after ten minutes of me ranting, made him cry. Oops!

Barbara, bless her, did not really need to work, being financially well off, but she enjoyed it, and enjoyed the social aspect. She was steady, was liked by all, and did a good job. So much so, that one evening at work she seemed a bit down. It transpired that her husband had died that day, but she still turned up for work! What a star!

A family staying in Maxton Lodge for two weeks had brought over a Canadian friend who was a blonde bombshell, a teenager who ticked all the boxes. Simon took a shine to her, and she to him. They seemed to spend a lot of time together, almost like the Mandy Smith and Bill Wyman thing decades ago. Being the manager, I had to talk to him. It seemed he was besotted with her and was even thinking of leaving his job to fly to Canada to be with her. He was acting irrationally, it was screwing with his head, and I tried to put things into perspective for him.

It came to a head one evening, maybe it was her last evening at Maxton Lodge, and Simon couldn't take any more, so he locked himself in his car and chain smoked. We could not get into his car, and I really thought he was going to try to kill himself. We waited outside for an eternity, but he just sat there, refusing to let anyone speak to him, the inside fogged up with cigarette smoke. I cannot remember the outcome that night, but the following day we had to part company. Never mind the fact that he had told me he might have to go with her to Canada! I can't remember having seen Simon since, and hope that life is treating him well. I was quite upset, because I had lost a friend.

Sadly, the trio of Simon, Jen and I had been broken. We had worked really well together as a team, but the bubble had burst. I vowed to myself that when Jen eventually found it time to move on, then so would I. We employed Andy Moates as an assistant manager and he was fine, and did as good a job as Simon, but it was never the same. I am pleased that life has turned out well for Andy with a successful career.

It was quite difficult sleeping in, which may be one reason for having a drink or two when on a late shift, which is to try to help you get to sleep. But often you would hear footsteps in the car park late at night or early in the morning. Most guests went to bed at a normal time, and you could guess if particular residents might be out late. If you got up to have a look, it meant turning the light on, by which time any miscreants would have vanished, so you would get dressed and go outside to find nothing amiss. If I shut the bedroom door, I could not hear the phone or any possible goings-on. If I left it open, the fridge motors in the kitchen kept me awake.

One morning I awoke to find that we had been burgled. Between the bedroom and kitchen there was a corridor leading to the back door. It contained a fridge and a freezer, a washing machine and dryer, with the dry stores off to one side, and our bathroom to the other. Above the washing machine and dryer, which were stacked one on top of the other, was a small slit type window. Someone, god knows how, had climbed through this narrow window, and proceeded to do whatever without waking me, or if they did wake me, they were long gone before I was up. That was embarrassing. I can't remember what they took, but I don't think it was anything valuable.

One time, some youths were messing around in Maxton Lodge's car park, so I went over to get rid of them. As the grounds were built on a slope there was a four foot wall in part of the car park, with a pedestrian area above, and I'm pleased to say that one of these lads fell over backwards off this wall when I was squaring up to him.

Jen reminded me of one occasion when she was sleeping in. She found a homeless person rummaging through the bins outside, so she took pity on him and made him a sandwich! We also lost our public phone box, which stood just outside the hotel office. Someone had grabbed the whole lot and pulled it off the wall and walked off with it.

We delivered milk, bread, and newspapers to the apartments in the morning, into numbered pigeonholes, but gradually items started to disappear. The culprit had to be a person living locally due to the frequency. Then one day I caught a local woman stealing a pint of milk from one of the lockers in the foyer, and that put a stop to our burglaries. Jen reminded me of one incident which she witnessed one night she slept over. There were two rattan style easy chairs/loungers and a small table in the foyer of Maxton Lodge, and someone stole them one night.

Another night Andy called me at home at about 1.30 am to say that he had called the police, as there were youths in the garden. He wanted me to come over, which was fair enough. I had been drinking, but I thought hey ho, this is legit, I'm on a case, so I can drink and drive. And break the speed limit! So off I hurried at full pace to the Red House. No sooner was I there than the police asked Andy to go with them to locate the offenders. So off Andy went in the police car patrolling around. They were not found.

There were some beautiful women at that hotel, either in the indoor or outdoor pool, either residents or club members, so time permitting, whenever there was 'totty' in the pool, you went to test the water, and by that I mean chemically checking the chlorine levels etc, not testing the women out! I would certainly test it when Rachel was doing her swimming lessons, and make sure I talked to her. All us male management were the same. I expect the female staff did the same when a male hulk went swimming.

Every January, Torquay held the Gift Fair. Our main regulars were a card company called Hunky Dory Designs, who I will always remember. They were all very pleasant. They exhibited their greetings cards in the Riviera Centre. I mention them not only because of their memorable name, but because of the faff we went through at the Belgrave Hotel, to be documented in a later chapter.

Our double fryer sprung a small leak, so it was inspected by our contractors, who found nothing wrong. This irritated me, because I knew it leaked, and not long after we re-installed it, sure enough there was a fire inside the unit near the gas burners, which we put out without much effort. I was furious with the contractors and stormed off to their showroom in Torquay and gave them a mouthful in public. I think they were taken aback. These various commercial catering suppliers and contractors always go from good to bad and vice versa over the decades, but since then I have tried my utmost not to have to deal with this particular company, even though I would regularly see the directors at functions in other hotels.

Eventually the inevitable happened. Jen's boyfriend was going to move back to Shropshire, which meant she would have to hand in her notice. When she told me, I was devastated, and I burst into tears once she had left the office. I could not contemplate life at the hotel without her.

We employed Amanda as junior assistant manager to replace Jen, who I think worked the afternoon shift anyway by that time, Mandine having long left, and I set about planning my resignation. Tim, the eldest of the Hassells' sons, was also around in the university holidays and he came in one day and asked if I or my father knew so-and-so, to which I replied 'Yes', and it turns out this person was Tim's godfather, and was an old naval colleague of my Dad's. Small world! This made it harder for me to plan my resignation, since we now had a mutual family contact. The Hassells were such nice employers that I felt it hard to do; besides, I knew I would get upset when the moment came. I could never force myself to do it or find the right opportunity or moment, so in the end it took me a year to resign!

We still operated manually, although we had, believe it or not, bought a calculator. I wanted a computer, but they would not buy one. I was getting stale and there was nothing further I could achieve at the Red House. And Jen had gone. So eventually it happened. I resigned, very emotionally, trying to hold back the tears whilst apologising for having to do this. Coincidentally Tim their son, had finished university, so I trained him to take over the reins. Eventually the Hassells proposed to me that instead of me resigning, they make me redundant, to which I agreed. They did not want to employ another manager (not surprised after me!), so if Tim did not want to run the hotel, they would sell it. That was a nice thing to say about me, which also meant that I could sign on the dole. And so ended nine very enjoyable years, and I would like to think I did a good job there. As it happened, Tim and Richard became directors and ran the Red House with their respective partners for a while, before selling it and moving to the Ilsington Hotel on Dartmoor, enjoying a solid successful career path and raising the standards of that hotel to become the success it is today.

The Hassells took me for lunch with champagne at the five-star Imperial Hotel and gave me a bonus of £5000, which in 1996 was very well received thank you, as well as my redundancy pay. They also presented me with a crystal fruit bowl, which I accidentally smashed years later. After lunch, I had to rush to the Job Centre for my signing-on appointment; there's not many people who go to the Job Centre wearing a suit, having just drunk champagne and lunched at a five-star hotel!

CHAPTER 10

Coaching hotels

So that was that. I had enjoyed a solid period of employment and put myself on the map as a hotel manager. I planned to enjoy some time off, which was great. No need to get up early, nothing to do, no commitments except drinking in the Saxon Bar. I still had my lodgers, most of whom were my friends anyway, all singly at some point, being Jeff, Rupert, Jane and Helen, along with a few short-term strangers.

One was a chap in his mid-thirties who was a tennis coach I think, and went off to Exeter at weekends to be with his girlfriend. His rent was paid direct by the council, but they eventually found out about his weekend trips, so they demanded the rent back from me. The lodger refused to pay, so I threw him out. Another was a young lady who had been deposited by her ex-boyfriend who had paid the deposit, but in terms of possessions she only had a few plastic carrier bags with stuff in. She was nice enough, and Jeff was also a lodger in my box room. It transpired that she did not even have her own toothbrush, but was using either mine or Jeff's or both, along with helping herself to our individual milk and food supplies from the fridge. She was about to be employed as a croupier at the local casino, but they turned her down, so she told me, due to a previous criminal record. It got so bad, and I believe the rent payment became a bit erratic, that I threw her out.

Another young lady was nice enough, but it transpired that her boyfriend was sleeping there every night. I didn't mind the odd night, but this was taking the piss. I would come home in the evening to find them watching TV in my lounge, so I would feel the odd one out! Invariably I went out to the pub. This couldn't go on. One afternoon they were both sitting in my lounge when she admitted that she had lost her front door key. I said I would get another one cut or change the locks and charge her. Then it dawned on me – how did they get in then? He was a mobile locksmith and told me he had broken in. He said he could break into any modern door without causing damage, which was a bit unnerving! I couldn't see any damage on the door or frame. My mind was racing and I didn't know what to think. He told me he had a spare lock in his van and could fit it, so I thought OK, fair enough, so he fitted it. No harm done, in a way. Then he asked me for £30 as payment. Incredible! I was so gobsmacked that I paid him, and a few days later I gave her notice. So that was the last stranger I took as a lodger over the years.

I caught up with DIY and the garden, and spent Christmas with my parents and generally chilled out. After a while, the novelty wore off and I got bored, so I volunteered with Rowcroft Hospice. I worked one day a week at the shop in St. Marychurch, which was amazing as the storage area in the basement was massive with tons of glassware, china, clothes, etc. Bags and bags of it came in each day, and all had to be sorted and checked. If damaged, it was thrown out. Clothes were washed and ironed. It amazed me how some people, buying something for a couple of quid, would still barter for 50p off. I had no time for these people. I would also work once a week on the transport as a 'helper', bringing in day patients and taking them home later, or even bringing in a new resident, which could be someone leaving their own home for the last time. This could be quite upsetting for the person concerned, which rubbed off on me a bit.

I also worked once a week, or more if required, on the hospice reception, answering the phone and dealing with visitors. This again could be quite upsetting at times but I had to keep a straight face. I won't delve into their procedures because that would not be fair to current occupants, but it was quite a humbling experience. I enjoyed it all and would have liked to have worked at Rowcroft full-time.

I went for a few interviews to no avail, including one at the Grosvenor Hotel in Torquay. This was owned by Dilip Patel, a Ugandan Indian, who it transpired had changed his name to Patel to facilitate his immigration. He was well spoken, spoke seven languages, was at ease with himself, and seemed a nice chap. He was looking for a deputy manager. The bar or lounge was plush, with ample sofas and deep cushions all over, with Indian-style decorative items strewn around the room, just the sort of place where you could sit down and fall asleep for the afternoon. There was a function room or two, and two restaurants, one of which, called Mima's, after his wife, was leased out and run by Chris Edwards, a well-known Torquay chef. My pay was £13,000 per annum which was dire I know, but I needed a job! So I took it. What a relief, out of work for probably ten months now, and now back in it.

He asked me to come over to talk about something before my start date, so I obliged, and we went off in his car. He wanted me to run another hotel of his as manager but wanted me to accept before seeing it. It must be bad then. But what choice did I have? I accepted. The Conway Court hotel, a coaching hotel, was on Warren Road, not the most salubrious in Torquay and known further along for its drug problems. It had a cosy bar, with the restaurant tables around the perimeter of the ballroom. The kitchen was tiny and basic, as were the bedrooms. It had one star I think. But it had superb views across the bay towards Brixham. I was the only manager. Breakfast and dinner were the highlights of the day, then the bar, along with any entertainment if booked. Was this a cowboy outfit or what? It was incredible, so bad that you just had to laugh.

Let's start with breakfast. The hot water boiler for tea and coffee was a manual fill electric one. This meant that if it had not been topped up at night, there wouldn't be enough hot water for breakfast. If this happened, it would take too long to heat up in the morning. There was a six-slot toast rack, but only two and a half slots worked. Patel would not pay for anything to be repaired, so doing the toast was time consuming.

Getting staff was difficult. I roped in Sarah (name changed), who had been massaging my back at the Riviera Centre, and we became friends. She was invariably late but tried to make up for it by bringing me a coffee, smiling and sweet-talking me. It did calm me down, even if I knew she didn't mean it.

If it rained, the rain leaked down the pass, so plates of food had to be positioned in a certain way. The rain ran down the back of the plate shelves, so if a stack of plates had been pushed back against the wall, the rain would dribble on them and they would all have to be washed again. Harry, the KP, cooked breakfast and was a nice chap. I had to be there as the first person on duty for breakfast because of the staffing shortage, and Patel would not employ anyone else or allow me to. One particular morning, no waiting staff turned up for breakfast! Fuck me I thought. And I have a coach load of fifty-odd guests.

With mind racing and in a panic, I waited for everyone to sit down and made an announcement. 'Good morning everyone! I've had a bit of a crisis with the staff this morning, so you will have to bear with me. I am going to put pots of tea and coffee on that table, toast on that table, and you will all be getting a full English breakfast, which I will put on that table, and you can all help yourselves. Thank you very much and have a nice day!' And with that I strode off and set to it. It was hard, especially with only 2.5 slots on the toaster, but I got through it, having to re-lay for dinner on my own.

Once the room attendants had finished, and if I knew that the coaches were out on a trip until a particular time, I could leave the hotel, locking the front door as I left. Sometimes I did this to go to the shops to get basics, but more importantly to sleep at home. The phone didn't ring much at the hotel, we didn't take many 'private' guests, so the main reception function was in allocating the rooms and preparing for the arrivals. A coach arrival often involved a welcome cup of tea, maybe cake or biscuits, but nothing was offered at this hotel. Luggage was labelled and taken upstairs by me. There was no lift. It was hard work and a relief to get everyone settled. You might come across the odd room move where someone is jealous of another person's room, so they complain to you as a matter of course.

Dinner wasn't so bad. The food was brought up from the Grosvenor hotel by Harry in the hotel van and reheated by the 'chef'. There were enough waiting staff and the barman helped with the wines and drinks. After service, breakfast was laid, then when things had died down, I let the barman go and carried on myself. This could be any time from midnight, but normally 1 am, sometimes 2 ish, sometimes 3 ish. Then I would lock the hotel and go home. And I would have to be back at 7 am for breakfast. There was no one to cover me for my days off, Patel didn't give a shit, so I worked seven days a week, doing up to 120 hours per week. I was beyond knackered. Most days I would work from 7 am until the bar shut at night.

There were a few staff from the Grosvenor who lived at the Conway Court. One was a receptionist, whilst her boyfriend was a hotel maintenance man or decorator. I think Harry lived there too. He was OK actually, and to my amazement seemed to be able to solve all sorts of issues. It was almost as if he was a supervisor working as a KP. I couldn't quite get my head round it. Almost like the KP years later at the Quayside Hotel in Brixham who, in his spare time, built computers amongst other things. These live-in staff were responsible for any night-time emergencies because there was no night porter on duty.

I had the keys to the derelict hotel next door which Patel owned, the Rock Walk hotel, which contained some really good kitchen pots and pans, so once a week I would nip in to have a nose around. Some of the bedroom radios would be turned on, despite me turning them off each time, and there were tell-tale signs of squatters like mess on the floor, the odd needle maybe, unflushed toilets and so on, but I never saw anyone. Not quite sure what I would have done! It was ironic that not one of the bedroom radios in the Conway Court worked. Music came from radio boxes, which were oblong wooden affairs normally screwed to the wall above the bed and wired centrally. You could listen to various radio stations. They were a standard feature in bedrooms at the time and can still be seen to this day in some hotels.

I gradually began to notice that the bar didn't look the same in the morning as it had the previous evening. At first I thought maybe someone had been in before me at breakfast (like who?), but after testing my theory, I realised that you could open one of the shutters from the outside by undoing the bolts and then climb over the bar to get drinks, so I presumed the live-in staff had been responsible. I reported this to Patel (he is not worthy of being called Mr) who admitted that he might have had something to do with it. Great! So what do I do about that? Liquor stock was being consumed by the owner or with his knowledge with no form of accounting for it, let alone payment. I was horrified. From then on when I closed the bar at night, I would position a pint glass on the bar top in such a position that if the shutter was moved, so would the glass, which would result in it smashing on the floor behind the bar. Yes, you've got it, I would find it smashed on the floor regularly. They couldn't be bothered to clear it up. I knew who it was mainly, and I didn't like being taken for a fool.

Not long after I had started work there, Patel had asked me to give all the live-in staff notice, which I did, saying it had come from him. He denied it, saying it was my idea. That's the kind of little shit he was. So the live-in staff took it out on me, mainly the maintenance man who wasn't blessed with much intelligence. He glared at me, called me names, gave me the finger and generally made my life hell. It was that bad that I drove at him once in the street as if to run him over, and if I had done, I would only have felt sorry for his girlfriend the receptionist, who I suspect, was under his influence to a certain degree.

After about six weeks of this nightmare, the hotel closed for December and I moved down to the Grosvenor to work. What a relief!

There didn't seem to be any management team at the Grosvenor, just Andy who was the sales manager. Being December, there were all the Christmas parties. Ah, back to a normal hotel, thank the Lord! On my first evening as duty manager, I 'zedded' the bar till, meaning you read it at night, first doing an 'x', then a 'z', which is normal procedure. I got a bollocking in the morning from Patel for doing this. What! We never ever read the tills. OK, you are the boss I thought. Over the next few weeks I realised why. During the evening, Patel would come behind the function bar, open the till drawer and take out all the notes. It wasn't as if he was doing a cash 'drop', whereby the management for security reasons take most of the notes out, and after counting them, put them in the safe. No, Patel was off to the casino. This meant the tills could never be balanced, and they were open to abuse by the staff. Any member of staff could have nicked a few tenners, and it could only be proved by CCTV, if it worked.

Andy managed to twist his ankle so badly that for a month he couldn't walk well enough to help with waiting. This really pissed me off because at some functions, it was just us two serving. There was a dinner for about twenty people on a large oval table, with just me waiting on. Normally that would require two staff. I thought I could handle it; I was doing my best and running around like a blue-arsed fly and getting wound up. It came to the dessert, which involved plating it in the restaurant. I picked it up in the kitchen, then let go of it so that it clattered back down onto the worktop, not caring if it was ruined and shouted 'I'm fucked if I'm taking that out on my own!' With that a startled chef came out to help, so I calmed down.

One day Patel asked me if I would like to go to Bristol to collect his Rolls Royce, possibly a Wraith, so I jumped at the chance. On the day, I took a train to Bristol railway station and was met by the person who had been borrowing it.

'There you go. It's that one over there,' he said, as he handed me the keys, and walked off. 'Whoooaa, wait a minute!' I replied, 'I've never driven an automatic, let alone a Roller! You'll have to show me how it works.' So he gave me the quick run through. And so, very nervously, I drove off, back down the M5 to Torquay.

It was a nice car though, even though it smelled of mould and cigarettes, and was a bit tatty inside. I stopped at the services to get more fuel, only to be really embarrassed at not being able to open the filler cap, so I had to look in the manual, all the while delaying the cars behind me. Further down the M5, it was getting dark, so I put the headlights on, but I started to be flashed by approaching cars. I was on full beam and did not know how to change it, nor could I stop. When back home I realised that you dip the lights by pressing a button with your left foot. How was I to know?

Being the evening, I drove it home and parked it on my driveway and took it to the hotel the next morning. Patel was very pleased to have it back and arranged for me to drive him and his cronies to lunch. His four business pals piled in and I got in the driver's seat, all set. The car didn't really move forward – I only managed a yard – and an approaching driver shook his head at me, as if to imply don't be an idiot! I got out to see if maybe there was a puncture, but the whole body of the car was almost touching the ground, as if there was no suspension. 'This doesn't look right,' I said to him, so they all got out and he arranged for me to take it to be serviced at a Rolls Royce garage in mid Devon, Ashburton maybe. A few days later I drove to the garage, whereupon the mechanic told me to go away for an hour, so I wandered about. When I returned, he asked where I'd driven it from.

'Bristol,' I replied with excitement.

'My God!' he exclaimed, 'Bristol!? You're lucky to be alive!'

'Why's that?' I enquired with morbid curiosity.

'The back end's gone. If you had accelerated too fast, or gone over a bump, the car could have split in two! Have you really driven it from Bristol?'

'Yes.'

'This car is grounded. It's going nowhere.'

'Oh,' I said, 'What does that mean?'

'This car's staying with me.'

'Oh, I will ask my boss to phone you. Shall I just go then?'

'Yes,' was his final word to me so I slunk off, not knowing what to do. What really pissed me off was that on my supposed return journey to Torquay, I had planned to put this roller through its paces. So far I had driven quite carefully, but I was getting the hang of it, so I wanted to let rip. It was also a damp winter's day and I had to find public transport back to Torquay, so I wasn't best pleased. The only consolation was that it was going to cost Patel some money, and he was going to be deprived of his pet toy. I think it actually cost him about £5000 in the end.

The Conway Court was planned to be closed over Christmas, but at the last minute he took a coach party, which annoyed me because I wasn't prepared. The waitresses would only work if they were paid cash. Normally the wages came from the Grosvenor Hotel, but Patel was renowned for his non-payment of wages; indeed if he saw (via the CCTV) a member of staff walking up the car park to the hotel, he would nip out of the back reception door and hide, so as to avoid paying the wages or other imminent confrontation. He was such a coward. Sometimes he would just give someone a bundle of notes from his pocket as payment. A very dubious system. Some staff became upset quite rightly about not being paid on time.

Normally every day or so I would take the cash takings from the Conway down to the Grosvenor, but over Christmas I didn't, so as to be able to pay the staff. I even used some of my own money. When it was all over, I presented Patel with an account of the bar takings, my own money used, and wages paid to the staff, and all he could do was to accuse me of stealing! Laughable really.

On New Year's Eve it was blowing a gale, and the wind had blown in a balcony door on one of the top floor bedrooms. The door was lying in the bedroom, with the wind howling. No way could I get any maintenance people, so I drove home, got my drill and some long screws, and somehow screwed the door to the frame. Patel was not happy, accusing me of damaging the door, but so what. The evening went fine, with the entertainment in the restaurant, which was really a ballroom. Everything finished about 2 am, whereupon

I realised that there was only me left to re-lay the restaurant for breakfast, so I finished about 4 am, and had to be back at 7!

A customer at the Grosvenor had complained about their stay, but Patel had refused to budge on any compensation, so it ended up going to court. This was in Birmingham, so on the day, I drove Andy up to court and waited around inside for a few hours for our turn. The judge then decided it was lunchtime, or rather his lunchtime, so he called it a day. And we'd just driven up from Torquay! No, that was that, end of story. We hadn't talked to the 'other side' but we decided to go and have lunch together, so we went to a pub, and came to an agreement which we all thought was fair. In our opinion the customer was actually in the right. We phoned Patel to tell him what we had done, but he was having none of it, so we had to scrap that!

Although I had already bought some petrol for my car to cover the fuel cost, I decided to nip into the Exeter services and get another tenner's worth. At the M5 roundabout, I couldn't decide which exit to take to the services, so on a whim I yanked the car to the left to change lanes, but side swiped another car. We both pulled over onto the grass verge, as did a witness, and it was totally my fault. The old lady I had hit was quite shaken up. I was furious with myself, because to save a tenner I had actually cost myself a lot more!

Patel did employ a part-time assistant manager for me, probably for Christmas, which was a help and a relief, but as far as I was concerned, the damage had been done. I did not particularly like working for someone who had a total disregard for accounting procedures, for paying wages or for the welfare of the staff, I had a major personality clash with the young decorator living at the Conway, and Patel accused me of stealing from him! I therefore resigned, so as to finish before the hotel reopened for the summer season, and was glad to have left. The Conway Court was such a dive as to be unreal. Both it and the derelict one next door have since been demolished and rebuilt as residential apartments. Patel's wife Mimi was charming and their school age son was also quite normal, so after they had to sell the hotels for financial reasons some time later, I have no idea what happened to them, because they lived in an extremely well-appointed flat inside the Grosvenor hotel. Patel died of cancer some years later. I don't feel sorry for him because he was an outright liar.

I had a few interviews, some for jobs outside Torbay, and even overseas. I even thought about emigrating to Australia, which after the checks, I would have qualified for. A coaching company called Alfa Leisureplex, with its head office at their Torquay hotel, the Regina, interviewed me. The company had maybe a dozen coastal hotels around Wales, the South West, South East, and possibly East Anglia. My preliminary interview was held at the Regina by the area manager then, a few days later, he drove me to Falmouth to look at the hotel. The Madeira Hotel was on the seafront, close to the harbour, and had some history. Its ballroom, used for entertainment, used to be a cinema, with the bar at the far end being the former ticket office, and the fire escape being the original entrance. It was fascinating. This being March (1998), the hotel was still closed, so we stayed at another hotel down the road. Falmouth seemed a nice seaside town, with its famous deep natural harbour, palm trees, and that Mediterranean feeling.

Before I moved down to work, I drove down for the day to meet the management, sort out rotas, and any other nitty gritty. The hotel was still closed, and the three of us were having coffee in the lounge overlooking the sea when a man came into the hotel wielding a baseball bat.

'I'm going to kill you!' he shouted to us, 'You've ruined my life!'

I looked at the others in alarm, hoping they would reply, or at least know who this was. Fortunately, they did know him, and managed to calm him down a bit, enough for him to leave without causing damage. It turned out he was a night porter, laid off for the winter. I thought to myself my God, is this what the people in Falmouth are like?

The management consisted of two sisters, one as head receptionist, and the younger one as a part time receptionist, both acting as duty managers. There was a ground floor flat for me at the back of the hotel. Later I drove home, which in those days took over two hours, without dual carriageways.

And so I moved down. My lodger could feed my cat, but I would miss my friends in Torquay.

The area manager came down for my first evening to settle me in, and I was due to start the following morning. We again went out for a meal, followed by a walk, then back to the hotel. I let the barman go about 10.30 pm, presumably to save wages, or maybe to make a good impression, so I had started work, even though I had no idea how to use the till, lock up etc. The area manager was amazed. I think his name was Trevor. That all went fine.

My flat did not have any heating or hot water, so I had to have a cold shower. Being a weekend, it was a few days before this was fixed by the maintenance team, and by this time I was not feeling well and never really recovered. Being a coaching hotel, every penny had to be accounted for. Every meal was costed out, for instance how many slices of bread, how many tomatoes (tinned). Incidentally I have never seen before or since a chef heating drained tinned tomatoes in a deep fat fryer. I still can't quite understand how or why he did it that way. Everything was costed according to the number of guests, so as to bring about a food cost per person of say 0.85p. (I've just picked that figure out of the air – I'm hopeless at remembering figures.) Same for dinner. These figures had to be sent daily to the Regina, along with their other hotels, and as the menus were identical in all their hotels, the costs should be the same. If there was a variance, you had to answer for it. Linen stocktaking had to be done daily, and presumably the same for liquor.

After a week, I went home and brought my cat down along with my bicycle. There was a cat flap in the flat, so that was OK. The head receptionist was very good at her job, but I found her sister to be annoying, so I diplomatically tried to do something about it, which didn't go down well with her sister! So, in a way, that was a bad move. I think they felt I was interfering.

My health still wasn't good and my social life was zero, with the only highlights being able to get an Indian or Chinese takeaway on an evening off, and 'living in' was depressing me. I only ever drank in a pub on my own. So things were not good. I would hardly ever go around to see the entertainment in the ballroom, and never go to the bar there, until a guest reported the barman smoking behind the bar. That was bad management from me I thought, I was losing my grip, if ever I had one. There was no CCTV, so without watching him constantly, there was no way of stopping him. I also sacked the housekeeper for some reason, and temporarily took the job on myself, which was a nightmare, having to count the linen as well as organise the department and even clean some rooms. After interviewing for the position, I took on a woman who had never been a room attendant but had been a council toilet cleaner. This was a random choice because I thought she would have the right character for the job. This was a bad mistake!

As the weeks went on, I felt worse and worse, not just health wise, but as a manager. You know when the staff like you or respect you. You might say that you are not there to be liked, but to ensure the job is done. That's fair enough. But you also know when the management do not treat you as a team member. Something wasn't right and things weren't gelling.

One day Trevor came down unexpectedly, took me into a room and asked me why I had done this and that, why hadn't I done that and so on, then sacked me on the spot. I went red with embarrassment and said I would leave at once. I'd had a feeling a few days prior that something was up, and maybe they had interviewed a new manager on my days off, when I would have been back in Torquay. So I packed as much as possible into my car, said goodbye to the receptionist, and left without a second glance behind. Good riddance! I was actually quite upset that I had been a failure and tried to assess my shortcomings. I had the awkwardness of having to return to collect my last things, which was embarrassing. I think I apologised to the receptionist.

So, unemployed again, but my cat was happy to be back home! Back to the job hunting. Quite soon, I was interviewed by Carol Smith, the joint proprietor with her ex-husband of Torquay Holiday Hotels, comprising the Burlington, the Richmond and the Roselands. Carol was a tall, elegant lady, very much in charge, very switched on, and quite intelligent, with a sense of humour. They were looking for a general manager for the Roselands. I was quite excited about the prospect of working there, because it was just along from the Conway Court, and walking past I had always felt the poorer cousin whilst employed at the Conway, and had dreamt of working at the Roselands, with its cream-coloured exterior and pinkish décor inside. It looked an inviting hotel.

Carol employed me as general manager and so I started. I was greeted by a tall, blonde and very good looking assistant manager, dressed smartly in the tiniest of miniskirts. Wow! She beamed at me, welcomed me, and showed me around, with those amazing legs striding out. I think she was called Jules. Like all the hotels on Warren Road, they worked in reverse, so you went down to the kitchens, restaurant and other public rooms. Departments were properly manned and all looked to be in order. I couldn't see much that needed immediate improvement; the bedrooms were functional, albeit a bit tacky with cheap furniture. The reception area was tiny, being a small area near the front door. Our office was what had once been a long broom cupboard, long and thin, with a fantastic view down the cliff to the sea front. You could not pass behind the chairs if someone was sitting at the desk, it was that narrow. We typed the daily menus, did rotas, wages, HR and the usual office things. We checked bedrooms daily, helped in the restaurant, it was relatively easy, and the customers and staff were all happy.

The coach bookings were all organised by Carol, based at the Burlington hotel, who seemed to work endlessly, and she would allocate the guests to hotels. Likewise 'privates' were allocated by her. She could be irritating though and move a coach or private around from one hotel to another at a moment's notice. She was very astute, often undercutting other hotels, I found out years later, making her not so popular amongst her competitors. But it was bums on beds. Coach bookings were given tea and biscuits on arrival, in which time the luggage was taken to the rooms by the management and maybe a porter, followed by a speech to the group welcoming them, introducing the team, explaining meal times, a bit about Torquay and so on. We had it sussed to a tee. Similarly on a coach departure, once we had collected the luggage from upstairs and given it to the driver to load onto the coach, I would go on the coach and speak to the guests using the microphone, wishing them a good journey, and hope they had enjoyed themselves, see you again etc, all the usual bullshit. Often they clapped, which was much appreciated.

Carol bought a fourth hotel, the Water's Edge, run by a manager called Neil I think, who in my opinion was a complete idiot. Anne, the general manager at the Richmond just round the corner from the Roselands, was lovely, and Carol herself was the general manager I believe at the Burlington. I took a great dislike to Neil. We interviewed staff who applied for a job whether we needed them or not, but if any good, we would recommend them to one of the other hotels in case they had a staff vacancy. We needed a waitress, so Neil sent over one he had interviewed. Great, thanks. This soon turned out to be a mistake. The waitresses left their bags and coats in an area open to all staff, and money started to go missing from their handbags or purses when the new waitress was working. She denied any knowledge, and it got to the stage where the waitresses were about to refuse to work with her. Then, one day she came to work with a short-sleeved blouse, complete with visible needle marks inside her elbow. *We've got a junkie,* we all thought. We looked at each other aghast. Was this for real? I thought, well that's it, I will have to get rid of her. After service I went up to the reception to talk to the receptionist about this new discovery, whereupon Jules' boyfriend, who was waiting to collect her, piped up.

'Did you say Karen Thompson?' he enquired. (I've changed the names.)

'Yes, that's right,' I replied.

'That's not her real name, its Laura Spencer,' he said.

'Oh, how do you know that?' I enquired, rather bewildered.

'She's well known to us,' he said, and continued to describe her appearance and characteristics. He worked in the police, so I had reason to believe him. 'You don't want her here,' he said.

I wrote Karen's real name down excitedly. This was a new situation for me, how exciting. A bit of drama about to unfold! I asked Jules and her boyfriend to wait five minutes whilst I dealt with the situation, in case I needed backup, then went back down to the restaurant and asked to have a private word with 'Karen'.

'How do you feel things are going for you here?' I offered as a sort of warm up to the main event.

'Ok,' she replied.

'I've had reports of money going missing from staff handbags. Do you know anything about that?' I continued. We had already had this conversation but it was adding to my attack.

'No,' she replied.

'I've also been told that your real name is Laura Spencer.'

'No,' she replied, in a slightly higher-pitched voice.

'Why are you using another name?' I continued.

'I'm not,' she replied, but she was squirming and clearly feeling under pressure.

'Well I don't care, this isn't going to work out. You are still on trial, so your employment has ended as of now,' I stated with finality.

She left without much comment, never to be seen again, much to the relief of all. Thank you, Neil, for that one. I had my revenge on him a few weeks later. He came to collect a small safe, which almost fitted in the boot of his car, but not quite. He slammed the boot down to make the boot lock catch, but to my intense amusement, the edge of the safe smashed his boot window, which fell in pieces into his car and onto the road. He drove off in a temper. One up to me!

I can remember early on Jules sitting close to me in the office, on a training session.

'I'll do anything for you Geoff, absolutely anything!' she exclaimed.

'Anything?' I said with glee, trying not to look down at those gorgeous bare legs.

'Not that!' she retorted with finality, and we both laughed. End of discussion, sadly.

The only other member of staff I can remember is Janet, who lived in an apartment further along the road and was either the head receptionist or assistant manager, once Jules had left to work elsewhere, due to her boyfriend being posted out of the area.

Brian was employed as an assistant manager at the Richmond. He had been an entertainment manager at holiday parks, and certainly had his strengths, but also his weaknesses. He was a lovely chap, a bit effeminate, and always swept into a room with a flurry, immediately commanding attention. He would answer a question before you had finished asking it, with a verbal tirade as to why you should or shouldn't do something, with a slight Scottish accent. Wherever he went, he ruled the roost, mainly because he persuaded the world around him that his view was the way forward, and even if someone could get a word in edgeways, it would be dismissed. He did however take on all the Christmas decorations for each hotel, putting them up himself which was a true blessing, and then came the management pantomime, which he instigated. The *what?* Yes, the management Christmas pantomime. Oh my God! I was to be Looby Lou, Brian was Teddy and Carol played Andy or something like that. Just the three of us. My costume, which Brian produced, was a skirt or frock, high heels, and a blonde ponytail wig, along with red lipstick. Our lines weren't too bad; it was a manageable effort only about fifteen minutes long, and some of my lines were quite amorous to Carol, which amused us, so after dinner on Christmas Eve we performed to the Roselands Hotel. Then, to my horror, Brian gathered the three of us up to perform at the Richmond. That meant walking out in the open along the street in drag. I couldn't do that. What would people think? I was so embarrassed, but we walked the ten minutes to the Richmond and performed again. Thankfully Anne gave me a pint afterwards!

One afternoon, Neil asked me if I could pop into the Water's Edge 'for five minutes' to cover because he had to go somewhere. Sure, no problem. On arrival (I had never set foot in the hotel before), he left saying he wouldn't be long, telling me as he walked out of the door that a coach was arriving, but not to worry he would be back to see to it. Yes, you've guessed it, the coach arrived, but Neil didn't. I had to sort the luggage, and I seem to remember that the room numbers were illogically numbered, so had no idea where to find the rooms. Then I had to do the speech; I couldn't tell them the dinner or breakfast times, or much else about the hotel, so I just welcomed them as best I could. I was fuming with Neil, who eventually returned maybe an hour later. He was a marked man from then on.

The Roselands had all the problems that Victorian era buildings have. Water leaks were never ending, either from a blocked flat roof where leaves had blocked a drain, or more commonly from a bathroom above. This can be due to people showering without using the shower curtain or screen effectively (most common), overflowing the bath through large people getting in or couples having sex in it (not so common) – broken waste seals on toilets (quite common), same reason as per baths, except large people don't get in toilets! – but their weight can move the bowl slightly, sometimes burst mains (very rare), so normally the water, always a stained colour, leaks below for maybe twenty minutes before stopping. Often they leak down through the ceiling light. But you become blasé about it over the years, just putting a wine bucket under the drip, sometimes two or three depending on the locations of the drips and leaving it to sort itself out. And you have to ring the bedrooms above to see if they have had a shower or left a tap on. Usually you get an inkling of who the culprit is, or from which room the leak has sprung. Hopefully any leaks are just onto the carpet or flat surface. If onto a bed or customers belongings, then you have to deal with it. If it continues beyond the twenty-minute stage, then you know it's something more serious. I've regularly repaired broken toilet flush handles with a wire coat hanger, which you cut and bend and fix in the cistern. Metal coat hangers are also useful implements for extracting corks from bottles when the cork has been pushed into the bottle. Bend the coat hanger into two, insert the looped end into the wine bottle, catch the end of the cork and pull. This doesn't mean the wine is corked, it just means that the cork (and coat hanger) has temporarily entered the wine.

Then there were the bedrooms. One at the Roselands was superior, having its own private entrance at the side of the hotel with a jacuzzi bath and sea views. But you had the best rooms, good ones, average ones, and poor ones. Coach drivers always went into the worst single rooms. Some rooms were 'zip and link' meaning they could be either a double or a twin. Internal coding for the room attendants in some hotels used (..) to denote a double or (xx) to denote a twin. If the guests arrived, but the room was made incorrectly, ie they wanted a twin but it had been set up as a double, then you could either move them to a similar standard twin or upgrade to a better twin. If they were nice about it, you would naturally accommodate them and maybe upgrade for free. If they complained nastily, then you would not do anything to help them, except change the beds around in their original room. As far as I was concerned changing a bed from a double to twin was such a faff. Not only do you have to get clean sheets, but also single blankets or duvets. It always put me in a bad mood! Sorry, let me clarify that; if we had made the mistake then we would do our utmost to correct it, but if the customer had booked the incorrect room type, then my description above applies.

Carol decided to sell the Water's Edge hotel, so we all wondered what would happen to its staff once she sold. We were a little apprehensive. One day soon after, Carol came along unannounced with her accountant, so I knew something big was about to happen. She told me that she was having to make cuts in the staffing so would have to let me go. Oh no! My mind was racing. Why? I had done nothing wrong. It didn't make sense. Carol and I had a good working relationship.

'Well. Supposing I worked for less money?' I offered. I was only being paid a salary of £13,000 and could only just survive financially anyway, so quite how I could manage on less was beyond me, but I was testing Carol to see how she would reply.

She thought carefully for a few seconds before replying with sincerity, 'Geoffrey, that's very thoughtful of you to think of the hotel like that, but no, I can't do that.'

'Well, I'm sorry if I have underperformed in any respect,' I replied, feeling that I should say something.

'No Geoffrey, your work has been fine, I just have to make some cuts,' she stated.

So that was that. A sentence which was becoming all too frequent! I felt really let down by her, and something was not right, but I couldn't put my finger on it.

Ironically about four weeks after I had left, I made an appointment to go and see Carol at the Burlington; maybe my final pay was incorrect. I had heard previously that Neil was going to be the spare 'manager' to cover holidays and illness at the three hotels, so I asked how he was getting on at the Roselands, having replaced me as the manager. Carol had sacked him after a few weeks for getting the rotas wrong and for staffing for a coach when there wasn't one etc etc, which produced a wry smile from me. She also admitted that maybe she should have kept me on. So Neil had stitched me up to Carol!

Brian had moved to the Roselands as manager I think, so the vacancy had gone, and the moment had passed. Although jobless, I was pleased that Neil had been sacked and that Carol realised that she should have kept me on. She was to re-employ me at the Belgrave hotel a year or two later anyway. As it happened I stayed and helped her with her paperwork for several hours, as one does!

So back to the drawing board, but this time, not for long.

CHAPTER 11

The Palm Court Hotel

After a few interviews locally, it wasn't long before I was offered a suitable position. I was interviewed by Tom Hart, an elderly man dressed in a suit, and his son Nigel, who was dressed in jeans and T-shirt, which I found a bit odd and almost offensive. The Palm Court Hotel is in Abbey Crescent, which is now nothing more than a curve on the Torquay seafront road. Ten Victorian terraced houses were built originally, interconnected by a communal passageway at the rear, which faces the cliff. I believe it opened in the 1930s, and it soon became a popular four-star hotel in a prime seafront position, with the Palm Court orchestra, I believe, which recorded on the radio. Back then the hotel had 120 bedrooms with hot and cold water. That would have meant a basin in the bedroom, at best. Baths in those days were communal and at the ends of corridors.

Roll on to February 1999. The Harts had operated the hotel for twenty years, which is a good record. It boasted four bars.

The Sands Bar and Restaurant was geared for families and all-day food, and Captain Pepper's Bar was a busy bar which also provided bar snacks. The Veranda Bar was a small outside bar on the first floor overlooking the road and beach and used in the summer, and fourthly there was the Restaurant Bar, open when the restaurant was in use and again on the first floor.

The restaurant itself was unique, with dark wooden panelling, a dance floor in the middle of the room with tables and chairs around the perimeter, stained lead glass windows, and a minstrel's gallery above, which stretched around three sides of the restaurant, along with enough space for one line of restaurant tables and chairs, which looked down over the dance floor. It was remarkable. Oh boy, the potential! The Hotel had 36 en-suite bedrooms and seven self-catering holiday apartments. Captain Pepper's bar terrified me; at weekends it was often full with stag nights and hen parties, certainly manic, certainly noisy, and certainly crammed – all the things that scare me, and here I was going from a timid little oik to being in charge of it!

The first paragraph of my General Manager's job description continues: 'It becomes very busy during the summer season when the General Manager is likely to have to work long hours and withstand exceptional pressures. The post of General Manager entails both the supervision of others and personal "hands on" involvement'. Hmmm, I'm sure I can hack that. My interview was in an office and went fairly well, despite the fact that Nigel seemed more intent on playing what I assumed was a computer card game, and would chip in the occasional comment, sometimes with a wide grin. Nigel seemed relaxed, which put me at ease. Mr Hart may have owned another hotel (can't remember) which he had sold or was about to sell, but he also owned the Palm Court Nursing Home in Dawlish. He was also a senior partner in a law firm and he lived in Crediton, so visited the Hotel weekly. Nigel would be the immediate contact.

Nigel involved himself with maintenance, and matters relating to the financial side. I started in March 1999.

We had a couple of weeks to get organised before the hotel opened again, so Nigel showed me around, explaining this and that and left me to it. I had a proper office with a large enough table, a computer and a filing cabinet and shelves. My first what I would call 'private' office, mine and mine alone. The other management consisted of Emma Hammond, who was the Head Receptionist, and Hossein or 'H' as Bars Manager. That was it. Emma was really switched on and as well as being chirpy and positive, had her department sewn up. Hossein, an Iranian, was built like a brick shithouse and had played international football in the past, so he was the ideal person to run the bars. He doubled as a bouncer, as one was required at weekends. Thank God there was some muscle to look after the bars – what a relief! Our beers were delivered by Courage.

The kitchens were adequate, with a large wash-up section with a conveyor belt system that went around a corner, which impressed me. From the restaurant you could walk outside to the veranda on the first floor to the bar with its patio seating, and along the front of the hotel. You could also sit outside the main bars below on raised seating from the pavement in what I would describe as alcoves, which were very popular!

The bedrooms were rather tacky, but the apartments were adequately furnished. I remember Debbie, who looked after the housekeeping, and was charming, polite, fit and lovely. The main maintenance man, who was shaped like Humpty Dumpty, being short and chubby, was called Angel and originally from Gibraltar. I found that a bit odd and couldn't quite work out why he lived and worked in Torquay. He had worked at the Palm Court for at least a decade, having been a lift engineer in a previous life, which was to come in handy many a time. He always wore a blue boiler suit with a blue engine driver's style blue cap. The other part-time maintenance man, more of an odd job person, was called John. I employed a restaurant manager who had previously been a supervisor, so he would do, given the short time in which to find someone. The chefs seemed OK, but there was no one to shout home about. Another Debbie was a bar supervisor who was fantastic in every respect and went on to marry, years later, a man who was probably her ideal partner. Other bar staff were employed seasonally, and we normally had enough of them, being a fun place to work.

And so we opened. All the departments knew how to operate their areas, which was a blessing for me. The hotel also took coach bookings, so I dealt with these, along with the normal management functions, mainly HR, ordering, stocktaking, checking of invoices/pricing, maybe helping out in the departments, but mainly left to my own devices, which was great. Nigel would have a quiet word if he thought something was wrong or if I was maybe doing something a bit off-line, or I could even ask him. He had his own office somewhere in the hotel and drove around in his white van. I soon became envious of him; I don't know why – he was tall and only ever dressed in jeans and T-shirt. Perhaps that was it. Maybe it was because he only seemed to work Monday to Friday in the daytime. His style was very different from what I was used to, and I found it hard to accept.

Captain Peppers operated a free jukebox with a DJ at weekends, with various fruit and gaming machines scattered about. Entertainment for the coaches was held in the restaurant. The bar could get very busy, with hordes of young energetic people, and an electric atmosphere. It was really good, and most people behaved themselves, but H was at hand to sort any problems. One of us had to be on duty. We would each take a couple of hours off in the afternoons, staggered. H always worked weekends, for which I was extremely grateful. The beer cellar at the back of the hotel was reasonably large, and for the main lagers like Fosters, we used

22-gallon barrels. The gas, supplied by BOC, came in six to seven-foot tall cylinders which could only be changed by BOC. Apparently, the pressure used was far greater than the everyday cylinders. These were too large and heavy to carry, even for H, and were trundled in on a trolley. They were industrial scale, and I have never seen them before or since.

We operated a carvery on Sunday lunchtimes in the Sands Bar, for which we had a carvery unit. I think I wore my chef's whites and did the carvery. I liked doing that. As well as the passenger lift, there was a little service lift that came down behind the food service area in the Sands Bar. All the carvery meats, potatoes, and veg came down in the lift in containers; likewise dirty plates went back up. Every couple of months the lift would jam; we could be in the middle of service, so it was frantic, and any delay was a frustration to all. This happened when the chefs put two meat trays in the lift on the same shelf so that they protruded over the sides of the shelf. As the lift went down, these trays would catch on the lift framework, I presume, and jam. Fortunately, Angel, being a former lift engineer, would come in and sort it out. But it still disrupted our food service and meant that whatever was in the lift could not be offered to guests. It also meant that anything else required for the carvery had be carried downstairs manually.

We had employed a Scottish Head Chef, who appeared to know what he was doing, and was a typical chef in that he didn't take any shit. I could relate to that! We designed a new bar menu; the chef for the food, Nigel and I the design of the menu, which was to be laminated. After an eternity of dithering by the chef, the menu was agreed and printed. What seemed like the very next day, Nigel passed me this chef's resignation letter. GREAT! Not. Fucking marvellous. I stormed up to the kitchen waving this letter, and shouted to the chef, 'Well, that's marvellous isn't it! Now what!' He came over and asked to have a private word with me. What! He wants a private word! With *me?*

'Sure, let's go,' I said, at my wits' end. Unbelievably, he gave *me* a bollocking, telling me never to shout at him in public again. What! How insolent! I was gobsmacked. Through gritted teeth, I had to ask him what was going on, was it anything we had done to cause him to resign? No, he was going to be a chef in the Caribbean. Well, I couldn't blame him, that was almost fair enough. I don't think I spoke to him again, I was so incensed at being dumped in it. This left us well and truly in the shit.

The second chef wasn't by his own admission up to being the head chef, so in the short term I had to step into the kitchen and run it; the bar snack menu was adapted to take off some of the more complex items, or we just told the bar staff that we were out of stock of certain products for that day. We had to use agency chefs and eventually found a head chef who lasted the season.

My Torquay friends clubbed together to buy me my first mobile phone, which was a huge present. I thanked them all profusely, even though I hated them at the time. I mean I hated mobile phones. I refused to buy one. I felt they were an invasion of privacy.

However, after only three days of using it, I was to realise its value. Mr Hart called me to say that there had been an accident at the hotel, and could I take care of it. Sure, so left my shopping at Sainsbury's, and quickly drove to the hotel. In the kitchen, John the maintenance man was running around screaming with arms outstretched in front of him, but his hands were limp and floppy. I think an ambulance was on its way. Angel and John had been painting the external wooden frame of the kitchen skylight, accessed by the flat roof, which is a wooden and glass framed hexagonal affair, and despite being told not to lean on the wood, he had ignored this, and consequently had fallen through into the kitchen, landing on his hands, which had been smashed up. He was in that much agony he could not be helped. He just ran around the kitchen like a headless chicken, not knowing what to do with himself, screaming and groaning. He was duly carted off, and after a long recovery, gradually came back to work.

My fortieth birthday was looming, and my parents were going to take me to Venice with them for a long weekend. How nice. When my parents and I boarded a BA flight from Heathrow, the stewardess exclaimed 'Geoff!' I was ecstatic to see Sue, my dear friend from the Riviera Hotel, who was on the same flight. She made me stand in the corner near her whilst she boarded the remaining passengers, then once they were on, she took me to some seats at the front of the plane, in the opposite direction to my parents, who were beginning to wonder what the hell I was doing. Dad must have been having an apoplectic fit!

Sue upgraded all of us to the front and had to delay the flight to bring on some extra food, presumably for us, then brought us all a glass of champagne. This is nice, I thought. A good start to the holiday. Once the plane had taken off, and everything seemed in order, Sue came along and said that the captain would like a word with me. What, me? What had I done? She smiled at me, so I realised it was going to be something worthwhile. My parents were bemused at all these proceedings.

So I proceeded to the flight deck and met the captain and co-pilot. They sat me down on the spare seat in the middle and put on headphones so I could hear them. Wow! I asked them silly questions, I'm sure, but it was brilliant. Then Sue came in and said that my lunch was ready, with more champagne, and after that I went back into the cockpit. I watched them operate the autopilot, which seemed quite simple, and as we approached Italy, they began to get out some maps. I nervously commented that surely these days with modern technology, you don't need maps. It turned out that none of the crew had ever flown to Venice before, which I found hard

to believe, and the homing beacon (or whatever it is called) from
Venice airport was out of order, so they were flying visually. 'Yes,
there's the railway line and the bridge over there,' they would say
at regular intervals, and so on, as they came to new landmarks and
checked them against the map. I was amazed. I kept quiet because
they were flying 'properly' in my opinion but watched them with
great excitement. They found the airport, we landed and taxied,
and parked. I carried on talking to them, and vice versa. After some
time, I suggested that maybe I should go, so they agreed, and shook
hands with me, and I thanked them.

Sue was waiting at the top of the steps for me, with a plastic bag
containing eight quarter bottles of Champagne as a present, (against
BA regs) so we embraced as I thanked her, and had a quick chat.
When I looked out of the plane, all the passengers were waiting in
the coaches, with my parents on the tarmac waiting for me. I felt
like a star, holding the whole plane up! Sheepishly, I went down the
steps, met my parents, who by now were getting a bit impatient,
and joined a coach. We enjoyed the holiday, despite the smell of the
canals, and I was convinced that my parents had arranged for Sue to
be present on the flight etc etc, but no, it was just pure coincidence,
and a very enjoyable one!

There's so much to write about my time at the Palm Court that
I don't know where to begin. The staff were great. Some of them
were friends of mine anyway before they started as bar staff, and
some became and remained friends afterwards. The summer was
busy and all a bit of a blur. I guess that because there was an outside
seating area off the pavement, we felt responsible for the pavement
and road; it almost felt as if we should charge a toll for cars using
'our' road. Indeed, if there was a car accident or an injury from the
nearby beach, they all came to us as the first point of call, which was
fair enough, and we would provide appropriate assistance.

At one end of the Palm Court, the last ground floor section of the hotel was rented out to a man who operated a very successful bucket and spade shop, selling all the usual paraphernalia for seaside tourists. I think there was also the Oasis café which, if it was rented out, didn't last long. The other end of the Palm Court housed some fish and chip shops. Two were in a separate building, whilst one was attached to the hotel and leased out. Further down in the direction of the harbour was the old council toilet block, built in stone back in the 1840s as a toll house. It became a gardener's cottage, then the Beach Manager's office before it became a toilet block.

The solar eclipse in August 1999 was approaching, and we didn't quite know what to expect. It was a normal morning, breakfast just about finishing for the residents, and the bar staff arriving early just in case, but slowly people began to gather on the seafront and the wide area of pavement opposite the hotel became jammed with parked motorbikes, hundreds of them. Shit, I thought, this is going to be big. I decided on the spur of the moment to sell a carvery-style breakfast, so I got the chefs to start cooking everything up, much to their irritation. I put my chef's whites on, got H to open up the bar, someone made a sign and so we sold a full English Breakfast with tea or coffee for a set amount – £5? £6? £10? I can't remember, but they were flying out. The barmaid poured the tea or coffee into mugs and took the money whilst I plated the breakfast. We didn't mess about with fancies like scrambled egg or vegetarian sausages. Full English; sausage, bacon, beans, hash brown, tomato, fried egg, black pudding, mushroom. Just take it or leave it. No discount if you didn't like black pudding, for example. It was a good move, and I was so glad I did this.

Gradually it became darker, slowly at first, then complete whilst everything became somehow quieter, people, seagulls, traffic, and a sense of calm descended on us all outside as the event took place. It was magnificent to see. And afterwards, people stayed around for hours. It was a major event.

The council, in their wisdom, decided to build a brand new 'bucket and spade' shop with public toilets across the road on the wide section of pavement, which was a safer place I have to admit because it meant that people did not have to cross the busy road to get to the existing shop and block of toilets. This new shop was operated by a new businessman, and it devastated the existing trade across the road. We were all annoyed at this new construction. It slightly blocked our view, and was more of an inconvenience. It made the old toilet block effectively redundant, and an application to turn it into a water bottling plant was granted, to my amazement. The building had that typical revolting council-operated toilet smell, at least the men's area did, but in due course the building was all cleaned and kitted out as a water bottling plant, complete with all the appropriate testing equipment. It looked impressive, like a laboratory, clinically clean, but in the most bizarre of locations.

I was aghast to hear that this so called 'Riviera Water' was using a spring in the cliff above as the water source. Not that I knew or had ever seen a spring above. What they did not know was that one of the Roselands Hotel's sewerage drainage pipes had a small leak down the cliff, yes directly above the new bottling plant room! I never tried the water, nor did I offer to sell it at the hotel, even though it was fairly popular for a year or so in catering outlets, until either the source ran dry or the income ran dry, or the sewerage leak had been fixed!

One week, perhaps in preparation for the solar eclipse, but more likely for the Young Farmers' convention, two Courage lorries arrived to deliver our beer. Usually your delivery is part of one lorry stopping at various pubs or hotels, but this time we had two. A lorry and a half arrived just for us, and the beer barrels were stacked three high in the cellar! I don't blame the Young Farmers for being a nightmare when they are on a bender. They work hard, so they play hard. Supermarkets drive down the price we should pay for farm produce, so I have every sympathy for farmers. Probably something to do with me being brought up in Shropshire. And they have a central fund to pay for damages, which is fair play. Obviously you don't want damage, but wherever they go, they spend a fortune. Do you take them or don't you? Always a quandary. 'Nice' hotels and B&Bs generally refuse to accommodate single sex parties, whether Young Farmers, stag nights, hen dos or just plain single sex groups. If you have elderly residents or families staying, they do not want to be upset by what they would regard as appalling behaviour, whether it be bad language, pissing in the street, having sex in public, being drunk or near comatose, banging on bedroom doors, shouting, screaming, and all manner of animalistic noises and actions, not forgetting fighting, which goes hand in hand with alcohol, whether boy or girl. You get a bit bored with it when you see it going on all the time.

Talking of alcohol, H and I began to find part-drunk half bottles of whisky, the flat sort of bottle and a brand we didn't sell. I would find them tucked away behind a speaker on a shelf in the corner, or random hidden places where no one ever looked, or an empty one in the main bins – not hidden away in a bin liner as part of something else, but on its own, which was a giveaway. By a process of elimination and checking the whisky levels of these bottles, I was sure it was one of the night porters. I had been discreetly told a few times by residents that one of the night porters had been asleep on the sofa, which is not part of their job description! I think they said he smelled of whisky. I decided one night to go into the hotel and see what was going on, so I set my alarm for 3 am, got dressed and drove to the hotel, parking along the street so as to be more covert.

Whilst walking up to the hotel, I noticed with annoyance that a couple had just got back from town, so they would have 'woken' the night porter. Irritated beyond words, I drove back home to plan another night's mission.

Second time lucky. The front door of the hotel was locked at night, so I naturally had a key, and the night porter can admit any late guests. So I unlocked the door at about 4 am, crept into the lounge, saw the night porter asleep on the sofa, and sat down in a chair opposite him. Not a murmur. Fast asleep. I sat there waiting for him to wake up and after ten minutes, before I fell asleep myself, I kicked the sofa. He woke up with a start, muttered something, and rushed off to the bin area. I was a bit slow to grasp what he was doing but I caught up with him to see what he had just put in the bin. I really wanted to catch him holding his bottle. Sure enough, an empty whisky bottle, on top of everything else. Even though I could not prove that he had just put it in the bin, or indeed that he had been drinking from it, I had it out with him there and then. He denied it, but I fired him on the spot. He didn't seem to object and went to get his coat, then turned around and asked me if I minded if he stayed until the morning because otherwise his wife would go mad! Fair enough, so I sat behind the reception desk until the receptionist arrived at 7.30 am, and he sat in the public area, while we had the odd chat. After he had gone, I explained to the receptionist and went home to sleep.

The hotel had quite a few safes, too many in my opinion. One was used by the bucket and spade shop, one was maybe used by the fish and chip shop, one was used maybe by Nigel and Mr Hart, and there was a floor safe for the bar takings. We frequently performed cash 'drops', meaning you would take out all the £10, £20 and £50 notes from the bar tills, for security reasons, and drop them through the letterbox on the floor. You might leave £100 in £10 and £20 notes in the till just in case someone came in with large denominations. No credit card machines then. Card payments were done in triplicate on a form with a manual swipe of your credit card. Most payments were made with cash, with only a few by card. Cheques were still written in those days. The key for this safe was probably kept in another safe. One safe was probably used for banking and change, and another for keys and sensitive documents, so that still leaves a spare one. I seem to remember having to lie on the floor and stretching my hand down to retrieve money from the floor safe, once it had been opened. I've never seen one since.

We often enjoyed a drink at the bar once we had got rid of all the customers and tidied up. It's natural. The drinks were all paid for by the staff, which is something I'm quite strict about, and always have been. The only time drinks were 'free' was when H cleaned the pipes. He would do this after service on say a Thursday, and, as the first couple of pints being poured off from each tap are still 100% lager/beer/Guinness/cider, he would pull them off into pint glasses and leave them on the bar top for us to drink. With the pipe run at the hotel, there was about a couple of pints worth in the pipes from the cellar to the beer tap. Then he would pull through the cleaning fluid until the purple liquid came through, from cloudy to clear, then leave it to 'soak in', pull a bit more through until clear again, and so on. But that was it, obviously – no more pints once we had drunk our free ones. Some nights were quite late, but all good fun.

The Veranda Bar was a small bar, more like a shed with a hatch that sold bottled beers, along with the main spirits, wine, soft drinks, and so on. It opened on hot sunny days, but mostly at weekends. Sometimes it could be busy, taking a worthwhile amount in a couple of hours, or other times quiet, not even warranting a member of staff running it.

One morning, more towards the end of the season, something wasn't right. The 'bucket and spade' shop hadn't opened. I looked through their window, only to find it empty. I got my key to the door and went in. Overnight, the owners had stripped the shop and done a runner, presumably owing rent to the hotel.

One of the receptionists worked some extra hours behind the bar, which was fine, and she did a good job. I came through one evening to check the Sands Bar only to find a complete stranger behind the bar, and the barmaid nowhere in sight.

'Who the hell are you!?' I shouted, and almost before he had a chance to reply, I told him to get out. It transpired that the barmaid had gone to the lavatory and asked her boyfriend to watch the bar. I was not impressed, especially with the amount of money and stock behind the bar. She could have asked me or one of the bar staff in the other bar, but no, she had just decided for herself. I sacked her, which may have been a bit hasty, but I was incensed. I was rather sad after the event actually. This also meant that she lost her reception job, which can't have pleased Emma. It ended up at a tribunal for unfair dismissal, where I think she won a week's wages and that was that.

Talking of being sacked, my favourite topic, I heard a good story about my predecessor. Tom Hart had come down to the hotel unannounced and phoned the Manager asking him where he was, to which the reply was that he was in the restaurant. A few minutes later Mr Hart phoned him again, asking him where in the restaurant he was. Well he wasn't – he was out on the golf course playing golf! So that was the end of him.

The summer passed. 'Celebrities', whether genuine or self-styled, often came in for a drink or a bite to eat, but you were often too busy to be bothered to notice, or more often than not, you did not recognise them if you didn't watch their programme. Besides they just wanted to be left alone. They didn't concern me.

Mr Hart and Nigel gradually started to mention the winter more and more often; would we stay open, or wouldn't we? I was quite happy to stay open, albeit with a reduced staffing level, and it meant that much-needed maintenance could be carried out in the bedrooms and other areas. But the level of business dropped off a cliff in October, so they decided to shut for the winter. They decided to develop Captain Pepper's bar and make a new kitchen downstairs, utilising a couple of store rooms, my office, and some other space. Nigel was in his element. Nigel, H, Angel and I took great pleasure in smashing up the bar with sledgehammers, once the stock and glassware had been stored away.

The Harts then decided that they wouldn't be re-opening the accommodation part of the Hotel. I couldn't believe it. OK, they hadn't invested any money in the bedrooms, some of which were getting a bit tatty, but I fought my case with them. I had worked hard for the following year's coach bookings, and had agreed sixty contracts for next year, with various operators. I had even arranged for one coach operator to pay for minstrels and jesters one night in the restaurant, which would have cost £350, for which we would offer more of a banquet than the traditional three-course dinner. I had it all planned out and the hotel would be busier in theory next year than this year, but no, they were adamant; the accommodation was finishing.

Even before I had a chance to ring the various coach operators, a rival hotel phoned me asking if they could take our business. I was furious with them – how dare they! I was actually furious with everybody at that time. All that I had worked on, which I was proud of, had gone to pot. I had to phone the operators and cancel. Some of them actually charged us a cancellation fee due to having adverts in their brochures for the year 2000. It felt like being stabbed in the back, and I wondered out of spite whether I should change jobs. And I would be bored over the winter at the Palm Court. I couldn't quite grasp that from now on, the entire operation, except for the Veranda Bar, would operate from the ground floor.

We converted one of the best apartments into an office for me, which was lovely. My new office had a sea view, a bathroom, kitchen and bedroom – that'll do nicely thank you! My previous one didn't have any windows at all. And that restaurant was going to go to waste. What a shame. A real, real shame. The Harts had just killed my enthusiasm for the success of the hotel. I didn't care anymore. We had worked our butts off in the summer, for what? I was quite upset. Worse still was that all the staff, with the exception of H, Angel and John had been made redundant or laid off. I was going to miss some of them.

But the Harts soon gave me a new challenge. They 'asked' me whether I would like to go to their nursing home for the winter. Their reasoning was that I would be wasted at the Palm Court, and their Head Chef at the nursing home was sick, long term. So I agreed, thinking that there could be some nice nurses over there.

The Palm Court Nursing Home was a smart-looking purpose-built building facing the railway line and seafront as you approach Dawlish from Teignmouth. Elaine, the Administrator, greeted me and I was shown around. Average sized kitchen, suitable for its purpose, and all the staff seemed pleasant. I was instructed to learn all the nursing rules and regulations (oh please!) and change or adapt the menus to a fortnightly rotation. I had my work cut out. The rules and regs didn't really interest me, but I had to go through it all and take it in. Normally there were three kitchen staff; the head, the second, and a casual, I seem to remember. The head was sick, and the second on holiday, or had resigned or been fired, I can't remember. For me it was a full-time job, but at least five days a week instead of six at the hotel.

I took existing menus home and started to work on a rotational set. Of course old people don't have so much chewing capacity so pork chops are no good, similarly they do not like veg cooked 'al dente', mainly because they are used to their partners overcooking it at home, and although less nutritious, it is easier to eat. Likewise they do not like overly-spiced food, and remember you are having to cook a choice of two meals that they will all enjoy. So this was quite different from designing restaurant menus. My previous experience at Stoke Mandeville Hospital obviously helped here, and as I still had a set of their menus, I cribbed off them.

It meant getting up at 6 am to drive to Dawlish to start breakfast. Porridge, the bane of every hotel chef, was a major breakfast item, and I hadn't cooked it for decades, so the first time I'm embarrassed to say it was dry and sticky. Some had a small cooked breakfast, or a combination of various hot items. All fairly straightforward. Some of the residents had bread or toast with the crusts on, some off. Some had marmalade sandwiches with the crusts off. Oh my God, chefs don't do this sort of thing! Frigging about with little triangles of crustless marmalade sandwiches. Come on, really...

Lunch was OK; the care assistants provided meal plans from each resident, which had theoretically been discussed with them the previous day, so I knew exactly what to cook and how much of each choice. There may have been one or two diabetics, but thankfully no special diets. Some would not eat tomatoes in any shape or form, which might mean that their main course had to be prepared differently; I was used to that from the diet kitchen at the hospital. Another wouldn't eat green beans. Some would not eat 'x' with 'y'. Someone else might have wanted only peas as a veg, and so on. Quite a few niggly little irritants, and for me, being predominantly a hotel manager, a bit of a challenge initially.

Technically the shifts were split, with an hour off after lunch, so I was asked to do some non-catering chores. Always happy to oblige! I might collect prescriptions from the pharmacy, in chefs' whites. One of the residents, would be taken for his weekly coffee in his favourite café. This was OK actually; I would wheel him along in his wheelchair to the café, order the coffees and have a chat. Another favourite was Frank, who used to sit in his wheelchair at the front door smoking. He would frequently forget his cigarette so that it burned between his two fingers. He would just stare out, and conversation wasn't great, but he was a really nice chap, bless him. Other residents all had their idiosyncrasies which you came to accept. I could not have worked there permanently, I can tell you that straight off! I had full admiration for all the care workers.

The 'tea', as they called it, was basic; maybe I had to make a soup, or just prepare salad items for the care assistants. Whatever it was, perhaps more of those pointless little crustless triangles of sandwiches with marmalade, cucumber or other filling, would be prepared and left for the assistants to dispense at the appropriate time. Then there was the food ordering, cleaning up, and the usual head chef stuff to do. The casual chef covered my days off. I implemented my new menus, with approval from the Harts and the Matron. The Matron might also discuss non-catering matters with me periodically, as if it was any concern of mine! But I would naturally oblige her or advise her as I thought fit, with sincerity. By late afternoon I would be exhausted, so while driving back to Torquay it was always a challenge to stay awake.

I would call in at the hotel to see how the transformation was progressing. Mr Hart told H and me that this new venture had to work. It was up to us two. If it didn't, we would all be out of a job. It was a wake-up call. Fair enough. I would also have a few managerial matters to deal with like wages, appointments with suppliers, meeting Mr Hart, and in February, interviewing bar staff. Some came back from the previous year.

We dismantled two ovens from the kitchen and carried them downstairs and refitted them, and I think the grill. I was expecting a brand-new kitchen, but no. I think we had a new fryer and fridge, but most was brought from upstairs, like freezers, other fridges etc. Nigel had installed white plastic cladding in the kitchen, so it looked nice and clean, and I had previously deep-cleaned the ovens upstairs, with their hobs or gas rings. Because the ovens had been dismantled and reassembled, I decided to give them a blast, so I turned both ovens on full and went away for an hour. When I came back, the plastic cladding behind the ovens had warped and sagged over the cookers! Oops...

We discussed who was to be Head Chef from the previous year's brigade, which I scoffed at, not holding either of them in any great esteem, and I volunteered to do it myself, which after a bit of discussion, they agreed to. Yes, my own kitchen from scratch! That WAS exciting. I set about designing the menu, with relish. The bar was beginning to look fabulous, all designed by Nigel I guess – all credit to him – and in the now redundant café installed purpose-built toilets, all brand new. About four cubicles each, and two basins each with plenty of worktop, soap dispensers, dryers etc, all new. They looked smart, and I intended to keep them that way. I set up cleaning procedures, to be carried out by the bar staff before it opened. They were given instructions as to what chemicals to use where and when, weekly cleaning for things like the cubicle sides, and daily toilet checks. As you can imagine, there was a lot of resistance to this new task, but after a lot of personal demonstration, they got to grips with it. They were the cleanest in the bay that year. Normally in a hotel the night porter, day porters or the housekeeping department are responsible for the cleaning of public areas, but now we were a pub in essence, and cleaning staff were superfluous.

Because the summer was going to be busy, my menu was geared for a quick turnaround, which was definitely of importance, with me being the only chef. I had sandwiches and baguettes, salads, soup, the usual pub grub like burgers, steak, spag bol, scampi (whole tail of course), kids' meals, and so on. Desserts were mainly bought in, not being my forte. So it all came together, and rotas were organised and an opening date set.

A couple of days before opening I made my prep, being potato salad, coleslaw, spaghetti bolognaise and so on, labelled the fridge into sections, raw meat/fish at the bottom, and so on. All items were labelled and dated in plastic containers; all neat, tidy and organised.

I came in the next morning and opened the fridge door only to find drips of blood all over everything. On the top shelf, yes, the TOP shelf, had appeared a raw chicken. This was not a chicken wrapped up in its plastic packaging, but a real chicken with legs up in the air, not even on a plate! Who the hell had been so bloody stupid to put that up there!?

I slammed the fridge door and stormed off to find some staff for an explanation. To say I was mad was an understatement. I was FULLY on one. NO ONE messes with my kitchen! It turned out that H had brought in a chicken to cook later on Iranian style, along with other bits and pieces in a plastic bag. I let rip like never before, and I think he was a bit taken aback. I was fuming for a couple of weeks over that. OK, I could have probably wiped off the blood from the container lids and cleaned the fridge, but taking no chances, I ditched anything that had blood on it, cleaned the fridge, covered and placed the chicken on the bottom shelf, and remade anything that had been thrown. After that, they knew I meant business in there. H's Iranian chicken was really nice actually when he cooked it later, which made me forgive him.

Some professional people go through a personality change once they put their business hats on. I certainly do the minute I step into a kitchen wearing chef's whites. No more Mr Nice Guy. Everything becomes black or white. There's no grey middle area. Throughout this book, you've read about me losing my temper, but I am actually quite a gentle soft-spoken person who wouldn't hurt a fly...

On the first day of opening, the bar staff were behind the bar with me in the kitchen. We had not staffed a waitress, because we weren't sure how busy we were going to be. But the kitchen printer soon started humming. I took out the first few orders but soon got in the shit, unable to perform both tasks, so H sent over an able person to take the food out. I think this was Jane, a friend of mine, who talked a lot and could be quite 'gobby', although she meant well. Straight away, before she had a chance to open her mouth, I said 'When you are in here Jane, you will be quiet, do whatever I say, and get on with it!' She stared at me gobsmacked, mainly at the fact that she had been instructed by someone to do something, no questions asked, not something she was accustomed to.

'Well,' she said, at a loss for words, 'there's no need to talk like that.'

'So Jane, I may need a hand with the sandwiches and baguettes, otherwise it's taking the food out,' I continued, ignoring her previous comment.

'OK,' she replied, looking almost upset.

I hadn't got time for niceties, so I carried on. I might have said thank you as an afterthought. All went well, although Jane was still smarting hours later from my directive. She still gave me the odd furtive glance just to check that this was the same Geoff she knew.

At weekends it became very busy food wise; I couldn't put baguettes in the oven fast enough. As soon as a tray came out, time for another one to go in. The bar helper, whoever it was for the day, prepared sandwiches and baguettes and took the food out, whilst I did the hot food. It was going well. No complaints. I settled into a routine, starting about 10 am to get ready for lunch service. If I had to make more bolognaise, I would start it first thing, but sometimes the kitchen became so busy that the big saucepan of it would be on the solid top all day before I had time to cool and refrigerate it.

Food was served lunchtime and evening, so in the afternoon H would take a couple of hours' break, then when he came back, so would I. I was shattered and really just wanted to power nap, but three times a week I would go to the gym, because it made me feel better, ready for the evening. After the evening service, I cleared up, did the ordering and ate something, sitting, more often than not, on a crate in the kitchen. I wasn't really hungry, having picked at food all day, and too tired to eat, but most evenings I forced myself to eat a 'meal'. Then I would stand at the bar and drink a pint before going home to sleep. Sometimes I stayed on for more drinks and took a taxi home.

We took on a lovely German student called Aleks for the summer who came from near Hamburg, and we gave her an apartment to live in, which must have pleased her, and it always looked strange seeing her underwear drying on an improvised line in the old kitchen upstairs, having been washed in the washing machine. Jane's younger brother Chris worked for the summer, so one day he was my assistant. He cut his hand slightly and promptly fainted in the kitchen. *Oh, I haven't got time for this shit* I thought as I tended to him, whilst the orders mounted up. I had to get H to phone Jane to collect and take care of him. He was fine, just squeamish at the sight of blood.

All the staff worked brilliantly over the summer. The only thing that pissed us off was that on previous years, the juke box had been free, operated by tokens which we used behind the bar. But now it was payment only, so music was played less and less. In our opinion, this was a major mistake on behalf of the owners. On my day off, which was usually Mondays, the bar only offered sandwiches and baguettes. I didn't trust anyone else to cook in the kitchen with my food. I received just one complaint from my cooking and that was that the kids' fish fingers were horrible; I cooked one and yes they were, they were reformed, not fillets, so we changed them to proper fish fillet ones. I hadn't realised. That was the only complaint to my knowledge, so I was very pleased about that.

The hotel was up for sale, as most are all the time at the right price, indeed I had known that from the start of my employment. Over the summer various people came to look, some covertly, some officially. One afternoon in October, I was preparing to do a liquor stocktake, and having a quick chat with Nigel and Mr Hart in their office upstairs, when Nigel just shook his head. I knew exactly what this signified, but I needed to hear it. So they told me the hotel was closing at the end of next week. I was instructed to keep this to myself for now but tell the staff on Wednesday 18th October that the Hotel will close on Sunday 22nd, for good. I was gutted, more so for the long-standing staff, especially Angel, who had been there for twelve years or so. All that hard work for nothing. So, on the appropriate day, I arranged a staff meeting and told them that the bank had closed the hotel, which would be shutting on Sunday. That was that. The end. We were all obviously upset.

Nigel and John stripped the bar of alcohol and put it somewhere. Suppliers came to take back stock and I helped them as much as possible. They were not amused. Nor was I! I could sell any fixtures and fittings. I sold all the crockery, after taking a dozen of each for myself with Nigel's permission. I went to the Belgrave Hotel next door to see if they wanted any of our dry goods, so this was agreed and a price set. I had been dealing with the Assistant Manageress, but when I brought the goods over and asked for her, there was a deathly silence. Something was amiss. She was not available. In fact, I was later told, she had been dismissed for stealing or something like that. All sorts of strange things seemed to be going on there between the owners and management, none of it my business, or relevant here. It would be nice to work there, I thought.

I stayed on for another five days to finish as much as possible, including doing the final wages. Oddly, in retrospect, I should have kept for myself all the money I had taken for the hotel since closing; it would have contributed towards my wages. So, on Friday 27th October, I gave Nigel my keys and finished. A very sad day. I felt as if my performance, whether good or bad, was somehow responsible for the demise of the hotel. I would never know.

I believe Mr Hart had received a deposit for the sale of the hotel, but had since received a better offer, so he reneged on the first. I was convinced that there was something fishy going on, but this was out of my league. I didn't know who or what to believe, and I still wanted to be part of the hotel, so I tried to keep up-to-date with events. I just couldn't let go of that lovely hotel.

Our wages were not paid, which incensed me, never mind the others. The hotel did not have any money. I couldn't understand this, as I was employed by Riviera Leisure Ltd as the parent company, which also owned the Palm Court Nursing Home and a flat somewhere. I think the potential hotel sale was subject to planning permission. It all got a bit messy. I was out of my depth, but not prepared to just sit back and forget about it, so I represented some of the staff who were owed money. Our expectations were made up of a combination of redundancy pay, holiday pay, notice period, and wages owing. Mr Hart had no money, so he would not pay us. I made an error at the time, in thinking that Mr Hart as a Director could be liable in the same way as the company. I didn't believe him, so I tried to turn the screw by informing his partners (he was a senior partner in a law firm) of what was going on, as well as his bank. I must have been mad because no one in their right mind takes on a senior solicitor! Or can afford to! That backfired totally, and he threatened to take action against me if I used malicious language against him again. I thought this was getting a bit too heavy, so I back tracked, saying that it wasn't personal, that I was just trying to find out how to get the staff paid. I also worry how he will react when he reads this!

Our claim went to a tribunal, which we won, but that didn't mean we would be paid. It just proved that legally we were entitled to it. One way we could be paid was through the National Insurance fund, but for this to happen, the business in question would have to be wound up, ie liquidated, which it duly was, instigated by me, so that meant the staff could apply to the NI fund. Most of the others were duly paid a reasonable amount, but all I received was £4.68, even though the Tribunal had awarded me £3660! This laughable amount, which I had pedantically claimed for, was a petty £6 error on one of my wage slips less tax, leaving £4.68. Never again. It's just not worth it.

All this took over a year to accomplish, and at one point I was a little worried that I had overstepped the mark and was going to be sued, but now it's water under the bridge. With the costs I incurred going through this process I would have been better off just walking away and forgetting about the whole thing!

In time the hotel was sold and the downstairs bar opened as Mojo's for a few seasons, then closed. Eventually the building burnt down, a sad end for an iconic building in Torquay.

CHAPTER 12

The Belgrave Hotel

So, time to relax a little after the Palm Court hotel. I spent a rare Christmas with my parents in Shropshire, and in January 2001 I went on a bizarre holiday to Tunisia. The previous November or December Lin, the Oxford Poly student I had trained at the Red House hotel, phoned me out of the blue to say that she was now staying in Newton Abbot, and could we meet. There had been no contact between us since, so it seemed a bit strange, but harmless enough. So we met and dated a few times, me always driving, not drinking a drop of alcohol, which was a supreme effort!

Her extended family ran a Chinese restaurant in Newton Abbot, whilst other relations ran one in Falmouth. When we went down to Falmouth, we stayed in a bedroom above the restaurant. Although we slept together, nothing happened from recollection, for I was on my guard, even more so the next day from the body language between Lin and her relations whilst they were talking Chinese, which in this case, I didn't need to understand. I knew what was going on. She was after something. What did she want? The main topic was that she wanted to go on holiday and had seen a cheap deal to Tunisia, so I thought, why not? I had nothing better to do. We booked it.

The date came and I was to collect Lin from Newton Abbot, on the drive down to the airport. A few hours before, I had packed and looked at my passport. Oh my God! It had expired at the end of December. What was I going to do? I was normally so organised with everything at work but had not done this simple thing. So I picked Lin up and on the way to the airport, I told her about my passport and said I wouldn't be on the same flight as her. She went ballistic, then upset and then quiet. I appeased the situation by saying that I would go into London in the morning to get a new passport and book the next flight. Fortunately, our holiday was for two weeks.

We stayed up all night at the airport, and after she had caught her flight, I drove to some friends in Wokingham where I crashed for a couple of hours, before going into London to get a passport, which I eventually succeeded in doing. I then phoned the travel agent in Falmouth and booked another flight and asked them to send the ticket to my house in Torquay. Then I drove home to Torquay. The ticket did not arrive in the post the next morning, much to my irritation, so I then repacked and drove back to Heathrow in the afternoon to catch the early morning flight. What a palaver!

Finally I got to Tunisia. Lin was still not happy with me. She had made some friends, which was good, one of them an Australian woman on her own, so she hadn't been totally alone. We booked some trips; we went to Souss, to Carthage, rode camels in the desert, and took a touristy train through the desert up into some mountains, and so on. All the trips were good. The town itself, Hammamet I think, was more or less shut being the winter, and you needed to wear a coat at night, it was that cold.

Carol Smith had just bought the Belgrave hotel and added it to her portfolio, so I rang her and asked if she had anything going in terms of a job. She might have, she confided, and shortly after she employed me as an assistant manager, and I started in April 2001. I was extremely pleased. The Belgrave was a well-established three-star hotel on Torquay's seafront with 70 bedrooms and conference and banqueting facilities, and two bars, one of which was operated as a pub, the Dickens Bar, which was a complete waste of a bar, having no music or entertainment, and appeared dark and dingy. It was probably the last traditional hotel which accommodated only 'private' guests, ie it did not take groups or coaches.

Since there had recently been some management changes, there was no general manager. Jonathan Crocker was in charge, me second, and a trainee assistant manager, Nicola. The restaurant was well run with Tony in charge, Jill second, and I remember full-time staff included Margaret, Lionel and Mary. John oversaw the bars with Faye and Katy. Steve, who never talked if he could help it, ran the kitchen efficiently, with Bob as second, and Adam from New Zealand as third. Heidi, a tall thin blonde lady, ran the reception with Yvonne, who was Tony's estranged wife, along with a good team who I cannot remember. They had been there for years. I remember Jack the tall porter from Finland, Mel, and an old porter who was part of the furniture. The latter was annoying, because he would come in on his day off when there was a big departure day to hang around getting the tips, which was unfair. I remember flirting with the deputy housekeeper a couple of times. The rest I can't remember except Pam and Maggie, who were 'black and whites' and came in to help at functions as well as the restaurant. All the public rooms were spacious, bright and airy. There was a solid team. Oh, the maintenance man, another Steve, was memorable because he wore the same shirt all week, so combined with his incessant smoking, he smelled awful!

The staff were genuinely concerned that Carol was going to turn the hotel into a coaching hotel, but at a staff meeting she assured us that everything would remain the same. That reassured us, but I did not quite believe her. I also wondered whether the staff thought I was her 'spy', having worked for her before. Some staff left because of Carol's reputation, which is inevitable with any new employer, but they were replaced easily enough. It all settled down.

Gradually Carol started to slip the odd coach in, and this increased as time went on, much to the consternation of some of the staff, especially in the restaurant because the coaches were getting the same food as normal guests. However, they were 'private' coaches to begin with, such as gardening groups or societies, so they were paying a bit more than a typical coach party. Groups were seated on long tables, whereas Lionel and Margaret looked after the regular guests who sat nearer to the windows. Lionel, a cheerful red-faced chap, did his station but nothing more.

Brian, who was by now manager at one of Carol's other hotels, the Roselands, was asked to come down on New Year's Eve to 'help'. All the dining guests had separate tables reserved for them in the ballroom after dinner. Regular guests had their favourite tables in the ballroom. It was all organised, and flowed. So what did Brian do? He brought the guests through and seated them all randomly, with complaints to me and Jono from the guests. I don't really want to slag Brian off because he was a really nice man with a heart of gold and could entertain the guests. He's one of those people that guests remember and ask for the next time. Unlike someone like me, who is NOT the life and soul of the party!

The reservation system used was called Innsite, the same as used by the Palm Court hotel, and I didn't find it very easy to use, so it was suggested to Carol that we update it with a new system. So

Avondata, one of the software companies we looked at, arranged for us to visit a hotel in Cornwall. I drove Carol down and we looked at this system which seemed logically set out, having been designed by a hotelier. So we opted for it, as well as considering other options.

Avondata came down to train Yvonne and me and give us a mock set up so the staff could practise, along with the real one, so we could start to transfer existing bedroom bookings across. This all happened in August, the middle of the summer of all times! Our changeover day approached and we weren't really ready, but we changed anyway. I can remember working out the morning and evening shift pattern with Yvonne, both of us unsure of the correct procedure. We were working it out as we went along. Carol came in the next morning and said 'Geoff, I want the shift procedures NOW!' with that pout of hers that signifies 'don't bother trying to reply'.

Fuck off Carol, I thought.

'Carol, NO! I haven't even written them yet! They're in my head. You'll get them later,' I replied, arms gesticulating with despair. She had a habit, bless her, of asking for the most ridiculous and irrelevant things (to me) at the most inappropriate time. Like you could be checking in a coach and she wanted the sales figures for the last month compared to the previous year; that's fair enough, but she wanted it NOW. However, she had that female touch, and she applied it to the fixtures and fittings, which gradually improved.

Every year the Russian ballet would stay for several nights while they performed at the Princess Theatre. Checking them in was a nightmare because most did not speak English. One year, their tour manager grabbed all the registration cards that had been laid out neatly on the desk and handed them out to the dancers, seemingly at random. I hadn't got a clue who was staying in what room. I went upstairs to do something only to find a group of Russians sitting in the corridor (the bedroom corridors were quite wide at the Belgrave) with a little gas stove with which they were heating up soup or something. I said 'No, No, No!' but you know what, I actually let them carry on it was that strange, and certainly futile trying to explain. Some of them had used their kettles as saucepans to make soup in. They were ruined, with dried pieces of food stuck to the elements.

I produced a breakfast menu in Russian, using my English/ Cyrillic keyboard, and had the hotel brochure translated into Russian by my teacher. I had started to learn Russian anyway at an evening class, which went well. We learnt in capital letters, but as soon as we started to learn lower case Cyrillic, we were lost. Some letters looked totally different in lower case, as in most languages. I took two terms worth of lessons, but then gave it up because I was missing out on one of my two evenings per week out drinking. Glasnost had come about in Russia and it was easing up, and so I thought it might be a cool country to work in. I'm glad that's as far as it went!

Two of the major conference events in Torquay were the Gift Fair in January, much appreciated at the quietest time of year, and the IWM in June, the Institute of Waste Management, covering all aspects of recycling and waste management including re-cycling equipment, bins and containers, and much much more.

For the Gift Fair in January, the Belgrave hotel was the venue for leather goods, which comprised anything from wallets and purses to luggage, so for the four-day event, the hotel was turned upside down. The function rooms were laid out with trestle tables, as was the restaurant, and the Shakespeare Bar became the restaurant. It meant that the staff had further to walk from the kitchen, so had to be quicker on their feet carrying hot food, and due to the size of the bar, it could not accommodate all the guests, so sittings were organised. The wine fridges had to be brought up, along with the 'drops' holding the cutlery. It worked, but the normal style and space of the restaurant service were compromised. People just wanting a drink spilled out into the reception area. One year after they had all dismantled and left, I noticed a bulge behind a curtain, and saw that a nice brown leather hold-all had obviously fallen off the display table and been missed. I still use it to this day as my overnight bag if going on a short trip somewhere, thank you very much!

The waste management event in June was big business. The event, held on Paignton Green, had grown for over twenty years, but it had outgrown the venue, so, much to the distress of both local businesses and some of the exhibitors, it eventually moved elsewhere. The Belgrave's car park filled up with an assortment of commercial vehicles, refuse trucks, street cleaners, sewage-pumping lorries and so on, all brand spanking new, ready to be driven to be displayed on Paignton Green. We treated our guests with first-class service. They might want us to provide a hot drinks station along with a waitress (pretty of course!) Whatever it was, we obliged.

For the salespeople on Paignton Green, it was big business. They might have an air force from anywhere around the world looking for up-to-date runway cleaners, or a council in the UK or Europe might buy a fleet of new domestic waste lorries. They made sales worth millions and millions. And they partied! The several IWM companies that stayed at the hotel, the major one being from Kent, spent a fortune on entertaining their guests, with bar tabs running into thousands of pounds. Money was no object, when their end result was sales worth millions.

Then Carol sold her other three coaching hotels. This meant that she would be moving into the manager's office, which was across the other side of the expansive foyer from our offices. This was the final straw for Jono, who resigned. The conference and banqueting were a major aspect of the hotel, which meant that I would be taking it over from Jono, whose whole time was spent dealing with the paperwork and sending letters. We employed Katja, the German girlfriend of a friend of mine, who did a good job. Function sheets were sent out the week before the start of the month, along with a summary of the business for that month on one sheet of paper. They listed the who, what, when and where of a function, including customer details, drinks required, menus, timings etc. Function sheets were held on a computer, updated throughout the month and printed. It all took time, as did photocopying the months' worth ten times and sorting them into piles for each department. I met with clients, showed them around, explaining how we carried out whatever it was, be it a wedding, a dinner dance, a conference, and so on, suggested what we might do. It was hard work, but I relished it. It was extremely hard for me to help in the restaurant, as became the norm, due to having a conflict of tasks, but it didn't bother me how many hours I worked each day as long as the hotel was functioning properly.

Carol was concerned about my stress levels, which were irrelevant to me, so she put me on a stress management course. Maybe this was after the incident when I threw my bowl of cereal across the foyer at her in a fit of temper! The night before the course, the night porter phoned in sick, so since there wasn't time to organise anyone else, I did the night shift myself. In the morning I asked the receptionist to phone the course to give my apologies and tell them I could not make it. A few weeks later I received a certificate stating that I had passed the course, so I proudly showed Carol, much to our amusement!

Talking of night porters, we had to replace one, and one night a couple of weeks after the new one joined, two gay men were staying. These weren't just gay men; these were full-on queers. Their language in the bar was filthy, crude and sexual. They bought me a drink so I felt obliged, reluctantly, to have a drink with them. I can take a lot of verbal innuendos, and I can give it, but these two were on another level completely. I was a bit shocked. I got to work at the usual time of 8 am the next morning only to find the receptionist waiting outside. I had a key so I was able to open the front door. A resident had let the chef in earlier. No sign of a night porter, and his keys were on the desk – the chef later explained that they had been found on the floor inside the front door, having been put through the letterbox. When the two gays appeared later, I asked them how the night porter had been, and they explained that they may have had something to do with it. They had terrified him so much with their language that he had locked the hotel, posted the keys through the front door and done a runner!

Invariably with late nights and the availability of alcohol, hotel staff start going out with each other. Adam the chef and Faye in the bars dated, and years later they married at Oldway Mansion, now sadly neglected by the council. Katja secretly dated a barman, which we frowned upon as this was management dating staff, but mainly from jealousy. Tony and Yvonne only spoke to each other about hotel business. Tony, who ran the restaurant well, was a bit of a lad in those days, and always had a cheeky grin to get around any misdemeanours, normally during the middle of dinner service! Jono, who left to work as assistant catering manager at Paignton Zoo, dated Katy in the bars and they married.

Equally you get the dramas. For example, a friend of Carol's worked as a receptionist while her husband worked as a porter. She was having an affair with someone close to Carol, which we all knew about before Carol, or at least if she did know, she put on a brave face. The porter husband was the last to know, and I seem to remember having to either break the news to him or console him when he found out. The receptionist in question had to leave. Lots more goes on in hotels than meets the eye, but you must be careful what you write, unfortunately, so some juicy bits have been omitted throughout this book.

Telephone calls made from the bedroom phones were logged and charged to the room account. We started to find large phone bills overnight from rooms that were unlet, so we guessed it was a night porter. Sure enough, after a bit of detective work, we found the culprit, who had been phoning chat lines and racking up large bills!

Pancake Day was approaching, so I asked the chef which pancakes he would be doing.

'Oh, I'm not messing about with that!' he retorted, scoffing at the idea.

'Why not?' I replied.

'It's a waste of time, do them yourself if you like!' he sniggered.

'Yes OK then,' I replied, not to be outdone, at which he grinned sarcastically at me and walked off, pleased with himself, as all chefs are. So on the night I set myself up. Two frying pans, the pancake mix, lemons, oranges, sugar, etc, everything ready, I was dressed in chefs' whites, and prepared to be rammed. Dinner started, desserts went out, but no pancakes, not one. I went into the restaurant to look at the menu; what an idiot, I had forgotten to add them to the menu! Of course the chefs were loving it, watching me make a prat of myself! What a fool.

One of the Abba Tribute bands, I think it was the Australian band Bjorn Again, booked some rooms, but they required an early check in and late check out, due to the nature of their business. In a small hotel like the Belgrave, bedrooms are only serviced in the daytime, so that means that you could be blocking off a room for three nights to accommodate a one-night booking. You might do this in the winter, but not the spring, summer or autumn, so I didn't promise anything but said I would do my best to oblige. They were offered a good rate, probably corporate, so they had nothing to grumble about.

They arrived about 7.30 am and demanded their rooms. I explained that they weren't yet ready, but we would do them as soon as possible, and offered them some coffee. The four of them sat in the foyer on the two sofas facing each other. Every twenty minutes or so, the two women would get up and ask me – I was on the reception shift – are the rooms ready? So, the same answer over and over, no I'm sorry, but we will do them ASAP. If they were that desperate, they could always sleep in their tour bus!

I could hear their muttering and whining from the sofas, so finally lost my patience. I stormed over to them and said, 'Look! I did not guarantee an early check-in, but we are doing our best for you. It shouldn't be too long. The best thing you can do is to sit down and be quiet! Grumbling to me isn't going to make any difference at all. All our rooms are occupied. Would you like some more coffee?' That did the trick. I think the women realised the futility of their actions and came down to earth a bit, and there was no more trouble. It did not dawn on me until later that I had told a major pop group to shut up!

The weddings held at the hotel all seemed to go well. I frequently ran them, or if not I was there to ensure all went tickety-boo. There was one wedding where the ex-wife of the father of the bride was not welcome, but she appeared, so the current wife stormed off in a huff and delayed the main course for forty minutes or so. She couldn't be found. As staff, we were extremely concerned due to the time delay and the food not going out at the correct time, never mind the labour cost. When it comes to evening buffets, if you have a hundred guests, you charge for a hundred guests. Frequently, you will find that the organisers will try to economise and if they have a hundred people, for example, they will say they will only provide a buffet for fifty, so as to keep the cost down. Well it doesn't work like that. I explained that if the food ran out, which it would, then it looks bad on the bride and groom, and it looks bad on the hotel. We charge for a hundred and that's that, and you put out a hundred plates. If however, all these plates are used and more are requested, that means there are more than a hundred people there, or some have used two plates, so I would charge for the number of extra plates. Years later Carol told me she had always looked up to me regarding my insistence on this. I was astounded; it was me that had always looked up to her! Carol also told me one time that she had always appreciated my meticulous and analytical attention down to the last intricate detail, working out if we had enough of everything for a function, how the day would flow, where everything would be down to the last teaspoon. She even used this planning approach, which to me was second nature, as a training tool for future staff.

I have always thought I could handle doing two jobs, in the sense of being the receptionist a couple of times a week as well as being the duty manager. It could get quite stressful at times, when you're trying to discuss a function with a customer who has just walked through the door and deal with the telephone, or check people out. It was not ideal and didn't look professional. At some point Carol asked me to propose a management structure for the hotel, along with salaries, so I thought, oh she's obviously going to promote me, so I put the general manager salary at a nice level, but kept the deputy manager at an average one, and assistant managers maybe lower. She was fine with that. We were recruiting for another assistant manager. Not long after, Carol asked to see me in her office. She informed me that she had taken on a general manager. She could see that I was devastated, though in reality, it was the correct way forward. What upset me more than anything was that had I known this, I would have increased the deputy manager's salary in my recent proposal to her. Grrr! So there was no change in my salary, which considering my responsibilities, was not great.

Ironically, this manager had applied for the vacancy of assistant manager and I had rejected him as being too old and overqualified, and here he was, coming in over my head! He was rotund, apparently past retirement age, with glasses, white hair and a jovial face, and was soon dubbed 'the Fat Controller'. He could look at things objectively, whereas I was involved more in the day-to day running of the hotel, for it was difficult for me to 'step back' and think outside the box. Did this mean I was a bad manager? I don't think so; I had been holding the hotel together, there were no real bad staff issues, and everything was functioning without complaints. I think to appease me, my title was changed to operations manager, but not my salary I hasten to add!

Our Masonic Lodge business increased quite substantially because of the manager's connections, so we hosted not just the run of the mill Ladies' Nights but Installation Dinners, and sometimes meetings like Initiation Ceremonies (if that's what they're called), often with access to the room restricted to Brothers only. His most annoying habit would be to say, 'Where's xxx folder?' to which I would say 'On your desk!' He would even ring me at 8 am on my morning or day off, always to ask the same thing, which even happened for a fortnight after I had left the hotel, until I told him to stop it!

He sat at his desk, used the phone frequently, ie for networking, and ventured out to the foyer for meetings. He was actually a welcome addition, and it was a relief for me not to have the weight of the hotel on my shoulders. He could not really use a keyboard, let alone a computer, so he relied on others for information. I remember once that a Brother had left behind by mistake his green 'bible' after a Masonic function and was desperate to get it back. This is their instruction manual, for want of a better word, on how to be a Mason, and not something that gets passed around. I had found it but delayed telling him for a day, to give myself time to read it, but I only skimmed through, being unable to decipher the coded words.

What did concern me was the fluctuations of our management safe float. This was normally kept in a petty cash tin and used to pay out odd amounts, to be recorded with a receipt. It worked fine, and just might be 5p or 10p up or down due to a mistake in counting. But after this manager had started it consistently dropped by anything up to say £10. If he was responsible, he was probably being a bit absent-minded, perhaps giving out petty cash without replacing it with a receipt or a slip. Paperwork was not his forte. Maybe he was just forgetful. I have always been a bit OCD on being accurate, so it began to niggle at me. It became such an issue that I had a private word with Carol, who thanked me for my concern, but it continued, and I was not happy. It also instilled mistrust amongst the management team because it could not be proved who was being inaccurate, so by rights any one of us could have been responsible.

It seemed that the heads of departments always took Sundays off, these being the bar manager, restaurant manager and probably therefore the head chef and Carol. This meant that I always ran Sunday lunch in the restaurant, which in itself was not an issue, but I could not be everywhere at once, and it meant that my split shift was a longer one. I seem to remember raising this and other issues, like communication, with Carol, and receiving a memo back to follow company policy etc.

The final straw came when a member of staff held a little function at the hotel. I think the payment only came to £290, but the manager suggested that we could maybe do something like splitting it between us. What? Then I thought, ah, is this a trick? If I said 'Yes', would he accuse me of stealing? If I said 'No', what then?

'No, do what you like with it, there's the money,' I replied, and left it on his desk for him to process, and walked off.

Certainly, years later I heard of a receptionist who was arrested for fraud. An accommodation bill was paid and put through the books. Fair enough. This receptionist was then refunding this amount to her own credit card. So the books balanced, but the revenue was down. How long this had been going on is anyone's guess.

So in the spring of 2003 I started to secretly look for a new job. The Headland Hotel in Newquay was looking for a food and beverage manager, so I went down for the interview, at short notice.

The Headland was a traditional Victorian square-built hotel, much the same size as the Victoria at Sidmouth. It held a good reputation, with the owners, the Armstrongs, coming from a solid Newquay hotel background; I had known of them when working at the Riviera hotel as a trainee manager. Being next to Fistral beach, famous for surfing, the hotel employed a higher than average percentage of Australian employees. Indeed the general manager was an Aussie, and was working out his notice, having been sacked I believe. Various other management levels were also Australian.

The Armstrongs explained that the position of F&B manager was a new position, and that I would find it difficult at the hotel to get along due to the general manager leaving and his colleagues being Australian. They asked whether I aspired to be a general manager, to which I replied in a non-committal manner 'Maybe.' It did not really appeal to me and the set-up seemed odd. Compared to the Belgrave, there seemed to be a manager for this, a manager for that, a manager for every conceivable department, secretaries for this department, that department; it was so top heavy as to be unrealistic, never mind the wage bill. They wanted to know my answer within twenty-four hours. The following morning, or probably later the same night as the interview, I was off on holiday to Florida, so I was under pressure to answer. Yes or no? Do I or don't I? Without having had time to consider the pro's and con's thoroughly, I reluctantly agreed to take the position, and resigned at the Belgrave.

I travelled to Orlando on my own, being my first trip to the USA, so I was excited. I picked a hire car up at Orlando and drove for hours trying to find my hotel on International Drive. My first night was good; I found a bar which had a live band playing. Once they realised I was a Brit, they got me up on stage to sing the chorus of 'Alice, who the fuck is Alice?' (based on the hit song 'Living Next

Door to Alice', released by Smokie). I was a hit with the audience and afterwards I was chatted up by some amazing women. I was offered a job, and got totally smashed, being oblivious to what was going on. The next day was a write off!

I did all the tourist stuff; Disney, Cape Canaveral and the Kennedy Space Centre, which was my primary reason for choosing Orlando, then drove down to Key West, after a night's stop at Key Largo. I had a good few days at Key West, including a few boat trips, and met some nice people. Then I drove through the Everglades. I had to stop for a reality check. I was driving on a dead straight road for what seemed like half an hour without any other traffic or people, except a few Indian tents. I had never come across such a straight road for so long. I saw the alligators and all that at the alligator farm, went on one of those shallow boats with a fan style propeller in the air behind you, and on to Sarasota for a few nights. The beach was amazing with white sand as fine as white flour, easily the best beach in the world for me.

I had planned to look for a job whilst in the States but had left it until Sarasota. I found an employment agency and decided to call in the next day, but the next day they were closed for training, so that was that, I'd missed my chance; the following day I had to drive back to Orlando for my flight home. Even though I was lonely a lot of the time, I did enjoy myself, ate loads and loads of nice food, met some nice people, and gathered an insight into the American people.

When I arrived at the Headland Hotel in Newquay, I was presented with an A4 envelope containing a letter from Carolyn Armstrong along with a job description and press cutting, as they had just attained four-star standard. Well done them. It seemed the main area of concern for me to concentrate on was their popular Sands Bar & Brasserie, as its manager had recently left, and the deputy was on sick leave. So it was in disarray, apparently. I was able to live in a small staff room at the top of the hotel until I had settled in. I met all the HODs and was shown around the hotel, and everything looked clean and orderly. I was impressed. I can't remember ever meeting the general manager, let alone talking to him, so there was no one to turn to for advice, except the head chef and restaurant manager, and I felt from day one out on a limb. And it was a newly created position, so no structure existed. I also felt it strange that the head chef would come up and ask me if he could do this or that; he was far more experienced than me, so if the head chef was deferential to me, then really I was the next in line from the general manager.

The problem to me in the Brasserie was obvious – the lift. The food came up from the basement kitchen in a service lift, like at the Palm Court hotel, and this one was about the size of an oven, with one shelf in the middle. Dirty crockery went down in the lift, but it was not always taken out of the lift by the kitchen, which limited how much service food could go back in. From day one, I could see this as being a major bottleneck, never mind a hygiene issue. Whether the issue was downstairs, that they needed someone on the 'pass', I don't know, but they never asked or seemed to want assistance down there. I tried to organise a system of stacking the dirty plates, cutlery etc behind a counter, to make it easier to put them in the lift.

The bistro staff were all fine and carried out their jobs as you would expect. They had a regular repeat trade, especially with the fantastic views. On my first day I met Sylvia Moret, the co-owner of the Riviera when I had worked there. I felt superfluous, being used to being a hands-on manager, especially with there being a manager for every department. I also became fixated with the liquor stocktaking, and in my spare time I set up a 'live' stock control programme, meaning that if you entered every purchase and equally entered the daily liquor sales it would tell you the exact theoretical stock. It took two weeks to set up, was probably never used, and I have never tried to do it again!

Weddings, wakes, parties, dinners and so on were held at the hotel, and all flowed smoothly. Weekly HOD meetings were held at the hotel. But I wasn't enjoying my job. The Armstrongs had told me it would be difficult and the management might be unfriendly, and I certainly found this. Only the personnel manager talked to me like a human being. So towards the end of my second week, I was looking forward to the return of the deputy in the Brasserie and meeting him. One night was awful; the Bar and Brasserie were rammed, being the beginning of June, and I went to help behind the bar. The food orders were piling in, and I thought, should we stop taking orders? But being the newbie, I was hesitant. I should have come off the bar and looked after the food element. There were many complaints about slow food service, and my fault really for not managing the situation.

The next day, Carolyn Armstrong approached me with a folder, and asked to have a word. Because she was holding a folder and a pen, as a form of ammunition for her, I knew exactly what this was going to be about. Her body language gave it away also. She asked how last night had gone, so I told her badly, and that the lift was the problem. She then steered the subject towards my progress, how I was settling in etc. With reference to all the above, I explained that I was finding the job difficult. So we amicably called it a day, and I left to go back home. I was quite relieved actually. Still to this day I believe they originally employed me as a stop-gap whilst the deputy in the Brasserie was sick, so I never actually met him, and at the same time to see whether I was general manager material for The Headland, to which I would have to admit to not being of the calibre required. I don't blame the Armstrongs, who were genuine people and have done wonders for the Headland; they were hedging their bets, I thought, and I would probably have done the same in their shoes. I vowed never to work in Cornwall again, having turned my previous 'loyalty' over to Devon, but that was not to be.

CHAPTER 13

The Northfield Hotel

Adam, the chef who had worked at the Belgrave Hotel, had briefly worked at the Northfield Hotel, and he told me they were looking for a deputy manager. I declined, as I was enjoying the summer off, not a bonus normally afforded to me. So it was with reluctance that later in August I rang Simon Deacon and made an appointment for an interview.

Although it was about time I found another job, I was in two minds about the Northfield. In terms of commuting it was a bit farther away than was ideal, but it was certainly a nice enough hotel.

I had to delay my interview due to a wedding, which was understandable. Adam and Faye's marriage ceremony was held in Oldway Mansions, a marvellous old mansion once lived in by the Singer family, of sewing machine fame, and now run by the council as a building for tourists and used as offices for Environmental Health etc. They also performed civil ceremonies and it was a lovely setting.

Currently 'Churchill; the Hollywood Years' was being filmed, so the car park was full of military paraphernalia and film crew trucks. It had been agreed that filming would be suspended for the wedding, but it seemed that it was going ahead anyway. They had forgotten about the wedding!

Everything had to be hastily stopped to start the ceremony. There were soldiers lazing around along with Grenadier Guards who were quite happy to be photographed as part of the wedding! Bizarre really, and it was certainly a wedding with a difference – they were incredibly lucky. Christian Slater was being filmed as Churchill, and Katja, with whom I'd gone to the wedding, was desperate to see and talk to him, which she managed, being German, attractive and blonde; but she's another story...

At my interview Simon was sporting a morning suit but with a morning coat and in my opinion looked a bit OTT, as did the other management. I guessed wrongly that there must have been a wedding on that day. I have worn one many a time in the course of my employment, but was a morning coat (often mistakenly referred to as 'tails') really necessary? Anyway, he showed me around, told me a bit about the hotel, the hours, the usual hotel shifts, uniform, holidays etc etc and said 'I don't want anything changed!' Fine. Then he asked when I could start, and when I suggested the following Monday, he replied 'Fine, see you about nine o'clock'.

'Oh ok,' I replied, a bit taken aback at being offered a job so promptly. 'Does that mean I've got the job?' to which he replied affirmatively, smiled and wished me all the best, nice to have you on board etc. That was a relief, I had a job, but I wondered with trepidation what I had let myself in for.

And so began a somewhat interesting three years. Judy Deacon owned both the Northfield Hotel (62 bedrooms) and the Valley View Hotel (43 bedrooms), which was just over the Devon border. Her sons ran the hotels, Simon the Northfield and Charles the Valley

View. The former was described as a 'Country House Hotel', and I suppose it was, despite being in a town. It had a nice little garden with well-kept grass and rose flowerbeds along with an outdated outdoor swimming pool (a modern one would not look right) and plenty of flourishing hanging baskets. It was easily the best kept visible garden in the area. Inside you were greeted by a small foyer and reception, more akin to that of a bed & breakfast but with the addition of a grandfather clock. As first impressions count, it was a bit of a let-down – shame.

The restaurant, which was on your immediate right, was fabulous I have to say, and was recarpeted and recurtained during my employment at vast expense. As well as several opulent chandeliers, each table had its own candle and at the far end was a magnificent 19th century golden candelabra on which each evening about ten new candles were placed and lit. Add to that gold curtains, a huge ornamental mirror, a glistening silver ornament, a grand piano, gold and brown chairs, gold napkins and orange flowers and I think you get the idea. Eating there was designed to be an experience, which it was!

The wine list contained over one hundred varieties of wine, varying from house plonk like Moreau red or white at £15.95 a bottle to Dom Perignon at £206 or Chateau Latour at £220 or so. There were some excellent wines on the list and a choice to suit most palates, but some had a virtual zero turnover with the result that some wines might become corked, especially the German ones, of which the good quality ones are vastly underrated in this country.

Corks are an interesting subject: most punters think a 'corked' bottle of wine is one that has a piece of cork left in when you have opened it. This is totally incorrect. A corked bottle of wine is one in which the wine is spoilt by tannin from the cork. The wine will smell off and probably be discoloured, and most customers will accept another bottle without making a fuss. It's amazing though what some people will drink: at various hotels I have had people who have ordered wine which I've noticed that upon pouring looks corked, so I've asked them to taste it and some have just asked me to carry on pouring and drunk the whole lot through ignorance. Some people just haven't a clue and if the corked wine has been something cheap and nasty, then I might let it go, but if it's something worth drinking I will intervene even if the customer doesn't, unless they've pissed me off of course!

It's also a shame that some people just order brands they know like Liebfraumilch or Sutter Home or Captain's Table, Merlot, Chardonnay etc – if they only took the time to read the list, they would find some lovely wines, something Simon was quite rightly proud of. Perhaps they were put off by the size, being ten pages of A4 along with extra pages of wine maps, especially as the expensive champagnes were on the third page – even house champagne was £48 and normal Moet £85, which in my opinion was quite expensive at the time.

To the left of reception one entered the Cathedral Bar, the main hotel and public bar. Again, there was that individuality which was part of the Deacon family philosophy. The two draught beer dispensers were old brass fittings with small product labels, each fitting dispensing two lagers and two bitters. It was only Guinness that had its own branded pump, probably because Pete, the Head Chef, drank it. Coke and lemonade were dispensed by the bottle and soda water from siphons; I think the latter should always be a standard bar product. This was partly to be old-fashioned and partly because there was no space to install a cooler or the post mix boxes. The back of the bar had a nice range of brandies and whiskies with only the basic spirits on optic. The wooden bar top was kept polished and it was a neat little bar, in keeping with the style of the hotel.

Further down were three lounges, the first of which was probably the original lounge of the house complete with log fire and was a comfortable little enclosed lounge, next an intermediate lounge, which to me was a kind of a no-man's land, and finally the Devon Lounge, which was glass fronted all round. Each lounge could be closed off to make three separate rooms. To the rear was the Dartmoor suite, which would once have been a summer-time lounge of the original house with its own bar and at the back, the main ballroom, complete with fully-sprung dance floor and bar. In the middle of all this stood the kitchen.

Three-piece morning suits were the order of the day, complete with a red carnation, whilst in the evening we changed into dinner jackets with white carnations. I eventually found out that the red/white difference was to do with the Wars of the Roses. Simon temporarily found me an old morning coat until I could buy one, and boy was it hot! Most of the first week I seemed to be behind the bar serving and cleaning glasses.

The bar manageress was a middle-aged, average-figured blonde whose appearance told you, without any shadow of a doubt, that she was in charge. My first encounter with her resulted in our first clash. I went behind HER bar to pour several pints of beer. In busy bars, you can stand an inverted pint glass on the drip tray, then place one on top and pour the beer. This means the pint glass is nearer the pump head, so you won't get so much froth, and you can pour more than one pint at a time, because you don't have to hold the glass constantly.

'Don't ever do that in MY bar!' she shouted, in such a manner as to signify the matter was closed. I was gobsmacked at being told what to do by an inferior.

'Well, I can serve quicker!' I exclaimed, after the shock had passed.

'That's not a professional way,' she added, 'I don't want to ever see you doing that again,' she continued with daggers in her eyes. That was it. Enemy number one! No one tells me how to pour a pint! I have been doing it for years. It's just as well there were no guests in the bar at the time, these drinks being for the restaurant. Being new, and duly smarting from her arrogance, I obliged. That was that – we never spoke again unless it was work related; anyway staff were not encouraged to talk amongst themselves in public.

A few weeks later, we were coincidentally both outside the kitchen having a smoke, sitting on upturned beer crates. We started to talk, a miracle in itself, and it turned out that we both thought in remarkably similar terms as regards the hotel profession, and enjoyed a really candid conversation. It was quite a relief; the ice had been broken. Then about five weeks later I was informed quietly one morning, on arriving at work, that she had died. What? No, that cannot be? Surely not, she was only in her thirties. She had died in her sleep overnight from low blood pressure. I was quite upset, even though I had hated her guts, but I had to get on with the job and cover her bar shifts. It was hard to believe for all of us.

A week or so later, Adam, Faye and I went on one of our frequent pub crawls and ended up at the Hole in the Wall, one of Torquay's oldest pubs, hidden away from the tourists and run by a great chap called Dave. I seem to remember Bombardier being the order of the day. Phil, a well-known local pub and hotel entertainer, was playing so Adam asked if he could sing a song, so at the appropriate time, Adam announced that he was going to sing a song but with different words. I was amazed and genuinely thought he was going to make a balls of it. What I did not realise was that he was about to do a tribute to the bar manageress who had died, even though he had only worked there a couple of months. He had obviously spent some time preparing for this, and he performed well, playing the guitar and singing improvised words. My eyes started to well up, and despite clenched fists, the tears started to roll, so I let it all out, blubbing like a little boy, all in public view. I don't think I had even cried when my grandparents had passed away, and here was I, crying for someone I had not even liked! I will never forget that night.

The restaurant was run by a French girl, Marie, who was Simon's girlfriend. The evening duty managers worked as the wine waiters for the restaurant. This involved preparing half a dozen ice buckets and stands and at least a dozen iced water jugs, making sure candles were lit, lights on, staff dressed appropriately, tables set correctly etc. Sweets were put out on the buffet table and a staff briefing done by the Restaurant Manager. Marie was quite rightly in charge of the restaurant. She appeared neat and tidy, and organised. But here was another person with whom I clashed on my first week! New guests were coming into the restaurant and required seating. Marie was seating some guests, so I gave her a hand and seated the next couple, according to the table plan. She went mental at me because she had changed the plan in her head, but not corrected the original. Her glare was impressive, indicating I was an imbecile. Not my fault!

After that I tried not to help her at all, or if I did, would be pedantic, asking her the most obvious things, as if I WAS an imbecile! In my first week I seemed to be polishing a lot of glasses; for the restaurant, for weddings – for arrival drinks, glasses for the tables, so three sets normally, wine, water and champagne. I nearly quit in the first week because I was so exasperated at the number of glasses that I polished, but Simon assured me that I would 'settle in'.

The restaurant staff, housekeeping and porters mostly consisted of Eastern European staff, employed via agencies, who lived in. Their first-floor accommodation in the hotel consisted of small single rooms with metal bars on the windows, presumably installed in the days of servants, with communal bathrooms. Not much had changed! Except for the odd one that didn't work out, they were brilliant at their jobs and I have made lifelong friends with some of them.

Each waitress had a plastic bucket somewhere in the kitchen where they emptied the dirty cutlery from their station. They then washed this so that they had exactly the same cutlery to go back to their station. Rosie, an elderly local waitress, always took a dozen or so teaspoons home in her handbag, which she then brought back to work, thus enabling her to always have enough teaspoons!

Certain events became routine on a weekly basis, namely Thursdays and Sundays. The first important event on a Sunday was Sunday lunch, and we were a popular venue for locals, so the management did the wines, as per the evening service. Coffee, also as per the evening service, was served in the lounge afterwards, organised by the porter. This helped the restaurant staff to get on and clear up. Most lunch guests would have retired to the lounge by 3 pm, but the next task was to prepare for the imminent arrival of Country Travel, the hotel's coach business, from a local tour operator. The driver would always give us ten minutes' warning, so upon arrival we served tea, coffee and biscuits from trestle tables in the lounge. It was sometimes quite a struggle to get cleared up from lunch in time for the coach.

Country Travel were VIPs. The Devon coach was originally owned and driven by Derek, Mrs Deacon's partner, who often displayed a short fuse. Silver tea and coffee pots were used, along with silver trays of biscuits. This was all part of the ritual of staying at the Northfield. Upon arrival we, the management, would get the cases out of the coach, chalk the room numbers on the cases, then line them up in sections, ready to be taken upstairs. Mrs Deacon would stand dutifully at the entrance, greeting them all, either by saying hello or hugging those who were long-lost friends, beaming at them all. Most of the trips came from South Wales, Bournemouth, and occasionally Cornwall, and we enjoyed a high percentage of repeat business, many on first-name terms with Mrs Deacon.

Once all the guests were inside, we could take the luggage upstairs. It amazed me that we older management carried the luggage instead of the younger porter. We packed the luggage into the lift from floor to ceiling, and delivered it to the rooms at breakneck speed, so that by the time the guests had finished their tea, their cases would be outside their bedrooms. It wasn't just that – it would have been impossible to achieve if the guests had started to go upstairs in the lifts. The hotel had two lifts, one of which was out of the ark, comprising a panelled carriage with a metal grille or gate that opened and closed, similar to those used to close off London Underground stations. Then there was the outer door, which shut normally. Both had to be closed for the lift to operate. You could, if you so wished, stick your fingers through the closed grille whilst the lift was in motion, and get your fingers sliced off between the floors! And as happened several times, you could catch your fingers in the grille when opening it, squeezing your fingers.

The bedroom corridors were always roasting, whether summer or winter, and bear in mind we were carrying luggage wearing three-piece suits. We would be sweating buckets by the time we had finished. Then we had to proceed to reception and assist the guests. They all had to be seen to their rooms and luggage taken inside, whether they knew where to go or not. A most tedious affair, but we treated them like lost sheep! My grey waistcoat had a permanent stain under the armpits from sweating so much.

Thursdays were an equally pompous affair. Country Travel departed that day. Most of the luggage would be brought down by the night porter, with the management checking the corridors upstairs for the last few cases. Then the coach pulled up and the driver loaded the luggage. Then all the staff on duty, chefs included, lined up outside, saying goodbye to the guests and waving the coach off. It was embarrassing, and we felt like children waving grandparents away after a weekend's visit. Then, the lounge had to be smartened up and tea, coffee, and biscuits prepared for the Thursday Club, a charitable organisation made up of businessmen, mostly retired. They held a weekly meeting involving coffee and biscuits to begin with in the lounge, followed by a meeting, which could be a lecture by a visitor. The porter, Mrs Deacon, Simon, and either one or two duty managers would dutifully stand behind the trestle table serving tea or coffee for up to 25 men as they drifted in over the space of 20 minutes. One person could do it, but this was all part of Thursday morning at the Northfield. The person I felt most sorry for was Simon, Thursday being his day off. Once this was finished, we all sat down for a coffee with Mrs Deacon.

The reception department worked well, staffed with British girls. Sharon dealt with the accounts. Housekeeping all seemed fine, with the foreign waitresses also working as room attendants. On the management side, Simon was GM, with John and me as deputy managers. We worked six days per week, between fifty and sixty hours, which Simon noted in advance on the right-hand side of our rotas.

My relationship with the kitchen was another matter in my case, warranting a chapter in itself, which I cannot include. The Head Chef, Pete, ran the kitchen with an iron fist. He had cooked for the Queen, which was his claim to fame, and was also brilliant at sugar sculptures and making naval battleships, some over two feet long. They were all stored high up in the kitchen, but bits had drooped due to old age.

I crossed paths with Pete on my first week. When the waitresses wanted the main course for a particular table, they had to wait quietly in line in the kitchen. Pete would ask 'Table?' The waitress had to reply, 'Table two please,' 'please' being the important word. If they omitted it, Pete would repeat 'Table?' but a bit louder. If it happened a third time, Pete might shout 'Which fucking table?' If the waitresses dared to talk to each other, even quietly, Pete would shout 'Shut up!' or if that didn't work, 'What part of fucking shut up don't you understand?'

I walked into the kitchen to hear Pete swearing away to the restaurant staff, so I asked him 'Do you always talk to the staff like that?' to which he replied 'Yes I fucking do! Table?' as he moved on to the next waitress, the discussion with me apparently being over. He would also at times go red in the face, maybe from the heat, and on bad nights he would froth at the mouth, like a rabid dog. I think both Pete and Gordon Ramsey had been trained by the same chef on kitchen language! You get the idea. He was a good chef and had the catering buttoned up, but he was getting older and liked a drink, which was making his job harder and harder for him.

The desserts were made by the pastry chef, and they all looked good. Every evening, including Sunday Lunch, new gateaux, cheesecakes, trifles, chocolate eclairs, fresh fruit salad and so on, would be displayed on the dessert table. Lots of decorative fresh fruit on top with chocolate and cream. All yummy. The Management had to assist in the serving, partly to ensure portion control. I remember it being extremely hard to avoid getting whipped cream on your jacket sleeve. It was always an impressive spread. But Pete took care of the kitchen and I believe Mrs Deacon had a soft spot for him, so that was that.

On my first night (maybe collectively it was the first week), I had crossed paths with three heads of departments, so on the face of it, it would appear that I was the one out of order. Maybe. As the new person, was I the fly in the ointment? The hotel was run in a particular way, militarily more than anything, and I had to adjust. At the Belgrave Hotel I had enjoyed a high degree of autonomy, making decisions all the time. Here I was to perform a function, as an automaton. You sometimes forget that when you're employed as a manager, your employer wants you to work to their specifications, not what you think is right. I can say that now in hindsight, but at the time I may have had a higher opinion of myself.

There were strict regulations. The hotel was being operated to a 4-star standard, but with a 3-star classification. One had to stand 'at ease' all the time. You could not lean against something, nor rest your arm against a wall. We were certainly not allowed to sit down in public, oh no! I have a lot of respect for Mrs Deacon as to her success.

I did not drink on duty, so Pete took umbrage against me very early on. Cans of Guinness would appear with the vegetable delivery and he would offer the other managers a can of lager or Guinness or glass of port before service, drinking in his office in the kitchen. I would not, so I was not one of the boys. I have never been drawn into this 'boys' club' thing involving alcohol with the management in various hotels I have worked in. Pete would line up several cans of Guinness near his service area, ready for the dinner service. Most of the main courses involved slicing a joint of meat, placing two or three slices per person on a plate, coating it with the appropriate sauce, and finishing it off under the grill. The second chef would produce the potatoes and vegetables, so it was quite easy for him. The meats were always nice, beef done rare, and so on, and the sauces were quite good. To be fair to Pete, the grill was quite small, so anything above a table of four was difficult, there not being enough space for more than four plates. However, I think it also had something to do with his ability to count above four, after having had a drink or two. Potatoes and vegetables were silver served.

After Pete had finished in the kitchen, he might come into the bar for a drink, and be all sweetness and light, as if Hyde had turned back into Jekyll. He could ask me nicely for half a Guinness, and obviously, being in the public eye, I had to oblige and speak back nicely to him. It grated every time I saw him, but it was another of those hotel rituals the public sees, not knowing what goes on behind the scenes, never mind the number of times I could have shopped him for drink driving!

The Deacons expected high standards, and the hotel enjoyed a good reputation with repeat business, and a solid conference and banqueting business. So the family knew what they were doing. Simon's hobby was vintage Rolls Royces, two of which were available for hire for weddings. That was his sideline. He lived in a flat inside the hotel. Hats off to them. Upstairs the rooms were traditional, for instance keeping lemon-coloured bath suites. For years and years, even after I had left, you would find old (maybe almost antique) table lamp shades in the lounge where the fabric had split, or the little coffee tables where liquid had penetrated the veneer to cause a ridge and discoloration on the table surface. But their standards were high, fair play to them.

The irony was that later in the evenings when no one is about, Simon's veneer could lose its shine. His waistcoat was just a waistcoat at the front, the back being the straps. This meant you could see the back of his shirt if he took off his jacket. On the odd occasions when he did take his jacket off and go out into the public areas, normally when all guests had gone to bed, everyone could see that the back of his shirt was crinkled. It had been nowhere near an iron, or if it had been ironed, it was without steam.

Another thing the hotel did properly was Melba toast. A loaf of pre-sliced thick white bread was toasted, not forgetting to cut off the crusts. This toast is sliced into two parts lengthways through the inside, then the two parts rubbed together so as to make the 'bread' part inside congeal into balls and fall off, leaving a thinner result. This was then toasted on the untoasted side, the result being a delicate crispy piece of Melba toast, served with pâté or parfaits. All too often these days people cheat by passing it off as normal toast or if sliced as above, not rubbing and removing the 'bread' part, resulting in a poor second-class affair. We were forever making Melba toast.

The hotel could hold two weddings on the same day, but at different times. The gardens, with well-manicured lawns and abundant hanging baskets and rose beds, were an ideal setting for an outside drinks' reception. The most popular item was Summer Punch, served on silver trays with each coupe glass sporting an orchid flower, cherry and half twist of an orange slice. They did look impressive. We management stood and dispensed the drinks, which we all enjoyed doing. Mrs Deacon always greeted the guests, looking immaculate as she always did. Sometimes it was a real rush clearing up the first reception and being prepared for the second. I have to say that the wedding brochure for the Northfield was the most comprehensive I have ever seen, including useful information for the bride and groom as to the dos and don'ts, where guests sit on the top table, things to consider for a wedding like flowers, chair covers, entertainment and so on, along with the wedding car brochure, menus and drinks packages, and a brochure including adverts for local suppliers of wedding-related items.

Guests were ushered into the 'breakfast' venue before clapping in the bride and groom. Wine was poured by the management, whilst the staff silver served the bread rolls. Normally a soup was the starter, so a huge pot of it would be brought into the corridor, where it was ladled into hot soup bowls and distributed. Most staff had their own round table of ten, or in the case of the Dartmoor, which utilised smaller tables of six, a table and a half. If the guests were on a drinks package, this would include two glasses of wine. So smaller glasses were used, and the wine poured at the start, then during the main course. This is the same for many hotels. If the guests are on 'free flow' wine (meaning no limit to the number of bottles used) or corkage (whereby the guests bring their own wine and we charge a small amount per bottle opened), larger wine glasses were used with frequent top ups, so as to use as much wine as possible. Again, the same as in most hotels. At the end of the evening the empty bottles were counted, and this amount charged to the account. But that is not correct. You should also have counted how many you started with, and how many unopened remain, to confirm the above. Guests may have taken a bottle upstairs, or an empty one could have been thrown away, or, unlikely, a member of staff could have nicked one.

As with other hotels, the whole room was cleared at once. The person running the show, John or me I guess, would wait until the last person had finished, and inform the chef that we were about to clear – VERY important – then signal with your hand for action. Once cleared, including side plates and side knives, the room would be checked before coordinating with the chef for hot plates to go down. This all had to be in military fashion. Staff were not expected to think outside the box or defer from their mission. Speed was of the essence. Once plates had been laid, the staff lined up, top table waiter first, then the other staff in order of table number, ready for the meats in the kitchen. Once all the plates were down, the signal was given to the chefs and out came the silver flats of meat from the oven. They were hot, and if you didn't have enough cloth protection, you could burn yourself. Once when serving a function at a hotel I melted my jacket sleeve, which was a synthetic material, which pissed me off! The meat flat was coated in the gravy or sauce, but if the chefs had poured too much sauce onto the flat, it had to be held level otherwise the sauce would run onto your arm, burning it, or dribble the other way onto a guest's lap, or sometimes down their jackets. These silver flats WERE heavy! Occasionally younger, more frail staff would be unable to hold a flat. Then the potatoes and vegetables.

Some hotels get each staff to do their own table, followed by the sauce or gravy, whereas at some hotels the staff 'sweep' the room, some doing vegetables and some doing gravy. You always serve on the left-hand side of a person, and clear from the right. Again, the chefs could fill a gravy boat up to the brim, so it was inevitable you would spill it. It was always a rush. Someone would deal with oddities, which over the years grew and grew, like vegetarians or gluten free, diabetics being the main ones. Then the room had to be checked, and each table asked if everything was fine. Some hotels go around with extra potatoes, vegetables and gravy. Then in the kitchen, it was like feeding time at the zoo. Any left-over roast potatoes or equally scrumptious items not required by the kitchen would be gobbled up by the staff before you could blink. Some hotels keep the remaining vegetables to use in a soup at a later date. I always tried to grab a bowl of soup, however the number of times I have splashed tomato soup onto my white shirt, thereby staining it permanently, is countless.

If two weddings were going on in separate function rooms, you could not relax for ten minutes. You would ideally coordinate them, so you did the starters on one, then the next wedding, mains on one, mains on the other, and so on, so it was hard work. But we all wanted everything to flow smoothly, so we all worked our best. You could always play for time a bit, to co-ordinate with the chefs, so you could clear a course slowly or do the wine top up before serving the mains, and so on. The guests would have no idea and would assume this to be 'as per'.

Then it is time for the desserts. Main course plates are cleared along with all cutlery except the dessert cutlery, and sauce boats of accompaniments like horseradish sauce, cruets, and then the tables are 'crumbed'. This means you sweep the area in front of the guest with a folded napkin onto a plate, or with a crumber, a pen-sized flattish piece of metal, which is much easier. Once you have done that, the dessert cutlery can be brought down to its correct place. Desserts are then served, mostly plated from the kitchen, but at some hotels, they are plated in the room to order. Cream is served separately, and/or custard or crème anglaise, depending on the menu wording. After the desserts are cleared, coffee cups and white and brown sugar are placed on the tables. Some hotels ask the bride and groom to cut the cake at this point, all pre-arranged with them. I think the wording at the Northfield was, as announced by a member of management, 'Ladies and Gentlemen, Pray silence for the Bride and Groom, who will now cut the cake'. They are escorted to the cake, where they cut it. Once the photographers have finished faffing about, the cake is taken away and the bottom layer or layers cut up onto side plates. At the same time coffee is poured, so half the staff do this, and the other half distribute the cake. Anyone daring to ask for tea or decaff coffee was deemed a pain in the arse, as it means we have to polish extra silverware and make extra trips to and from the kitchen.

Then the toast wine is poured into champagne flutes. This could be sparkling wine or champagne. Some budget weddings just have another glass of wine, and some these days, no toast at all, but ideally you want to sell a 'package'. Once all that is done and checked, it's time for the speeches. These are announced in turn. In this time the staff have a bit of a break, and wash and polish their cutlery. At the Northfield the management were responsible for the glassware, which all came to a little room off a corridor, containing glass boxes and a glass washer. Glasses were washed and polished only by the management.

After the speeches, guests are encouraged to leave the room, either to the garden, to the bar, or wherever they liked. This is to enable the room to be changed around for the evening. The top table could be moved and become a buffet table, and some of the round tables might be dismantled so as to create the dance floor and make little seating areas with maybe six chairs with a coffee table. The DJ or evening entertainment can then be set up. Guests return about 7 pm onwards with a buffet being served between 8.30 and 9 pm.

There is a bit of psychology involved with buffets, believe it or not. I prefer the plates at one end. The stodgy items like chips/ French fries/ roast potatoes are the most popular items, so they need to be furthest away from the plates. If they are one of the first items, guests will take more than they need. Sandwiches are normally placed first, and it helps if items are labelled. Likewise, items like sausage rolls are popular, so again they need to be at the far end. I hate it when staff set out plates at both ends, thinking it will speed up the process. It only creates a bottleneck, because guests will go from one end to another in case they have missed something, and take another of the same item. Hot food items are brought out as required. At the Northfield, the staff stood behind the buffet and silver-served it onto the guests' plates, which helped portion control. Dirty plates had to be collected. Some hotels leave the buffet out until the end of the evening, which I like, so that the staff can then nibble at any remains, even if they have been out for over three hours; some hotels take the buffet in after say an hour, when it seems that everyone has finished. The entertainment in those days at the Northfield ended at midnight, which was good, allowing staff to clear up sooner than later.

Green seemed to be a favourite colour of the chef. Apart from tomato, most soups he made were vegetable, asparagus, or maybe broccoli and Stilton, so were all a shade of green. When the soup pot went back into the kitchen, the soup was strained and the liquid cooled, to be used for a future soup, maybe as a base for that evening's soup. Once, for an important function, I had arranged for the soup to be carrot and coriander, but this was not listed on the function menus. The chef went ballistic. How dare I? The function arrived, and strangely enough Pete was not working that day. We served the soup. We were so used to serving either a red tomato or greenish soup that it hadn't occurred to me that the green soup we were serving was supposed to be carrot and coriander, which in my book is orange! I went into the kitchen and said to the second chef, 'I thought it was supposed to be carrot and coriander soup today?'

'Yes,' came the reply, looking at me as if I was a moron.

'But that soup is green!' I exclaimed.

'Well, it's got carrot in it,' he replied, as if to imply that I was an idiot. I looked at him in disbelief that a chef could not make something as basic as carrot and coriander soup. We were so used to the food from the kitchen being spot-on that we didn't check the menu. So they had used their 'base' green soup, and maybe liquidised a few carrots into it. Had this come from Pete, in direct contradiction to a function sheet?

We had to watch the buffet sandwiches. These were often made in advance and placed on oval/round silver flats which had doyleys on them, to keep the sandwiches away from the metal. These were cling filmed and placed in the walk-in fridge. Sometimes, if one of the doyleys had slipped, the sandwiches around the edge would come into direct contact with the metal, resulting in the bread going green, looking like mould! It was probably direct contact where the silver plating had worn off. It had to be checked before being taken out, and the odd quarter sandwich thrown away.

So what goes on before and after a wedding? The function room must be emptied and vacuumed, and anything else that's dirty cleaned. The night porter sets the tables, which can either be round 'tops', which are rolled along the floor and placed onto a square table, or purpose-built round tables with legs that fold, again to be wheeled. It is quite an art form rolling some of these tables. Chairs, according to the table plan supplied by the management, are placed around. The top table is set out where it should go. Base cloths are laid on, with a top tablecloth over the base cloth. In the morning, the tables are laid with crockery, cutlery, glasses, cruets, candles and flowers as ordered by the bride. Place cards have to be set according to the bride's instructions, along with other things like favours, decorations and other bespoke items. A table has to be prepared for the cake, the cake set up, and various tables for extras that may have been ordered like one for presents, one for sweets which is a popular extra, all supplied by the bride. Chair covers must be put on, normally by the supplier. They take forever to put on, and my only recommendation about these is to pay a bit more to get good ones with which the bottom tucks under the chair leg, so that the whole leg is covered. Economy ones are just not worth the effort.

The reception drinks glasses must be prepared, all wines chilled if required, all counted. Presents for the bride and groom to distribute must be stored ready, the car park and entrance swept, red carpet vacuumed and prepared. All place settings must be checked, along with checking that table legs are locked – oh yes, during my hotel career I have seen tables collapse due to the legs not being put up properly, not having been checked by the person running the show! The whole room needs to be scanned to ensure it is ready.

Photographers, some of whom can be extremely irritating, need to be shown where to take photos and told of the timeline of the day. Some go over this time slot, much to our annoyance, because we are on a time schedule ref food, wages etc. Staff need to be organised, maybe to serve canapes or to collect dirty glasses. So the event proceeds as described above. After the event, the room has to be stripped and hoovered. All glasses need to be washed and polished, and maybe, if you have time and space, you can prepare for the next day's event. The bars must be tidied up and closed. Then we might have a drink if Simon was in a good mood.

A few weddings bring back memories. I was trying to get a wedding seated in the Dartmoor, but some guests would not sit down. Gradually you have to become more forceful, to such an extent that I almost became annoyed. It turned out that the bride had missed a table off her plan, so six people had nowhere to sit. In what was already a cramped room, we had to quickly bring in another table, lay it up, re-arrange the others slightly, and inform the chef. Phew! At another wedding, one of the 'bank' waitresses, stood right by her table, invading the personal space of the guests if you get my drift. You just don't do that. Upon asking her to stand by her drop, which is a piece of furniture against the wall containing cutlery etc, she went to it, but pulled it across the room to her table. Oh my God! Later, I was cutting the cake in the room and she grabbed a piece and started to eat it.

'You can't do that,' I exclaimed, horrified.

'No, it's all right, don't worry,' she replied.

Exasperated, I asked her to go to the kitchen, to be out of the way. Another wedding opted for a bespoke drinks package. They required Laurent Perrier Rose champagne throughout. The sale price in 2007 per bottle was £75. This was a good wedding for the hotel. We ordered boxes and boxes of this lovely champagne on a sale or return basis as they required it throughout. There was even a pre-wedding drinks reception, later the actual drinks reception, and served throughout the wedding breakfast, for the toast, and maybe during the evening if required. At all times, to increase the number of bottles used, we were going round topping up glasses like there was no tomorrow. Simon was certainly rubbing his hands that weekend!

Simon normally produced all the departmental rotas on Sundays, often leaving it until the evening. Having done rotas all my life, I know it can be difficult. Regularly I would leave work on a Sunday evening, not knowing my shift for the next day. So you had to ring early in the morning just to see if you were 'on' for breakfast. Invariably Simon would give me Mondays off, which annoyed me because it gave you no time to plan anything.

I went to work one morning to be immediately told to sit on a chair on the public side near the reception and wait to be called. What, me? The Deputy Manager? Fancy being told by a member of staff to sit down in a place where we never sat! I was called through after a few minutes into a room, maybe Mrs Deacon's office, to be greeted by two policemen. Alarm bells began to ring, naturally. They asked me if I knew what this was about. 'No,' I replied with a mixture of intrigue and incredulity. So they began to question me about where I had worked yesterday, and whether I had been down to the basement. The basement was a storage area for spare cutlery, crockery, and odd bits of furniture etc, including an old display stand similar to the one used at the reception entrance with gold lettering to denote what function is in which room etc, as hotels use daily. It turns out that someone had re-arranged the letters to write something that I assume was insulting to Simon, but whatever wording was used, it was offensive. How long these words had been there is anyone's guess because you might only go down there once a fortnight. So two policemen had been called in to question all the staff, one by one. I laughed at the police, saying firstly that did they really think I would do something so puerile, and secondly hadn't they better things to do than waste their time on a little insult? They did agree somewhat. I suggested that it could have been a member of staff that had just left the hotel's employment. I lost some respect for Simon that day. How pathetic! I've no idea as to the outcome, but we all carried on working, very nervously.

John, the other Deputy Manager, left the hotel to go and run a pub chain, to be replaced by Rob, who turned out to be the wonder boy. He was young, tall and good looking, with a pleasant disposition, so Mrs Deacon liked him. Simon's office was a partially partitioned area off the reception, which had enough space for two small work areas, Simon's being the first, the other for whoever. As I dealt with the conference and banqueting side of things, this was where I sat to use the computer for correspondence. Really a manager had to be out front, supervising, but to do what when it was quiet? You could not talk to the guests too much because you were deemed to be 'not working.' Someone was employed in the new position of Sales Manager, and that made it even harder for me to do my job, because he sat at 'my' desk. Every month or so, and too frequent to be coincidence, Simon would tell me to come for a chat, somewhere private, where he would give me a bollocking. This could have been for something petty, but most warnings came the day before a holiday. How nice of him!

It got really bad in November 2004, resulting in a disciplinary meeting against me for several misdemeanours, resulting in a written warning, received the following January. In my defence I was fairly depressed at the time; I had recently fallen over in the kitchen and damaged my back, which hurt, and I was paying for chiropractic treatment. I was fed up with the verbal and written abuse from the Head Chef, which I tried to tolerate, and the fact that they did not always feed me. My face did not fit. Let's be honest, when any manager in any organisation gives someone a written warning, it means they want to get rid of that person. Never mind the fact that the Head Chef had worked there a long time and had his department wrapped up, whereas I was the newcomer upsetting the applecart. It was a no-brainer.

Thursday 30 December 2004 was a major day for me. I had been taking abuse all day from the Head Chef who was on one, Christmas being a stressful time for everyone, and about 8.30 pm I finally flipped. I threw my tray down in the restaurant and went home. I had taken all I could handle. The next day, Simon phoned me at home and due to the time of year, advised me not to come in until the 3rd January, by which time the New Year guests would have departed. As the hotel was shutting down on the 3rd January for ten days, a meeting was scheduled for the 13th January. So I went out for a rare New Year's Eve night off and got pissed in Torquay with some friends.

The disciplinary meeting of the 13th January was attended by Mrs Deacon, Simon, and Sharon. Whilst appalled at my behaviour, they could understand why. They had issued Pete with a warning and confiscated all alcohol from his office. Mrs Deacon did not want either of us to leave but expected to lose either one or both of us.

I started back at work on 16th January and a meeting was held between Pete, Mrs Deacon, Simon and me to discuss the situation. I received a final written warning relating to the disciplinary held on 13th January! So there you go. Simon had me by the balls, and I could be out of the door for any further little misdemeanour. But I could not afford in terms of my career to have another short-lived job, having lasted only a short while at the Headland Hotel in Newquay. I was not going to let them get the better of me.

Things must have settled down, because I do not have any more documentation at home relating to disciplinaries at the Northfield. The abuse, including written abuse, from the chef may have continued. Certainly he stopped drinking cans during service, but after a couple of months, his routine reverted to the norm. The only bonus of working at the hotel was that I enjoyed a good social life with the staff. We went out to pubs and clubs, and I would take my female friends on days out by car, to local attractions. Sometimes I had parties at home, during which the Polish drank vodka like there was no tomorrow. They would all crash the night, public transport long having finished for the night. One girl, Magaly, was from Ecuador, her father being a general in the Ecuadorean Army. She stayed in my house as a lodger, but we had to keep it secret from the staff. To pick her up from the hotel she had to walk around the corner, where I would wait in my car, so that none of the staff could see us. It also meant she had to hang around sometimes to wait for a lift from me. She was charming, a little pocket rocket, but even in the summer she found it cold. When I took her out in my car in the summer on trips, she would wear a fur coat and I would have to have the heating on full! Many times I nearly fell asleep from being too hot. Many of the foreign staff have remained friends and I have since been to Varna in Bulgaria and Gdansk and Krakow in Poland visiting some of them.

The hotel held regular weekly dancing sessions in the ballroom, perhaps line dancing or ballroom. The function bar had to be opened, but it was so tedious. A few might buy a glass of squash, the odd sherry, maybe a G&T, but 99% of the time you just watched them. Line dancing to me is particularly tedious.

The other extraordinary thing that is unique to the Northfield in my experience is that the dry goods were put away by the Duty Manager. We actually looked forward to it, as a change of routine. Dry goods were delivered in metal 'cages', so they were checked off against the delivery note and placed in stock rotation on the shelves. Once unpacked, the empty cages were left outside the kitchen, which was around the side of the hotel. One day I looked outside to see an unattended cage trundling along the carpark, across the pavement and on to the main road, where it collided with a bus. It was a windy day! Finding it quite amusing, I went to retrieve it to find the driver taking photos. He told me not to worry about it!

The hotel was busy with Christmas parties, maybe a lunch or dinner with a disco afterwards. Whichever it was, the Christmas pudding service was almost iconic to the Deacons. Every single home-made Christmas pudding was served in the restaurant or function room in front of the guests. It was irrelevant how busy you were; we performed the same for everyone. Lights would be dimmed, the Christmas pudding torched with brandy, then cut up and plated. Another waitress spooned on the brandy butter, someone else the brandy sauce. It was a time-consuming affair, but each Christmas pudding was flamed, and the guests appreciated it.

One New Year's Eve we had a vacancy, which was luckily booked by a young couple that same day. They immediately ordered the most expensive champagne, to be brought to their room. This was Dom Perignon at £206 per bottle (2007 price). We only stocked one or two bottles and after the couple had consumed these, we had to offer the next one down, being Taittinger Brut Reserve at £91 per bottle (2007 price). After their third bottle, Simon offered them a complimentary bottle of house champagne. They still bought more, and their bill that night was about £1000!

A year or two passed. One day Mrs Deacon asked me to take some guests and their luggage over to the railway station, to which I agreed. I went to get my car to bring it to the hotel entrance, passing Derek, who was talking to the gardener. I duly took the luggage and guests to the railway station and re-parked my car. When I walked past Derek, who was still talking to the gardener, he bawled at me 'What the bloody hell do you think you are doing!?'

'Sorry?' I replied, a bit shocked.

'What were you doing taking those guests to the station?' he shouted.

'Mrs Deacon asked me to,' I replied.

'I was supposed to do that!' he continued. 'You've made me look like a fool!'

'Well, I'm just carrying out instructions. I didn't know you were supposed to take them,' I replied.

'We'll see about that!' he said, as he strode off towards Mrs Deacon's office, mouthing obscenities at me.

'Don't speak to me like that!' I shouted, furious with rage.

He had managed in a few seconds to turn a normal quiet day into a blazing row. Why oh why? We both stormed off to Mrs Deacon's office, and I beckoned Simon to join us, whereupon Derek let rip at me. I may have sworn back at him; I was going to stand my ground. I wasn't going to let that bad-tempered chap have the better of me. Mrs Deacon backed me up. Derek completely lost the plot. Over what? My god, is life so small? Does it really matter? The purpose was to look after the customer, which I had done. I matched him word for word, until he gave up and stormed out of the office. Mrs Deacon and Simon actually found it comical.

The Manager and Manageress quit suddenly from the Cottage hotel, which Mrs Deacon had recently bought, meaning they owned three hotels, and Rob was offered the position of General Manager, which he accepted. It was a finger in my face and upset me that I had not been asked, in fact I had been by-passed by the much younger Rob. But I could understand why. My working relationship with the Deacons was not brilliant, whereas the sun shone out of Rob's arse. As it happened, he did a good job over there, so fair play to him. That left me alone with Simon. Just the two of us as management. Great, as it probably meant working longer hours.

In 2006 Simon wanted to change the reservation system, so I recommended Avondata, which we went for. I took charge of training all the receptionists and wrote a training manual which even the Avondata trainer took copies of, he was that impressed! I was in my element, training them all and setting up all the systems. If there was a problem, I would sort it out.

One day in August that year I found I couldn't log in. Simon informed me, followed up by a memo, that he was restricting all users of the system to be unable to process refunds. This meant that any refund had to be authorised by himself or Sharon, and it would mean them needing to log on to be able to do it. I was put back to a basic user, and I was the person who had set up the procedures. Really!? As if I was going to fiddle the system. He just did not trust anyone. That's what hurt the most.

There was an Italian waitress who wanted to progress her career, so Simon took an equal interest in her and showed her the ropes. This progressed and she wanted to know more about the function side of things. First, she became a duty manager, much to the disgust of the staff, who realised that a former equal was now a superior.

I wasn't that impressed either as I was asked to train her on the function side of things. Simon was going to take the functions off me and give them to her! I could not believe him. He was going to give the function side of things to a person who had no experience? She could not even speak proper English. Come on! But she could smile, and she wore a skirt, which I did not.

After a few weeks' training from me the handover day came, and I wished her good luck. It was the final insult that Simon could throw at me. When we next went for one of his 'chats' in the Dartmoor, aka bollocking, he said 'Why don't you leave if you don't like it?'

'Yes, Ok, you'll get my resignation later,' I replied, and walked off. I think I wrote it there and then. Wow, I had finally done it. Thank god, the nightmare would soon be over. When I came back in the evening, Simon appeared, and glided up to me. He had a habit of somehow being able to move across a room in one motion, like forwards breakdancing. He wrung his hands in front of me, and in a subservient manner, said 'We all say things we don't mean.'

'Do we?' I replied. 'I don't.'

That took him aback. I do not go back on my word.

A few days later Mrs Deacon called me into her office to ask what this was all about, so I told her, lock, stock and barrel. There was nothing to lose, so I spoke from my heart, mainly about the way I had been treated by certain people working at the hotel. She suggested that to help both the hotel and me I should retract my notice, but look for a job, and give my notice in when I had found one. That was fair enough, it helped both sides, so I agreed.

A few days later I went for an interview at the Riverview Hotel, who were looking for a Deputy Manager. It was a lovely setting. Mr Smith and her daughter Jane, the General Manager, interviewed me. It went well. I remember Jane asking me which department I liked working in, to which I replied whichever was the busiest. With that she shot a look at her Dad, so I knew I was in with a chance.

And I got it. So I gave my four weeks' notice back to the Northfield and finally departed, much to my relief! It was not the happiest of episodes of my life that had just come to an end, but the hotel is still there and still has a good reputation.

As a Deputy Manager wherever I have worked, I have always tried to strike a balance between the wishes of the management and the well-being of the staff. I don't mean that I am the union representative for the staff or anything like that, but my style of management did not really fit in with what the Deacons wanted, which was probably the reason why I found life so difficult there.

CHAPTER 14

The Riverview Hotel

Whilst waiting for the Riverview Hotel to send me a contract, which took over a week, I was offered another interview, to be a manager for a Holiday Cottage Management Company, which appealed to me, except they wanted to interview me at the Riverview, which, it transpired, they used for meetings and interviews. I had to explain to them that it would be inappropriate to hold it there, and we met at a nearby hotel. The interview didn't go brilliantly but it didn't particularly bother me. Months later, talking to Jane, she had seen me going into this hotel, so she thought I was going to work there; I explained that I had had another interview booked, as I hadn't yet received my contract from her. We were both worried about each other! Amazing coincidence that she saw me go in there.

And so started an amazing eight years as deputy manager. Oh boy, what a difference. Staff talked to you, they smiled and were happy. James and Juliet were brilliant bosses, enjoying a laugh, seemingly concerned about everyone's welfare. They had loads of friends coming in for a drink or a meal; the difference from my previous employment was like chalk and cheese. I enjoyed going to work. And no more morning suits, just a business suit for daily operations. I wore my morning suit at weddings, or my dinner jacket for important evening events.

The Riverview Hotel is in a nearby town along a south Devon river estuary with scenic views, with a multitude of boat and bird activity, along with copious amounts of tourists and walkers. The Smith family have owned it for about twenty-five years, and in that time have added a second floor of bedrooms in the roof space, making about thirty in total, added the Dolphin Room, being the main function room. They have extended the bistro and bar outwards, added an indoor pool and other leisure facilities, and generally improved the standard and facilities so that the hotel restaurant now has an AA Rosette, and the hotel itself recently attained four stars. James is the managing director, Juliet, his wife, deals with the function side of things, their daughter Jane is the general manager, and their son James worked elsewhere. Most of the staff were young, with most of the management and HODs being older.

I found the hotel busy and vibrant, with cheerful guests, which rubbed off on the staff, and vice versa. If you have happy staff, it reflects on the guest experience.

I soon settled in. I didn't have a choice actually, it was that busy. You didn't have time to think. You just had to get on with it. There was always lots to do, and you had to be organised. This is what I thrive on, a challenge. Except in the winter, the bistro was always busy on sunny days and weekends. A duty manager HAD to be on the 'pass', where chefs place food ready to go out. The duty manager checks the food order (received in triplicate – one for waiting staff, one for the cold food chef, and one for the hot food chef) for content and quality and collates the order ready for the waitresses. You could not leave the pass, so if you needed the loo, you had to wait. The pass had to be controlled. The orders would stack up, but it was great to be manic. There might be a wedding happening as well, or another function, just to add to the melee.

One duty manager would be 'out front', another on the pass. If the bar needed change or a barrel changing, or a guest wanted to talk to the duty manager, it was the job of the manager out front. One particular duty manager would frequently disappear. You could look for him quickly, or ask a member of staff to, but it all takes time, and in that time you could have dealt with the issue yourself. Sometimes if you had to leave the pass, you could come back to find it a shambles. Grrr! It was not until after this person had retired that I found he had been taking a break in the housekeeper's office upstairs, sitting quietly with the light off!

The bistro menu was comprehensive with the addition of about five daily specials. The main bar operated two tills, one of which we called the food till, being the primary one for food orders. At busy times, people could be queuing out of the door, waiting to be served at the bar for food and drinks. It was great, but you could easily run out of glasses, or the outside patio could become swamped with dirty plates and glasses. You could not let yourself become bogged down serving blindly – that was the bar staffs' job – so you had to always think what needed to be done next – allocate a glass collector? Wash glasses yourself? Allocate a plate clearer? Clear plates yourself? And so on. It had to be a team effort. The 'inside' bistro staff often felt it beneath themselves to go outside and clear; the serving staff outside didn't always have the time to clear, as they were still bringing out food orders, so they all needed managing. The bar wash-up area was tiny, so it didn't take long for that area to become overrun with dirty glasses. You might be passing through the bar to get change but find they were rammed, so you helped with glass cleaning for twenty minutes, which I actually quite enjoyed, then on to the area next most in the shit.

Food in those early days was served lunchtime and evenings, with sandwiches and cream teas available during the afternoons. Chefs worked split shifts, so the duty manager had to make the afternoon sandwiches and do the cream teas. Every single day this wound us up. Sometimes you could be stuck there making food for an hour, an hour you did not have, when you just wanted to sit down with a coffee and have a smoke for five minutes, just to have a bit of silence away from people.

The scones were another matter. They were freshly made but then could be frozen and defrosted to order in a microwave. If you knew what to do and monitored it, you could get it right, but a novice might 'nuke' a couple of scones so that they came out red hot, only to turn rock hard upon cooling. There would be one waitress on a middle shift of midday to 10 pm, so they would have their break at 6 pm, when the supervisor returned for the evening part of her split shift. But you were trying to get the evening ready, and people's eating habits changed so that the bistro could be busy right from the start, so you'd find yourself on the pass and taking food out. It could be a frantic nightmare, trying to manage two areas. If, as a duty manager, you were on the early shift, 8 am to 6 pm, you could sometimes find yourself still there at 9 or 10 pm, because it was too busy to leave the late duty manager to be on their own. It pissed us right off, but it's teamwork, and we helped each other.

Our only sane moments as management were when we could take a few minutes' break in the courtyard out the back of the kitchen, with a Coke or coffee and a smoke. Oh such relief! We didn't need to speak, we were all in the same boat, so we all felt the same – hot, bothered, and knackered! Your head was spinning with different thoughts about this bar, that bar, who's doing what, what do I need to do next etc. You might not have the headspace for a conversation. Or you were catching your breath. We might get a meal as well. We wouldn't necessarily eat it all – you were too busy to eat, you'd seen so much food already, and only really want to smoke and drink. What really wound us up was if a member of staff came to find us wanting change or such like, interrupting our short break. Some days were real battles, seemingly never ending, but at the end of the shift, phew, a long sigh of relief! Some days walking back to my car in the car park, out of sight of the public, I would walk with my eyes shut and head tilted facing the sky with a long sigh, just to try to let it all go out...

We employed porters at weekends to sweep outside and generally clear up. They were usually schoolboys and didn't need a brain. Thinking wasn't part of the job. But you just would not believe how inept some of them could be. You would give them a broom, a dustpan and brush, a black plastic bag and show them where to sweep and what to do. Some were quite good but others you could watch for ten minutes sweeping the same piece of tarmac over and over, like a robot on a five-second repeat sequence. They were in another world, dreaming of a partner or holidays or whatever. Never mind not needing a brain, these people didn't have one. So it was part of the morning ritual chasing the porters around the car park. Woe betide if Mummy or Daddy called them in sick in the morning! That meant you had to do it yourself. Other managers might get Peter to rob Paul, but I could never see the point in that, as it means two departments are compromised. So I would do it myself, which meant that my tolerance level for the rest of the day would be teetering on the brink, but it didn't take long, and as you had to check it anyway, you may as well do it yourself, by the time you've found someone and checked it.

One day the porter phoned in sick, so I did the job, and I happened to look up at a shrub in front of me only to find a £20 note in it! Wow! Thank you very much. That day, my tolerance level was far better! Strangely enough the same porter did the same thing the following weekend, so whilst on my rounds sweeping, I looked deliberately at the same bush and lo and behold, another £20! I had a good rummage around, but that was it! I still smoked in those days, so I didn't mind so much picking up fag ends, which could be strewn all over the place especially after a wedding. When I did give up smoking, maybe a year after starting at the Riverview, you soon found the smell of old cigarette butts revolting.

On Sunday lunchtimes the hotel served a carvery, accompanied by a pianist in the winter or a brass band outside in the summer. Everything was fresh and looked good. We offered a one, two, or three-course carvery, which was extremely popular. The bonus for us staff was that we could have a carvery after service. There was one particular chef who had a chip on his shoulder (no pun intended) and would throw away left-over roast potatoes that had come back from the carvery rather than leave them as a freebie for the staff. So pointless and puerile.

Oh and before I forget, no more of that awful (sorry entertainers) coaching hotel style evening entertainment that you have to listen to. Most couldn't sing in tune, and what enthusiasm they showed whilst performing reflected on the type of customer listening. Praise the Lord!

We seemed to do a lot of birthday parties and wakes, meetings and exhibitions, indeed there was always something going on. Boxing matches, held annually, were a new sort of function as far as I was concerned. The boxing ring – or square as they are now – was set up in the Dolphin with long tables for dinner for a hundred or so guests. A separate changing room, the Cormorant, was set for the boxers. The guests enjoyed their dinner followed by the boxing. The officials, judges, trainers, medic and so on all had to sit around the edge of the ring getting 'in our way'. The first time for me I had visions of huge meatloaf types arriving, but instead they were teenage boys. The dinner had to be served quickly because the boxing had to be completed by law by a certain time, so from our point of view, a bit of a rush. But great to do something a bit different!

We would only entertain one wedding per day, making the day private for the bride and groom. One manager would stand in the car park ready to direct guests around the outside of the hotel, past the patio to the drinks reception area, and to ensure the driveway to the hotel was kept free of vehicles. I have stood out there for an hour before now, waiting for the wedding party. If their wedding had taken place say over 10 miles away and the photographer had gone over time or the traffic had been bad, it could happen. Drinks were served attentively, canapes served if requested, and the senior manager made contact with the Bride as to timings and the procedure. The wedding went in the same way as described in the Northfield Hotel chapter.

Amongst all this, the bistro would be busy; there would be noise and a bustle in the still room (the waiters' side of the kitchen), so if there were enough managers, one would do the wedding whilst another did everything else. Otherwise you were everywhere as a manager, balancing ever-changing priorities, without a moment to stop. Except for a bride and groom. Then you would proceed slowly and calmly as you announced them into the room, and you could catch your breath. You acted professionally out front. Then it was full steam ahead again.

We were licensed to hold civil ceremonies, which could be held either in the Cormorant for smaller ones, the Dolphin, or the Dolphin Garden. The latter was a faff, because the venue was weather dependent, so if it rained beforehand, chairs would have to be brought in. I think we might have been geared for an inside venue as well as the garden, just in case.

We would often do the music for the ceremony, being the bride's choice. Music for guests entering, for the bride's entrance and for the exit. It was imperative to test their CD prior to the day, as some CDs recorded by the bride would not work. One in ten weddings lost their CD prior to the ceremony (we normally requested the CD along with all the other bits and pieces the day before) so we had to play our own music.

I mainly ran the wedding music from behind the Cormorant bar, taking cues from the Registrar. You had to stand there for the whole ceremony. Being a softie, I found some to be quite emotional, so I had to control myself!

Some weddings were memorable. At one a photographer, walking backwards taking pictures of the bride arriving, tripped and fell into the fountain, which was highly amusing! At another wedding, a civil ceremony for two, just the bride and groom, I had to act as a witness. Amazing really. At another small wedding, the groom kept getting up from the table during the wedding breakfast to go and play the fruit machine in the bar, which irritated his new wife, as well as us! It was so bad that he had to be called back for the speeches, and being the worse for wear, he gave the flowers out to the wrong people, despite me telling him who they were for and where they were sitting. I wonder how long that one lasted!

Other weddings I have been told about, not necessarily at the Riverview, did not go to plan; one couple fell out on their wedding night, so they had their wedding annulled the next day. Another was not happy with her wedding video, so at vast expense she arranged for the whole wedding to be redone at a later date using the services of a more professional video company. Another bride was so ill that she had to go to bed, and just made an appearance in the evening. You get 'best men' who misplace wedding rings, CDs or speeches, causing a last-minute panic. Some strange vehicles are used for the bride and groom's departure – one left in a tuk-tuk, another in a gleaming brand new green tractor.

The evenings were another matter. We left the buffets out until the end of the night. As an alternative to buffets, we could do a spit roast, as these were extremely popular, carved by a chef outside. Sometimes we placed the buffet trestle tables outside in the garden, and on one occasion I boxed a buffet table and placed maybe a hundred plates at one end, only for the table legs to sink into the ground at that end, resulting in all the plates sliding off onto the ground with a cacophony, resulting in some smashing. Not a good move, Geoff. They all had to be washed, quickly!

But this was the good thing about my employers. If you had an accident and broken a few plates, that was the way it went, so quite rightly there were no recriminations or warnings. At the Northfield the entertainment stopped at midnight and guests had twenty minutes to vacate the room, but at the Riverview the entertainment stopped at midnight, or sometimes 1 am, and we let the guests carry on drinking. We would slowly encroach more and more around the tables, clearing as much as possible, and if a table had been cleared of guests completely, we would dismantle it. This could go on for a long time. Sometimes we called 'time' earlier, sometimes later; it all depended on how many guests remained, whether they were spending at the bar or just chatting, how well behaved they were, and of course, what mood we were in. We were usually all tired, we had all worked long enough, we all wanted to go home, and we were beginning to think we couldn't give a shit anymore, especially as the customers were invariably pissed by now and becoming tiresome. But as a manager, you can't think like that. The staff must be chivvied up, and organised if need be, to help. We certainly did as much as possible to clear down the room to help the night porter. They had a long night after a wedding or similar event. The room could be a mess, and all wedding paraphernalia, including shoes and all sorts of items of clothing left behind, had to be piled up on a table, except the odd pair of knickers, which would be binned.

Sometimes we would not finish until 3 am, and then I would have to drive back to Torquay to sleep before returning in the morning to work, about 45 minutes each way.

One particular night I will never forget. The wedding that day had been brilliant; all happy, all good. On the tables the bride had arranged flowers in tall glass vases which also contained those little clear balls which absorb moisture, so they go from hard to soft. Some guests had been throwing these balls all over the room, so the floor was a real mess. All of it. There was no way that Mike the night porter could clear up in time, so I volunteered to do the hoovering for him. Bad move Geoff. I couldn't use the normal Henry hoover head because it squished these balls, so you had to suck them up with just the tube, meaning you had to suck each one individually. Then the bag burst after getting damp, so I ended up vacuuming without a bag. Every square inch of the room had to be covered in this manner. I finished at 5 am!

If we finished work at a reasonable time, we would all have a drink outside on the patio. That was bliss! Fresh air, a pint, a smoke, and a chat. It would be totally peaceful with no one around and no one to hassle us. This made it all worthwhile. James might be with us, joining in. Even on a normal night, without a function, he would offer the staff a drink, either inside or out. Once work was finished we were all on a par, as far as he was concerned. If he had given a member of staff a bollocking that day, it would all be forgotten about with a drink.

One such evening at around 1 am, Juliet appeared looking distraught. They both lived in the cottage adjoining the hotel. She had obviously had a medical mishap in the cottage, so bad that she had to retire and rest for several months and was sorely missed. Anyway, that changed things. So Jane took over the function side. She worked harder and harder, six days a week, even coming in to manage the pass on busy Sunday lunches. That was commitment.

John at some point finished his job and joined the hotel as an assistant manager. By his own admission, his weakness was paperwork, whilst his strength was maintenance. It was handy that he could be called upon if there was a problem, even if off duty, which annoyed him no end; the down side with him was that he had his own agenda. I think he would be happier being say maintenance manager, and only covering duty management for holidays.

James asked me one day how I would feel about running the Dragon Hotel in North Cornwall, the sister hotel to the Riverview. I thought, why not? I knew the hotel because there had been the odd occasion when I had driven down with two or three waitresses for us to help on a function, silver service waitresses being in short supply at the hotel. We would do the function, then hit the bar, stay the night in hotel bedrooms and return in the morning. James wasn't happy with the general manager there, so he wanted to bring him up to the Riverview for 'training', doing a direct swap with me. I had vowed never to work in Cornwall again, but this was different.

And so I moved down, staying in a single room. I started mid-afternoon, and after half an hour together, to my amazement the duty manager said she was finishing for the day and left me to it. She had worked something like 8 am to 4 pm. That was barely a half day to me. It was a lovely hotel with lovely staff, and the restaurant had a panoramic view out to sea. I just had to keep things ticking over, I presume in hindsight, being a temporary position. Life, as you can expect in Cornwall, did not include the word 'urgency'. It was very laid back. I was used to working with all cylinders firing, but after breakfast, all the staff would sit down for half an hour for their breakfast. What? Unheard of anywhere else. I gradually wound down to their pace and wondered if it would 'hit me' upon my return to the Riverview.

They ran functions in a strange way, maybe due to the lack of silver service staff. If there were ten tables with six silver service staff, then those staff would do the first six tables and the remainder a 'free for all'. I had come across this when visiting for the night with Riverview staff. I found it a bit of a shambles with no one knowing who had served what where, or if someone was on their way to the kitchen to get something for a particular table. They muddled through. So when I started, I changed it. Staff had specific tasks; their table, then meat for table seven for example. I think they found it difficult to adjust. The starters and desserts were served collectively; in other words, the whole room was swept. You didn't just serve your own table. Very confusing. At one function, there was a table with a dozen or so children, and during the main course the middle of the table dropped to the floor! The table had been made up of two squares at either end, with an extension in the middle, which had become unhinged.

On my days off I would return to Torquay and often pop into the Riverview, if only to update James and Jane. After a month or so, this manager had been 'trained' and he returned to his hotel, but not for long. It has since been run by a successful manager who is liked by all. There are some lovely staff there, all of whom I missed on my return to the Riverview.

Each year we took on a few schoolkids for a couple of weeks' school experience, and we put them through different departments. I was amazed by one of them, who on only his second day of working started training a 'newcomer' on the bistro operations! They were only sixteen years old! The four of them then decided that as they had enjoyed themselves so much, they would like to work the summer. So they all did, and weekends in term time, holidays, etc for years. Indeed two of them still work at the hotel full time. That group of four were memorable as to the service they provided.

Don't get me wrong, there were also some brilliant full-time staff. They came from all sorts of backgrounds, and I would like to personally thank them for all the hard work they did for me. I hate to say it, but I think a lot of women are better at supervising than men. One was quite capable at seventeen of running the restaurant and supervising the bistro, and more importantly, organising the staff. Equally there were some time wasters. One particular member of staff would walk quickly along the corridor from the still-room to the bar, as if he was going to do something, but it was all a sham. He would walk back a few moments later at the same speed. I used to watch him regularly and tackle him to ask what he was doing. Another youngster came into the kitchen to talk to me on the pass about a complaint. Being under pressure I used kitchen language and said something like 'Go tell him to shove it up his arse', upon which this waiter proceeded to tell the customer. Oh my god! This customer demanded to see me at once, so reluctantly I had to leave the pass, and grovelled to the customer saying that he had misheard me and I had been referring to one of the chefs…

After I quit smoking, which was a miracle with the pressure we were under, staff smokers began to niggle me with their pleas about going for a cigarette break, making it unfair for non-smokers. Staff who were on an early finish, ie when things have quietened down, would display that style of body language that indicates that they've worked their bit and they think it's time to go home; you are still busy on the pass, you haven't got the head space for whining staff, so you wait for the inevitable whine and reply something like, 'Soon, go and check outside.'

One member of staff drove me mad. She had two speeds: slow and stop. The world could be ending but still she would walk at a snail's pace. OH MY GOD you think, MOVE, SHIFT IT! But the customers loved her, and the job seemed to get done. If she went on that SAS Who Dares Wins TV programme, she wouldn't even get there in time!

Another member of staff sometimes took her break under a boxed trestle table, where she would fall asleep! One lad who was doing a catering course at college told me that he had been trained to silver serve using a knife and fork! Quite how is beyond me, so he was probably quite glad to use the customary spoon and fork.

The stronger staff are expected to help the weaker staff, and we have to monitor it. You get other staff who don't really want to work hard. It's beyond their ethics and their ability. We all know who they are and they know that we know. It's a little game. One barman decided overnight without notice that he would be better off not working because his partner had just had a baby. Good riddance to that sort! Another member of the bistro staff poured himself a spirit from behind the bar and necked it there and then. It turned out he had a bit of an alcohol problem, and he had been pouring a shot or two, placing them on his tray and leaving the bar via the wash up area, as if he was going to a customer. But he would just neck one or both of these spirits!

You must deal with people when they have personal mental health problems, which seem to be far more prevalent now. You try to help them sort out their problem. You get thieves amongst staff at any hotel, whether it be stock or money. We know what's going on, normally by a process of elimination. In one such case, a warning had recently been issued to the two senior chefs to keep the back lane clear of empty bread and milk crates. A few days later I heard that one of these chefs had tripped over a bread basket in the back lane and cut his wrists on glass, which turned out to be from a bottle of hotel wine, and food items belonging to the hotel were found in his friend's car, which had been left in the car park overnight, with drips of blood leading up to it. Served him right. He eventually did admit to stealing the wine and food, and it cost him his job. How stupid. I have since found out that one female member of the kitchen staff virtually always had a large pack of hotel bacon in her fridge at home.

Staff parties were always interesting. The Riverview often held theirs at the hotel at the beginning of January once all New Year guests had departed, when John's disco equipment would still be up in the bar. There would be a buffet with wine on the table and discounted drinks, followed by a disco. Most youngsters would get smashed, sometimes with the inevitable fights; some staff would be so inebriated you'd find women spread-eagled on the floor showing their knickers. One such night a chef was the worse for wear and had passed out. His legs remained upright while his body rotated at the hips so that his head hit the floor. He stayed in that position for a few seconds almost bent double before falling over onto the carpet. We put him in a bedroom for the night for safe keeping. I always stayed in the hotel on these nights and had the following day off. In the morning I casually went downstairs to get a coffee to appease my hangover, only to find the kitchen in darkness, with all electrics off and water pouring through the ceiling. I ascertained that Jane was in the bedroom this chef was in, so I went upstairs. Jane was standing in a few inches of water in the bathroom with water shooting out of the toilet water-main pipe. It transpired that this chef had gone to the toilet but slipped, grabbed the pipe and pulled it out of its joint!

Jane asked me to organise breakfast, which pissed me right off being a day off with a hangover, but obviously you muck in. So I basically had to work out where to make coffee, do the toast etc for the few residents we did have. Juliet, bless her, was cooking the breakfasts in the cottage. So that was sorted, coffee being the prime objective!

Other staff, in a seemingly normal relationship of boy and girl, would split up, with the girl becoming lesbian, either as a fad before going back to boys, or permanently to other girls. Some of them got married.

One of the chefs drank Red Bull like it was going out of fashion. One day he left the gas blow-torch on the central pillar in the kitchen, with the result that it heated up, exploded and shot across the kitchen, making a hole in the wall. Lucky no one was in the way! Another chef had a serious alcohol problem and another a drug problem, which we tolerated for a while. I could go on forever about the idiosyncrasies of some of the staff, likewise the way they talk about the management!

One afternoon in the summer, having worked the morning, I went along to the park to join some of the staff who were having an afternoon playing football and chilling out. One of them asked how my morning was.

'Oh, it was all fine, except the porter did a sickie,' I replied. A short while later, who should appear but this porter. He said hello to everyone and settled in.

'I thought you were sick?' I enquired.

'Oh yes,' he replied, and then it sunk in that I had been at work in the morning and was a member of the management. 'Ohhhh.....' he continued, having been rumbled and unsure what to say.

'Don't worry about it!' I said, grinning. He slunk away from me, obviously embarrassed, and sat down with some of the staff.

Jane roped me into her netball team, which I found a bit strange, being an all-female sport. I played a few games, but could never 'hassle' my opposite number as they do. By 'hassle' I mean standing right in front of an opponent, invading personal space, moving around invariably with arms raised, doing anything to put you off being able to throw the ball, or just getting in your way. I was rubbish at it, so I was either dropped after a few games or the season ended.

At some point Jane started to rent out the local gym once a week for a team-building exercise with the hotel staff, which was a good idea. We would hold five-a-side football, so I joined in. I crippled myself by kicking the ball at the same time as my oppo, a tall fit chef in his twenties, also kicked it, so our ankles clashed, which sprained mine, forcing me to limp off to the bench and sit down.

Christmas parties were a nightmare. All the different groups, whether four or forty guests, were put on trestle tables around the Dolphin room, so table legs and place settings had to be checked. Menus were pre-ordered, and an A3 chart was made with the starters, soup, main, dessert, and coffee courses along the top and the names of the groups down the side, so either Jane or James would be on the pass, asking the staff things and shouting to the chefs for a course to 'go'. Niceties were irrelevant. It was too busy to say please or thank you. They would shout 'do this' or 'do that', 'have you done this', 'have you done that', 'check that table'. John always did the early shift because he later became the DJ. Normally my job was to greet the groups and after they had all bought a drink or two in the bar, bring them through. The room was not served as a whole but by each group, so trying to get them in on time was paramount.

Staffing wise the room was split into two groups. One group did the main courses and the other group did starters, soup, desserts and coffee. Nothing could be served or cleared unless authorised by Jane or James. It was frantic. The soup course was ladled from the pot in the room by someone. It was a real battle to get through the courses. There was no time to serve coffee and it would be easy to forget about it, being the least important part of the dinner. But I would splinter off a group of two competent waitresses just to serve coffee, so that I didn't have to worry about it. Over the years I had been putting on weight, so found it hard to get between the trestle tables. Best left for the slim waitresses! John always played his disco music too loud, having, I guess, become slightly deaf from being a DJ.

Then there was the Holly Ball, held once a year and open to the public, in a sense. A couple could book a table and it was extremely popular, using the same format. It was manic, with seemingly all the locals out for a bash. You could guarantee that two local brothers would drop their trousers and pants and display themselves along the corridor! I was so glad when James and Jane decided to drop this and hold a Christmas party night instead.

One night a local charitable group were having their Christmas bash and had booked the entire room. All proceeded as planned, but we started to get some complaints about the Christmas pudding; the sauce tasted funny. So some came back. It turned out that one of the chefs had grabbed a bucket of white sauce from the fridge, except he had grabbed cheese sauce, so they were all served with that! Amazingly some people didn't realise or didn't care, and ate it anyway, but we had to quickly sort out another fifty or so portions with brandy sauce!

Christmas itself was hard work, and for us it involved a seemingly never-ending supply of food. On Christmas Eve there was the obligatory drinks reception for the residents, followed by a speech by James about the events of the year, which was always a drag. Christmas lunch, a six-course affair, always worked well with the staff in sections, one waiter with a commis. The management supervised. Although we served hundreds, it was a far more pleasant operation than party nights. It was great to welcome back repeat guests.

The same for the New Year lot, who also had their drinks reception followed by the same speech from James. Staff dressed up in a theme such as sailors, or pirates, or wenches. I particularly enjoyed the sailor's year, because I added gold braid to my jacket sleeve, giving myself a higher rank than James, who had been in the Navy. For New Year's Eve, the main bar was stripped of fixtures and fittings, the dance floor was laid and John's disco set up. Residents and guests ate in the Dolphin, with a self-service three-course buffet followed by entertainment including a band. Other guests could pay a fiver to use the main bar with its disco. This was a packed area with everyone on form. The noise was deafening. Just before midnight, Champagne was poured for everyone in the Dolphin, mince pies served, and the frivolity continued into the small hours.

One New Year's evening in the main bar, one of the barmaids sounded a bit more gobby than usual. It seemed that she had been drinking. We wouldn't necessarily reprimand a member of staff if they had a drink on that night, but it became apparent that she had a bottle of vodka in her handbag, which she had been sharing out with some other bar staff when they went for a cigarette break. We tried to take it off her, whereupon she walked out, followed by two barmen. What a night to do this! We management had to jump onto the bar, which did not please us at all. She lost her job because of that.

Jane married her partner Jack, and her wedding at the hotel was probably the most important I have presided over. She duly became pregnant, so when the time came, I took over the reins. Boy did I work hard, six days per week, also covering the function side of things. I worked my arse off until she returned after maternity leave. Dealing with the function side of things is a full-time job in itself, so Jane found it hard to juggle management shifts, what with the needs of her baby.

Some residents randomly started to complain that money had gone missing from their bedrooms. This was very perturbing. Were they making it up? Was it a member of staff? Was it external? A pattern began to emerge. We questioned some staff quite thoroughly, without any outcome, before we realised it was external, and always the same set of bedrooms. The police became involved and did some research. I told them how I thought he was accessing the hotel grounds, so Operation Hilton, as the police called it, began. John, in the meantime, had installed covert external CCTV cameras. We knew who it was. The police said that one day they would ring us, and they did. We marked a couple of £10 notes and recorded their numbers. Then we placed some lost property in an empty bedroom, along with a purse containing the marked notes, and carried on as normal. I instructed all the staff not to go out the back for a smoke or break until authorised, the back lane being his access point from the woods. The police were blacked out hiding in the woods I guess. They knew he was on his way, having parked his car up near the layby at the start of the woods, which is why they had called me. Sure enough, he arrived, stole the planted money, and was caught. The little oik was also stealing from another couple of local hotels. Job done! And if anyone else gets any ideas, you can't open these windows any more in the same way.

I managed to get an inguinal hernia, I presume from lifting heavy water-logged pond plants out of my pond at an awkward angle, so that meant a few weeks off work, which didn't impress the boss, as we were in the summer! I couldn't believe that the hospital discharged me as soon as I had woken up from the operation.

Film crews were a regular occurrence, whether just staying at the hotel or filming in the town. They were always welcome due to the publicity that could result. One such film crew covered a wedding where the couple had dated each other ten years earlier but split up. The boyfriend had written a letter to his now ex-girlfriend which she had never received, and it had been forgotten about, having dropped behind her parents' mantelpiece. When they changed their mantelpiece ten years later, they found the letter, so the girl received it. She was so impressed that they got back together and became engaged and were married at the Riverview. This story made international headlines.

The film crew staying at the hotel were from Japan, and most didn't speak English. They were a pain in the arse, wanting to commandeer a third of our busy patio during a busy afternoon for their filming and displace other guests, which we couldn't permit.

They filmed all weekend, so there is a high chance I have been on Japanese TV!

Our major excitement involved the Princes Trust. They wanted to hold a meeting at the hotel for several days concerned with the 'sustainability of fishing'. It was all very hush hush due to a certain VIP who would be visiting, namely Prince Charles. Months in advance, undercover police were involved, mostly incognito, and nearer the time, also formally, searching bedrooms and public areas with sniffer dogs. The Princes Trust even installed up-to-date audio-visual equipment. For three days we were to provide breakfast, lunch, and dinner for our residents, 90% of whom were involved with the meeting, as well as for guests staying in other local hotels. So it was a big event for the hotel. Prince Charles was due to visit for one lunchtime. We even bought a red carpet for the VIP's.

The day came. I wasn't impressed though with the Prince's chauffeur, who drove over our brand-new carpet! We all lined up to meet him. As he shook my hand, he glanced at my name badge, and smiled. 'Ah,' he said, 'It's the poor old deputy manager!' How right, I thought! Camilla was tittering in the background. I did not know how to reply to this, but by the time I had thought of something, he had moved on. Then it was Camilla's turn, which was fine. Prince Charles enjoyed himself and the sandwiches and went over his allotted time, I believe.

So what about the customers? Most are law-abiding citizens, enjoying themselves and appreciating the food and service they receive along with the view. Others think that because they have watched a couple of cookery programmes on TV, they have a divine right to criticise. One woman springs to mind. She would complain almost to attract attention; the food in her opinion might not look 'as it should'. Or she would sit at a table the furthest away possible outside and order mussels. You have to carry the bread, the bowl of mussels, chips, and hot water for rinsing, so you cannot rush with all these items on a tray. She might complain that the mussels were cold. She complained so much and in such a manner, which she considered to be acceptable, that we dreaded her coming in.

Another customer ordered a crab sandwich on a Saturday lunchtime in the summer. But he wanted half the bread white, half brown, so that he could share it with his wife. The chefs agreed, and it came out after a reasonable wait, considering how busy we were. He brought the sandwich uneaten back up to the bar and said that his wife had gone off the idea now and could he have his money back. Well no! No way! There was a queue of people all the way to the door, and I had not got time for this. He seemed to think we could give it to someone else! Get real man! Anyway he kept on like a blubbering schoolkid, so I lost patience, grabbed the plate off him and threw it and the contents into an empty cardboard box, smashing the plate.

'There you go!' I said, through glaring eyes, as I gave him his money back.

'We'll be back in a few days,' he replied.

'WILL YOU?' came my retort, through hissing teeth, and with that I moved on to the next person. One woman used to push her sick dog around in a pushchair, but we had to ask her to refrain the next time she brought it, because we learnt that the dog had died a few days earlier, but she was still pushing it around. Then there was the lady who fancied a sweet wine, so I sold her a half bottle of dessert wine, which she found too sweet, so she added a bottle of bitter lemon! Give me strength!

A local businessman comes to mind. 'Three gin and tonics!' he would announce to the bar in general, and then turn his back and carry on talking to his friends. He wouldn't necessarily look at any of the bar staff, who would be serving other people. Come on man! This is Devon, not some private members' club in London. An astute bar person would pick up on this and serve him in line. He wouldn't necessarily pay, expecting without asking to have a 'tab', and regularly he would leave without paying, resulting in us having to charge the bill to his account.

This same person was once a guest speaker at a function. All guests were dressed formally, so our chap arrives late, dressed in jeans and T-shirt, doesn't eat the food, gives his speech, then leaves. How rude and disrespectful to the local community!

Some customers have a right to complain, and if we have got it wrong, then of course we will rectify it as soon as possible. Some people do have a good knowledge of food, more than me, so I admit that there have been times when I didn't know who was right, the chef or the customer. Some complain to get a cheap meal, but you can spot these a mile off. You can tell by the body language before they even sit down whether a table is going to be a problem or not. I have seen it all. By the way, you only remember the complaints, you don't remember the 95% of people that have enjoyed their food. And people jump on bandwagons. Let's say a table complains about something, rightly or wrongly; you deal with it. If another table does the same, again you deal with it. But by then everyone sitting in that room will know that there have been two complaints, so if you have given a discount, which I try not to confirm to the guest until after their meal, others will try the same. You can end up with half a dozen tables complaining, so it has become a bad night.

One evening a woman came in to complain that her car was covered in paint. I had visions of someone pouring a pot of white emulsion over her car, so with an alarmed expression, went out to the car park with her. Her car, parked under the trees, had little yellow spots all over. My immediate thought was John who, the other side of the car park in his garage was spray painting his car. You fucking idiot I thought, thinking the wind had carried the spray over. I went up to John to tell him about the woman's car. He came over all concerned. The fact that he was using another colour to yellow was irrelevant. In the woman's opinion, because he was spray painting, it had gone over her car and reacted with her paint to go yellow, and that was that.

'What are you going to do about it?' she demanded. I thought shit, this is a tricky one. Then John realised that the yellow spots were insect sap or honeydew from the trees above! The woman was having none of it, claiming that was just an excuse, so John volunteered to wash her car, which he did, thus removing the problem, but she wasn't satisfied. She still thought it was paint and would make a written complaint.

Once a year I used to go to the local school for a 'What's my line?' day. This involved four or five people from different professions going to the school, dressed in casual clothes and answering questions asked by a hundred or so schoolkids. We could only answer 'Yes' or 'No', as in the original TV programme. The kids had a list of professions in front of them, and at the end they had to guess ours. Then we went off to change into our work clothes. So there might be a nurse, a construction worker, an artist, and myself. In turn we would talk for ten minutes about our profession.

During my ad hoc speech, I would ask them how many drank tea. Half the hands might go up. How many drank tea from a teapot? Only a few hands would go up. So I would explain that in a hotel, people are served a pot of tea with a separate pot of hot water, a milk jug, sugar, a cup and saucer, a teaspoon and a biscuit. We had to train new staff in even the most basic of functions.

I started to notice that my feet were uncomfortable in my shoes after a late night if I had just say four hours' sleep. I had also opened a fire exit door, as you do, by hitting the metal bar with the palm of my hand, which jarred my hand in an unusual way. That didn't feel normal. I even told James that there was something wrong with me, but I didn't know what. I can remember running a wedding on the Saturday, and because walking was so painful, was mainly standing in the middle of the room and shouting orders, about which the bride complained. I felt awful, and embarrassed at the time, knowing how unprofessional my actions were, but in such pain that there was no choice.

I couldn't put my shoes on the following morning, so I drove to work in my slippers, which was difficult, and once inside, I sat in the hotel wheelchair and trundled about in that. I was almost in tears from the pain, just from sitting. I waited until the next manager came in, then went home. The next day, the doctor straightaway gave me six weeks off, not that he could tell me what was wrong! He put me on the maximum dose of Paracetamol. All I could do was lie on my sofa watching TV. It hurt to hold a book. It hurt to sit at my computer. It hurt to stand up, which took about five minutes to achieve, so if someone rang the doorbell, by the time I answered, they would be long gone. It hurt to do anything. My feet, legs and hands had all swollen up.

Over the next few weeks I went to a bone specialist, then a skin specialist at the hospital, but no, nothing wrong there. I even once checked myself into A&E at Torbay Hospital, who could see I was in pain and checked me in straight away. They performed tests on all my organs, which were all fine, so that was good news, and they sent me home. I was alive and everything functioned, which was all they were interested in. Even they couldn't tell me what my problem was, or what to do. Weeks passed, and I was on the point of resigning my job, thinking I would never return and would be sofa-bound for the rest of my life. I went again to my GP, who told me to drink water like there was no tomorrow, no limit. And so I did. I forced it down, and over a couple of weeks the swelling gradually went back to normal, which it has been ever since.

Months later I went to another specialist at the hospital and described my symptoms. 'Ah… this is what you've had,' he told me. 'It's reactive arthritis,' he explained. 'You have a normal cold which goes after a few days, but then your body's immune system kicks in and you get this swelling. It's a genetic thing which mainly happens to men in their forties. It could happen again anytime.' So there you are! But I was really scared at the time, not being able to walk or hold anything and not knowing what was wrong, let alone what to do about it.

And so the years went by. I was tired, and every Sunday I worked on autopilot. It went without saying that you worked every weekend. It was a tiredness in the bones, almost. Worn out! Maybe I was getting too old? I was about fifty-five by now, but I had and still have a lot more stamina than some twenty-year olds. 'Do a proper job,' as my dad always used to say. You just go on and on and on, and then you realise how the years, then the decades have gone by. And you don't always have time to talk to the guests. If you do you're only half listening, because your mind is racing thinking about the next urgent matter.

It was also time to question my personal life, which was pretty much non-existent. I wanted to resign, feeling it was time to think about number one, but the hotel was too busy, and I could not leave the other management in the shit, so I stayed on and never actually left. I didn't really want to anyway.

The following January, instead of letting me go, Jane offered me the position of Front of House Manager, which had just become vacant. This would be a new challenge in more ways than one. I was dying to get my hands on the reception department and have a bash at it. On the other hand I didn't think I would be able to achieve this, but I accepted the position anyway, although it involved a £2000 per year pay drop!

I gave myself six months as a personal trial to see if I could achieve what I thought needed changing. Having updated a couple of hotels' reservation systems before, I felt I knew what I was talking about. I wanted to improve the ergonomic functioning of the reception department, which in my opinion, would not be too hard to achieve. Another issue was that it was always so busy in there that you didn't have the time to think outside the box. So, as suspected, I did not get anywhere.

It was hard work in reception. People were checking in or out, the phone was ringing, waitresses wanted menus typing, people want to go swimming, tills had to be balanced, and so on. The whole shift would go by in a blur, and you end up working like an automaton. You hardly had time to go to the loo. Towards the end of your shift you think, have I done this or that? You might have little scraps of paper with reminders for yourself, do you balance, can you hand over yet? At the end of a morning shift your head was fried. It was a challenge, and I don't think the food & beverage staff had any idea of the stress you were under. But Katie, one of life's angels, was a darling as a breakfast waitress bringing me coffee and toast in the morning.

One of my January chores was to complete the 'Asset Register'. This listed all the fixtures and fittings of the hotel, so I had to count everything, from pictures to staplers to computer screens to cookers, and collate it all on a computer print-out, by department. I usually rushed to do this before going on my January skiing holiday. But when I moved to reception, I could hand this over to John, which was such a relief. I never noticed it being done though afterwards.

Sometimes it became too much, and a couple of times I blew my top at Jane. I was shouting at her, almost screaming, ready to commit murder! Any staff who heard would be visibly shocked that someone had dared to shout at her like that. I just had to let it all out, then that was that. Except maybe I had gone too far? Would I be dismissed? We would meet after ten minutes, and both being professional, carry on working. Maybe I would apologise.

I had tried to give a year's notice for a holiday in Cyprus the following June, but it had been point blank refused. Nobody else had booked holiday for that time. So I was a bit miffed. My dad had booked it anyway, so in a way he forced my hand, and I knew I had to leave before this holiday started. So I resigned in the spring and told Jane that it was for definite this time. It was very upsetting for both of us because it felt like the end of an era. I enjoyed working there, despite what I've written above, and I was going to miss many friends, both staff and customers. And it was a big risk on my part, leaving without a future job at my age. Ironically, I was phoned a few weeks after I had left to see, if I could work some of that holiday week in June, because, so I heard, Jane had given too many receptionists time off! But no, I couldn't help, as I was on holiday. I sure would have otherwise.

And so ended a fabulous eight years. I learned a lot at the hotel, which goes from strength to strength, and I would like to think that my contribution was well received. The kitchens produce a remarkable amount of catering, and all credit to the family for constantly improving the standards. Some nights after work, drinking in the bar with staff and customers, and James, who regularly recites his set of stories, always as if for the first time, were superb. It would be sorely missed.

I vowed never to work again as a hotel manager. I was sick to death of pricing wet and dry goods, housekeeping, stationary goods, of fire training, Health & Safety matters, HR issues and so on. I had had enough.

CHAPTER 15

The Quayside Hotel

Oh, how lovely to have time off and to catch up on sleep. Bliss! Financially I was fine, having paid off my mortgage a few years earlier, courtesy of my mother, who as I mentioned very sadly passed away after a heart problem and cancer. The summer was enjoyable, but in the autumn it was time to get my act together. I was ideally looking for a Monday to Friday 9 to 5 job, not necessarily in catering. At my age I found it hard breaking into a new industry, but I did have some interviews. To keep myself occupied, I took some random jobs. I delivered phonebooks to my area, which meant stuffing my sports car with 900 phonebooks, and over five days I delivered all but thirty to my patch using my own petrol, and for this I was paid about £78! A joke. I went to work for a photographic company at a local town where I was to cut up photos, ie your holiday snaps. I had visions of sitting down with a guillotine with a sheet of photos and cutting them into four or six, so I was amazed at the size of this factory. They printed clothes, mugs, pictures – you name it, they did it. I took a huge reel of photos, almost two feet in diameter, and loaded them into my machine. You pressed the button and TACK TACK TACK TACK TACK! The first set was chopped at breakneck speed and it sounded like a machine gun. You then packaged them a certain way, according to which retailer they were to go to, eg Boots, then pressed the button for the next set. Each worker cut thousands of photos per day. It was fine, though you had to concentrate, but my problem was that there was an infra-red light flashing quickly whilst it read the barcodes, which perturbed me with regards to my epilepsy, so after a few days I asked to do something else. That didn't seem to amuse them, but I moved to the canvas pictures. The canvas had been stapled onto the frame, but the excess canvas at the back needed tidying up. We used Stanley knives for this. It's harder than you'd think. The excess canvas had to be held tight with your left hand whilst you sliced with your right. If you held it loose, you would not get a clean cut against the frame. You needed the right speed and angle of attack to slice to the corner, where the folds bunch up. If you used the Stanley knife at the wrong angle, you might slice the actual picture, so it had to be reprinted. If the blade wore out, it would not cut cleanly. By wearing out, I mean after about ten frames! So, we frequently changed the blades for new ones. Then the canvas, now being the same width as the frame, had to be taped, neatly with no crinkles. I began to get an ache in my left hand from holding the canvas tight. This repetitive strain injury in my left hand lasted about six months.

I requested a day off to go for an interview (which in hindsight is something you don't tell an employer), which they granted, but when I asked for another, they got rid of me. I was amazed that they did this; it was December and there was a rush to get all the Christmas orders finished. Staff were being asked to come in early to work extra. I volunteered, but to no avail. As a manager, I would have thought OK, this guy isn't going to last, but we'll use him for the Christmas rush, then get rid of him. Their staff turnover was high anyway.

After Christmas, which I spent at my dad's, it was time to get back to the hotel trade. It was so pleasant to spend a normal Christmas for a change. I had given it six months trying to change direction, but January and February is always a good time to get a job in the hotel trade, so it hadn't necessarily bothered me being out of work. Within a week I was offered interviews at the Palace Hotel in Paignton and the Quayside Hotel in Brixham, both as general manager.

The Palace was part of a group of well-established three-star hotels in Torquay and Paignton, but Steve Furness, the owner, had a reputation of hiring and firing on a whim, so, I was a bit cautious. He had said that the Palace could operate without a manager, but the hours were 8 am to 8 pm, with probably split days off. Oh, and food wise you would be given a sandwich at lunchtime. My reasoning was that if it ran without a manager, why would you need one twelve hours per day? A manager in my opinion should be paid to do the job, not just be on the premises.

I was also a member of their leisure club, so if I had accepted, I could not have enjoyed the club in the same way, although it would certainly have been cleaner! All my friends and family warned me not to take it, due to the hours, so I didn't. I might say that Steve's daughter Kim does a very good job of running the Belgrave Sands Hotel, which they had bought, being the old Kistor Hotel, which they had gutted, showing me the structural changes that they were making at the time.

I had already been for my interview at the Quayside Hotel, and subsequently I was offered the job. Beforehand, Bridget had told me that there were a few applicants, but afterwards she admitted that there was only one other. What she did not know was that I knew who that person was! Carlos, a very good friend of mine, had applied, and it had been agreed that I call him afterwards. There was no way he could cope with the stairs due to his dodgy hip. I duly called him and told him about the job, which he thought sounded dismal, so he cancelled his interview. Therefore I knew it would be offered to me.

Chris and Bridget Bowring, the owners, were off to the Caribbean for a holiday, so they didn't mind whether I started whilst they were away or when they were back after a couple of weeks. I decided to start fairly quickly; they had run it without a manager for six years, so it would still run whether I started or not. It raised the question regarding both of these hotels; are hotel managers superfluous?

The 30-bedroomed hotel had 'sea' views, mainly of the harbour. It had a quirky little bar with loads of character, a restaurant, which was the focal point of the hotel, and a pub called the Ernie Lister bar, run with its own manager. Being built on a slope, the five fishermen's cottages that made up the Quayside Hotel had quaint staircases here and there, at varying levels. Virtually all the bedrooms were different, some quirky, some furnished to a good standard. There was no space for a lift. The building next door housed a self-catering apartment, with the owners' accommodation on the floors above. The car park was three hundred yards away.

The hotel itself was run by the popular Vicky (aka Vix) who was the front office manager, with Ota as restaurant manager, and to a certain extent by Andy, the head chef. Ota had resigned to go to pastures new, so to begin with I kept out of his way and started to organise the filing system, which was all over the place, with no seemingly logical order. 'Sleeping in' three times per week formed part of my contract. Whilst Ota was still working, I didn't have to sleep in because he lived in the staff bedroom. The bar manager slept in one night and Geoff the night porter did a couple, in a spare bedroom, but he sadly died suddenly from cancer during my first week.

So my first task was to employ a night porter to work three nights per week. This was a difficult one to fill, due to the shift pattern. They started at 9 pm, shut the hotel bar normally at midnight, locked up and went to sleep in the staff bedroom. They went straight home in the morning. We could be woken up for late arrivals. Foreign pilots would be booked by MTS, the worldwide marine agent based in Brixham. Basically, as the English Channel is right hand drive, pilots get on a cargo ship or tanker at Cherbourg and get off at Brixham. These ships have to have a pilot to go up and down the English Channel. Pilot boats go out to these ships to take them on or off. They could be booked to arrive at 3 am. That's fine (in a way). You can go to sleep and be woken at threeish by the front doorbell, which rings in the bedroom, get up, check the guest in and go back to bed. It could be midnight when they arrived, or any time. You could hardly ask the ship to circle around Torbay for a few hours until a civilised time like 8 am for check-in.

The British pilots were housed in an accommodation block owned by MTS, but the foreign pilots, who I came to know, were given to us. The pain in the arse was when MTS booked in a few of the ship's crew, who could be joining the ship. If they were arriving via Heathrow, normally flying from the Far East, they had transport booked to the hotel. MTS might book them in for a midnight arrival, so you stayed up waiting. Then it was 1 am, then 2 am, and you think, shall I go to bed or wait another fifteen minutes? You might go to bed, only to be woken five minutes later. Their arrival could be delayed by so many factors; late plane, delay at customs at Heathrow, bad motorway traffic, and so on. MTS operated 24/7, so we obliged their booking requests. Donna, who worked for them, was a charmer, having been one of my three wicked witches, aka receptionists, at the Northfield Hotel.

I employed Earl as the night porter so that I worked three nights, Earl did three and the bar manager did one. When Ota left, most of the staff had never seen his room, which had been strictly private, so they were keen to have a look. Basically, it was a bedroom with a four-foot bed and a bathroom, not decorated to a hotel standard, but that didn't matter. It seemed to be a storage area for spare pictures, so I put some of them up on the bedroom wall. The hotel kitchen was below, so when the extractor fans went on in the morning, you knew about it, especially as the vent went up through a cupboard in the bathroom. You slept with one ear open and were awake at the slightest noise. I never really slept properly in that room, so by midday I was struggling to concentrate and only wanted to go home and catch up on sleep.

Earl was a huge man to begin with, but he soon lost weight. He could not stand for long, having to rest his hands on his knees with his body horizontal, but that soon changed to being able to walk around without resting. He was charming, having had a career in the oil industry, laying pipelines and working on oil rigs I believe. He seemed to know everything, but what he didn't know he managed to blag his way out of. He seemed to display one long tooth; it always intrigued me why he didn't have it out and get dentures fitted. He also chewed gum of some description. I detest chewing gum, and never let anyone chew it at work. But Earl was different, almost an enigma, and his chewing gum seemed to go with that. Maybe I was getting old and soft. He was brilliant with the guests, who loved his pleasant demeanour and his habit of looking at you with his face only six inches away from yours. I think he was short-sighted, although he never admitted it. God knows how he has been coping with the Covid-19 spacing restrictions!

In his own time, he got up early in the morning so that everything was ready for the restaurant, the milk and bread had been brought in, something which to begin with the chefs hardly seemed able to do, even though they walked past it every morning, and the money had been brought down for the receptionist and all lights put on. It was appreciated by all.

I was a bit anxious when Chris and Bridget returned from their holiday because I didn't really want any interference from them as I regarded it, but was expecting to be taken down a peg or two. Bridget was impressed that I had already employed a night porter, remarking that previous managers hadn't done that. I presumed that meant it was a good start! Both were past retirement age, Chris being tall and without an ounce of fat on him, Bridget small. Chris had been an accountant for a large multi-national company in the past. They were a pleasant couple with vast experience around the world, which they applied to the hotel and well-being of the staff.

Ben, who I knew from having worked at the Riverview was glad that I had started, and he naturally took over the reins in the restaurant once Ota had left. Because there were stairs down to the restaurant, with a low ceiling, anyone tall had to bend down. Ben tilted his head instead, but he had developed a habit of doing this anyway, every minute, like a nerve had been activated. Bizarre really. I helped in the restaurant and ran it on his days off. Ben had issues with his personal life, and we all tried to support him to overcome his various predicaments, and it can't have been easy for him.

The other restaurant staff in my early days were good enough but some frequently messed around. One of them was invaluable due to being able to work in other departments, but there came a time when he was bored, and from my point of view it was time to move on along with the others and go off to university. The evening receptionist helped with the dinner service if need be, or the breakfast layup. There was no bar person as such, this being covered by the receptionist, who stayed until the night porter started his shift at 9 pm. The night porter really covers the bar, helps in the restaurant if need be, answers the phone, and deals with any guest requirements. Earl's primary objective was to converse with guests, so he would head straight into the restaurant and talk to each table. This killed two birds with one stone. He was saving me doing the chatting which as a waiter I didn't always have the time for, having other things to think about.

After finishing as a waiter, there was the office work. Everything for me was time critical. It seemed bizarre to me that the manager was rushing around clearing, but Earl was just chatting to the guests! I'm sure people thought he was the manager. It didn't bother me. And remember, when I was working in the restaurant on a sleep-over night, I didn't have a night porter to come in and help!

Vix sat at her desk and bossed everyone else, including Chris and Bridget at times. She talked so much that you didn't have a chance to object, and with her cheeky smile, you felt obliged to obey. There was space for one other chair, which was frequently occupied by a member of staff, either chatting to Vix, or signing in or out for their shift. That would have to change. Basically there was no room for me to sit down, so eventually I installed a clocking-in machine near the entrance to the kitchen. This freed up the other chair for me. Vix didn't understand this machine (or didn't want to), so I had to analyse it weekly and pass it on to her for her to complete the wages. I was used to it, having performed this function at the Riverview Hotel. Vix had been working there for something like twenty years, likewise Alli who worked Saturday daytime, and Sandra, who did a couple of shifts, as well as the accounts. It was a happy little family. Anne also worked in the reception, and I found out later that she had referred to me as a 'back of house manager' or something similar, having applied for my job herself. She could have probably done it, albeit it in a different style.

Andy ran the kitchen with Phil as second chef and then a trainee, whose name escapes me. They also cooked bar snacks for the pub. Andy controlled the kitchen well and managed to cook the food quickly and was popular locally due to his charisma, and the fact that he had produced a recipe book. I have never known a head chef work less than forty hours a week, but even though they worked split shifts, he seemed to be the first one to leave. We didn't always see eye to eye. He had had the run of the place without a manager and didn't like being told what to do by me.

It was about this time that I had to change my car. It was my pride and joy, being a Tuscani, which is a special edition Hyundai Coupe, in other words a poor man's Ferrari, and Ferrari red in colour. That and the sports car shape were the only similarities. It wasn't particularly powerful being a straight two litres, but the good thing about this car, of which there are not many around, was that no one knew what make or model it was. The badge at the front and rear was a 'T' logo, for Tuscani, and I changed the central wheel caps to the 'T' badge, bought from Korea. Some people even thought it was a Tesla - with twin exhaust pipes? Nothing, except the radio when turned on, denoted the make as Hyundai, let alone the model. Amazingly, traffic wardens couldn't issue a ticket, because they have to include the make or marque and they couldn't tell what it was, so I parked where I liked, on double yellow lines, and in non-camera operated council car parks. It would actually irritate me if a kind member of public let me know that a traffic warden was at my car! I wanted them to try and give me a ticket!

The pedals seemed miles away, so that for me, being short, the seat was too far from the pedals. This meant that to exit the car, I had to step sideways and backwards, like a crab. This motion had caused a repetitive strain injury in my groin, which was affecting my walking, so the car had to go. Parking in a car park was a nightmare, because the door, being long, could only be opened slightly, again meaning that you had to climb out at a 5 o'clock angle, or park at one end so that you had space to open the door properly.

After a lot of research, I bought a Skoda Octavia. Really I would have preferred a Beemer, but practicalities came first, and I needed a four-seater to ferry around my then girlfriend's parents when they visited (which never actually happened because we fell out), also to drive to an airport when we lads went on a short break in Europe.

Earl and I came to an agreement that he would work Friday and Saturday nights, and normally Tuesday and Wednesdays. This was beneficial in two ways. The hotel was likely to be busier at weekends, so more guests for him to chat to, whereas I tried to do office work after the restaurant had finished for the evening, so I didn't particularly want to be involved serving the odd couple here and there, let alone chat. Sometimes you realise that you are not going to achieve your office work, so then you would have a drink with the customer, often sitting with them, if they were regulars.

Despite assurances to the contrary, Ben's personal life did not improve, and it was affecting his work more and more. He had been living with his ex-girlfriend, which in itself was stressful enough for him, but then she moved up country with their baby, which he quite understandably found hard to handle. He visited her occasionally, but on one such trip he didn't come back. He apologised profusely to me on the phone, which I accepted, as it was the best thing he could have done to get out of Brixham. He was a nice man, and I have a lot of time for him, and wish him all the best.

This gave Earl the opportunity to edge into working more restaurant shifts. At breakfast one person takes the orders whilst the other does the tea or coffee, with toast. Coffee goes in metal cafetières, tea served in teapots, and shock horror, one teabag per person, none of this one teabag per person and one for the pot. So at the age of fifty-seven, I had to relinquish my teabag philosophy for the first time in almost forty years of catering. Sob sob!

If not taking orders, I always worked in the stillroom as above. At busy times, the restaurant had to be re-laid for up to twenty guests, so it was imperative to turn the tables over. Earl's natural friendly habit of chatting to the guests could drive us mad at times because we wanted them to leave, never mind the fact that there was other work to do! He really didn't seem to understand. If not rota'd to do a dinner shift starting at 7 pm, he would frequently arrive before 9 pm to see if he was needed in the restaurant; sometimes he was, so he clocked on. Other times he would just talk to the customers, clocking on at 9 pm. But he was worth his weight in gold. He liked vacuuming the restaurant, and always produced a cleaning cloth from his immense pocket, whether it be for brass, glass, or another hard surface.

May was always a busy month. The first bank holiday coincided with the Pirate Festival, which was the first excuse for a piss up, then towards the end of May there was Brixfest, the next excuse for the proverbial, which included cookery demonstrations from the likes of Andy and other local chefs. Devon produce was available, entertainment was laid on, and it was a good few days.

The hotel's stocktaker retired, so I took this on myself, which I came to regret. The bars had different prices, and the Ernie Lister also operated a happy hour from 4-6 pm or so, so that had to be factored in, along with the staff discount, which from memory was 20%. The first result produced a loss. I had a good idea where this came from, as it fitted the previous pattern. When the bar manager left to work elsewhere, his daughter Megan became bar manager, so we tried to split the stock, so that the hotel bar just used 70 cl bottles, whereas the Ernie Lister used 1.5 litre bottles for the main optic spirits. Over a year, I managed to pinpoint the main deficit to a few optics, and small bottles of wine in the Ernie Lister bar but it became harder and harder in terms of time available to do the stocktake, let alone deal with the results, which I eventually more or less abandoned.

Andy left to pursue other interests, so Phil naturally took over. The commis at the time was not capable of stepping up, so we used agency chefs or whoever we could get. We ended up with Tony, who lived in. He was above budget, but worth it. His career had included working with famous chefs at Michelin-starred restaurants, and he knew his stuff. His repertoire far exceeded Phil's, who, like me, was old school. I had a lot of time for Tony, who was genuinely concerned about the success of the hotel, and I loved all of his food. He wouldn't take any shit off anyone and enjoyed a drink in the bar. But I know what it's like to live in a hotel. It eventually drives you mad, so after four or five months, he would need a change. This would tend to coincide with us finding a second chef who might last a year, followed by a stint with Tony, then another second chef, then Tony. His only Achilles heel was to involve himself with me in the politics of the staff, which was none of his business, even though he could be right. We had quite a few frank discussions in the bar over a drink or two about various aspects of the hotel. The style of food fluctuated according to whether Tony was working or not.

I started going to pottery classes at The Shed in Chelston on Wednesday afternoons. I had always wanted to make more pottery since doing the 'O' level back in 1976, so this was my chance. Again, it was for social reasons that it interested me. I soon began to enjoy the afternoons, making crabs and octopuses (octopodes to be correct, from the Greek), experimenting with techniques, and after a few months I started a website -www.geoffparispottery.com. Bridget suggested I make a seagull, of all things, a bird that I detest, so reluctantly made one and displayed it along with several other ceramic items made by me in the restaurant windows. One such item was a plaice, which our fishmonger thought was real when I showed him. I did sell a few of these ceramic masterpieces!

Christmas and New Year were a doddle. The hotel struggled to get maximum occupancy for Christmas, so for the arrival afternoon tea there might only be a dozen people. Easy. Time also to sit down with them and chat. That was a first! On Christmas Eve, sparkling wine was served pre dinner, for the carol singing. I always made sure that I was too busy serving the bubbly and canapes to be involved in the carol singing. The Christmas day quiz had, in the past, been handed out in the day, collected in the evening, and prizes given. But that meant people could cheat! So I did it live after the Christmas evening buffet, and it went down well.

On Boxing Day evening, we held the horse races. All guests were seated on long tables so that they all sat together to our plan. A screen was erected at one end to show the races. The dinner menu, the same for everyone, consisted of seven courses, so it worked in sequence. We took bets for the first race then served the first course, then showed the race and distributed the winnings, took bets for the next race, and so on. It was a fun night, enjoyed by all. New Year's Eve was similar, except the room would be full up with a maximum of fifty-five. That was hard work, serving the courses and taking the bets. Both nights were strictly time controlled, because on New Year's Eve there was also the piper at midnight, followed by Auld Lang Syne outside. There was no time to stop inside, having to clear the restaurant and prepare for haggis and neaps and tatties and a tot of whisky for everyone. Then of course after all that, the restaurant had to be moved back to normal and be re-laid for breakfast.

The commis waiters came and went, but one of them stands out. He was a fresh-faced seventeen-year-old blond lad, with all the energy, never having had a job before. His naivety at the time was intriguing. He announced to everyone he spoke to in the restaurant that he had been out that day on the jet ski his parents had bought him for getting a job at the Quayside! Lucky him. He didn't seem to realise that boasting about his new toy might upset some of the other staff, for whom life was more financially difficult. But he did a fairly good job, even if he took it personally when told off about his bragging, which we all found rather comical.

One night I had just got to bed at the hotel when I heard an unusual tapping or banging. It persisted, but I just couldn't place it. With reluctance I had to get up. I went to the second floor to listen. Then a Swedish woman appeared calling for help and glad to have found someone. I went into her room, which was close by. Her husband had been stuck in the bathroom for an hour and couldn't open the door, so he had been banging on the wall. I couldn't explain to him how to undo the bolt, so I went to get my electrical screwdriver and passed it under the bathroom door. He unscrewed the bolt, a little brass one, and got out. I screwed it back up and tried the bolt. Fine, no problem. I honestly think he was trying to slide the bolt the wrong way. Really odd.

You also get random naked people. They go to their bathroom, but the door they have opened is the main door, which closes behind them, leaving them stuck in the corridor without a key. One such naked woman didn't even bother to hide her parts from me. She couldn't remember her room number, but I knew, having previously clocked her as someone to keep an eye on, meaning potential trouble.

The annual Brixham Trawler Race is another of those eagerly awaited excuses for a piss up. Most staff want the day off so that they can either go on a trawler as a guest or just join in with everyone else drinking in town. The Quayside has the same lot staying every year, invariably in the same rooms. There's the Dutch contingent, all nice people, to support the few Dutch trawlers that come over to participate in the race. One set of friends who come for these events drink port and brandies (mixed) at breakfast, so by the time breakfast is over, they will have drunk at least six shots. These are VIPs to the Quayside. They drink more at breakfast than I can in a whole day! There is a strong connection with the Dutch, who are all well-liked by the British, also because I believe most of the Brixham beam trawlers were built in Holland.

Staff came and went. Some were good, some terrible. One year due to staff shortages I had to spend a lot of time in the housekeeping department, supervising or cleaning rooms, which isn't my forte.

I don't know how I did it. Over a certain period, after a really efficient stretch, our laundry supplier seemed to be having training issues with their office staff so that our deliveries were frequently incorrect; this meant that I had to unpack the linen delivery and check it off against the delivery sheet and also help the girls in housekeeping, which took up so much time, especially checking the invoices against the monthly statements. One keen young lad we employed in housekeeping was quite good, but after a few weeks his work rate dropped through the floor. He had found that his pay rate was about half that of adults, so thought he should do half the work. He didn't last long!

Because the hotel's car park was three hundred yards away, it could not be policed by us, with the result that all and sundry parked there to do their shopping in town etc, Brixham being devoid of adequate parking. This was a real issue with residents, who quite rightly complained to us. One day I was approached by a parking management company. In essence they would pay for all the installation costs and make their money from the fines they issued. It sounded good, so after looking at their plans, we gave the go-ahead. It involved three electrical boxes being installed, power from the road, a camera on a pole, and several warning notices dotted around the car park. Guests registered their car registration at the hotel upon check-in via the parking company's device, and staff cars were similarly logged in via their computer program. This program enabled us to view who had been fined and when.

However, time dragged on without much action. It transpired that the hotel, being the primary contractor, had to get quotes for the services side, being the electrical installation from the road, ie digging a trench and installing a mains cable. But due to the inactivity of the parking company, the quote would expire, so a re-quote would have to be given. I think it took two years before it was finally finished, which I'm told was about average! This was my baby. I wanted it to 'catch' all those who parked 'illegally'.

I've no idea how many it caught out, but to begin with there was an error resulting in legitimate parkers being fined. I could get the fine cancelled by first emailing the parking company, and then the driver, once it had been cancelled, but it became a pain, with a whole ring binder filled up with incorrect fines. This was becoming an issue, and something was wrong. Eventually the company admitted this, and the issue was resolved. No more fines. Thank God! It was taking up too much of my precious time.

In January and February when the hotel was quiet, I knew there was an illegal parker, but on the system no fines were being registered. Hmmm... I tested it by unregistering my car as a permanent parker to see if I was given a fine. No I wasn't, so I rang the company to tell them that their camera wasn't working! They duly re-activated it, or did something, and from then on we didn't seem to have too much of a problem. Would I go through this again? Doubtful, but due to the location of our car park, probably.

One member of staff warrants a mention. He started as a KP, having had previous experience in Brixham. He was good, turned up, and did his job. So we were happy. After a few months his partner threw him out, so he was effectively homeless. It was early spring, so it was still cold out at night. I gave him my sleeping bag, and he had a tent which he pitched every night on some grass somewhere, but physically and emotionally he was at rock bottom. Sleeping in the cold wasn't doing him any good, he had pleurisy or something similar, and his cough wasn't healthy; indeed one afternoon he came into the kitchen crying his eyes out, because he didn't know what to do. I talked to Chris & Bridget, asking them if we could put him up in the hotel, and they agreed on the proviso that he must find himself a flat or bedsit. His room at the hotel would be room only, no charge. He was so grateful, virtually kissed our feet, and said he would do anything for the hotel. He would be forever grateful. Yeah right! After three weeks he found a flat and moved into it. But soon after he dumped us in it, to go for another job. Thank you kindly. Maybe nine months later, we were looking for a commis chef in the kitchen, and someone suggested this former KP. You've got to be kidding! The trouble is, sometimes it's better the devil you know than the devil you don't. So we interviewed him. We were aware of his liquid and other abuse levels, which we advised he needed to control if he wanted to succeed. Reluctantly, he started back as a commis. He started off fairly well, citing how grateful he would always be to the hotel, and then, on a very busy night in December, he didn't appear. OK, not amused, but we let him off the once. Then at Christmas he did a runner, so as to avoid all the busy nights. Thank you so much mate.

The hotel was on the market for two million and various people were shown around over a year or so, but an Indian family took an interest. The man stayed a few times with some business colleagues, arriving from India, the last time culminating in a meeting with Chris and Bridget, me, and our HODs. They had a corporate hotel group in India, a hotel in Penzance (which I visited, combining it with a trip to see a friend), and he was looking at buying another hotel as a birthday or wedding present for his daughter! Very nice. One of his colleagues was a corporate hotelier, so he asked the detailed nitty-gritty questions. One of them was how we communicated between departments. In his world, departments emailed each other. He couldn't quite get his head round the fact that we talked to other departments because they were just around the corner. We rarely emailed each other. He asked me the technical questions, but they were too simple to understand. Don't get me wrong: I was talking to a professional, far more experienced than myself, but he could just not relate to the fact that our different departments intermingled with other departments in terms of their job content. It was like a

747 pilot asking how to fly a Spitfire. We were too small for him. It was a bizarre conversation. When they left by taxi, the owner said to me 'See you very soon!' which I acknowledged. I thought they were going to buy the hotel, but that was the last we heard, them not being confident of being able to operate the hotel from afar with me as manager.

Over a ten-day period in one summer, all three of the main restaurant staff left for one reason or another, meaning there were no dedicated restaurant staff. This meant I had to run the restaurant, which in itself was not a problem, but it meant split shifts all the time. I knew laying up tables would soon become tedious for me, day after day. Earl was in his element, having more or less dinner and breakfast shifts in addition to his night portering, Vicky helped more, being a solid all-rounder who could supervise any department, as did Megan I think, from the Ernie Lister bar, as well as the receptionists. We got through. We employed a youngster who soon picked it up, but I was just desperate to get a body in the restaurant, so my standards slipped, and I allowed her to wear black jeans and trainers. My back was against the wall, and I was knackered from sleeping in, with only a few hours' light sleep each night.

One particular couple deserve mention. They arrived on a Friday for a weekend, and after a few hours their bedroom power tripped. No problem, it happened quite regularly if people used too many appliances or say boil a kettle without water, you just re-set the trip switch. No problem, guests OK. It happened again later in the evening, so the warning signs went up. Either something major was wrong electrically, or the customer was doing something abnormal to cause the tripping. I asked to go into their room to have a look around, but they denied me access! So now, from my point of view, they had something to hide. They asked to have a meeting with me in the morning to discuss the failings of the room. There was nothing wrong with the room from my point of view; sea view and balcony with a nice walk in shower in the bathroom. I warned Earl about them, as well as Megan in the bar.

So we had our meeting in the morning. He was a big man and he almost protruded from his armchair, whereas I sank into the sofa, being small. Kind of like David and Goliath. His partner was a regular size. Their first comment was something like 'So what are you going to do?' It automatically puts you on the defensive; you have no ammo because you don't know what or where the problem is, and access to the room has been denied. I have every right to go where I like, which I do 100% of the time normally, but they still would not let me into the room. I reiterated that I needed to go into the room before commenting.

'Did you know that such and such member of staff was talking with another member of staff in the bar last night about another member of staff lying or being dishonest?' he said.

'Well, thank you for letting me know, I will investigate that,' I said, after digesting the implications of what he had just told me. So again I was put on the spot. Were they right or was it totally fictious? It was quite a shocking statement about my staff, which obviously I knew nothing about, something I would have to sort out. They wanted to know what I was going to do to their room bill, and they added little things like saying they had to wait for their breakfast table, or the coffee took too long – little sidelines to add to the general dissatisfaction.

I had had enough by now and could see this was going nowhere so I ended up giving them that first night free, much to my own irritation. Everyone was warned to watch this couple.

The next night their power tripped again a few times and Earl had to call Chris over from his flat at night-time. They wouldn't even let him into the room! Chris told them to go in the morning, with no charge and never to come back! It turned out that the bedside light fixed to the wall was broken, which I presume was why they had denied us access, certainly it would have been the reason for the electricity to be tripping; they had even put up the 'Do Not Disturb' sign on the door so that the room attendants could not go in during their stay. I talked to Megan about what they had said about the bar staff, which she laughed at. It wasn't until a day or two later that it dawned on me how clever this couple had been. They had managed to get a weekend free and wound up the management and directors.

One evening, I was called outside in the pouring rain to assist. An elderly man had fallen over in the road and was lying there. I quickly told the receptionist to call for an ambulance, then fetched a foil blanket and went back outside. The man couldn't move, so I covered him with the blanket, and after checking the pupils of his eyes as best I could in the rain, I waited for the ambulance, directing traffic around him, which was by far the most important matter, than any attempt at medical assistance. I waited and waited. He was conscious, but didn't want to be touched.

Eventually a young man arrived, who it turned out was his nephew. They then had a full-on row with swear words like there's no tomorrow. The nephew was trying to help, but the uncle was repeatedly telling him to fuck off. We tried the ambulance again, both of us. After an hour, someone with more medical knowledge than me walked down the road and offered to help, for which I was grateful. Then I called the police. I had now been standing in the road for over an hour, in the rain, directing traffic, and told the police this. When they eventually arrived, they effectively blocked the road with their cars, even getting in the way of the ambulance! This man had broken his hip, so it transpired. It was fortunate that I was not working on my own in the restaurant, so I could be spared to be outside!

Then Vix had to retire on health grounds, which was another blow. This meant we were without a head receptionist, so Anne became a reception supervisor, and I took over the wages etc. I was also required, at least once a week, to do a reception shift, normally an afternoon shift followed by a sleep-in. The afternoons were the most appropriate time for Bridget to talk to me about personnel matters, including how to help those with personal problems, or about hotel procedures. Her input was invaluable, being able to look at situations from a different angle, which I might have missed. These meetings could go on for quite a time on the occasions of being interrupted by phone calls or check-ins. My whole time was spent working in either the restaurant or reception with maybe a half day per week for 'management' duties. Yes, I was saving the hotel on the wages, but it wasn't doing me any good. I was in a rut. It was also very difficult to take holidays. If any of the reception team were on holiday, I couldn't go, likewise if any heads of department were away, and Chris and Bridget went abroad for two sets of holidays annually, so all of this began to niggle at me. I always managed my skiing holiday in the first or second week of January, before Anne went on her four to six weeks holiday, which Chris and Bridget always authorised, something that in all my years of hotel work was unheard of, which astounds me to this day.

A mature person was employed in the restaurant to take over, so for me it was a welcome relief. It soon became apparent that she was out of her depth, but the positives outweighed the negatives, so we kept her. However, after a few months her health deteriorated, including I guess her mental health, so we called a meeting to discuss the options with her. To be fair to her we reassigned her to the position of waitress and re-advertised for a manager. It was our fault really, because we had given her a position above her station. Then Jacqui arrived, a veteran in the restaurant world, what a relief! Straight away I knew she was the right choice. I just hoped she would stick it out, seeing that she lived in Torquay. My life began to improve; the pressure was off from one department.

It didn't last long. Anne went off on her long holiday, to Australia I believe, with her boyfriend. She was well organised and had prepared all her department's rotas in advance, including her start back shifts, but on the Sunday morning she was due back, she never turned up, so I was called and had to come in. What joy. It was feasible I suppose that her flight had been delayed or something similar, but there was no communication from her, nor did she appear for her next shift, as rota'd by Anne herself! So I began to make some enquiries, including emailing Anne. We eventually received a reply saying she had resigned with me before her holiday and that I had the letter. What a joke! If that had been the case, I would have advertised her position six weeks ago. And I'm not in the habit of throwing away resignation letters, or of letting a department get in the shit. Nor was I in the habit of lying. So there were a few tense emails sent back and forth.

What I found really strange was that Anne was doing a really good job. She had, off her own bat, reorganised the reception and taken charge of the procedures for our reservations systems upgrade, Guestline to Rezlynx, which are like chalk and cheese, and she seemed to be enjoying her job far more, and earning the respect from other staff. For maybe a year afterwards I thought about this every day. Did she, or didn't she say anything to me before she left? I've thought about it so much that even now I'm not sure whether she did or didn't. What the hell...

The sleeping-in thing was beginning to niggle more and more, so I suggested one evening to Chris and Bridget, on one of the occasions when they came in for dinner, that I should cut my sleep-ins from three to two nights. Earl would gladly do a fifth. I realised there might be a salary adjustment. A few weeks later we had a meeting. They asked what I was proposing so I discussed it with them, but then I realised that I would be worse off – not in the financial sense, but because most of my office work was done after the restaurant and bar had finished on my sleep-in nights, and now I was reducing that precious time, a time which was too valuable to lose. I was in a quandary. I wasn't really happy anyway, and I didn't feel I was doing my job properly as a manager, or not to my standards, because of being so hands on in the departments, and this situation was not going to improve.

'I think I'll resign,' I found myself saying, before realising what I had said. Well that was it. A bit of a relief. I've done it.

'Oh dear, it's the end of an era,' Chris replied.

'Sorry, but I've been on the fence for some time now,' I stated, feeling the need to say something further.

'I thought you had,' Bridget acknowledged.

I can't recall whether they advertised for a manager or not, but certainly they are running the hotel themselves now. There were lots of reasons for resigning, and I knew that my lodger and friend Rob would be moving into his own house that year, meaning I would have to be at home every night to feed my cat. My Dad had had a stroke, so visiting him was going to be more of a priority.

My health was also a real worry. In January I had gone to my doctor about my constant tiredness. My worry was always trying not to fall asleep at the wheel; I had to pinch myself to stay awake, have the air con on low, or windows open, it was seriously worrying me. This had been going on for years, if not decades.

The doctor asked about my alcohol consumption. I drank at the hotel, a bottle of Peroni a night or sometimes two. If I went out, it was a couple of pints, if at home a couple of cans. He took a blood test and stopped me drinking for three weeks. OMG! Well amazingly, after a week I had so much more energy, and felt less tired. Basically, my liver was knackered from alcohol abuse; even though the amounts were small, it's because it was regular. I have never given my liver a rest from alcohol. Even two days per week abstaining helps. Fortunately for me the liver is the only internal organ that can repair itself, so he told me.

A blood test three weeks later showed an improvement in my liver, so I was on the right track. He told me that now it was up to me. Thanks! So now I drink alcohol-free lager at home, and sometimes I drink alcohol-free in pubs or restaurants, if driving. I limit my alcohol to once or twice a week, until the Covid lockdown in the spring of 2020 put paid to that! I was drinking most nights at home.

So the sad day approached for my departure from the Quayside Hotel. They produced a cake and we had a glass of bubbly with the staff in the lounge. Chris and Bridget kindly gave me a picture of the hotel, painted by a local artist, and the staff had clubbed together to buy a huge collection of pottery tools, all of which I use, which was really thoughtful.

Had I just retired? Did I want to be a manager again? No, not really. It was great to finally relax without a care in the world. I wanted to concentrate on the pottery side of things and coincidentally my pottery teacher suggested that I could teach or hold workshops. That was a great accolade. Someone else suggested I join the Torbay Guild of Artists, which I duly did, and before I knew it, was exhibiting with others at the Spanish Barn in Torquay. I had never in a million years considered that I would ever be exhibiting, but here I was – a whole new world! And I was thrilled. It didn't matter that I didn't sell anything, just being part of it was good enough for me. When you're focused on the hotel trade, you sometimes find normal things outside work a bit tedious and tiresome, so I had anticipated being bored stiff on the days that I did my stewarding for the exhibition. But amazingly, the other stewards all had their own fascinating stories to tell, and I was not bored one little bit.

I produced a business card and printed flyers to advertise my lessons, which began in July 2020. It works like this; you give half your income from the students to the owner, and in return you can use the facilities for free any time you like.

I saw a financial adviser to discuss my finances, and duly put all of my ISAs, pension policies etc into one pot (yes, risky I know), from which I could take an income drawdown. That meant I needed to get a job; it didn't matter what, maybe four days a week on minimum wage. Therefore, I classified myself as semi-retired. I was so happy.

This is where this book ends, because it is the end of my management career. I have, for the most part, kept my private life separate from this book. As it happens, I went to work in a local hotel in February 2020 as a receptionist. It was just what I wanted. No management responsibility, despite being offered the position of head receptionist, which I refused. The difference in income is just not worth the extra hassle.

During my professional life I have met some amazing people; royalty, popstars, film or TV stars, politicians, or other great people. Equally I have met some scumbags. To all these people you have to portray a happy demeanour, with a positive attitude. You have to be psychic, intelligent, headstrong and determined, and you need eyes in the back of your head. You have to be friendly and make conversation, often working when you're ill, or for long hours and over weekends, for little financial reward. You have to be thinking about several things at once, be multi-functional, and do as asked by the customer, some of whom display manners that are appalling. It is not always easy. You have to deal with drunks and tolerate verbal abuse. You have to clean up mess when guests have had a personal accident, some of which you would not believe physically possible.

I have had the pleasure of working for some really professional hotel proprietors who have taught me a lot; equally I have worked for crooks. In terms of managers, most have been professional, whereas a few weren't worth the clothes they were wearing, and some treated me like a piece of dirt.

As regards staff, there have been the great ones who always smiled, worked above and beyond the call of duty, were quick and efficient and never complained, and for a manager, they were a dream. They would work overtime in other departments, sometimes sacrificing personal social occasions. Most staff are good to average. Then you get the ones who have either one or a combination of mental health issues, alcohol and/or substance abuse, and who generally have no interest in anyone or anything around them. The root of their affliction is probably not their fault, with their life a depression; I feel sorry for them in a way, caught in a rut.

To all of these staff, in the size of hotels I've worked in, you have to treat them as part of the family. You have to listen to their issues (which can be numerous) and try to deal with each issue. You get all levels of employees who steal, whether it be hotel property, cash, customers' property, or even by refunding your credit card for cash in one instance. You have to deal with all of this. If you put a foot wrong as a manager, as I have done a few times, they will give you hell, whether it be accusing you of unfair dismissal, taking legal action, or physical abuse. Gone are the days when you could get rid of bad staff just like that.

My journey through hotel life has been interesting and varied. It has been hard work, but enjoyable, and rewarding to see people enjoying themselves. I've met some fascinating people. The hours are anti-social and long with poor pay, which maybe is why I'm single.

Have I been a good manager or a bad manager? And from whose viewpoint – the staff? The management? The directors? The customers? I would like to think so, but who knows. But would I do it again? You bet!

BV - #0041 - 110621 - C6 - 229/152/24 - PB - 9781861519757 - Gloss Lamination